The Megacorp and Oligopoly

The Megacorp and Oligopoly

Micro Foundations of Macro Dynamics

ALFRED S. EICHNER

Professor of Economics
State University of New York, College at Purchase
and Senior Research Associate and
Senior Research Coordinator
Conservation of Human Resources
Project, Columbia University

CAMBRIDGE UNIVERSITY PRESS

Cambridge

London New York Melbourne

CAMBRIDGE UNIVERSITY PRESS
Cambridge, New York, Melbourne, Madrid, Cape Town, Singapore, São Paulo

Cambridge University Press
The Edinburgh Building, Cambridge CB2 8RU, UK

Published in the United States of America by Cambridge University Press, New York

www.cambridge.org
Information on this title: www.cambridge.org/9780521208857

First published 1976
This digitally printed version 2008

A catalogue record for this publication is available from the British Library

Library of Congress Cataloguing in Publication data

Eichner, Alfred S.
The megacorp and oligopoly.
Bibliography: p.
Includes index.
1. Oligopolies. 2. Price policy.
3. Economics. 4. Microeconomics. I. Title.
HD2731.E48 338.8 75-17115

ISBN 978-0-521-20885-7 hardback
ISBN 978-0-521-06861-1 paperback

To the many economists who, over the years, have chipped away at the foundations of neo-classical economics so that a more serviceable edifice might be erected and who, by so doing, have made this treatise possible.

Contents

Preface ix

1 Introduction 1

2 The nature of the megacorp 19
Appendix: Alternative behavioral assumptions 49

3 The pricing decision 55
Appendix: Antecedent formulations of the entry factor 103

4 Extensions of the basic model 108

5 The distribution of income 144

6 Micro and macro 189

7 Conventional policy instruments 224

8 Toward social control 271

Notes 288

References 327

Index 353

Preface

For someone seeking to change the way economists perceive their world, there are two opposing strategies that can be followed. One is to emphasize the novelty of the theoretical schema being offered, showing how it leads to conclusions that contravene some important part of the accepted body of economics. This is the Keynesian strategy, as reflected in *The General Theory*. The alternative is to present the schema as though there were no intrinsic conflict between it and the prevailing doctrines, the new approach, it being suggested, simply serving to bring out some previously neglected points. This is the Marshallian strategy, as reflected in the *Principles*.

Neither strategy is without disadvantage. To stress the errors in economics as presently taught is to threaten the authority of the older generation of economists, thereby increasing their natural resistance to the new ideas. Since it is the older generation who determine what the younger generation will learn, this additional ground for hostility will hardly improve the chances of the new theoretical schema gaining acceptance. Yet to minimize the extent to which the new approach represents a discontinuity with past modes of thought is to run the risk that its significance will go unrecognized.

The present work wavers between the two strategies. On the one hand, it clearly seeks to supplant much of the existing body of microeconomic theory - or at least shrink it to the emphasis which it realistically deserves. Instead of the usual assumption of perfect competition in product and factor markets, this work is based on the notion that large corporations have considerable discretion as to the prices they will charge and that trade unions have a similar degree of power with respect to wage rates. Only an economist, of course, would consider this a radical set of premises upon which to erect a theoretical model. The result, nonetheless, is a quite different theory from that found in the standard textbooks, this microeconomic theory in turn laying the foundation for a quite different macrodynamics.

On the other hand, it must be admitted that hardly any of the ideas contained in this work are original. Almost without exception, as careful attention to the notes and appendixes will attest, they can be traced to some previous writer - even if the ideas have not all made their way into the mainstream of economics. There is, in fact, only one clearly novel idea to be found in the work. It is this idea, however, which forms the central core of the work, making it possible to tie together many previous strands of thought in a synthesis which is itself unique. The idea is that the pricing decision, when some degree of market power exists, is ultimately linked to the investment decision; that, indeed, under the circumstances, prices are likely to be set so as to assure the internally generated funds necessary to finance a firm's desired rate of capital expansion. It is this insight which makes it possible not only to provide the long-missing determinate solution to the oligopolistic pricing problem but also to reintegrate micro with macroeconomic theory.

It must also be admitted that the present work, rather than requiring that the prevailing microeconomic theory be scrapped entirely, merely suggests that it be taken far less seriously. Indeed, the work deals with competition as a special case of oligopoly, and the resulting polypolistic model - identical under extreme assumptions to the model which appears so prominently in the textbooks - is still held to apply to at least one part of the business sector, even if it is the less important part. For this reason, the present work can be viewed as simply one further step in the gradual evolution of microeconomic theory, providing as it does a more generalized framework for analyzing price and wage decisions, as well as output, investment and financing decisions.

Just as there is a Keynesian and a Marshallian strategy for presenting some radically different theoretical schema, so too there is a Keynesian and a Marshallian view as to how quickly the new ideas should be made public. To Keynes it was desirable that the novel way of thinking about things find its way into print as soon as possible so that the ideas could be honed, and the errors discovered, in the ensuing debate among economists. To Marshall it was more important that the ideas be sharpened, and the errors eliminated, before publication, this to avoid leading economists down false paths.

Again, neither alternative is without disadvantage. Many needless controversies might have been avoided, and larger numbers of neophyte economists attracted to reading it, were *The General Theory* a more finished work. On the other hand, while the *Principles* sets a standard for clarity in exposition and avoidance of error that no other major work in economics is ever likely to match, the development of economics was seriously impaired by the fact that the *magnum opus* was so long delayed in appearing and, even more important, that so much of the Marshallian theory existed only as part of an oral tradition.

This volume, unfortunately, suffers from both these disadvantages. In retrospect, it seems that the work has been much too slow to appear - even though the delay has served a useful purpose. Having read through all of the Kefauver Committee's hearings on the steel industry before even beginning the serious study of economics - the suggestion by the late C. Wright Mills to read those hearings in fact prompting the initial interest in economics - I found it impossible, as a first-year graduate student in 1960, to reconcile what I was being taught about prices and wage setting with what I already knew of the real world. That same year, in Alexander Erlich's course dealing with the Russian economy, the critical insight occurred: the way in which Soviet planners used the turnover tax to finance planned investment in that country was remarkably similar to what corporate executives told the Kefauver Committee was the way they used the profits which they added to costs in determining their own prices. It has taken over ten years to work out this idea so that the resulting theoretical model could stand up under the criticisms which persons trained in the conventional microeconomic theory are likely to mount.

Part of the time was taken up writing my doctoral dissertation. Bowing to the advice that a theoretical thesis, especially one so at variance with accustomed modes of thought, stood little chance of being accepted, I wrote instead on a historical topic, describing the process by which oligopoly arose in a representative industry, sugar refining. The exercise, aside from permitting my thoughts on oligopoly to mature, was important for two reasons. First, it showed how limited in time was the existence of competitive conditions in the American economy's manufacturing sector and, second, it showed how unstable and unviable those conditions were even for the brief period they lasted. Indeed, the dissertation suggested that, because of price competition's capital expropriating effect, some control over prices is absolutely essential to the maintenance of a private business sector. If this be so, then oligopoly must be viewed, not as the perversion which most economists consider it but rather, as simply a historical necessity.

The time required to complete the study of the sugar refining industry which forms the historical backdrop to the present work has not been the only source of delay, however. The appearance of this work has also been retarded by the hostility of other economists to the ideas which it contains. It is important to recognize the phenomenon, for few readers, especially those well-trained in the conventional economics, are likely to be entirely free of a similar resistance to the book's conceptual framework.

I was at first quite taken aback by this hostility. I had assumed that economists would warmly welcome a solution to the problem that had long confounded them - how prices are set under oligopolistic conditions. The resistance which I instead encountered forced me to think more seriously about the sociology of knowledge. It was not until I read *The Copernican Revolution* and *The Structure of Scientific Revolutions* by Thomas Kuhn, however, that I actually began to understand the phenomenon I was observing. The fact is that, in Kuhn's terminology, the treatise is based on a quite different paradigm from that found in the standard textbooks. Indeed, it is disorienting for someone trained in neo-classical theory to read a work which does not assume that price competition is necessarily good or that market power is necessarily bad, that income distribution is based on marginal productivity theory or that inflation is due to supply shortages, generally in labor markets. A reader, reacting viscerally to his disorientation, is likely to reject the present work out of hand. Indeed, it has been my experience that anyone who has grown comfortable with the conventional microeconomic theory is unlikely to see much merit in the present work until he has been exposed to its ideas for at least the second time. It should also be noted - and this is a caveat I pass along from Adrian Wood - the book as a whole cannot be digested by trying to read it straight through. It should be put down after a chapter has been read, and time allowed for the ideas to percolate. At the very least, the reader should pause between the first four chapters and the last four. Otherwise, he will find it difficult to absorb what is being said. These warnings are given so that reaction to the book will come as no surprise.

While quite naturally I would have wished that this work could have been published much sooner, the delay has nonetheless had a beneficial effect. It has provided the time to correct a number of errors, smooth out a large part of the exposition and deal more thoroughly with some of the implications of the analysis. No one has been more influential in this respect than Joan Robinson. It was she who, with her insistence that the macrodynamic implications of the microeconomic model be made fully explicit, was responsible for the sixth chapter being completely rewritten - much to the advantage of that chapter. Her criticisms and comments have also made their mark on other parts of the work. Indeed, it has been her aid and encouragement which almost alone have helped sustain me during a period in which the response of economists in the United States has been almost universally either negative or indifferent. I would like to acknowledge similar support and encouragement from Robert Averitt, Robert Lekachman, Adrian Wood, Jan Kregel, Edward Nell, William Vickrey, Peter Kenen, Jesse Markham and Alfred Chandler. Aside from support and encouragement, many of these same colleagues have made helpful comments and suggestions which have now been incorporated into the finished manuscript. Valuable as this assistance has been, the above persons are nonetheless to be absolved of any of the defects which still remain, for I have not in all cases been able to follow their advice as well as I might. It is to Aaron Warner that I owe the particular perspective on labor-management relations found in this work, and to Eli Ginzberg the particular perspective on manpower generally. Donald Dewey's contribution, besides providing the initial exposure to the field of industrial organization, has been a degree of tolerance for antipathetic ideas which is somewhat unique in the academic world. Joel Koblentz, Solomon Honig and Stanley Eichner have given valuable research assistance, and Paul Robertson, Roman Frydman and Ralph Bradburd - especially the last - noteworthy editorial assistance. Finally, I would like to acknowledge the support, and most important the understanding, of my wife Barbara. Most of the true burdens of writing this volume have fallen on her shoulders.

Financial assistance during many of the summers when this work was proceeding came from the Royal Meeker Fund of the Columbia University Economics Department. A Guggenheim Fellowship during 1971-2 made it possible to move expeditiously to put the finishing touches on the work and, especially, to review with care the recent economic literature. This financial assistance considerably shortened the delay in these ideas reaching the public, and it is gratefully acknowledged.

Yet, despite the unintendedly longer time that has been taken to work out the kinks in the analysis, numerous flaws still remain. I would be the first to concede this point. No doubt later generations will greatly modify what I have written. Indeed, I have suggested what two of the needed modifications are - (1) to take into account the growing transnational scope of the megacorp and (2) to deal more explicitly with the increasing importance of the service and governmental sectors. What I do assert, however, is that the theoretical framework provided here, based on the postulated linkage between the pricing and investment decisions, is a better paradigm for understanding a modern, technological society than that now relied upon by most economists; and that whatever modifications are to come will most advantageously be made within that framework.

Alfred S. Eichner

March, 1976

1. Introduction

The purpose of this volume is to provide a theoretical understanding of how prices are determined in the oligopolistic sector of the American economy and how those prices, so determined, affect the growth and stability of the economy as a whole.

The need for such an understanding would appear to be unquestionable. Persistent inflation in the period after World War II, manifested as a continuing rise in the various price indexes, has thwarted the application of the Keynesian insights to assure steady economic growth at full employment. In the process the pre-war business cycle has been replaced by what Joan Robinson (1962b), following Michal Kalecki (1943), has termed the political trade cycle. This involves the deliberate suppression of aggregate demand by the government, once high levels of employment have been attained, to meet the complaints of rentier groups that the value of the dollar is being eroded - followed by the deliberate stimulation of the economy, once the rise in the price level has been halted, to calm fears of spreading unemployment. Forced to choose alternatively between full employment and price stability, the government has been unable to achieve either with consistency.

Why the American economy should find itself caught on the horns of this Phillipsian dilemma cannot be adequately explained by recourse to the existing body of economic theory.[1] While one might expect on the basis of this theory that prices would rise if aggregate demand should grow more rapidly than aggregate supply, one would not anticipate that prices would remain constant or even continue to rise if aggregate demand should begin to decline. This is because in the conventional pricing models there is nothing to suggest that the industry supply curve is not positively sloped. A decline in aggregate demand and, *pari passu*, a decline in the demand for any particular industry's product should, according to the existing body of theory, lead to a fall in industry price levels. Yet, as recent experience reveals, prices do remain constant and even on occasion continue to rise when aggregate demand begins to decline.[2] Meanwhile, the American government, like the political authorities in other Western nations, continues to rely almost entirely on monetary and fiscal policy for dealing with inflationary pressures, despite the fact that the efficacy of these instruments derives solely from their ability to affect the level of aggregate demand. Thus the failure of public policy can be traced more basically, as Keynes suggested in another connection, to the failure of theory. In this case, it is the failure of theory to provide an adequate explanation of the inflationary process or to suggest some means of bringing it under control without, at the same time, sacrificing the growth of real output.[3]

The failure of theory can be traced, in turn, to the lack of a suitable pricing model for the type of industry which plays such a prominent role in the American economy. This type of industry is what is known as oligopoly. While superficially it is the fewness of the sellers that is the essential characteristic, actually it is the recognized interdependence to which the fewness of the sellers gives rise that sets oligopoly apart from other types of market structure. What this means is that no single member of the industry can expect to take action without evoking a response from the other firms which are its rivals.[4] Considered as a whole, the industries which evidence this prerequisite interdependence constitute the oligopolistic sector of the American economy, a delineation which cuts across manufacturing and similar sectoral lines. As one of the underlying themes of the present work, it may be stated that not only is it essential to make a distinction between the oligopolistic and non-oligopolistic sectors of the economy but that, in addition, the former gives rise to a pricing dynamic which is a significant source of autonomous inflationary pressure.

The dynamic derives from the substantial market power - or pricing discretion - which the firms in the oligopolistic sector possess and from the interaction between these firms and certain trade unions which results in the establishment of the national incremental wage pattern. Implicit in the oligopolistic pricing model which forms the core of this work is a cost-push explanation of the inflationary process - with equal emphasis on wage and profit factors - that supplements the more generally recognized excess-demand theories.

The purpose of this volume, then, is to provide a valid micro foundation for Keynesian - and post-Keynesian - macroeconomic theory.[5] The aim is to make it unnecessary to rely on the neo-classical model for microeconomic analysis, thereby removing a major source of the resistance to Keynesian ideas. This purpose is accomplished, first by developing a model based on assumptions that more accurately reflect conditions in the oligopolistic sector and, second, by relating the variable to be explained to the same key determinant as that found in the basic Keynesian system. In the oligopolistic pricing model that follows, a change in the industry price level is held to be a function, costs remaining constant, of a change in the rate of growth of investment relative to the rate of growth of internal funds generation. Put another way, prices in the oligopolistic sector are set not to maximize short-run profits but rather to enable the firms in that sector to finance the level of investment necessary to maximize - or at least move further toward maximizing - their own long-run growth. It is this crucial link between the pricing decision and the investment decision which, among other things, sets this oligopolistic model apart from others.

Aside from its greater compatibility with the Keynesian system, the pricing model developed here has several other important characteristics. For one thing, as already alluded to, it is predicated upon realistic assumptions, that is, assumptions descriptive of actual conditions in oligopolistic industries. These assumptions, justified more fully in the next chapter, pertain to the representative firm in the oligopolistic sector, a firm which, for communicative convenience, shall henceforth be referred to as a megacorp. The assumptions made about the megacorp are threefold: (1) that it is characterized by a separation of management from ownership, with the effective decision-making power residing in the former; (2) that production occurs within multiple plants or plant segments, the factor coefficients for each of these plants or plant segments being fixed due to both technological and institutional constraints, and (3) that the firm's output is sold under conditions of recognized interdependence, the members of the industry engaging in what has been termed 'joint profit maximization'.[6] Each of these assumptions is of critical importance analytically. The first bears on the motivation of the firm, determining the behaviorial rule that will be followed for pricing decisions; the second assumption bears on the shape of the megacorp's cost curves, determining the incremental expense incurred over the relevant range of output, and the third assumption bears on the nature of the megacorp's revenue curve, or function.

Another important characteristic of the model developed here is that it leads to a determinate solution. It is this determinateness, together with the realistic nature of the underlying assumptions, which makes the model unique. On the one hand, other models which also provide a determinate solution, such as the classical Cournot duopoly model, lack realism. They are based on premises that either contradict the behavioral definition of oligopoly or are in some other crucial aspect incompatible with observed conditions.[7] On the other hand, previously available models which are realistic, such as the frequently employed percentage markup or cost-plus model, are indeterminate. They lead to a multiplicity of possible price levels (R. Hall and Hitch, 1939; Lanzilotti, 1958). Falling somewhere between these two polarities is the 'game theory' approach. Whatever its merits, this approach has so far failed to produce a model of oligopolistic pricing that is both determinate and realistic.[8]

The determinateness of the oligopolistic model presented below in chapter 3 is, however, of a special type. First, the solution is discernible only from the long-run perspective of the industry as a whole, with one megacorp, the price leader, acting as surrogate for all the members of that industry. As long as the focus remains either on the individual firm acting independently and/or on the short-run situation, the price in an oligopolistic industry will continue to appear indeterminate. Second, what is determinate from the long-run perspective of the industry as a whole is not the absolute price level but rather the change in that price level from one time period to the next. Thus the price in an oligopolistic industry can be understood only in terms of the marginal adjustment that occurs with respect to a historically established figure.

That marginal adjustment, however, is fully determinate within the hypothetical model. The price leader, on behalf of the industry, will vary the industry price so as to cover (1) any change in per unit average variable and fixed costs, and (2) any increased need for internally generated funds. Whether additional internal funds are needed will depend on the prospective return from the investment of those funds relative to the real costs incurred should the industry price be increased. These real costs, which serve as the effective restraint on the pricing power, or discretion, of the megacorp, derive from three sources: (a) the substitution effect, that is, the loss of market to substitute products as the relative price rises; (b) the entry factor, that is, the probability of new firms entering the industry as the absolute price rises, and (c) the fear of meaningful government intervention, that is, the probability of action by public authorities to impair the long-run growth prospects of the megacorp. From these costs it is possible to derive the equivalent of an interest rate, it then being possible to compare this implicit interest rate on internally derived funds with not only the megacorp's own marginal efficiency of investment but also the cost of external funds. Any resulting change in industry price will be one that is designed to maximize the long-run growth of the price leader - if not the other megacorps in the industry - by providing the price leader with an optimal quantity of internally generated investment funds.

The oligopolistic pricing model developed here is thus an elaboration of the cost-plus model cited so extensively in the survey literature - with one crucial refinement. The 'plus' in the cost-plus formula - why it varies both over time and among industries - is fully explained (Eichner 1973a). In the course of explaining this 'plus' item, the model builds on the earlier work of Baumol (1967) and Marris (1964) as to what motivates the megacorp's executive group and on the previous work of Bain (1949) and Sylos-Labini (1962, part 1) as to how potential entry affects the pricing decision. The precise relationship between the present work and these earlier efforts to explain oligopolistic pricing behavior is spelled out in separate appendixes to chapters 2 and 3. At the same time, the analysis points out the irrelevance of the conventional Chamberlin-Robinson monopoly model insofar as oligopoly with homogeneous products is concerned (Chamberlin, 1962; J. Robinson, 1969), it being shown that if there is to be a determinate price in such an industry, with the elasticities of demand actually observed in the oligopolistic sector, it will almost certainly reflect the unexercised monopoly power which Galbraith (1957) has on occasion pointed to (see also Galbraith 1952, 1967a). But this 'unexercised monopoly power', rather than indicating the type of satisficing behavior postulated by Simon (1955) and Cyert and March (1956, 1963), is instead simply one of the factors which, more appropriately termed the substitution effect, determine the shape of the megacorp's supply curve for internally generated funds - the latter being the analytical device for linking the pricing decision to the investment decision.

Once developed to fit the simple case of a megacorp-price leader which is a member of but a single oligopolistic industry, the model can be altered and extended to cover other types of enterprises, including the unregulated monopolist, the regulated monopolist and the conglomerate or multi-industry firm. By assigning the proper values to certain of the key variables as well as by making certain other modifications, even the perfectly competitive - or polypolistic[9] - firm can be analyzed within the same general framework. The effect is to cast in a somewhat different light the pricing model which has until now dominated microeconomic theory. These alterations and extensions of the basic oligopolistic model are described in chapter 4.

To complete the reformulation of microeconomic theory, it is necessary only to supplement the oligopolistic pricing model with an explanation of factor pricing or, viewed differently, the distribution of income within the megacorp. For this purpose, because of the fixed nature of the technical coefficients - at least in the short run - the traditional marginal productivity approach is irrelevant. Instead it is necessary to adopt an alternative approach, one that combines the institutional economists' emphasis on power relationships and the sociologists' focus on societal norms with the Marxian theory of surplus value, the Keynesian stress on aggregate demand factors and the linkage between the secular growth rate and the savings propensities of different groups brought out in post-Keynesian macrodynamic models.[10] This is done in chapter 5. There, in a return to one of the themes brought out in chapter 2, the megacorp is viewed as being confronted by various constituencies whose claims against its revenue are mediated by the executive group. The two most important of these constituencies are (1) the members of the laboring manpower force, a significant proportion of whom, it is assumed, are represented in collective bargaining by one or more trade unions, and (2) the equity debt or stockholders. The latter, it should be emphasized, serve as rentiers rather than as the recipients of the residual income share. They differ from the other constituent groups only insofar as the legal conventions enable them to bring to bear certain unique forms of pressure *vis-à-vis* the executive group. Since this view of the megacorp's nominal owners permeates other chapters as well, the entire treatise can be included among the growing body of managerial theories of the firm.[11]

The theory of income distribution developed in chapter 5 suggests that, as a result of practices that have evolved over time, the compensation received by the megacorp's other constituencies, including the equity shareholders, is geared to that obtained by the organized portion of the laboring manpower force. This means that the trade union, in bargaining for its own members, is in effect putting forth the claims of all the households dependent on the megacorp for income. The trade union, in turn, is likely to insist upon - and the megacorp to grant - that increase in compensation which has, in a social sense, been deemed 'fair and reasonable' through the mechanism of the national incremental wage pattern. This pattern can be established in a number of different ways, as the practice of other countries attests. In the United States it most typically arises from the 'key' collective bargaining agreement negotiated in one of the major industries, usually steel or automobiles, often only after Presidential intervention with its implicit socio-political sanction. In a period of active government involvement in the economy, the agreement negotiated in the 'key' industry may have to obtain explicit sanction from a Presidentially-appointed tripartite board. This, of course, was the case under the anti-inflationary program announced by President Nixon in the fall of 1971 and later endorsed by Congress. But it should be noted that the same was true during World War II and the Korean conflict.

Thus the increase in compensation obtained by the megacorp's principal constituencies - and *a fortiori* any increase in per unit costs - will depend, time lags aside, on the national incremental wage pattern established at the macro level. What in effect is determined in that key bargain is the nominal division between the household and business sectors of that portion of the current national income not already commandeered by government. The key bargain therefore represents the first step in the allocation of resources in the private sector between present and future consumption. In Marxian terms, the issue with which the key bargain is concerned is the disposition of the incremental surplus value created by individual megacorps, this incremental surplus value in the aggregate constituting the marginal social surplus arising in the oligopolistic sector. Any increase, either in wages or dividends, represents an apportionment of part of that incremental surplus value to households.

Yet the issue is not fully resolved, even after other trade unions have forced the megacorps with which they bargain collectively to grant increases in compensation equal to the national incremental wage pattern. For after the nominal wage rate has been agreed to, and per unit costs as a result determined, megacorps still retain the power to alter the various industry price levels and thereby, unconcertedly but none the less effectively, fix the real wage rate. With the theory of income distribution provided in chapter 5, it is possible to go on and explain in chapters 6 and 7 this process by which the real wage rate is determined - at least within the oligopolistic subsector of the economy. Chapter 6 uses the microeconomic base developed in the earlier chapters to sketch the outlines of a macrodynamic theory. Among the important points brought out are the following:

1. Because of the behavioral principle followed by the megacorp, investment within the oligopolistic subsector depends primarily on the expected rate of growth of industry and, *pari passu*, of aggregate demand. The oligopolistic pricing model which forms the core of this volume thus lends theoretical support to the accelerator model of investment now increasingly employed by empirical investigators - and in particular to the lagged industry sales version of that model developed by Eisner (1963, 1967). This model contrasts sharply with the determinants of investment in the competitive subsector, as well as those emphasized in economics textbooks.

2. With the oligopolistic sector in fact accounting for most of the private investment actually undertaken, the savings-investment equilibrium adjustment process needs to be reformulated. Assuming household savings to be relatively constant and only a minor contributor, in any case, to capital formation in the business sector, it follows that the critical savings decisions are those made by megacorps. These decisions are reflected in the margins above contracted costs at which price levels in the oligopolistic sector are set. Thus, as in the pre-Keynesian schema, the decisions of how much to save and how much to invest are in the hands of the same party. However, because the price levels must necessarily be set on the basis of expected sales volume - forecasts of which are subject to considerable error due to fluctuations in aggregate demand - the possibility of *ex ante* and *ex post* savings diverging, at least within the oligopolistic sector, nevertheless remains.

3. Given the first two propositions, a post-Keynesian macrodynamic model along the lines first set forth by Robinson (1956, 1962a) and Kaldor (1957) then emerges (see also Kaldor and Mirrlees, 1962). The model follows the earlier work in almost every important respect, including

the assumption of a flexible savings ratio and the rejection of a neo-classical production function. The one significant modification is that the flexibility of the savings ratio hinges, not on a presumed difference in the marginal propensity to consume out of wages and out of profits - and the effect that this difference has on aggregate savings as the share of national income accruing to property owners varies - but rather, on the power of megacorps, through the control which they exercise over prices, to alter the savings ratio. In this model the possibility of achieving steady growth, ignoring the influence of the government sector, depends on the ability of megacorps to set their prices so as to achieve a rate of growth of real savings equal to the rate of growth of real investment dictated by industry growth trends. This need not, however, be an optimum growth rate nor one unaccompanied by inflation.

Chapter 7 picks up on this last point, first exploring what might determine the optimum, or 'potential' growth rate. The conclusion reached is that the limit set on the rate of economic expansion by the availability of manpower and the rate of technological change is merely that - a limit which the economy can only approach - and that the real explanation for why growth rates in an advanced economy like that of the United States are not greater than observed is the difficulty of engineering any change in the secular growth rate. The oligopolistic sector, because of the factors determining the level of investment and the rate at which it generates internal funds, tends to exert pressure on the economy to maintain whatever growth rate has previously been established; and efforts by the government to put the economy on a different growth path are unlikely to succeed unless a complex set of adjustments can be made. The conventional policy instruments available to government, both fiscal and monetary, are ill-suited for this role. Indeed, they are likely to make the task of achieving macrodynamic balance at a higher growth rate all the more difficult. These shortcomings of the conventional policy instruments form the underlying theme of the chapter, and this theme is carried through in a final section reviewing what happened to the American economy during the 1960s.

Chapter 7 also points out that the aggregate supply function is quite different from what it is generally assumed to be, at least insofar as prices are concerned. The argument is based on the earlier showing that the price level in oligopolistic industries depends not on fluctuating levels of sales but rather on changes in costs and/or changes in the long-run demand for and supply of investment funds. This means that the aggregate price level itself - at least that portion attributable to the oligopolistic sector - will be insensitive to, that is, independent of, short-run fluctuations in demand. It will instead reflect the adjustment necessary to bring the need of megacorps for additional investment funds into line with the claims against revenue arising from forced acceptance of the national incremental wage pattern. In this respect, as several writers have suggested, the aggregate price level serves as a 'safety valve', dissipating otherwise unmanageable pressures by both the household and business sectors for additional current resources.[12] It also, of course, makes the aggregate price level less amenable to control through the conventional policy instruments available to government.

The final chapter draws out the policy implications of the preceding analysis. There a strategy is set forth for remedying the lack of effective social control over the megacorp revealed earlier. The key recommendation is that a system of national indicative planning be established. This recommendation is based on a proposition which emerges as the major policy conclusion of the study - namely, that effective social control over the individual megacorp can be achieved by no more and no less than regulating both the rate of growth, and the composition, of aggregate investment. If this conclusion is valid, Keynes (1936, p. 278) will turn out to have been more prophetic than is generally realized when he suggested that 'a somewhat comprehensive socialization of investment will prove the only means of securing an approximation to full employment.' For the principal reason that unemployment has been as high as it has been since the end of World War II is that governments have mistakenly attempted to arrest the wage-price inflationary spiral by curtailing aggregate demand. If the arguments to be presented in this volume are correct, the wage-price spiral can be prevented only by bringing the megacorp, not to mention trade unions, under more effective social control via the regulation of aggregate investment. What should give some heart to those who fear the government assuming an overbearing role in the economy is that this form of regulation is far less stifling than the alternatives which others have insisted are necessary - and indeed far less stifling, in important ways, than the type of regulation so recently instituted in this and other countries to deal with the problem of inflation.

Before proceeding further, it might be worth while to pause and make clear the conceptualization of the economic system that underlies the entire work.

In the analysis that follows, the economy will be viewed primarily in terms of three sectors - household, business and government - each characterized by a different type of decision-making unit.[13] In the household sector the pertinent decision-making unit is the family. Its unique role in the economic system is two-fold. First, it alone supplies the manpower resources indispensable to the production process. Second, it alone provides the economic system with a rationale, the ultimate justification of the system being its ability to reduce the material barriers to the realization by the family of its goals in life. Despite the obvious importance of the household sector it will be dealt with only peripherally, largely because the primary concern is with price determination in the business sector. The behavior of the family as it affects prices follows a relatively stable pattern and can, for that reason, be taken largely for granted.

The pertinent decision-making unit in the government sector is the political sovereignty exercising, through its monopoly of coercive power, exclusive jurisdiction over specified activities within a given geographical area. In the United States there are numerous such political sovereignties, including the many municipalities and states; however, this volume shall be concerned primarily with the Federal government because it alone exercises control over aggregate fiscal and monetary affairs. Much of what will be said about that political sovereignty will, of course, apply to the national governments of other countries, too.

The political sovereignty's unique role in the economic system is again two-fold. First, it alone determines the rules by which the economic system is to be operated. These rules include, in the case of the Federal government, what may constitute legal tender and monetary reserves. Second, it alone is capable of transcending the economic system by using its taxing power to commandeer resources outside normal market channels.

The pertinent decision-making unit in the business sector is the firm or enterprise. Its unique role is simply to direct the production process, determining what goods or services are to be made available, in what quantity and by what means. A fundamental premise underlying this treatise, as already noted, is that for an adequate understanding of how the economic system presently functions in the United States it is necessary to divide the business sector into at least two components, one consisting of all oligopolistic industries, the other, all remaining industries (cf. Averitt, 1968). Each of these industries consists of a cluster of firms, all of whom keep a watch on the same set of prices. Indeed, this description provides the operational definition of an industry that will be used throughout this work – that group of firms which share a day-to-day interest in the same set of price quotations for a class of goods they are each capable of producing.[14] While the manner in which these price quotations are established will vary according to the type of industry, this is not the basis for distinguishing the oligopolistic subsector from the rest of the business sector. The critical distinction has to do instead with the nature of the representative firm. In the oligopolistic subsector, the representative firm is the megacorp; in the rest of the business sector, it is the vestigal neo-classical proprietorship.

The analytical importance of this distinction between the oligopolistic and non-oligopolistic subsectors forms the principal subject matter of the chapters that follow. Suffice it for now to indicate the actual empirical significance of oligopoly in the American economy.

Taking value added as the measure of an industry's relative impact on the economy, it would appear that only in manufacturing and, to a somewhat lesser degree, in mining is oligopoly the predominate form of market structure. In manufacturing, for which the only reliable data are available, oligopolistic industries account for approximately two-thirds of all value added (Kaysen and Turner, 1959, ch. 2; Shepherd, 1970, part 2). This prevalence of oligopoly in manufacturing would by itself make the phenomenon worthy of understanding, despite any low incidence in the rest of the business sector. However, the prevalence of oligopoly in manufacturing has a significance which goes beyond what can be measured in terms of value added. To appreciate this fact, it is necessary to further schematize the business sector.

Each class of goods or services produced by the business sector can be viewed as having traveled, before emerging in final form, a production path uniquely its own, beginning with the initial extraction of raw materials from nature and continuing through the further processing, transportation, distribution, etc. of those raw materials at each successive stage. This progressive flow of total output is perhaps best represented, though still quite imperfectly, by the triangularization of an input-output table. At different points along the various paths, usually where two or more flows come together to create a new product, different industries are located. What is particularly true of industries in the manufacturing sector is that they lie astride a large proportion of all production paths - and at points where the volume of flow is perhaps most easily regulated. The pervasiveness of oligopoly in manufacturing thus takes on a special significance; it is no mere coincidence that oligopoly first emerged in that sector when it did. As the historical record makes clear, oligopoly was established primarily as a means of offsetting the downward pressure on prices during the latter third of the nineteenth century resulting both from the ability of supply to outpace the secular growth of demand and from the susceptibility of the economy to cyclical declines in activity (Eichner, 1969; Porter, 1973). The manufacturing sector, because of its strategic location, was the logical point at which to attempt the stabilization of prices. If, because an industry is oligopolistic, the member firms possess a certain degree of market power, this market power will be felt by those industries situated both antecedently and subsequently along the production path. To the extent that these other industries are without a comparable degree of market power, the range of discretion enjoyed by the oligopolistic industry in the manufacturing sector will, in fact, be all the greater. The significance of oligopoly's pervasiveness in manufacturing, then, is that such industries are strategically located in the economic system and possess sufficient market power to influence, somewhat independently through their pricing decisions, the flow of output throughout the business sector.

The economic system as a whole is defined not only by this flow of goods and services within the business sector but also by other flows as well. In one direction, providing the economic system with its rationale, move the various goods and services produced both by the business sector itself and by the other two sectors. This flow, with numerous feedback loops to handle factor inputs, constitutes the 'real' economy. In the other direction, serving as payment for the goods and services received, move the claims against total output which take the form of money. This flow, with the Federal Reserve Board serving as the overall regulating authority, constitutes the monetary economy. The two flows are equilibrated - except for certain of the governmental connections - through markets such as those for consumer goods, raw materials, etc. The adjustments necessary to equalize the contrary flows can come about in one of three ways: through a change in the quantity of goods or services being supplied, through a change in the amount of claims being given up in return, or through a change in the price ratio that defines the exchange relationship between the two flows. Assuming an initial equilibrium, a change in any one of these three variables will, of course, require a change in at least one other.

One of the most important controversies among economists at the present time centers on the question of the extent to which, by regulating the monetary economy, it is possible to regulate the real economy as well. Some economists would argue that the potential for effective control already exists; others would argue that, with certain changes in the authority of the Federal Reserve Board, effective control could be established.[15] The premise underlying this volume, however, is that the function of the monetary system is primarily to provide lubricating fluid for the real economy. To use it instead as a hydraulic control device is to run the risk not only that the regulation will be clumsy and ineffectual but that it will also seriously impair the working of the entire system. With hydraulic control resting on the ability to restrict the total availability of claims, only generalized restraint is possible; there is no way of directing pressure to the particular parts of the economy where it is specifically required or desired. Moreover, if price ratios are simultaneously being used to adjust the conflicting claims of households and business firms on current resources, and if business firms possess sufficient market power to assure that the prices they decide upon will prevail, then the burden of adjustment will fall on the real economy

- with socially undesirable consequences for output and employment. For this reason, the treatise assumes that it is better to seek out those critical variables in the operation of the real economy that are susceptible to social control, allowing the monetary system to function instead as a sympathetic facilitating mechanism. This is not to suggest that monetary policy be eschewed entirely - if indeed that were possible. It is merely to point out that the role of monetary policy is essentially complementary and subordinate.

When families and business firms, in exchange for the goods and services they provide, receive more claims than they choose to exercise the two types of decision-making units will necessarily emerge as net savers. This they will do by increasing their stocks of financial assets - with the output against which they have not exercised their claims thereby becoming available for capital formation. In the usual conceptualization of the economy it is the role of families as savers that is emphasized. This volume, however, plays down the importance of households in this respect. It does so for two reasons: first, because much of what the family does save is the result of involuntary action, the financial assets being accumulated through life insurance and pension programs over which the family has little or no control; and second, because the family accounts for only a minor portion of total private savings.[16]

Instead, as already noted, this treatise emphasizes the role of business firms as savers, the savings themselves taking the form of 'cash flow', that is, a combination of depreciation allowances and retained earnings.[17] Since it will be argued that the cash flow is not simply a residue or balance figure but is in fact a quantity deliberately chosen to enable the megacorp to achieve its investment goals and since, moreover, the cash flow does not include all of the megacorp's discretionary income, the less passive and more inclusive term 'corporate levy' will be used throughout. It includes, besides cash flow, the cost of advertising, research and development (R & D) and similar expenditures designed to enhance the megacorp's long-run market position; and it will be used interchangeably with such terms as discretionary income, internally generated funds, and individual megacorp savings.

The counterpart of the corporate levy in the government sector is, of course, the excise tax, whether it takes the form of a levy on sales, imports, luxuries, alcoholic beverages or the like. While this type of tax might at first seem less significant than others, the phenomenon of a government levy being incorporated into the price structure is, in fact, a fairly general one. As this volume attempts to demonstrate, the tax on corporate net income is simply passed along to customers in the form of higher prices and thus it serves as the equivalent of a generalized sales tax. Even the personal income tax, which stands as the one important type of government levy that is not an excise tax, influences to some degree - the extent to which it affects work incentives - the price structure of labor inputs. Needless to say, it is the total revenue from all taxes, excise and non-excise, that constitutes the level of savings generated by the government sector.

In this conceptualization of the economy, the megacorp and the political sovereignty both occupy similarly strategic positions - even if there nonetheless remain crucial differences in their respective powers. Both play a critical role in the capital accumulation process, the megacorp by seeing to it that facilities are created for the production of marketable goods and services, the political sovereignty by seeing to it that facilities are created for the provision of non-marketable, that is, public or collective goods and services. In developing those facilities, both the megacorp and the political sovereignty are able to tap savings in one of the other sectors - even though for the most part they prefer to adjust their respective levies to generate a level of savings equal to the level of desired investment. Finally, since the amount of revenue actually realized from their respective levies depends on the level of aggregate economic activity, both may find themselves running an unexpected surplus or deficit of savings. It is the ability of the megacorp and the political sovereignty to initiate the process of capital accumulation, then finance investment expenditures through levies of their own that makes these two types of economic decision-making units the logical points within the real economy at which to attempt to exercise control - for the first prerogative largely determines, in the aggregate, the rate of economic growth, the second the stability of the system and the two together the relative welfare of individual family units.

The economic system is a mechanism not merely for maintaining existing material standards of living but, more important, for improving upon those standards. In other words, the system for all its feedback loops is not closed or circular. It is open-ended, with a built-in capacity for increasing the output of goods and services. That built-in capacity derives from the ability of business firms - megacorps in particular - and political sovereignties - primarily the national government - to obtain control over resources, withholding those resources from current consumption so that they can be used to increase the system's productive capacity. The resulting increase in goods and services is what is meant by economic growth. The theory of pricing contained herein is predicated on the assumption that economic growth is continuous - even if the rate itself fluctuates. Its conclusions apply only to an economy in which such a positive rate of growth is the normal expectation.

In an economy that is either stagnant or in secular decline, the theory developed in the chapters which follow has little or no applicability. It is precisely for an economy of this type that the neo-classical microeconomic theory is best suited. Thus, just as the theoretical model outlined below is inappropriate for analyzing a stagnant or declining economy, so the neo-classical model is inappropriate for an expanding economy. Indeed, as Joan Robinson (1971, chs. 1 and 2) has pointed out, the use of the neo-classical analysis in a growth context involves a fundamental contradiction. A positive rate of economic growth has, however, been the predominant experience of American society since at least the origins of the megacorp around the turn of the century. For this reason, the theoretical model developed below is the more appropriate one for understanding contemporary problems.

Economic growth, however, occurs within limits set by the larger society's current stage of economic development. Thus it is necessary to distinguish economic growth from economic development. The latter depends, not on the output of goods and services at any one point in time but rather on the extent to which the society's human resources have been developed, both in terms of producing individual skills and of establishing the complex of institutions necessary for giving those skills full scope. In other words, economic development depends on the growth of institutions and human skills, economic growth on how completely those institutions and skills are then utilized. It is, of course, possible to develop new institutions and to increase the skill content of a society's population; but the time horizon is quite long and significant results cannot be expected in less than a generation. The current state of economic development, then, serves as the ultimate constraint in the intermediate run - what is referred to here as the planning period - on the rate of economic growth which a society can hope to achieve. Put another way, the increase in output cannot exceed the expansionary limits of the existing stock of skills and institutions.

It should be noted that the intermediate run, or planning period, is the time required to bring a new plant into operation, beginning with the decision to build it. In addition, reference will be made throughout this work to the pricing period - the interval between changes in the industry price level; to the short run - a duration of time less than the planning period; and to the long run - a duration of time greater than the planning period, extending potentially into the indefinite future.

The current stage of economic development is important for another reason. It determines the appropriateness or relevance of any particular body of economic theory. An underlying assumption of this volume is that as an economic system continues to evolve, creating new types of institutions to replace the old, the currently preferred conceptual framework with its attendant theoretical models becomes increasingly less relevant until finally, when an entirely different stage of development has been reached, it becomes an actual handicap to understanding. Thus the neo-classical theory of the firm, devised with the institution of the nineteenth-century proprietorship in mind, is a poor analytical device for explaining the behavior of the twentieth-century megacorp.[18] This point about the relativity of economic theory applies as well, of course, to the oligopolistic pricing model presented below.

The upper limit to the rate of economic growth set by the current stage of development is merely that: an upper limit. The actual growth path, it can be assumed, will in fact be quite erratic, with pronounced cyclical fluctuations in aggregate economic activity. This is because the economy will necessarily find itself beset from time to time by a major shift in some exogenous factor. It is this bombardment of the economic system by forces from without that precludes a theoretical stationary state from ever being actually realized. Thus it is the tendency toward disequilibrium rather than the tendency toward equilibrium which is the fact of actual economic experience; and both the megacorp and the political sovereignty in their respective planning and operational activities must be prepared to take that fact into account.

Were the economic system capable of reacting to the change in the exogenous factor quickly enough by making the appropriate price adjustments, the adverse affects might easily be contained without the need for any conscious intervention. But this is more than can be expected of the price mechanism. Consequently, the shift in the exogenous factor will necessarily lead to some change in real flows - even if the change is somewhat muted by whatever price adjustments have occurred. If sufficiently pronounced, the change in real flows can, in turn, be expected to cause a change in expectations which, when made the basis for subsequent decisions in the private sector, will tend to be self-confirming. In the absence of some further shift in one of the exogenous factors, such as a change in government policy, the working of the economic system *per se* will tend to reinforce whatever trend has previously emerged, whether that trend is consistent with an optimum growth path or not. In presupposing this underlying dynamic, the treatise merely accepts the thrust of the Kenyesian argument that, because price adjustments cannot be relied upon to completely neutralize the effect of exogenous shocks to the economic system, a continuous situation in which some significant portion of society's resources remains unemployed is not only likely but, indeed, highly probable.[19]

The duration and amplitude of any cyclical deviation from the optimum growth path will depend to a large degree on what response the various megacorps and the political sovereignty make to the change in real flows. To the extent that any one of them continues to generate a level of savings that is greater than its rate of investment, it will contribute to the slackening of aggregate economic activity; to the extent that it continues to generate a level of savings that is less than the rate of investment, it will contribute to the stimulation of the economy. In these matters the megacorp and the political sovereignty both enjoy considerable discretion. The power of the latter to alter the level of its expenditures and/or taxes is widely recognized, as is the power of the megacorp to alter the level of its investment outlays. But the power of the megacorp to alter its rate of savings through a change in price is no less critical to the stability of the economic system. What is required, if fluctuations in aggregate economic activity are to be minimized, is that any imbalance between savings and investment which arises in one sector, whether it be business or government, be offset by a deficit of the opposite sort in the other sector. Yet this is not likely to happen with sufficient speed or certainty unless there is some specific mechanism for coordinating *ex ante* decisions between the business and government sectors.

The point of reference for this volume is the economic welfare of the individual. That welfare, it can be demonstrated, will depend both on whether the growth rate of household income is, over time, being maximized (i.e. how close the society comes to the optimum growth path permitted by the current stage of development) and on whether fluctuations in aggregate economic activity are minimized (i.e. how little the economy deviates from that optimum growth path). Since the megacorp plays such a critical role in the growth and stability of the economic system, it seems clear that the economic welfare of the individual is closely tied to the performance of that institution. But the megacorp affects the economic welfare of the individual in yet another way. Basic to this treatise is the recognition that different households stand in different relationship to the megacorp. Some are merely final consumers of the products which the megacorp turns out. Other households have members who, in addition, are employees of the megacorp. Still other households have members who, as stockholders, hold legal title to the megacorp's residual income. These different relationships bear significantly on the economic welfare of the individual, for they determine the extent to which as a member of some household the individual will share in the bountifulness of American society.

As a final introductory word, it might be well to state precisely what is claimed of the theory presented below. Like any theory, it does not encompass all the phenomena of its universe - the universe in its case being that of the oligopolistic sector. But, it can be argued, the theory does encompass more of those phenomena - with respect, for example, to prices, investment and wage rates - than the alternative body of theory derived from neo-classical assumptions. As such it provides, not a final vantage place for viewing those phenomena but rather, a better point of departure for further analysis and empirical study. In other words, since resort must be had to some body of microeconomic theory in policy formulation and scholarly research, the theory presented below, it is asserted, is the better choice - at least with respect to the oligopolistic sector. Certainly its assumptions, if not its conclusions, are more consistent with what is known about the industries and firms that comprise that sector. The conventional neo-classical analysis, on the other hand, has only the comfortableness of accustomed modes of thinking to recommend it. To fit the reality of the oligopolistic sector its conclusions and its assumptions must be drastically altered.

2. The nature of the megacorp

The analysis of how prices are determined under oligopolistic conditions must begin with an examination of the megacorp, the representative firm found in that type of market structure. The megacorp, as the name implies, is a large corporation, typified by the companies included in Fortune Magazine's annual directory of the 500 largest corporations. Size alone, however, whether measured by sales or assets, is not what distinguishes the megacorp, either analytically or descriptively, from business firms in general. There are three other characteristics - each of which requires a specific modification of the conventional microanalytical apparatus - that define the megacorp as the representative firm in oligopoly. These characteristics are (1) the separation of management from ownership, this leading to a different behavioral pattern from that usually assumed in pricing models,[1] (2) multi-plant operation with fixed factor, or technical, coefficients, this producing a different set of cost curves, and (3) membership in at least one oligopolistic industry, this giving rise to a different type of revenue curve for the individual firm. Each of these characteristics, together with their respective theoretical implications, will be discussed in turn.

The separation of management from ownership

The widespread separation of management from ownership in American corporations, first pointed out by Adolf A. Berle and Gardiner C. Means in their classic 1933 volume, has now been confirmed by a more recent study. Individual stockholdings in 169 of the 200 largest non-financial corporations, that study reveals, are so widely distributed that effective control can be assumed to have fallen into the hands of a self-perpetuating management group without a significant proprietary interest in their own particular company.[2] While a comparable investigation has yet to be made of lesser corporations, there is no reason to assume that the phenomenon is limited only to the 200 largest such firms.

This separation of management from ownership, a characteristic observed in other countries with a similarly well developed market-type of economy, reflects two historical trends: first, the proliferation of stockholders in large corporations over time as personal considerations have necessitated the selling off of portions of the original blocks of stock and, second, the indispensability of professional, technically trained managers for the successful operations of a large company. These historical trends, themselves the result of creating a business organization the life of which extends beyond that of any single individual, have led to a shift in the locus of control within those firms which have become megacorps. While the stockholders may retain their nominal property rights, the actual power of decision-making has come to reside in the hands of the executive group, consisting of the chief executive officer, the active directors and the various vice-presidents (R. A. Gordon, 1945, ch. 5). The stockholders, diffuse, lacking leadership and unable to give more than occasional thought to the affairs of the megacorp, have become passive *rentiers* whose major concern is the size of the dividends and/or the current market price of their shares.

This change in the nature of ownership in what, under advanced economic conditions, is the most important form of property has transformed the capitalism of the nineteenth century into an economic system of quite a different sort. Sometimes referred to as 'managerial capitalism' (Marris, 1964), the new system represents the latest working out of what Marx called the dialectical laws of history and what Veblen spoke of as the evolutionary process. The former system of property rights and social relations, having come under attack because the means of production that were privately owned transcended in importance any one person's individual interest, has not been replaced, as some had hoped, by an antithetic socialism. Instead, in those sectors of the economy where the issue was germane, it has evolved into an entirely different system, one in which certain of the old property rights, primarily those relating to income, are still respected; but others, principally those relating to the disposition of the actual physical facilities, have been abrogated and turned over to a new class of men with a different mandate of responsibility. In the process, as it has become virtually impossible for sons to succeed fathers as heads of businesses, the very nature of inheritance has been drastically altered.

Thus the stockholders have become but one of the megacorp's several constituencies, albeit with certain unique powers. Only they, for example, have the *de jure* right to depose the incumbent executive group, a right which, though seldom exercised,[3] nonetheless gives them an advantage in bargaining power over at least some of the megacorp's other constituencies. These other constituencies are the fixed-interest debt holders, the laboring manpower force, the suppliers of material inputs, franchised distributors and the final consumers of the product. But though the stockholders may find themselves in a better bargaining position than some of the megacorp's other constituencies when it comes to the distribution of revenue, their influence over the operating policies that determine the size of that revenue is no greater. Of all the prerogatives of control, they retain only the right to ratify certain decisions of the management, a right which in most cases is more apparent than real.

Since it is the executive group that wields the effective decision-making power, it is the psychological propensities and goals of that body which will determine the megacorp's behavioral pattern and, following from that, the decision rule which will be observed in setting price and output levels. In the case of the neo-classical proprietorship, it is not unreasonable to assume that the behavioral pattern is to maximize net revenue, that is, the returns above contractual costs, in the short run. In view of the uncertainty as to how long the firm will be able to continue in business as well as the owner-managers' direct financial interest in whatever net income is earned, such a behavioral pattern is not irrational. Anyway, it is the behavioral pattern assumed in the conventional theory of the firm. In the case of the megacorp, however, the situation is quite different.

To begin with, the megacorp is a permanent institution. While it may suffer temporary reverses, its strategic position within the overall economy - its large share of one or more markets, the combination of skills, knowledge and experience embodied in its work force, and its ready access to capital markets - assures against outright demise in all except the most unusual of circumstances.[4] This sense of permanence pervades the actions of the executive group, and its members are able to make decisions based on long-run considerations that would be unthinkable to those in charge of a firm with a less certain life expectancy. By the same token, the megacorp's managers are unlikely to try to capitalize on short-run opportunities if to do so will jeopardize the company's long-run position (R. A. Gordon, 1945, pp. 331ff; Marris, 1964, p. 63).

This tendency to take a far-sighted view is reinforced by the fact that, except to the limited extent that its members are also stockholders, the executive group has only an indirect personal stake in whatever net income the megacorp may earn in any one year. The way in which stock option plans, bonuses and other forms of executive compensation are structured gives the members of the executive group even greater incentive to avoid short-run gains at the expense of the megacorp's long-run position.[5] Although the incumbent management runs the risk of incurring stockholder displeasure if reported earnings unexplainably fall below either the previous year's results or those of megacorps in general, this consideration places only a minimum restraint on its actions.[6] Of course, the executive group would prefer that the megacorp earn more rather than less net income. But net income is desirable, not so much because of the dividends which it makes possible as because of the overall financial strength which it affords the megacorp. The executive group's primary loyalty, in fact, is to the megacorp as an ongoing institution, not to the stockholders as owners. Whatever status or sense of accomplishment the megacorp's managers may have is but a reflection of the standing which their company has in the larger community. In working to enhance that position, they are simultaneously adding to their own prestige, and thus there is a considerable harmony between the goals of the executive group and those of the megacorp its members direct.[7]

This is not to deny that, as some writers have pointed out,[8] an individual megacorp executive will often find himself faced with a conflict between what is in his own best interests and what is in the best interests of his company. But the extent of the conflict is likely to be exaggerated if the best interests of the company are necessarily assumed to be identical with those of the stockholders. That the equity debt holders constitute but one of several constituencies associated with the megacorp has already been suggested. Carrying the logic of this conceptualization one step further, the megacorp must be viewed as having a life - and interests - entirely of its own, separate and distinct from that of any individual or group of individuals. Thus the important point is not whether the actions of an individual manager are inconsistent with the best interests of the stockholders, but rather whether they are inconsistent with best interests of the megacorp *qua* megacorp.

Even so, some divergence of interests between the megacorp and the individual manager can be expected. Several factors, however, serve to mitigate the potential conflict, at least insofar as the members of the executive group are concerned. The first is the process by which a person is chosen to serve on that self-perpetuating body. Each megacorp official is carefully screened as he rises through the organizational hierarchy so that only those deemed to have the necessary loyalty to the company are permitted to advance to the next higher position. Thus by the time a person is selected to serve on the executive group the identification of his own interests with those of the megacorp are likely to be quite substantial. The second factor is the dynamics of a body such as the executive group. The effect of the interaction between its members is to reinforce the group norms which have evolved over the many years, norms which are likely to emphasize a higher duty to the megacorp. As a result, individual interests tend to be subordinated to what is felt to be the more general interests of the organization itself. In fact, it is the interaction between the members of the executive group which enables those more general interests to be defined and articulated. Thus, while the exceptions may be instructive - they may explain, for example, the decline of certain firms or, short of that result, certain aspects of income distribution - it can be assumed, at least for the moment, that the goals of the executive group are coextensive with those of the megacorp.

The goals of any organization presumably are, as a minimum, to survive and, as a maximum, to grow to the full extent permitted by external circumstances.[9] The difference between these two limits may not, however, be very great. On the one hand, if external circumstances foreclose the possibility of growth, survival is all that can be expected. On the other hand, if the organization faces a dynamically competitive situation, simply to survive may require that it grow at the highest rate possible.

To the extent that a megacorp exists independently of any one industry, that is, to the extent that it has evolved into a conglomerate enterprise, it is likely to find itself in the latter type of circumstance. To survive in the long run, it must grow at the highest rate possible. There are two reasons for this, both related to the types of resources which give the megacorp whatever economic power it may possess. First, a conglomerate megacorp that grows less rapidly than its counterparts will be handicapped in its efforts to obtain command over the investment funds necessary for further expansion. Even more important - and this is the second reason - it will experience increasing difficulty in attracting the quality of management essential for long-run survival (Penrose, 1959, ch. 2; Downie, 1958, chs. 7-9; Leyland and Richardson, 1964). Since every firm may potentially evolve into a conglomerate enterprise, the broadest generalization that can be made about the goal or goals of the megacorp is that it will seek to maximize its own long-run rate of growth - depending, of course, on what it perceives to be the possibilities for growth.

How the rate of growth is to be measured is less important than this emphasis on growth itself. Still, if there is any one variable upon which attention should be focused, it is the amount of cash flowing into the megacorp over and above current expenses. Any increase in this sum - more broadly termed the corporate levy as on p. 13 above - will mean an increase in the amount of discretionary income accruing to the megacorp, and thus a lessening of the budgetary constraint on expansion. The most generally applicable prescription, then, if the megacorp is to maximize its own long-run rate of growth, is that it should seek to maximize the secular growth rate of the realized corporate levy.

In most cases, maximizing the rate of growth either of sales or of assets will achieve the same end.[10] Still, there are some situations in which to use the corporate levy either to increase sales or to augment balance sheet assets would not contribute to the megacorp's long-run growth. This would be the case, for example, if sales were to be increased through advertising outlays representing a larger sum than the additional net income subsequently generated; or if a particular asset which was purchased then failed to produce sufficient incremental revenue to cover its acquisition cost. By the same token, there may be ways for the megacorp to grow in terms of the realized corporate levy without necessarily adding either to sales or to assets. This would be the case, for example, if expenditures on research and development were to lead to a reduction in the cost of production. Since, however, it is unlikely that a megacorp will deliberately spend its funds with a promise of negative returns; and since, moreover, most of the gains in productivity that show up as a reduction in costs seem to derive from other than the megacorp's own efforts,[11] it follows that the maximization of the rate of growth of sales or assets is a close approximation to the maximization of the growth of the corporate levy, and all three maximands can in most cases be used interchangeably.

While the above may suffice as a generalized statement of the approximate behavioral pattern for a megacorp, it needs to be modified to take into account the constraints which the megacorp faces as a member of a particular oligopolistic industry. Prices, it must be remembered, pertain only to specific industries. This means that the generalized goal of the firm must be translated into a goal applicable to the individual industry or industries in which the megacorp finds itself. It is this rooting of even a conglomerate megacorp in specific industries that permits the simplifying assumption, at least as a first step, that the megacorp is a member of but a single industry. The analysis throughout the remainder of this chapter and the next will rest on that assumption. However, the basic model does not depend on it, and the assumption will be relaxed in subsequent chapters.

The most important constraint which the megacorp faces as a member of a particular oligopolistic industry is that it cannot use price cuts - at least those likely to come to the attention of its rivals - as a competitive weapon to increase its sales volume and thereby augment its share of the market. The reasons why this is so will be brought out below. For now, it must simply be accepted as a given condition of oligopolistic existence. The prohibition on price competition does not, however, preclude the megacorp from growing in size. The fact is that the industry to which the megacorp belongs is likely to grow itself over time as the general economic expansion increases the demand for the product being supplied. The rate of growth may not be as high as in some industries, those which, enjoying the heady boom of their first years, have not yet settled down to the somewhat more modest growth pattern found within the oligopolistic sector (Abramowitz, 1938);

still, it is likely to be a higher growth rate than that for the economy as a whole.

This growth over time of the industry to which it belongs is the primary source of expansionary opportunity for the megacorp, and simply maintaining an existing share of the industry's market will assure the firm a certain minimum rate of growth. In addition, of course, the megacorp can try to increase its share of the market through non-price forms of competition[12] - even though the chances of success in this regard are slight. Because of the recognized interdependence which exists in an oligopolistic industry, any stratagem by the megacorp to obtain a larger share of the market, even if it goes beyond simply cutting the price, is likely to be neutralized by its rivals' countermoves. Indeed, one of the outstanding empirical characteristics of an oligopolistic industry, and a sure sign that it has reached maturity, is the stability of relative market shares over time.[13]

The only realistic goal, then, for a megacorp within a specific industry is to maintain its relative market share. However, to provide the necessary internal dynamic, that is, to avoid the danger of complacency within the organization, this goal is likely to be modified in practice. The megacorp, it can be assumed, will seek to increase its long-run share of the market even though it recognizes that maintenance of the current market share is the more reasonable expectation. The 'rule of thumb',[14] then, likely to be followed by the megacorp in its efforts to optimize[15] long-run market share is at least to maintain, and if possible perhaps to increase, its current market share.

From the separation of management from ownership, it can thus be inferred that the overall goal of the megacorp is to grow at a maximum rate while the goal within any specific industry is to optimize its long-run market share. Under oligopolistic conditions, these two goals are consistent not only with each other but also with a number of other goals which megacorps are said to pursue - such as maximizing sales and maximizing net revenue over the long run.[16] They are not, however, consistent with maximizing net revenue in the short run - or even with maximizing the present net worth of the firm as reflected by the market price of equity shares. The differences between these two sets of maximands are important, and need to be elaborated on.

Two conditions must hold before the optimization of long-run market share will result in the maximization of a firm's present net worth. First, any increase in net revenue in the long run must ultimately be distributed to the equity debt holders in the form of higher dividends. Second, the capital funds market must function well enough so that any increase in the long-run yield of an asset is immediately and accurately reflected in the rise of its capital value, or price. Doubts as to the plausibility of this second condition need not detain us. The plausibility of the first condition is questionable enough.

In the face of the legal conventions it seems reasonable to expect that any increase in net revenue will ultimately be distributed to stockholders in the form of higher dividends. After all, it is the stockholders who, according to the law, are the megacorp's owners. It is faith in this principle that leads the average Wall Street investor to assume that any permanent increase in net revenue presages an eventual rise in dividends. Yet the reality, as already suggested, is quite different from what the legal conventions would suggest. In exercising its *de facto* control over the megacorp, the executive group will distribute as dividend payments only that portion of any future increase in net revenue which suits its own purpose and that of the megacorp whose destiny it directs. This means that, in practice, dividends will be limited to what is needed to forestall a take-over bid by an outside management group plus whatever additional amounts may serve to minimize the cost of obtaining external investment funds.[17] The rest of any increase in net revenue will be retained by the megacorp for its own benefit, largely to finance its desired rate of growth. This is but another way of saying that the interests of the megacorp and those of its equity debt holders are separate and distinct.

The fact that the megacorp retains a substantial portion of its earnings is, of course, widely known. But the dividends not paid out, so the conventional wisdom runs, are reinvested in the business, thereby leading to even higher dividends in the future. The trouble with this argument is that it must be taken largely on faith. Indeed, what little evidence exists on the point would suggest that the argument is part of a myth which has been created to disguise the disparity which exists between the stockholders' legal status as the owners of the enterprise and their actual position as merely one of several constituencies. Were it true that the megacorp's retained earnings are simply held by the firm in the best interests of the stockholders, two conditions would necessarily have to hold: (a) the present net worth of the stockholders' equity in the firm as measured by the market price of common shares could not be increased by raising the current dividend rate at the expense of retained earnings, and (b) the returns on earnings reinvested in the firm are not less than what can be obtained by purchasing new equity shares in other companies. In fact, neither condition prevails. An increase in the individual rate, it has been found, leads to an increase in the value of a company's stock - a dollar increase in dividends having two to four times greater effect than a dollar increase in retained earnings.[18] Moreover, it has been found that the returns on new equity debt are substantially higher than the returns on reinvested earnings, indicating that stockholders would be substantially better off financially if retained earnings were distributed instead as dividends and reinvested through the capital funds market (Baumol *et al.*, 1970; see also Whittington, 1972).

To the extent, then, that not all of any increase in net revenue will ultimately accrue to the stockholders in the form of higher dividends - and the divergent interests of the executive group and equity debt holders suggest why not all will - the optimization of long-run market share will not necessarily lead to the maximization of the firm's present net worth. If one assumes that the capital funds market functions as well as economists generally hypothesize, this conclusion is simply reinforced.

The preceding counterpoise to the conventional wisdom, it should be noted, is not critical to the argument that follows. If one persists in believing that any increase in net revenue will ultimately accrue to the stockholders, the maximization of present net worth becomes merely another way of talking about the maximization of the firm's growth over time. Making it, rather than the growth of the corporate levy, the variable upon which the executive group will hereafter be presumed to focus requires only a slight, though not insignificant, modification of the pricing model set forth below. It would mean that dividends could not be considered, as they are below, to be a claim on the megacorp's revenue similar to wages, salaries and interest, and therefore a part of fixed costs; and that consequently the megacorp must be assumed to try to maximize the growth of all net revenue, not just that portion accruing to the firm itself in the form of depreciation allowances and retained earnings. It would mean, moreover, that the executive group was constrained in determining the dividend rate only by the prospective return from reinvestment of earnings, and not by the desire to avoid any unnecessary payment to the stockholders.[19] Still, the maximization of the firm's present net worth is not inconsistent with the maximization of the firm's growth over time - if the firm is seen as being identical with its nominal owners. The maximization of net revenue in the short run - or, as it is more commonly phrased, the maximization of profits in the short run - is, however, an entirely different matter. On the distinction between this goal and the optimization of long-run market share rests the question of whether the oligopolistic pricing model developed in this treatise has any novel aspect to it.

Keeping in mind that, for a megacorp, the optimization of long-run market share is equivalent to the maximization of net revenue in the long run, the question is really whether such an enterprise cannot best achieve its goals by maximizing 'profits' over a series of short-run periods.

Put another way, the issue is whether the maximization of net revenue in the short run is inconsistent with the maximization of net revenue in the long run. In response, it is necessary only to point out that a megacorp, by attempting to increase its 'profits' in the short run, may well diminish its future earning prospects.[20] A rise in price, for example, which leads to an immediate increase in net revenue may, at the same time, encourage the entry of a new firm into the industry, thereby reducing the megacorp's long-run market share. That same rise in price may also provoke retaliatory action by the government in the form of an antitrust suit, thereby hampering the megacorp's future freedom of action.

But even beyond this somewhat obvious point, there is a more fundamental reason why the maximization of net revenue in the short run is incompatible with the maximization of net revenue in the long run. It has to do with the decision rule for maximizing net revenue in the short run. That decision rule requires that a firm produce and dispose of through the market that quantity of output for which the marginal costs are equal to the marginal revenue – even if it does not do so with conscious foresight. The megacorp, however, due to the nature of the cost and revenue functions which it faces, is not able to follow that decision rule.

The full explanation of why the megacorp cannot equate its marginal cost with its marginal revenue must wait until the nature of its cost and revenue functions has been specified. This will be done once the two other salient characteristics of the megacorp have been brought out. At this point it is possible only to assert that, reflecting the separation of its management from ownership, the megacorp's behavioral pattern within a specific oligopolistic industry is to seek to optimize its long-run market share; and that this behavioral pattern is analytically different from that postulated in the conventional pricing models. While the latter point still remains to be demonstrated deductively, the first half of the above statement is at least consistent with all that is known about the expressed goals of firms that would likely qualify as megacorps.[21]

Multiple-plant operation and fixed technical coefficients

In addition to the separation of management from ownership, the megacorp is characterized by a divisible capital stock and fixed factor, or technical, coefficients. This means that it consists of a number of smaller producing units, called plants or plant segments, and that within each of these smaller producing units the proportion of capital equipment, laboring manpower and other inputs required to turn out the final product cannot, as a practical matter, be altered in the short run. The first aspect, the multiple-plant operation, is directly observable among America's largest corporations;[22] the second aspect, fixed technical coefficients, is readily inferred from other observable characteristics of these same firms.

A plant or plant segment will consist of all the capital equipment necessary to the production process, and since different pieces of equipment have different output capacities, the numbers of each type of equipment found within a given segment will vary. The megacorp's total productive capacity consists of many such segments, either because it is a multiple-plant firm, because combining several segments to form a single plant leads to economics in overhead costs, or because of a combination of the two.

The factor coefficients, meanwhile, are fixed, at least in the short run, for non-economic as well as economic reasons. From basic engineering studies made at the time the capital equipment is first developed for the market, it will be determined what is the most efficient size crew to operate the machinery, together with the most efficient quantity of raw materials to be fed into or through it. These estimates may be modified by later operating experience, but the objective is nonetheless to develop a 'single-best' set of standards for combining inputs, standards which can then be applied by lower-ranking megacorp officials in charge of the plants or plant segments.

In some cases, the nature of the technology is such that the factor proportions embodied in those standards are incapable of being varied. For example, two and only two men may be required to operate a certain type of die-cutting machine; one and only one steering column can be added to an automobile body moving down the assembly line. But even if the nature of the technology does permit variations in the factor proportions, the inclination of the plant or plant segment managers may nonetheless be to go 'by the book', preferring to follow the standards that have been laid down for combining inputs rather than run the risk of seeming to violate established procedures. Still, one or two bold souls can be expected to arise even in the most rigidly bureaucratic of organizations, and their experiments in varying factor proportions may even result in more efficient combinations. The question, however, is whether such successful experiments can then become part of the information flow on which top management officials base their pricing decisions.

To the extent that the experiments reveal a new optimal combination of inputs, they may simply lead to the establishment of new standards. But to the extent that they reveal what are the most efficient combinations of inputs at sub-optimal levels of plant utilization, they provide information which is of little value in the price determination process. For at the time that the executive group must decide upon a price, it cannot know what the rate of utilization for individual plants or plant segments will be. It must therefore base its decision upon a cost figure which most closely approximates the costs being incurred in most of the plants or plant segments for most of the time during which the new price is expected to prevail. This cost figure is the cost figure associated with the standards that have been developed for combining inputs.

In other ways, too, these standards, once developed, tend to take on a life of their own. For example, the standards as to how many men are to be used to operate each type of equipment will, upon receiving the tacit approval of the workers involved, become part of a plant's work rules, and in the case of those plants in which the labor force is represented by a trade union the work rules are likely to be incorporated into collective bargaining agreements with the full force of law behind them. This is not to argue that the technical coefficients embodied in managerial practices and work rules will not change over time. Through the adoption of new types of equipment, together with the reevaluation of old practices and the assertion of managerial prerogatives, they are, in fact, quite likely to change. But - and this is the crucial point - not in the short run.

The significance, analytically, of a divisible capital plant with fixed factor coefficients is that it results in the megacorp having a cost curve that is significantly different from the familiar U-shaped cost curve of traditional analysis. The latter is based on the fact that at least one factor of production, generally the capital plant but also, in some formulations, the supervision and coordination of activities which the owner-entrepreneur provides, cannot be increased in the short run; and that therefore, in order to expand output, increasing quantities of the variable inputs, such as labor and raw materials, must be combined with the one or more fixed inputs. It can be shown that there necessarily exists some optimal combination of inputs in the production process, and that as increasing quantities of the variable inputs are combined with the fixed input, the law of variable returns will manifest itself - that is, the firm will at first experience increasing output per unit of input, both total and variable, and then decreasing output per unit of input. In this way there is traced out, geometrically, a U-shaped average variable and average total cost curve with a corresponding mathematically derived marginal cost curve. There is a second explanation, aside from the above technological one, for the U-shaped cost curve. As production expands, the argument runs, the resulting increase in the demand for variable inputs will cause their prices to be bid up, leading to a rise in costs for the firm. Such an argument assumes either that all resources in the economy are fully employed or that the relevant factor markets are imperfect. This second explanation of the U-shaped cost curve will be treated only parenthetically.

The technological considerations which, in the case of a polypolistic firm with but a single plant, give rise to a U-shaped cost curve are obviated in the case of the megacorp. On the one hand, the megacorp is able to alter its rate of production by either starting up or closing down one or more of its many plants or plant segments. While this implies that the megacorp cannot vary its output except by large, discrete quantities, the judicious management of inventories, together with a flexibility as to the degree to which all inputs together are utilized, nonetheless makes possible a smooth adjustment of output or supply to sales or demand. To illustrate, if sales are less than current production, one of the plants or plant segments currently in operation can be shut down; and if this causes output to fall short of sales, the balance can be supplied out of finished goods inventory. Similarly, if sales are greater than current production, one of the plants or plant segments presently idle can be started up; and if the resulting expansion of output exceeds the level of sales, the megacorp can then proceed to add to its finished goods inventory.[23] Uncertainty as to the future level of sales may complicate the making of decisions in this regard, but it will not alter the underlying adjustment mechanism itself (cf. Johnston, 1961; Whitin, 1968; Fair, 1971).

Alternatively, especially if the custom is to produce only to order, any discrepancy between sales and current levels of output can be overcome by operating the various plants or plant segments more or less intensively. The fact is that the most important source of variation in the production process is not the variation in the ratios at which inputs are combined but rather the variation in the degree to which the several inputs together are utilized within a given time period. Such a variation in the degree of utilization, however, affects both the 'fixed' and 'variable' inputs simultaneously; indeed, during the time period specified, even the 'variable' inputs will be 'fixed' in the sense that the contracts for their services cannot be cancelled or abrogated.[24] This implies that this second adjustment mechanism pertains only to very short periods of time, that is, for a day or at most a week, or to those situations in which the size of the market limits a plant or plant segment to less than full operation most of the time. To the extent that the latter type of situation prevails, the cost figure associated with the standards that have been developed for combining inputs will be increased to reflect the average expected utilization rate. Once this adjustment has been made, however, the revised cost figure is likely to be regarded by the megacorp's top officials as the cost of operating their plant or plant segment with the single-best combination of inputs. For this reason, the above situation stands as no exception to the general rule postulated, namely, that for the megacorp the technical coefficients are fixed in the short run.

On the other hand, because the technical coefficients are fixed, each plant or plant segment, when it is operated, either produces at what is perceived by the megacorp's top officials to be the plant's minimum average variable cost point, that is, at full efficiency, or it does not produce at all. This, in turn, means that as output expands (or contracts) through the starting up (or closing down) of plants or plant segments - and this, except for the more intensive utilization of plants or plant segments already in operation, is the only way in which production can be varied - the megacorp's average variable costs, and hence its marginal costs, remain constant. Average total costs, because of the fixed cost element, will of course decline steadily as output increases, but since it is only the average variable and marginal costs which are germane to short-run pricing periods, this decline in average total costs is somewhat beside the point.

As for the possibility that average variable and marginal costs will rise as output expands because the megacorp will be forced to pay higher prices for its inputs, the fact is that each megacorp will have attached to it a relatively permanent labor force upon which it can draw as the need arises (see below, chapter 7, pp. 227-8). Since the wages which the megacorp offers are likely to exceed the remuneration from alternative sources of employment, the members of the labor force, if temporarily laid off, will prefer to wait until called back to work (cf. Kuhn, 1959; Reynolds, 1960. pp. 199-200). They may, in the meantime, seek interim employment elsewhere as a source of extra income, but they will still consider themselves to be a part of the megacorp's work force; and once the plant or plant segment to which they are attached starts up again, they will return to the job at the same wage rates as before.[25] It might, of course, be argued that workers will tend to be laid off in reverse order to their degree of efficiency so that variations in the effective cost of labor, that is wage rates adjusted for efficiency, will still occur. The fact is, however, that layoffs in the case of megacorps are determined by overall plant efficiency and by seniority, not by individual efficiency. This means that within certain ranges as specified below the megacorp is able to alter the rate of output without the effective cost of labor itself varying.

Similarly, given the ability of other firms to expand output at constant average variable and marginal costs, the megacorp will be able to obtain whatever additional material inputs it may require as output increases without the per unit expense rising. Generally, to assure an unlimited supply of material inputs at constant prices the megacorp will to some extent have previously integrated backwards. If fluctuations in the price of a particular raw material can still not be avoided the megacorp may have to settle for something less than full control over the price of its final product. In that case, the 'price' set by the megacorp is simply the margin between the price of the material input and the price of the final product.

Finally, the megacorp will be able to alter the rate of output without suffering decreasing returns to management. Administrative salaries as part of the overhead expense, will vary on a per-unit basis even if, as is likely, the total sum remains unchanged. But this variation in average fixed costs is again beside the point. The important fact is that an increase in the number of plants or plant segments in operation will place no strain on managerial resources. The executive recruitment, training and advancement policies which most megacorps have adopted will assure an adequate supply of managers, not only for the number of plants already owned by the company but even for any new plants that might be added. These executive development programs together with the management techniques that have been refined over the years (Chandler, 1962) enable the megacorp to transcend the entrepreneurial limits on the expansion of the firm which were long thought to be immutable and which still govern in the case of most neo-classical proprietorships.[26]

With the megacorp able to alter its rate of output at constant average variable and marginal cost, its cost curves will take the shape shown in figure 1.

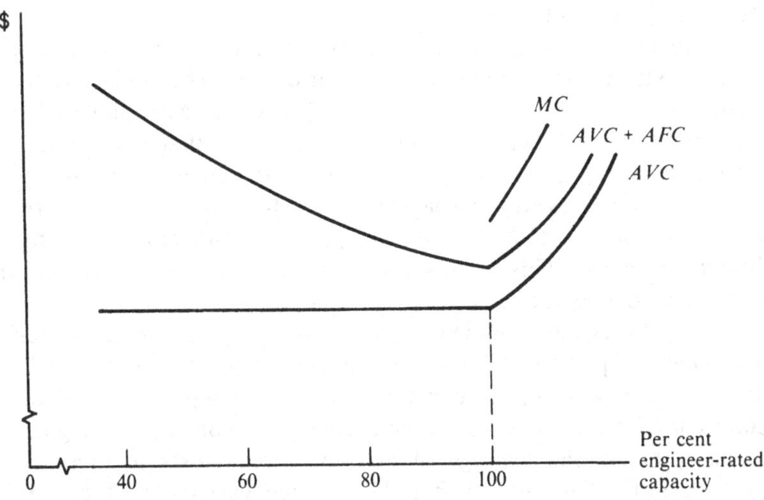

Figure 1

There are several things to be noted here. First, the fixed costs refer to those financial obligations of the megacorp, *de facto* or otherwise, which cannot be attributed to the operation of any single plant or plant segment. They thus include, unlike the customary usage, all dividend payments. While the megacorp is under no legal obligation to make such payments - the law taking the view that dividends are simply the residual income of the firm's owners - the truth of the matter is that the executive group's control of the megacorp would be jeopardized if it failed to meet that financial commitment to only a lesser degree than if it defaulted on some more formal obligation. At the same time, the fixed costs exclude all expenditures on advertising, research and development and other activities designed to protect and enhance the megacorp's current market position. The reason for this exclusion, as well as for the above treatment of dividends, will be brought out more fully in the next chapter. For now, suffice it to point out that the costs incurred from such expenditures are neither inescapable in the short run nor related to current production.

Second, the average variable and marginal cost curves depicted as an unbroken straight line are in fact discontinuous, representing as they do the locus of least-cost points for the various plant segments. They are shown to be parallel to the horizontal axis and coincidental with one another for most of their length only because it has been implicitly assumed that all of the megacorp's plant segments are equally efficient. If this is not the case - and with secular technological progress and plants built at different points in time it is difficult to believe it will be - the two curves not only will have a different shape but will also diverge from one another.

A marginal plant or plant segment of lesser efficiency, one that is likely to be started up again or shut down if output needs to be expanded or contracted, will necessarily have a higher least-cost point and thus can be operated only at a higher average variable cost than the megacorp's other plants or plant segments. Of course, it can produce all of its output at that higher average variable cost, and for this reason the marginal cost will still be constant over that range of output represented by its additional capacity. This means that the marginal cost curve for the firm as a whole will rise in step-like fashion, as shown in figure 2, the number of steps depending on the number of operating cost differentials among the plant segments. At the same time, the higher average variable cost of any marginal plant or plant segment, when added to or subtracted from the average variable costs of the other plant segments, will cause the overall average of per unit direct costs to increase as output expands. This means that the average variable cost curve for the firm as a whole will also rise, though more slowly than the marginal cost curve.

To ignore these effects of operating cost differentials among the various plant segments, however, is not a serious matter. The operating cost differentials themselves are not likely to be very great - or else the megacorp will certainly take steps to eliminate them. This pertains particularly to the plant segments most likely to be operated marginally. In any case, it can be shown that the upward drift of the average variable and marginal cost curves - an upward drift which is quite different from the rise in average variable and marginal cost curves postulated in the more conventional models - is of virtually no analytical significance. The upward drift of the marginal cost curve would be important only if the curve then intersected the marginal revenue curve. As will subsequently be brought out, however, this is not likely to be the case. The upward drift of the marginal cost curve simply means, therefore, that average variable and marginal costs cannot be assumed to be constant for all possible levels of output. Even in this regard, since the differentials in efficiency among plants or plant segments are likely to be small and since, in any case, the cost information received by the executive group prior to making a pricing decision is likely, due to organizational constraints, to represent an averaging out of these differentials, it may well be that insofar as the executive group is concerned the average variable and marginal costs are constant. The latter explanation is at least consistent with the empirical evidence on the cost functions of megacorps cited below. Thus no harm is done, and greater simplicity of exposition is obtained, if it is simply assumed that all of the megacorp's plant segments are equally efficient.

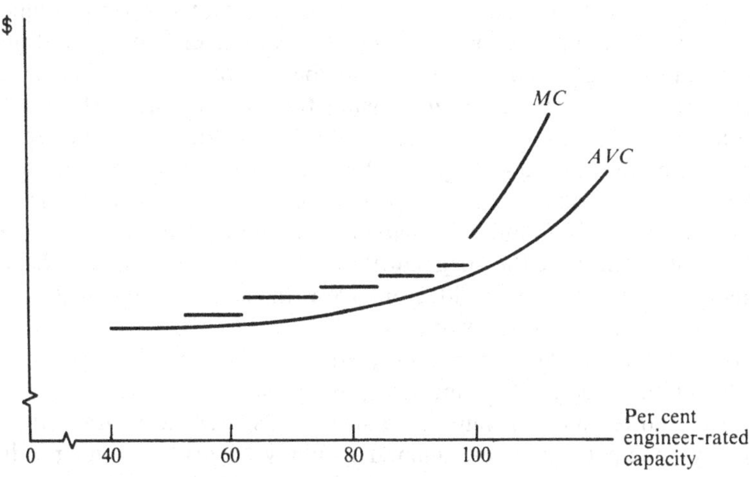

Figure 2

Third, the variable measured along the horizontal axis is not the same as the one generally shown in such diagrams. Instead of quantity per unit of time, the variable measured is the percentage of engineer-rated operating capacity being utilized at a particular moment in time. Aside from conforming to general business usage, this approach has the advantage that the resulting analysis can be generalized to apply to all megacorps, regardless of what their actual output capabilities may be. In the short-run examination of costs, then, the assumption is that capacity as an abstract concept, unrelated to any specific quantity of goods, is the most significant independent variable. It is not necessary to know how much the megacorp is actually producing, only what proportion of total capacity that output represents.

Such an approach has the disadvantage, however, that it is not always clear what is meant by the term 'capacity', especially as the word is sometimes used by megacorp officials themselves (Creamer, 1964; Gift, 1968). In the analysis that follows the term will be defined as the sum of the capacities of all plants or plant segments, these capacities in turn being defined as the quantities which, in the judgment of megacorp officials, each of the plant or plant segments is capable of producing when operated at maximum efficiency, that is, at the lowest possible average variable cost. The megacorp's total capacity thus corresponds to the point on its average variable and marginal cost curves where, as depicted above, they both rise - the marginal cost curve discontinuously. It should be noted that, due to the influence of declining average fixed costs, this point occurs at a lower rate of capacity utilization than that at which average total costs reach a minimum. This leads to the third point of importance.

Once the megacorp has brought all of its plant or plant segments into operation so that each is operating at maximum efficiency, additional output can be achieved only by using the existing capital stock more intensively, for example, by increasing the number of work shifts or by extending operations into the weekends. In other words, beyond a certain point, the megacorp will be able to expand production only if it is willing to incur increasing per unit costs, just like a neo-classical proprietor with his familiar U-shaped cost curve. This being the case, one might argue that the megacorp's cost curves, except for the flat, elongated portions, are no different from those employed in the more conventional theory of the firm.

The point is, however, that only the flat, elongated portions need be taken into account. If the megacorp is to achieve its goal of optimizing long-run market share, it must take steps to assure that it has sufficient capacity to meet whatever demand is likely to arise for its product. It cannot allow an order to go unfilled, since a customer turned away may not return after being forced to establish another source of supply. Even if all the other members of the industry are similarly short of capacity, the danger to the megacorp's long-run position still remains. An outside firm contemplating entry into the industry will be greatly encouraged to incur the risks involved if it perceives an existing demand that is going unmet. This last possibility, that of a new firm entering the industry, is particularly unwelcome to the executive group. A new firm, once it gains a foothold, is not easily dislodged, and the established enterprises whose domain has been invaded will find themselves with little choice but to surrender some small portion of the market to the newcomer. Not only are their respective market shares likely to be reduced but, in addition, the task of price coordination will be made more difficult.[27] For these reasons the megacorp will, as a normal rule, try to see to it that it has a certain amount of reserve capacity (see below, chapter 3, p. 89). This, however, means that the megacorp is unlikely to operate at more than 100 per cent of engineer-rated capacity. Its doing so, in fact, is a sign either of an extraordinary increase in demand, one that could not be anticipated in advance, or of management incompetence.[28]

The relevant portions of the megacorp's cost curves, then, are the portions below 100 per cent of engineer-rated capacity - more specifically, the portions between 65 and 95 per cent of engineer-rated capacity.[29] That these are the relevant portions and that they display constant average variable and hence constant marginal costs is confirmed by what empirical evidence is available on the subject. For nearly thirty-five years economists have been investigating the cost curves of business firms. Since the necessary data are most readily available from the records of larger companies, most of the studies have focused on firms which, on the basis of the criteria set forth in this work, would qualify as megacorps. After reviewing the results of those investigations, J. Johnston (1960, pp. 136-48, 168) has declared in his definitive text on statistical cost functions that 'the various short-run studies more often than not indicate constant marginal cost and declining average cost as the pattern that best seems to describe the data that have been analyzed.' See also Walters, 1963, pp. 1-66; Gold, 1966; Koot and Walker, 1970; Zudak, 1970, 1971.) While Johnston's conclusions and the underlying studies themselves have drawn criticism from other economists,[30] the fact remains that the evidence is most consistent, not with the U-shaped cost curves that are usually postulated but rather, with the type of horizontal cost curves depicted above. Given the prevalence of multiple-plant-segment operation and relatively fixed factor coefficients among the largest corporations in the United States, these empirical findings are hardly surprising.[31]

Membership in at least one oligopolistic industry

Finally, the megacorp is characterized by membership in at least one oligopolistic industry. This is implicit in the very definition of the megacorp as the representative oligopolistic firm. The fact that the megacorp is an oligopolist means that, unlike the neo-classical proprietorship in a Walrasian situation, it is not a price taker (Wiles, 1956, ch. 4; Machlup, 1952, pp. 85–92, 111–15). First, it does not simply throw on the market for whatever price can be obtained the output which it has decided to produce. Rather it sets a price, then produces and sells at that price whatever quantity the market will take. It is for this reason that the price in an oligopolistic industry is sometimes referred to as an 'administered' price – that is, a price which is seller determined. While the phenomenon of the administered price is not confined to oligopoly, it is nonetheless an almost unfailing characteristic of that type of market structure.[32] Of course, in a static model in which adjustments to exogenous disturbances occur instantaneously, how a firm responds to a change in industry demand is of little consequence. Whether it varies the price charged for its product or varies the quantity of that product supplied, the new equilibrium that will be reached is the same. But in a dynamic economy such as that of the United States, the manner in which the firm adjusts to the ever recurring disequilibria in the product markets will itself partially determine what growth path is followed. Varying the price charged rather than varying the quantity supplied does make a difference as to how things turn out.[33] This is why pricing models based on the assumption that the firm simply throws it output on the market for whatever price can be obtained must be rejected as inapplicable to the oligopolistic sector of the American economy. It should be noted that these models include, beside the conventional polypolistic model set forth in economics textbooks, the entire body of neo-classical pricing models – thus making most of what passes for contemporary microeconomic analysis irrelevant insofar as the oligopolistic sector is concerned. Among the general equilibrium systems thus called into question are those associated with Walras, Cassel, Lindahl, Hicks, Samuelson, Patinkin and Solow. For if these models are inapplicable to the oligopolistic sector, as significant as that sector is in the overall economy, one cannot help but question how useful they are for understanding the economy as a whole.

Second, because the megacorp supplies such a large share of the market, it cannot assume that its own individual actions will have no discernible impact on the industry. Rather it must anticipate that any change in price or other move it may make to improve its relative position will lead to a reaction by the other firms in the industry. It is this recognized interdependence among the members of the industry, not the number of such firms or the shares of the market they supply which, as pointed out earlier, defines oligopoly.[34] What this recognized interdependence means is that no individual firm can, by itself, alter the current price level. If a megacorp should attempt to raise its price unilaterally, in the hope of increasing its profit margin, it will find that so many of its customers will switch their purchases to other firms in the industry that its total revenue will fall. On the other hand, if a megacorp should attempt to lower its price unilaterally, in the hope of increasing its sales, it will find that the other firms in the industry will quickly follow suit to prevent the loss of customers. Thus relative market shares will remain unchanged, the only consequence being that the industry price is lower. But since the industry's short-run demand curve is likely to be price inelastic, the megacorp's total revenue will once again fall.[35]

The above argument assumes that the oligopolistic industry produces a single, homogeneous product so that any small variation in price is sufficient to cause all buyers to switch their purchases to the firm or firms quoting the lower price. If this condition does not hold, that is, if the industry supplies a product which is capable of being differentiated on the basis of which particular firm has produced it, the situation is more complicated - though not fundamentally different. In that event, one has a case of oligopoly with product differentiation.

The distinction between an oligopoly with product differentiation and one without is the distinction, for the most part, between an industry selling to the consuming public, that is, to households, and one selling to other groups of business firms. Actually, there is no such thing as an industry producing a single, homogeneous product. What one finds is that almost every industry produces a full line of products, the line including many different items. In the case of industries which sell to other business firms, especially on a continuing basis, the customer is generally able to evaluate objectively the relative merits of the different items in the product line and knows with some degree of certainty which particular item meets its own technical needs. It is the price of this one, homogeneous item which the customer is alone concerned with; and in a market of this type, because of the need to quickly match any rival firm's quotation lest a sale be lost, only a single known price can prevail.[36] This need not be true, however, of an oligopolistic industry with a differentiable product - that is, an industry which sells primarily to households or to other business firms on an infrequent basis. Due to the buyer's inadequate knowledge, different firms can charge different prices for what, ignoring superficial differences, are essentially identical items.

It is important to recognize, however, the purpose which these price differentials serve. It is to stabilize relative market shares, that is, to equalize any supposed advantage that one firm's product may have over another's, whether that supposed advantage arises from long-standing reputation, more intensive advertising, better servicing arrangements, or the like. Thus the above argument can be extended to include oligopolistic industries with differentiable products by noting that not only can an individual firm not alter, by itself, the current price level but also it cannot, by itself, alter the customary differential in price between its own products and those of the other firms in the industry - unless the change is necessary to offset a shift in consumer preferences that would otherwise lead to a shift in relative market shares (Schneider, 1966).

Since no individual firm can alter the current price level, any decision to revise prices must be made by the industry as a whole - or at least by all the leading firms acting together as a collective entity. This, in turn, gives rise to what William Fellner (1949, ch. 1) has termed 'joint profit maximization'. The firms that comprise the industry are likely to have learned through historical experience[37] that it is in their own self interest to avoid price competition among themselves and seek instead to maximize the net returns for the industry as a whole. While the simplest and most effective means of assuring this unity of pricing action is for the members of the industry to meet together formally as a cartel, such an approach is illegal under United States law (cf. Dewey, 1959, ch. 12; Neale, 1960, ch. 1). This does not necessarily eliminate collusion as a possibility (see Eichner, 1962, pp. 46-50; Sultan, 1975); but the fact is that, in order to avoid direct violation of the Sherman antitrust act, the members of oligopolistic industries will have, over time, devised various other means of coordinating their pricing decisions. The most widely employed of these, and the one which will therefore be taken to be typical, is price leadership. This is the practice whereby one firm, the largest and/or most powerful, assumes the role of initiating price changes. It is, of course, necessary to distinguish between firms which are, in the aggregate, large and firms which, in a particular industry, supply a large share of the market. A firm may be large in the aggregate because of its diversified activities, yet supply a smaller share of a particular market than one or more other firms in the same industry. Generally, it is the firm with the largest share of the market which acts as the price leader, though a smaller firm, one with lower costs and expanding more rapidly, may arrogate to itself that role (see Markham, 1951, pp. 891-905; Stocking and Watkins, 1951, chs. 6-8).

The 'joint profit maximization' or price leadership model of oligopoly which follows is to be distinguished from the 'dominant firm' model in which the largest firm sets the price on the assumption that the potential demand for its product is simply the total industry demand less whatever the other firms within the industry are capable of supplying. In this alternative model, the other firms do not necessarily match the price announced by the dominant firm, and as a result, the latter's share of the market will vary as industry sales vary. As Worcester (1957) has pointed out, the 'dominant firm' model is an unstable one, since it will, unless the industry is subject to decreasing returns to scale over time, necessarily evolve into monopoly or oligopoly with price leadership. This does not mean that the model may not be relevant at a certain point in an industry's history (Eichner, 1969, pp. 159-60). Nor does it mean that the price leader in an oligopolistic industry will not occasionally find it convenient to overlook what the competitive fringe of firms in its industry may be doing. It simply means that the 'dominant firm' model, since it implies an eventual decline in the market share of any firm which follows the model for any extended period of time, is not generally relevant to the oligopolistic sector of the economy where stability of market shares is the general rule. No matter how large a share of the market a price leader as the dominant firm may have, it cannot long tolerate the erosion of that position such as will occur when a significant number of other firms are free, in the face of declining demand, to pursue an independent pricing policy. Eventually, the price leader will be forced to take some type of retaliatory action, reminding other firms of the interdependence which exists among them.

The very fact that it is the largest and/or most powerful firm means that the price leader has sufficient financial strength to force any errant member of the industry back into line on prices - by means of a price war if ultimately necessary. Usually, however, the mere fact that the price leader is prepared to take such drastic action is sufficient to assure uniformity of pricing action. While the element of coercion lies at the base of the system of price leadership, it is by no means the sole factor. These is also the common interest which exists in an oligopolistic industry of avoiding price competition. For in an oligopolistic industry price competition is apt to lead to a price war - and a price war, for large firms with significant fixed costs, can be quite destructive, both because of the extent to which prices can be cut while still covering 'out-of-pocket' or variable costs and because of the considerable resources which can be consumed in such a struggle (cf. Telser, 1966a; Cassady, 1963).

Even aside from the element of coercion and the recognized community of interest, however, there is the important fact that the pricing decision in an oligopolistic industry is, in a real sense, a collective act. While the laws of the United States prohibit the members of any industry from conferring together over prices, various informal channels of communication nonetheless exist. Interviews granted to trade magazines, statements made at stockholder meetings and similar public utterances by megacorp officials serve to create an industry-wide consensus which the price leader must necessarily take into account before making its pricing decision. This is not to deny that the actual price decided upon is likely to be the one best calculated to advance the price leader's own interests or that the other members of the industry, if the decision were theirs to make, might choose some other figure. But - and this is the premise on which the analysis that follows will be based - the price leader in deciding upon a particular price is in effect acting on behalf of the entire industry (cf. Henderson, 1954; Almarin Phillips, 1964; see also Almarin Phillips, 1961, 1962). Through the mechanism of price leadership it is possible to coordinate prices without directly violating the Sherman antitrust act.

Not only must pricing decisions in an oligopolistic industry be coordinated, but also the price, once determined, must be maintained, that is, adhered to, by all the members of the industry until such time as they are able collectively, with the price leader in the forefront, to decide on a new price level. On the one hand, there is little point in developing a common position on prices, this to avoid the dangers of price competition, if all firms are not then going to follow those prices. On the other hand, because of the difficulty in developing such a consensus, price changes cannot be too frequent. The interval over which the industry price can thus be expected to remain unchanged is what is meant by the pricing period. It falls within the short period of Marshallian analysis (J. Robinson, 1971, ch. 2), and it varies from industry to industry, depending on the characteristics of the markets involved. In the automobile industry, for example, the pricing period is a year, the same as for many other consumer durable goods; in the steel industry, it is six months, an interval not untypical of metals that serve primarily as material inputs. This tendency for the price in an oligopolistic industry to change only infrequently follows from the fact that the price is an administered one, with time required not only to coordinate the setting of a new price level but also to assess the impact of the previous change in the price level.[38]

Of the several methods that have been devised for assuring that the industry price is maintained throughout the pricing period, the one which will here be taken as typical is the open price list - the publication and distribution of prices to customers by each of the firms in the industry. Since the prices are identical, the lists, too, will be identical. Indeed, it is not unknown for the firms in some industries simply to distribute as their own the price leader's list.[39] For those industries in which transportation costs are significant, the open price list is likely to be supplemented by a multiple basing point system. Certain cities, usually those in which plants are situated, are designated as base points and the price of the article then calculated on the basis of the price published in the open list plus the cost of transportation (generally specified as by rail) from the nearest base point to the place of sale.[40] In this way, two companies, one with a plant located at the base point and another with a plant some distance further away, can be certain of quoting identical prices to any prospective customer regardless of where the customer may be located.

It might be expected that the temptation to shave prices below those published in the open list would be irresistible, especially since this would enable a firm to increase its relative market share. But such a ploy, to turn out advantageously, must be concealed from the other members of the industry lest they retaliate. The very fact that a particular firm was suddenly gaining customers at the expense of its rivals would be *prima facie* evidence that the firm was secretly cutting its price. Thus any success which price shaving might have is likely to lead immediately and automatically to its detection and to reprisals from the other firms in the industry.[41] Oligopoly being in a certain sense a description of behavior that has been learned over time, firms in oligopolistic industries can be expected to have had sufficient experience with the untoward effects of price shaving to eschew it as a competitive weapon in all except periods of unusually depressed demand (cf. Cyert and DeGroot, 1971). This reinforces the point made earlier, namely, that in an oligopolistic industry no firm can or will, by itself, alter the current price level.[42]

The analytical significance of this fact is that, for the individual megacorp, a demand curve in the conventional sense cannot be said to exist (R. Robinson, 1961). The price that will be charged by the megacorp for its product during the current pricing period is determined by the industry as a whole acting through the price leader. The individual megacorp has no control over what that price will be nor, once the price has been determined, can it unilaterally alter that price. This limitation on the firm's discretion is even true, to a large extent, of the price leader itself. To the individual megacorp, then, the price that can and will be charged at varying levels of capacity utilization is constant. At what level of capacity the megacorp will actually operate, given that constant price, will depend on two factors over which, for all practical purposes, the megacorp has no control: (1) the quantity demanded from the industry as a whole at that price, reduced to the portion of total industry demand the megacorp has currently succeeded in capturing through non-price forms of competition, and (2) what is by far the more important factor, any shift in the industry demand curve resulting from

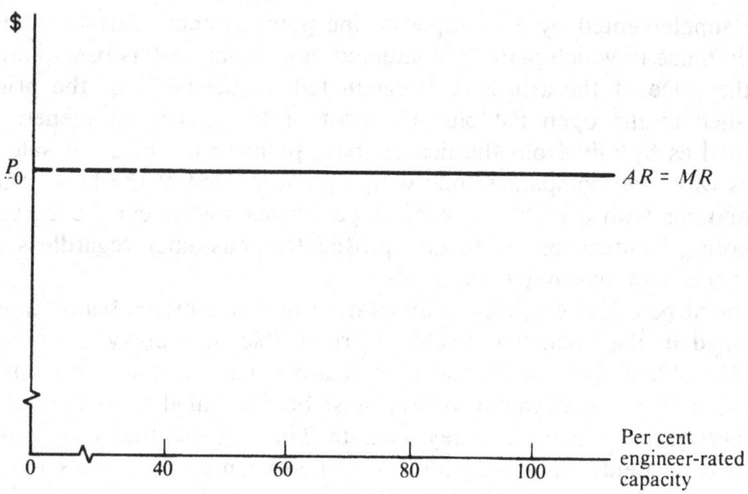

Figure 3

changes in aggregate economic conditions. It is because the megacorp cannot, as a practical matter, affect the demand for its product by altering its price that a demand curve in the conventional sense does not exist.

Still, a demand curve in the sense of a revenue function can be stipulated. This revenue function, as depicted in Figure 3, is a line parallel to the horizontal axis at a height equal to the price P_0. Since the price charged by the industry as a whole during the current pricing period will be constant whatever the rate of capacity utilization, the average revenue and marginal revenue will also be constant. This gives the revenue curve the appearance of an infinitely elastic demand curve.

The megacorp's individual short-run revenue curve would thus appear to be identical to that of a polypolistic firm. While geometrically similar, the two are quite different behaviorally. In a polypolistic industry, though a firm is likely to view the current industry price as something which is exogenously determined when deciding how much to produce - and it is in this sense that its demand curve will appear to be infinitely elastic - it will at the same time be continually testing to see if the industry price cannot be altered to its benefit. If the firm has a sense that demand is unusually strong at the current price level, it may quote a higher figure to a prospective customer; and if the customer, feeling that he is unlikely to obtain a better price from any other source, agrees to the figure quoted, then a new industry price will be established on which all the firms in the industry will thereafter base their output decisions. Of course, the prospective customer has the option of refusing to make the sale at the higher quoted price, in which case the industry price remains unchanged. On the other hand, if the firm has a sense that demand is weak, if in fact it finds that the goods currently being produced are simply being added to inventory, it may quote a price below the current industry price; and again, if this offer is accepted, a new industry price will be established. Though fixed and ascertainable at any given moment of time, the industry price level in a polypolistic industry is a constantly fluctuating figure as changing supply and demand conditions affect the bargaining between buyer and seller.

This continual testing of the industry price level, with the resulting fluctuations in price, is not to be found in an oligopolistic industry. Instead, as has already been indicated, each firm is likely to adhere scrupulously to the industry price schedule until at least the end of the current pricing period when, at the price leader's initiative, the schedule may be changed through collective action.[43] Even though demand may be unusually strong or unusually weak, an oligopolistic firm will forgo the opportunity for improving its own position by deviating from the industry price level, for experience has taught it what the reaction of its rivals is likely to be.

In conclusion, then, the characteristics of the megacorp which are analytically important are (1) the separation of management from ownership with its resulting effect on decision-making criteria; (2) the multiplicity and/or segmentation of plants, enabling the megacorp to produce over those ranges of output at which it customarily operates at constant marginal cost; and (3) the membership within an oligopolistic industry, in which all firms are aware of their interdependence and behave accordingly, thereby giving rise to an individual short-run revenue curve that is infinitely elastic. Of course, in the actual world, even among the companies included in Fortune Magazine's annual directory of the 500 largest corporations, these characteristics will not be observed, in their entirety, in all cases. In this sense, the portrait of the megacorp which has been sketched represents an ideal or pure type - just as the neo-classical proprietorship, with its profit-maximizing entrepreneur operating a single plant firm in a competitive industry, is also an ideal type.[44] Of the two hypothetical prototypes, however, it would appear on the basis of the available empirical evidence that the megacorp comes closer to reflecting actual conditions in the oligopolistic sector of the American economy. It thus represents a better *a priori* foundation upon which to begin the analysis of oligopolistic pricing.

The megacorp's short-run pricing situation

Having specified the megacorp's analytically significant characteristics - these characteristics, in turn, determining the nature of the megacorp's

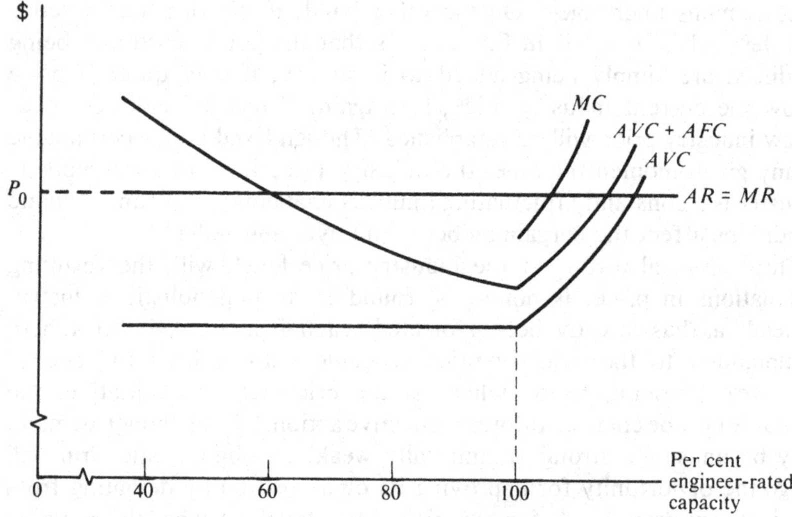

Figure 4

cost and revenue functions - it is now possible to examine the short-run pricing situation which the individual megacorp faces. To do so, it is necessary only to superimpose the stipulated cost and revenue curves on the same set of axes, as is done in Figure 4. What the diagram reveals is that from the short-run perspective of the individual megacorp the price in an oligopolistic industry still remains indeterminate, as it is in other models. Over the ranges of output at which the megacorp customarily operates, that is, between 65 and 95 per cent of engineer-rated capacity, marginal cost and marginal revenue are both constant. Since the two curves at no point intersect one another, the rule for short-run net revenue maximization - the equating of marginal cost with marginal revenue - cannot be applied. This conclusion still holds even if, due to operating cost differentials among the various plants or plant segments, the average variable and marginal cost curves have a slight upward tilt to them. Only if the marginal cost curve rises sufficiently to intersect the marginal revenue curve will the price be determinate; as long as the megacorp has reserve capacity, however, even if those reserve units are less efficient, no such intersection is likely to take place.

Of course, if the megacorp should operate beyond its normal range of output, and in particular beyond 100 per cent of engineer-rated capacity where marginal cost rises sharply, the maximization of net revenue is possible. There are even occasions when, due to extraordinary circumstances, the megacorp may find itself operating in that range.[45] But those occasions are the exception. For the reasons already indicated, the megacorp will make certain that it has capacity to spare. This capacity can be fully utilized in the short run only if the megacorp is prepared to shave its price below that of the industry. However, this is an option foreclosed to the megacorp by the very nature of the industry to which it belongs. Put another way, the price in an oligopolistic industry will normally be set so as to result in the members of that industry operating at between 65 and 96 per cent of engineer-rated capacity - and hence over ranges of output at which marginal cost and marginal revenue cannot be equated.

Thus, there is no answer to the question of how prices are determined under oligopolistic conditions as long as the focus remains on the individual firm. In seeking a determinate solution to the oligopolistic pricing enigma, it is necessary to shift the focus from the level of the firm to that of the industry as a whole. This can be done easily enough, given the ground already covered in this treatise. Since it is the megacorp-price leader which acts as surrogate for the entire industry in the setting of price, all that need be done is to indicate how the cost and revenue functions of that one firm are transformed when it acts, not just on its own behalf but on behalf of its fellow oligopolists as well.

If it can be assumed that no other member of the industry has a lower average variable cost curve than the price leader - and, for the reasons indicated above, this is not an unreasonable assumption to make - then no change need be made in the cost curves depicted in figure 4. With no other firm able to produce the same article at a lower cost, and with price shaving precluded as a means of increasing relative market share, no other firm is likely to be willing to offer that product at a lower price. Any additional supply will be obtainable only at the price announced by the price leader, and this means that the price leader's cost curves are the relevant ones for decisions made at the industry level. Indeed, it is to the cost curves of the price leader that one must look for an explanation of both the height and shape of the marginal portion of the industry supply curve.[46] The case is quite different, however, with respect to the revenue curves depicted in figure 4.

When acting as surrogate for the industry as a whole, the megacorp-price leader need not accept the current industry price as exogenously determined. It can announce a change in that price - either an increase or a decrease - confident that the other firms in the industry will follow suit.[47] Under these circumstances, when it varies its own price, the megacorp-price leader is in effect determining both the new price that will then prevail throughout the industry and, given the industry demand curve, the quantity of output that will be sold at that new price by all firms together. Since its own level of sales will change along with

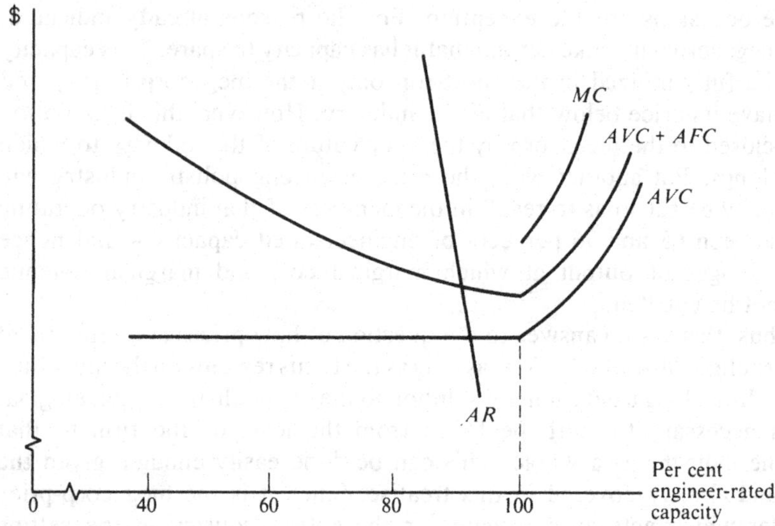

Figure 5

those of the other industry members - in proportion to its share of the market and in the direction opposite that of the price movement - the megacorp-price leader will have an average revenue curve that is negatively sloped such as the one shown in figure 5 (Triffin, 1949, pp. 28-9; see also Dewey, 1969, ch. 2). Though the magnitude of the slope will be different, this average revenue curve will have the same price elasticity of demand, at any given price level, as the industry demand curve itself.[48] For this reason, when the megacorp-price leader acts on behalf of the entire industry, its average revenue curve can be viewed as simply the marginal portion of the industry demand curve.

Yet even when the analysis is shifted in this manner to the industry level, the price under oligopolistic conditions still remains indeterminate. According to the best available empirical evidence, the demand curve in any industry the size and significance of most oligopolies is price inelastic in the vicinity of the prevailing price (cf. Houthakker and Taylor, 1966; Stone, 1954; Hirsch, 1950-1). This means that the marginal revenue curve, such as the one associated with the average revenue curve depicted in figure 5, must necessarily be negative. There being no way to equate a negative marginal revenue curve with a positive marginal cost curve, the rule for short-run net revenue maximization still cannot be applied.

The import of the above argument is twofold. First, it implies that the Chamberlin-Robinson model and its derivatives are irrelevant to the oligopolistic sector of the American economy - irrelevant even insofar as the megacorp-price leader is concerned.[49] To provide a determinate solution, that type of model must presume an average revenue curve that is not just price elastic but, indeed, sufficiently price elastic to take into account the existence of positive marginal costs. Yet, as just pointed out, any average revenue curve which would be that price elastic is hardly the type of average revenue curve which a megacorp-price leader is likely to face. Second, the above argument implies that the firms in an oligopolistic industry do not seek to maximize net revenue in the short run. This, of course, merely bears out the proposition advanced earlier as to the megacorp's behavioral pattern. To maximize net revenue in the short run, the firms in an oligopolistic industry would, acting together through the megacorp-price leader, have to raise the industry price well above the levels actually observed in the oligopolistic sector. Why they do not generally do so will become clear once the analysis has been shifted from the short run to what is the perspective of the megacorp itself - the long run.

Appendix to Chapter 2
Alternative Behavioral Assumptions[1]

Economists who balk at accepting the assumption of short-run profit maximization that is basic to neo-classical theory fall into two distinct camps, each pursuing at an oblique angle to the other the goal of providing a more realistic micro level analysis. In the one camp are those economists who question whether business firms maximize anything. In the other camp are those who propose that short-run profits be replaced by some other maximand.

The economists who, like Simon (1955), Cyert and March (1963), and Monsen and Downs (1965), question whether business firms maximize anything start with a recognition of the same institutional development emphasized in the main body of the chapter - the emergence of the megacorp with its hierarchical structure and separation of management from ownership (see also Margolis, 1958). Because of the organizational factors which this development introduces into the decision-making process - for example, the conflicting goals of different departments, the blocked lines of communication - it is unreasonable, these economists argue, to expect a megacorp to maximize anything. The most that can realistically be anticipated is that the megacorp will achieve a 'satisfactory' level of profits - or whatever else may be essential to the organization's survival. Those who hold this view may conveniently be labeled 'behavioralists', even though the term leads to some oversimplification of viewpoint.

However valuable the behavioralist approach may be for injecting a greater note of realism into theoretical discussions, it nonetheless has an inherent limitation, one that marks this approach as a conceptual box canyon. The implications of satisficing behavior cannot logically be analyzed except as a departure from maximizing behavior. This means that, unless some other 'satisficand' besides short-run profits is posited, the conventional neo-classical pricing model is still central to the analysis. For only after noting the consequences of firms seeking to maximize their short-run profits can the effects of a weaker thrust in that direction be determined. What this means is that the 'satisficing' part of any behavioral assumption is likely to be only modificatory, and not metamorphic.[2] The motivational engine remains the same; it is just that the engine has less power. Indeed, one can argue that a pricing model will lead to the same conclusions whether one assumes satisficing behavior or maximizing behavior, the only difference being the time required to reach the long-run equilibrium position (cf. Day, 1967; Day and Tinney, 1968).

Of course, it is not necessary to posit short-run profits as the sole satisficand. Most behavioralists would, in fact, consider profits to be only one of the many goals of the firm. Still, the essential point remains – that to und°rstand the implications of satisficing behavior one must begin by indicating the consequences of maximizing behavior. If the goals of the firm are no longer one-dimensional, then it is the consequences of pursuing multiple maximands simultaneously that must first be determined. It is only in this way that one can learn whether the several goals are actually in conflict with one another, thereby imposing satisficing behavior as a necessary part of constrained maximization (cf. Encarnacion, 1964); or whether, in fact, the several goals can be collapsed into one by more precise specification. What is here being argued is that, before the assumption of satisficing behavior can be allowed to inject a greater note of realism into the discussion of pricing behavior, the implications of other maximands besides short-run profits must first be examined.

A number of economists, beginning with Higgins (1939) and including most recently Ferguson (1965) and Horowitz (1969), have posited that there is a generalized utility function which the managers of megacorps seek to maximize (see also Scitovsky, 1943; Reder, 1967; Cooper, 1949; E. Edwards, 1961). Among the variables besides profits suggested for inclusion within this utility function have been survival, security, control, managerial salaries, staff, prestige, power, leisure and the 'quiet life'. This approach, like the theory of consumer behavior from which it is derived, suffers from a fatal defect to the extent that there is no way of assigning specific values to the relative weights attached to each of the multiple goals. Moreover, since there is hardly any form of corporate behavior which cannot be explained in terms of some additional objective sought by management, it can easily degenerate into an exercise in *ex post* rationalization. The generalized utility maximization approach, then, simply creates a set of empty boxes; and for this reason, as Papandreau (1952) pointed out not long after the idea surfaced in the literature, it is of little help in developing an operationally useful pricing model with general applicability.

To the extent that any one of these other goals can be measured separately and its impact then distinguished empirically from that of the profits objective, the above criticism does not hold. Two different kinds of maximands which meet this criterion have been suggested, and each has led to a different kind of behavioral model. One approach, following the lead of Berle and Means (1933), emphasizes the conflict between the interests of the executive group which controls the megacorp and the interests of the persons and/or the organization whom the managers are supposed to be serving in a fiduciary role. This is the 'individualistic' model. The alternative approach, one that builds on certain sociological concepts, emphasizes the commonality of interest between the members of the executive group and the organization whose destiny they direct. This is the 'organic' model.[3] Both approaches fall under the general rubric of managerial theories of the firm.

Economists who, like O. Williamson (1964),[4] adopt the individualistic approach are in the mainstream of a tradition which has always assumed that each person will seek to maximize his own personal welfare. They have merely transposed this view of human nature to the corporate setting, one in which those with the decision-making power are excluded from any significant profit share. In such a setting, these economists argue, the members of the executive group will seek to maximize the income which accrues to them directly. Such income may take several forms, including direct compensation, other emoluments such as pensions, bonuses and stock options, various perquisites such as expense accounts, executive aircraft, hunting lodges and lavishly furnished offices, and staff assistants.

The shortcoming of this approach is that it makes no difference insofar as the setting of price levels is concerned. If their own welfare is the only goal which the members of the executive group pursue besides short-term profits, they will still want to maximize the megacorp's net revenue. Since the various types of income which accrue to the executives themselves are all part of the overhead expense, they will have no bearing on what price is chosen in pursuit of the executive group's goals. Indeed, the only difference is that part of the revenue which might otherwise show up as corporate net income will appear instead under some expense heading. In other words, the pursuit of their own personal interest by the members of the executive group affects only the distribution of income within the megacorp, not the manner of response to external pressures. This distributional effect is not unimportant. It gives rise to a type of economic rent that may be distortive of values in general. Still, the price and allocative impact is probably negligible. This means that, insofar as providing the behavioral foundation for an alternative to the neo-classical theory of the firm is concerned, the individualistic approach does not lead very far. Its underlying assumption - that the members of the executive group seek to maximize their own individual welfare, and not profits - is thus also modificatory rather than metamorphic.

The 'organic' approach does not suffer from the same limitation. To the extent that the interests of the executive group and those of the megacorp itself are identical, they will both want to see the firm *qua* organization grow at a maximum rate. Maximum growth of the firm as a desideratum has two important advantages - aside from being operationally definable and empirically meaningful. The first is that it encompasses a number of other maximands (and optimands) which have been put forward as alternatives to short-run profits. These several other variables upon which, it has been suggested, the megacorp's executive group focuses are (a) market share, (b) the absolute level of sales, (c) the rate of growth of sales, (d) the rate of growth of assets, and (e) net revenue over the long run. Depending on the context, each of these variables can be considered the appropriate proxy for gauging whether the megacorp is achieving maximum growth.

That the firm struggles for relative market position has been suggested by a number of economists, including Abramowitz (1938), Helflebower (1954) and Duesenberry (1958, ch. 6). As the main body of this chapter points out, the optimization of long-run market share is the equivalent, under the type of pricing constraint that prevails in an oligopolistic industry, of maximizing the long-run growth of the megacorp. The secular expansion of the industry to which it belongs will, if the existing share of the market is retained, assure the megacorp a certain minimum rate of growth; if the market share can be increased, the megacorp's rate of growth will be even higher. Viewed in this dynamic context, the absolute level of sales is simply a proxy for relative market share, and it is hardly surprising that Baumol (1958 and 1959, chs. 6-8), in the consulting activity out of which arose his sales maximization hypothesis, found that business executives attached primary importance to this variable.

The emphasis on sales by business executives has, of course, been interpreted as more than just a concern with relative market share. The megacorp, so the argument runs, is willing to sacrifice some of its short-run profits in order to obtain a larger sales volume. This point, carried to an extreme, has led to the development of a pricing model in which sales are maximized subject to a minimum profit constraint.[5] To the extent that this constrained sales maximization model implies that prices will be held down by the industry as a whole in order to stimulate sales over the long run or that individual firms will use part of their sales revenue to try to increase their relative market shares through expenditures on advertising and other modes of non-price competition, it is fully in accord with the arguments presented below. However, to the extent that the sales maximization hypothesis is taken to mean that the megacorp, acting alone, can manipulate its sales volume in the short run through the price variable, it flies in the face of all that is known about oligopolistic industries - including the implicit curb on unilateral pricing initiatives and the price inelasticity of the industry demand curve.

Unfortunately, it is the latter interpretation which is sometimes placed on the constrained sales maximization model.[6] Since such an interpretation requires the least departure from the short-run, static framework of more conventional pricing models, it is not surprising that it has proven attractive to some economists. Even the alternative interpretation, however, that firms are concerned with sales over the long run, cannot be accepted without further refinement. As Baumol himself quickly came to realize, a dynamic version of the constrained sales maximization model must rest on the assumption that it is the rate of growth of sales, and not the absolute level, that is being maximized.[7]

Marris has, in a separate seminal work, posited that what megacorps actually seek to achieve is a maximum rate of growth of assets, rather than of sales (Marris, 1963 and 1964, ch. 2). But a little reflection makes it clear that the two maximands are roughly equivalent to one another, the differences being of little practical import. As the main body of this chapter points out, both are close approximations to the maximand which, assuming an optimal investment program, will lead to the highest rate of growth for the megacorp over time. This third, and most basic, maximand is the rate of growth of the corporate levy - taken to mean the discretionary or residual income accruing to the megacorp itself over and above projected dividend payments.

Once the time horizon has been pushed forward to encompass a maximum rate of growth over an extended period of time, an important transformation occurs in the theory of the firm - whether growth is measured in terms of sales, assets or the corporate levy. In a dynamic model of this sort, one cannot assume a fixed capital stock. This change in underlying premise implies more than just the possibility that output can be expanded without encountering rising marginal costs. It means, even more importantly, that the megacorp's growth rate will be governed not just by the industry price level but by the type and amount of investment being undertaken as well. Indeed, the two types of decisions are inextricably linked. A change in the industry price relative to costs will alter the amount of investment that can be financed internally, and the rate of investment will, in turn, partially determine what price can be charged. This last point is especially true if the concept of investment is broadened to include advertising and other forms of non-price competition.

With the emphasis placed on growth over the long run, the amount of profit - or net revenue - ceases to play the same critical role that it does in the neo-classical theory of the firm. Rather than being an end in itself, it becomes merely an instrument for achieving the more fundamental goal of growth. In fact, a 'satisfactory' level of profit can be defined as the amount of revenue in excess of costs which enables the megacorp to maximize its growth over time. This metamorphic impact on the theory of the firm is the second advantage of postulating growth as the megacorp's desideratum.

Before profits can be relegated to this secondary role, however, explicit account must be taken of the third group - in addition to the managers and the megacorp itself - whose interests are directly bound up with the behavior of the firm. This third group consists of the stock, or equity debt, holders. In the neo-classical theory of the firm, it is usually assumed that whatever profits are earned will ultimately be distributed to stockholders in the form of dividends. This makes it possible to argue, following Lutz (1945, p. 56) and Buchanan (1940, pp. 179-87), that maximizing the growth of the firm over time is the equivalent of maximizing the present value of the firm, measured by the market price of outstanding shares (see also Modigliani and Miller, 1958; Jorgenson, 1963; Vickers, 1968).

Net revenue distributed to stockholders as dividends represents, however, a diminution of the internal funds, or cash flow, available to finance the megacorp's expansion. There is thus a basic and unavoidable conflict between the interests of the stockholders and those of the megacorp itself - just as there is a similar, though less significant, conflict between the interests of the megacorp and those of the executive group. This conflict is reflected in the difference between maximizing the rate of growth of dividends over the long run and maximizing the rate of growth of the corporate levy over the same time period.

Single-minded pursuit of the latter goal - that of maximizing the role of growth of the corporate levy - is, of course, not possible. It would imply a dividend rate close to, if not actually equal to, zero; and the present socio-legal climate precludes this as a possibility. Indeed, as pointed out below, the existing institutional arrangements are likely to require that the dividend rate be increased over time by a certain fixed percentage. For this reason, the goal of maximizing the rate of growth of the corporate levy must necessarily be subject to a minimum dividend (or rate of growth of dividend) constraint. The same is true if the growth of sales or of assets is posited as the maximand. It is thus a minimum rate of growth of dividends, and not a minimum level of profit, which is the limiting factor in the dynamic version of the constrained sales maximization model of megacorp behavior and its two close substitute formulations.

No comparable constraint need be taken into account if one simply assumes that the megacorp seeks to maximize the rate of growth of dividends or - what is the equivalent under perfectly functioning capital markets - the present value of the firm measured by the market price of outstanding shares. The reason for not adopting this simpler alternative, for assuming instead that the megacorp will seek to maximize the rate of growth of the corporate levy subject to a minimum rate of growth of dividends, is given in the main body of the chapter.

Whatever approach is followed, however, the dynamics of the pricing decision remain the same. As long as the concern is with the growth of some target variable over time, the capital stock can no longer be assumed to remain unchanged, and the pricing and investment decisions must be viewed as being inextricably linked. To assume therefore that the megacorp seeks to maximize the rate of growth of dividends, rather than the rate of growth of the corporate levy, is to employ no less metamorphic a behavioral assumption. The growth rate of the megacorp *qua* organization will, it is true, be somewhat lower and the growth rate of income flowing to the equity debt holders somewhat higher,[8] but short-run profits must still be treated as being largely instrumental in nature. What this means is that economists who substitute the present value of the firm for short-run profits are making a far more significant change in the maximand than they usually realize.

With the rate of growth of dividends assumed to be an exogenously determined fixed percentage, it can be demonstrated that maximizing the growth rate of the megacorp - whether that growth rate is measured in terms of sales, assets or the corporate levy - is equivalent to maximizing net revenue, or profits, over the long run. This is because, with dividends viewed as a quasi-contractual cost and thus a part of the overhead expense, any increase in net revenue, or profits, is also an increase in the corporate levy. The equivalency of maximum growth and maximum long-run profits is, of course, even clearer if the growth rate is measured in terms of the increase in dividends paid out. The purpose of this chapter has been to show that all of these variants of long-run growth maximization are quite different from short-run profit maximization, and that indeed short-run profit maximization cannot realistically be pursued as a goal by the megacorp. Once the distinction between maximizing net revenue over time and maximizing net revenue momentarily is recognized, the behavioral foundation for a more relevant microeconomics has been laid.

Such a behavioral foundation is, of course, to be found in a number of earlier works. The dynamic models of Baumol (1962), Marris (1964) and John Williamson (1966) warrant special mention in this connection.[9] If one insists on identifying the interests of the megacorp with those of the nominal owners, then Vickers' book (1968), along with the contribution by Lintner (1971), must be added to the list. But whatever the merit of these various works in providing a more realistic view of megacorp behavior, they nonetheless all suffer from a crucial deficiency. They offer no theory of price determination. Careful examination of the models will reveal that in each instance the industry price is treated as something which is exogenously given - the megacorp's discretion being limited to the question of what proportion of its net revenue should be retained and what proportion paid out in dividends. This may be adequate for dealing with a megacorp that is a price follower, but for a megacorp that is a price leader, it leaves unexplained the most significant aspect of behavior - the price that will be announced on behalf of the industry. And this in turn means that the question of how oligopolistic prices are determined is left hanging in the air. It is this deficiency - the indeterminancy of price in the oligopolistic models hitherto available - which the chapter that follows will attempt to correct.

3. The pricing decision

For an understanding of how prices are determined under oligopoly it is necessary to examine, not the conditions affecting the individual firm in the short run but rather, the conditions affecting the industry as a whole over the long run. This extension of the analysis to multiple periods not only introduces time as a factor, it also means that the pricing decision cannot be divorced from the industry's investment planning.

To speak of the industry in this connection is, of course, to speak of the megacorp-price leader. Its practice of acting as the surrogate for its fellow oligopolists arises out of a real necessity - the need of an industry to avoid price competition that will be destructive to all its members. Still, the question remains of how one firm can decide upon a price that will be acceptable to other firms within the same industry despite the inevitable divergence of interests.

The megacorp-price leader's task in this regard is greatly facilitated by two conditions inherent in the very situation in which it finds itself. The first is the fact, already noted in chapter 2 (pp. 47–8), that when it acts on behalf of the entire industry the megacorp-price leader's own cost and revenue curves can be treated as the marginal portions of the industry supply and demand curves respectively. This means that, on the one hand, assuming the megacorp-price leader to be the least-cost producer, no other firm is likely to prefer a lower price; and that, on the other hand, since all the members of the industry will be faced with equally inelastic revenue curves, no other firm is likely to suffer a greater loss of sales should the price be raised. In other words, no other firm is likely to announce a price that would be more acceptable to the industry as a whole. The second condition that greatly simplifies the megacorp-price leader's task is the fact that it need not determine a price *de nouveau.* A price already prevails in the industry. Given its long-run goals as well as those of the other firms in the industry, all the price leader need determine is what change in price - insofar as the subsequent pricing period is concerned - will be optimal.[1] The new price announced by the price leader will thus depend on (1) the absolute price that prevailed during the previous pricing period, and (2) the change in price decided upon. That is,

$$P_1 = P_0 + \Delta P \tag{3.1}$$

where P_1 is the new industry price that is announced, P_0 is the previously prevailing price and ΔP is the change in price decided upon.[2] It is from this *ex ante* perspective of the price leader that the pricing decision in an oligopolistic industry needs to be analyzed.

The absolute price that prevailed during the previous pricing period will itself depend on price changes that have occurred antecedently. Each oligopolistic industry thus has a pricing history, this pricing history providing a base line for any subsequent marginal adjustment. But though the previously prevailing price is something the price leader must accept as historically given, that absolute price can nonetheless be understood in terms of the uses to which its component parts will be put by the megacorp. This gives rise to a pricing formula for oligopoly which is a more refined version of the commonly used 'cost-plus' approach. Under this formula, the 'plus' added to variable and fixed costs is the corporate levy - that is, the amount of internal funds required by the megacorp to finance its planned investment expenditures.

It follows that any change in price will necessarily reflect a change in one of the pricing formula's components. Assuming variable and fixed costs remain constant - a *ceteris paribus* assumption relaxed in later chapters - the change in price will, then, be due to a change in the required corporate levy. Any change in the required corporate levy will, in turn, depend on the megacorp's demand for and supply cost of internally generated investment funds. Thus the pricing decision in an oligopolistic industry is intimately bound up with the capital accumulation process. This linking of the price level to the industry's investment program is, in fact, the single most important feature of the pricing model set forth below.

In this model the firm is viewed as using the price variable to alter intertemporal revenue flows. Specifically, what will be argued is that, because of the market power which it possesses in conjunction with the other members of the industry, a megacorp can increase the margin above costs in order to obtain more internally generated investment funds, that is, a larger corporate levy. As a result of any such price adjustment, the intertemporal revenue flows will be altered in two ways: (1) from the returns to investment thereby being financed, and (2) from the decline in sales over time caused by the higher price. The first effect is encompassed by the firm's demand curve for additional investment funds, the second, by its supply curve for those same funds. The nature of both curves will be explained once the components of the absolute price level have been described.

The absolute price level

The absolute price level in an oligopolistic industry can be analyzed in terms of the following formula:

$$P = AVC + \frac{FC + CL}{SOR \cdot ERC} \tag{3.2}$$

where P ≡ absolute price level
AVC ≡ average variable costs
FC ≡ fixed costs
CL ≡ corporate levy
SOR ≡ standard operating ratio
and ERC ≡ engineer-rated capacity
Each of the terms in the formula will be explained more fully.

Average variable costs. The definition of average variable costs is that usually employed by economists. They are the costs incurred directly in the production process; that is, they are the costs the megacorp can avoid by curtailing current output. Specifically, they represent, on a per unit basis, the wages paid production workers and the price of material inputs. A change in these average variable costs will depend on either a change in the price of labor and material inputs or a change in the technical coefficients governing the manner in which labor and material inputs are combined with the capital inputs to produce the final output. While a change of the first type, that is, a change in the price of direct inputs, is possible in the short run, a change of the second is not. This is because, as previously argued, the technical coefficients are fixed in the short run. Of course, through the addition of new plants or plant segments designed by engineers to reflect the secular shift in relative factor prices, these technical coefficients will gradually change over time. But the effect even within a single planning period - not to mention a single pricing period - is likely to be negligible since all but the new plants or plant segments, and thus most of the megacorp's operating capacity, will be governed by the old technical coefficients. (A somewhat more extended discussion of technological change will be found below in chapter 5.) Although it must still be recognized that average variable cost may change in the short run as a result of changes in the price of material and/or labor inputs, this possibility will be temporarily excluded by invoking the *ceteris paribus* assumption.

As already suggested, the megacorp's average variable costs can be assumed to be constant and thus equal to marginal costs over the ranges of output at which the megacorp is likely to produce. To the extent that this condition holds, it is possible to substitute marginal costs for average variable costs in the pricing formula.

Fixed costs. These are here defined as those costs of current production which are independent of the actual operating ratio. They include, in line with the common usage of the term, both the salaries of managerial personnel and the interest paid to fixed debt holders. However, because of the special nature of the megacorp, it is best to modify the conventional notion of fixed costs in two ways: (a) to include the dividends paid the stock, or equity, debt holders, and (b) to exclude expenditures on research and development as well as expenditures on advertising and other activities designed to enhance the megacorp's long-run market position.

With respect to dividends, the reason why in the usual analysis they are not included among the fixed costs is that those to whom these payments go, the stock, or equity, debt holders, are viewed as being the owners of the firm entitled to whatever income remains after all contractual costs have been met. Their function, in fact, over and above that of any other supplier of capital funds, is to assume the risk that the residual income may be smaller than anticipated. This view of the equity debt holders, in turn, reflects the belief that they are the equivalent, insofar as the megacorp has an equivalent, to the erstwhile owner-entrepreneur. However, to treat the equity debt holders in this manner is to foster a myth which, as previously noted, has little basis in reality. The equity debt holders are neither owners in the sense of controlling the property to which they nominally hold title nor *de facto* recipients of the megacorp's residual income.

As pointed out above, the effective decision-making power within the megacorp rests with the executive group. The corollary to this is that the equity debt holders have no real voice in determining policy, not even with regard to how the firm's net revenue is to be distributed. They are merely one of the megacorp's several constituencies, albeit in a strong bargaining position as a result of their legal right, acting collectively, to depose the incumbent management. For this reason, they must be viewed, not as owners but rather, as *rentiers*, little different from the fixed-interest debt holders in receiving compensation for the investment funds they have at some point in historical time supplied the firm.

Of course, the equity debt and fixed-interest debt holders exercise differing degrees of influence over the megacorp's affairs and incur differing degrees of risk. But the difference are not necessarily what they are often assumed to be. While it is true that only the equity debt holders have the formal right to select new corporate officers, as a practical matter it is the fixed-interest debt holders who are more likely to be able to effect a change in management. This is because the fixed-interest debt holders are usually a smaller, more cohesive group and because, since they tend to be financial intermediaries, they are in a better position to shut off the flow of external funds. On the other hand, while it is true that the fixed-interest debt holders are contractually entitled to a certain nominal rate of return, as a practical matter it is the equity debt holders who are more likely to receive the anticipated real rate of compensation. This is because dividends, while they may fluctuate somewhat in the short run, are nonetheless more likely to rise over time to offset the effects of inflation. Yet these differences in the degree of influence exercised and the degree of risk incurred are less important than the similarity of function which both the equity debt and fixed-interest debt holders serve as suppliers of investment funds to the megacorp. The similarity is made all the greater by the complementary nature in the short run of equity shares and fixed-interest obligations within the megacorp's debt structures.[3]

The risk of the residual income being smaller than anticipated is, in fact, borne for the most part not by the equity debt holders but instead by the megacorp itself. Of course, if the megacorp's revenues decline drastically, the dividend rate may be temporarily reduced. But the executive group is likely to take such a step only as a last resort;[4] and the equity debt holders are amply compensated for this additional risk they run over and above that of the fixed-interest debt holders by the substantially higher rate of return they receive. Chapter 5 will discuss at some length the factors that actually determine the dividend rate. All that need be noted here is that the payment itself is a *de facto* obligation of the megacorp - an unexplainable failure to meet it placing the executive group's control in jeopardy - but that the amount of the payment will depend only slightly on the megacorp's current earnings per share. A decline in net revenue will be felt, more generally and more directly, by the megacorp itself - through the concomitant decline in its cash flow, or corporate levy. The latter, not the dividends paid the equity debt holders, constitutes the megacorp's true residual income. But since it is the megacorp *qua* organization to which this residual income accrues, it is also the megacorp on which devolves the risk that the residual income may be smaller than anticipated. The equity debt holders, meanwhile, can expect that their own compensation, if not somewhat higher than the previous year's, will probably be no lower. It is because the equity debt holders have thus been stripped almost entirely of any entrepreneurial function that the dividends paid them, like the interest disbursed to the fixed-interest debt holders, are treated here as part of the megacorp's fixed or overhead costs.

The reason for avoiding the term 'profit', as has been done for the most part so far, should now be clear. While suitable for describing the returns to the owner-entrepreneur of a neo-classical proprietorship, it simply leads to confusion in the case of the megacorp. What is generally referred to as the 'profit' of a megacorp actually lumps together two quite different income flows, a return to stockholders in the form of dividends and a return to the megacorp itself in the form of retained earnings - the latter comprising part of the corporate levy, or residual income. For analytical purposes, as will be argued below, it is best to keep these two quite different income flows separate.

With respect to the expenditures on research and development as well as on advertising, the reason why, in the usual analysis, they are included among the fixed costs is not entirely clear. It may simply reflect the fact that, under normal accounting procedures, these types of expenditures are allowable costs to be deducted from revenue before determining the firm's net profits - a practice not critically examined by economists since, in the conventional theory, research and development as well as advertising are dealt with, if at all, largely as an afterthought. Whatever the reason, it seems clear that such expenditures have little to do with current production. If they were to be terminated, the megacorp's sales and output are unlikely to be seriously affected, at least for some time. Expenditures on research and development as well as on advertising are intended, rather, to enhance the megacorp's long-run market position. In this respect, they are similar to the more conventional forms of investment. Like the latter, they will influence only future, not current, revenue; and though they are contractual obligations of the firm once entered into, they are nonetheless entirely discretionary beforehand. It is for this reason that they are herein treated, like the purchase of new plant and equipment, as part of the megacorp's investment expenditures to be financed out of the corporate levy. (This point will be dealt with more fully later in this chapter.)

It should be noted that these modifications of the conventional notion of fixed costs - whether it be the inclusion of dividend payments or the exclusion of research and development along with advertising expenditures - are not critical to the pricing model that follows. They are suggested here simply in the interest of greater realism and because some of the judgments made in later chapters depend on these points. Even if these modifications of the conventional notion of fixed costs are rejected, however, the pricing formula set forth above, along with the pricing model to which it gives rise, still pertains.

A change in fixed costs will, like a change in average variable costs, also depend on a change in the price of inputs or a change in technical coefficients - in this case the price of those inputs and a change in those technical coefficients reflected in the overhead cost structure. Here the inclusion of dividends among the fixed costs is a complicating factor, for it is not clear what input is provided by the equity debt holders. If the salaries paid managerial personnel should rise, it follows that the cost of that type of labor has increased. But if the dividends paid the equity debt holders should rise, one cannot be sure that the cost of capital - or even the cost of obtaining additional investment funds - has similarly increased. It may just be that the cost to the executive group of placating the stockholders, and thereby avoiding the possibility of a take-over by an outside group, has risen. For this reason it is necessary to add that a change in fixed costs may also occur through a change in the rate of compensation received by the equity debt holders.

In the short run, the possibility of a change in the technical coefficients relevant to the overhead cost structure is excluded for the same reason it was excluded in the earlier discussion of average variable costs. The development of new managerial techniques, no less than the construction of new plants embodying more efficient factor combinations, is essentially a long-run phenomenon. The possibility of a change in the price of overhead input and/or a change in the rate of compensation received by the equity debt holders will also be excluded, at least for the remainder of this chapter, by again invoking the *ceteris paribus* assumption.

The corporate levy. This is here defined as the amount of funds available to the megacorp from internal sources to finance investment expenditures. It includes not only what businessmen themselves refer to as the 'cash flow' - depreciation allowances plus retained earnings - but also whatever is currently being spent on research and development, advertising and similar means of enhancing the megacorp's long-run market position. The corporate levy can also be viewed as the difference between the megacorp's total revenue and the payments it is obligated to make, *de facto* as well as *de jure*, to its various constituencies. It thus consists of the funds that accrue to the megacorp *qua* organization. The distinction between this concept and the more conventional notion of profits can readily be seen. On the one hand the corporate levy excludes, for reasons already indicated, that portion of the megacorp's accounting profits that are paid out to the equity debt holders in the form of dividends. On the other hand it encompasses, unlike the conventional notion of profits, both depreciation allowances and any expenditures on research and development, advertising and the like. An underlying premise of this treatise is that the corporate levy is a more useful concept for understanding oligopolistic pricing behavior - and that, moreover, it is not simply a residual figure, the sum left over when all costs, including dividends, have been subtracted from gross revenue. Rather it is an amount deliberately decided upon by the megacorp so that it will have sufficient internal funds to achieve its long-run investment goals.

The required corporate levy, like fixed costs but unlike the realized corporate levy, is a sum which does not vary with the level of output. To convert it to a per-unit-of-sales figure comparable to price, it is necessary to determine the appropriate divisor. If one is interested in the *ex post* result, that is, in the average corporate levy already being realized, the appropriate divisor is simply the quantity of output currently being produced or sold. However, if one is interested in the *ex ante* calculation, that is, in the average corporate levy to be realized in the future, a different divisor is needed. This divisor, given in the pricing formula above, is the standard operating ratio multiplied by engineer-rated capacity.

The latter has already been defined as the sum of the capacities of all plants or plant segments, these capacities in turn being defined as the quantities which, in the judgment of the engineers who designed them, each of the plants or plant segments owned by the megacorp is capable of producing when operated at maximum efficiency. It corresponds to the level of output at which, all plant facilities having been put into operation, marginal costs begin to rise sharply and continuously. The standard operating ratio, in turn, is the percentage of total capacity at which, based on past experience, the megacorp can expect to operate on the average over the business cycle. It takes into account the fact that the megacorp will already have acquired sufficient reserve capacity to meet any likely fluctuations in demand.[5] This ratio, applied to the engineer-rated capacity, gives the quantity of output which the megacorp is most likely to produce at any given moment in time. It therefore provides the best basis for estimating, *ex ante*, the probable per unit fixed costs and the probable per unit corporate levy. Thus,

$$ACL = \frac{CL}{SOR \cdot ERC} \qquad (3.3)$$

where $ACL \equiv$ *ex ante* per unit or average corporate levy.[6]

The inclusion in the oligopolistic pricing formula of the term ($ERC \times SOR$) as the best estimate of the expected rate of output and/or sales has an implication worth noting even at this point. It means that any likely fluctuation in industry demand, and thus in aggregate demand, has already been allowed for; and that therefore a change in the level of industry sales will have little or no effect on the price level, at least during the current pricing period. Indeed, the use of the SOR to estimate the likely level of sales satisfies the final of the three objections commonly raised against cost-pricing models. These three objections are (1) that costs, especially average variable costs, will vary with the level of output; (2) that sales volume will depend on the parallel behavior of rivals in the industry, and (3) that sales volume will also depend on the level of industry and aggregate demand (Skinner, 1970). Objections (1) and (2) have already been met by positing that marginal costs, and hence average variable costs, are constant over the relevant range of output, and by positing that prices are set through a system of price leadership with relative market shares likely to remain unchanged in the short run. Still a fourth objection - that the margin above costs is not invariable but depends on 'what the traffic will bear' (J. Robinson, 1969, p. vii) - will be dealt with shortly.

In addition to the *ex ante* per unit corporate levy, it is possible to specify a marginal corporate levy, that is, the change in the total corporate levy that will be realized from the sale of an additional unit of output. Assuming that the *de facto* obligations represented by fixed costs will have already been allowed for by the megacorp - assuming, in other words, that the fixed costs are treated as having a prior claim on the megacorp's revenue - the marginal corporate levy is simply the difference between the absolute price level and average variable costs. Thus,

$$MCL = P - AVC \tag{3.4}$$

where $MCL \equiv$ marginal corporate levy.

If, as previously suggested, average variable costs are constant over the ranges of output at which the megacorp normally produces, the marginal corporate levy will not only be constant as long as the absolute price level remains unchanged, it will also be equal to the difference between that price level and marginal costs.

A geometric presentation. Its various components having been described, the oligopolistic pricing formula can now be translated into a geometric diagram as is done in figure 6. The only change from the earlier diagrams is that the average corporate levy has now been added to average variable and average fixed costs. Since the required corporate levy is a fixed sum which does not vary with the rate of capacity utilization, it will, when converted to a per unit basis, decline at a constant rate. In this respect, it differs not at all from fixed costs. Mathematically, in fact, the required corporate levy can be considered simply an addition to the fixed cost component.

The absolute price level prevailing at any given moment in an oligopolistic industry will thus be equal to the price necessary to cover, not only the average variable and average fixed costs but, in addition, the

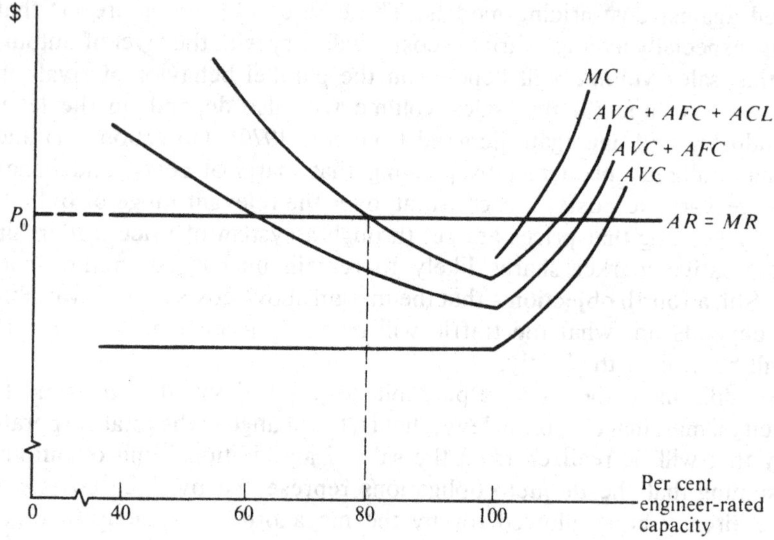

Figure 6

average required corporate levy at the standard operating ratio. Assuming the standard operating ratio to be 80, as in figure 6, this will be the price level P_0 as indicated in the diagram. It is this price level which the megacorp-price leader, acting on behalf of its fellow oligopolists, will have previously announced and this price level which, until the next pricing period, will then be maintained by all the firms in the industry.

A price which has been set and then maintained at level P_0 implies, of course, that insofar as the actual operating ratio differs from the standard operating ratio, the total corporate levy realized *ex post* will differ from the corporate levy planned *ex ante*. Even though the standard operating ratio will have been computed so as to average out these differences over the normal business cycle, the fact is that, at any given moment in time, there is almost certain to be a discrepancy between the two – with the total corporate levy actually realized being affected accordingly.

The total corporate levy realized *ex post* depends, of course, on the actual operating ratio. Indeed, with the marginal corporate levy necessarily being greater than the average corporate levy,[7] the total corporate levy actually realized will both rise and fall more sharply than the rate of capacity utilization. The larger the marginal corporate levy, that is, the greater the difference between P and AVC, the greater will be this sensitivity of the realized corporate levy to the actual operating ratio. Since the realized corporate levy is identical to the savings being generated by the megacorp, it then follows that the greater the marginal corporate levy, the greater too will be the megacorp's marginal propensity to save, this marginal propensity to save being equal to the ratio of the marginal corporate levy to the price level, MCL/P.[8] The significance of this point will become clear when, in chapter 6 below, the macro-dynamic impact of the oligopolistic sector is analyzed.

In figure 6, the price level is fully determinate only because specific values for AVC, FC and CL have been explicitly assumed. How these values themselves are determined must now be explained. This can be done, starting in the next section, by analyzing from the megacorp-price leader's perspective the desired change in industry price when costs have either not changed or, if they have changed, been exactly offset by productivity gains.

A change in price

With average variable and fixed costs held constant, a change in the price level of an oligopolistic industry must necessarily reflect a change in the required average corporate levy. Since the latter's sole function is to provide internal financing for capital expenditures, a change in the required average corporate levy must, in turn, reflect a change in the demand for investment funds over the next planning period relative to the supply cost of those funds.

The planning period, it should be noted, is the megacorp's time horizon for capital expenditures. It is at least equal to the gestation period for an additional production unit, that is, the time required to bring an entirely new facility into operation starting from scratch. With the pricing decision inextricably linked to the investment decision, the planning period thus corresponds to what, as a minimum, the megacorp must construe the long run to be. In deciding what price should prevail, the megacorp cannot avoid peering at least that far into the future - even though the price decided upon can be changed precipitously, if necessary, at the end of the next pricing period.

It follows, then, that with average variable and fixed costs held constant, a change in the price level in an oligopolistic industry must be a function of a change in either the demand for or the supply cost of additional investment funds over the next planning period. Thus,

$$\Delta P = f(D_I, S_I) \tag{3.5}$$

where $D_I \equiv$ demand for additional investment funds
and $S_I \equiv$ supply cost of additional investment funds.

Each of these determinants will be considered in turn, beginning with the latter.

The supply of investment funds. The megacorp can obtain additional investment funds internally through the corporate levy or externally through new debt financing. In the conventional analysis the cost of internal funds is held to be the same as that of external funds. By retaining a portion of the net revenue for its own use rather than allowing it to recirculate through the capital funds market, the megacorp, so the argument runs, incurs an opportunity cost equal to the rate of interest it would receive if, instead, it lent out those funds to others. That rate of interest, assuming the capital funds market works reasonably well, should be equal to the rate of interest the megacorp itself would have to pay on borrowed funds, adjusted for any difference in the relative degree of risk involved. The argument, however, ignores two important factors. The first is the margin between what the megacorp can earn by investing funds in its own business and what can be earned by lending out funds to others instead. This margin reflects, in addition to the cost of brokerage services, portfolio management and the like, the megacorp's differential skill in employing investment funds in the industries to which it is committed (this point will be elaborated below, pp. 119-20). The second, and far more significant, factor is the real cost incurred when additional investment funds are obtained through the corporate levy.

The conventional analysis obscures the real cost of internal funds because it implicitly assumes that the megacorp has no control over how large an amount of those funds will be generated. In the usual microeconomic treatment the current level of accounting profits, on which the amount of internal funds generated will depend in the first instance, is determined solely by the intersection of the marginal revenue and marginal cost curves; while the retention rate, on which the amount of internal funds generated will depend in the second instance, is determined solely by the ability of the firm to reinvest those funds on behalf of the stockholders at a more favorable rate of return than the stockholders themselves could obtain. By now the inapplicability of this conventional line of reasoning to the megacorp should be readily apparent - first, because, the amount of net revenue realized in the short run does not depend on the intersection of any marginal revenue and marginal cost curves and, second, because the retention rate does not necessarily depend on what is in the best interests of the equity debt holders. Rather, what is here being suggested - and it is a fundamental premise upon which rests the pricing model that follows - the megacorp-price leader, acting with the tacit acquiescence of its fellow oligopolists, is in a position to increase its net revenue in the short run by raising the industry price. Moreover, by doing so its intention is to augment, not the returns to the equity debt holders but rather, the megacorp's own residual income as reflected in the growth of the corporate levy over time.

What limits the megacorp-price leader in its willingness to increase the industry price level, and thereby obtain additional investment funds internally, is the real cost incurred as a result of any rise in industry price. This cost, it will be argued, derives from three sources: (a) the substitution effect, (b) the entry factor, and (c) the possibility of meaningful government intervention.

The substitution effect. Any increase in the relative price charged for a product will cause that product to lose part of its market to competing goods. This is because, as the relative price rises, other goods - including both those supplied by rival domestic industries and those imported from abroad - will become more attractive as substitutes. The resulting loss of industry sales is what is meant by the substitution effect.

A decrease in the relative price will, of course, have the opposite impact. While an announced price cut is somewhat rare in oligopolistic industries for reasons to be brought out later in this chapter, an increase in the price of competing goods while the price of the product in question remains unchanged - a set of circumstances equivalent to a fall in the relative price of the latter - is quite common. In fact, in a dynamic system, it is more generally the differential rates of increase in the price levels among competing industries that give rise to the substitution effect.

This effect, it is important to note, will be a function of time (cf. Pollack, 1970; Scherer, 1970, pp. 213-16). The ability to substitute other goods for any product the relative price of which has risen will be limited by the need to make certain prerequisite adjustments. In the case of a product sold to other business firms, production techniques will have to be revised; in the case of a product sold to households, taste preferences will have to be altered. (The distinction between production techniques and taste preferences is the distinction between objective and subjective considerations; thus there will be an element of taste in the purchasing decisions of business firms and an element of production technique in the purchasing decisions of households.) Moreover, unless the change in relative price can be expected to persist over time - and only by waiting can one have confidence in this regard - the necessary adjustments are not likely even to be attempted.

For these reasons the full impact of the substitution effect will not be felt at once. In the time period immediately following the rise in price the impact will be similar to the one shown in figure 7. With

AR the portion of the industry's short-run demand curve that is identical in terms of elasticities with the megacorp-price leader's own revenue curve, an increase in price from P_0 to P_1 will lead to decrease in output sold from Q_0 to Q_1. Net revenue will thus, on the one hand, be increased by an amount equal to the rectangle P_1ABP_0. This represents the additional net revenue that will be realized, as a result of the higher price, on the quantity of output still being sold. But net revenue will, at the same time, be reduced by an amount equal to the rectangle *BGFE*. This represents the net revenue (price less marginal cost) which will no longer be realized as a result of the decline in sales caused by the higher price. Since a change in the megacorp's net revenue position is the same, in this context, as a change in the realized corporate levy, the one term can be substituted for the other. Thus the rectangle P_1ABP_0 represents the increase in the total corporate levy as well as the increase in net revenue realized while the rectangle *BGFE* represents the reduction in the total corporate levy as well as the reduction in net revenue.[9]

Whether the megacorp-price leader will, on balance, be better off as a result of the price increase will depend on the relative size of the two rectangles, P_1ABP_0 and *BGFE*. In figure 7 the former is larger. This means that the net effect of the rise in price will be to increase the total corporate levy realized. Such a result was assured, however, by positing a revenue curve for the megacorp-price leader that is price

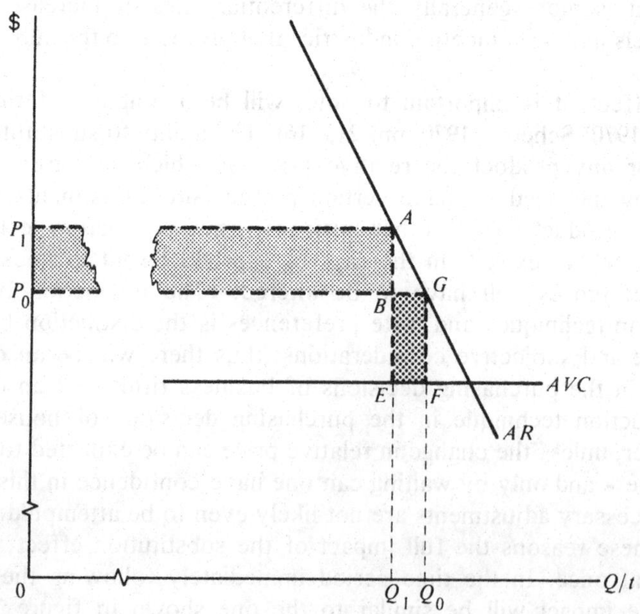

Figure 7

inelastic at the prevailing price level. For the reasons brought out in chapter 2, this is not an unreasonable assumption to make about the megacorp-price leader's revenue curve in the time period immediately following an increase in price. Thus the immediate impact of any rise in price is likely to be an increase in net revenue, that is, an increase in the total corporate levy realized.

But in subsequent periods, whether time is measured weekly, monthly, quarterly or annually, the megacorp-price leader's revenue curve is likely to become more elastic. This is because buyers will increasingly have the time necessary to make whatever changes in production techniques or tastes are needed to take advantage of the lower relative prices being charged for substitute goods. In fact, each succeeding time period should bring a revenue curve which, for any given price coordinate, is more elastic than that of the previous time period. As a result, the rectangle P_1ABP_0 should, over time, become smaller and the rectangle $BGFE$, bigger.

At some point in time following the increase in price, the relative size of the two rectangles may even come to be reversed, with rectangle $BGFE$, representing the corporate levy no longer realized as a result of the ensuing decline in sales, exceeding rectangle P_1ABP_0. If this occurs - and it is by no means certain that it will - the price increase may be said to have imposed a real cost, due to the substitution effect, on the megacorp-price leader. The internal funds generated through the corporate levy will henceforth be even less than they were before the rise in price. Indeed, if the industry demand curve continues to become more elastic with the passage of each additional time period, the total corporate levy realized will not only be less than it was initially, it will grow smaller and smaller.

Still, the megacorp-price leader - not to mention the other firms in the industry - may be better off as a result of the higher price. Though the megacorp-price leader may ultimately suffer a decline in the total corporate levy realized, this will not happen for some time. In the meantime it will have the additional internally generated funds to use as best it can to improve its long-run market position. To determine whether the megacorp-price leader will, in fact, be better off, it is necessary to compare the prospective rate of return from investing those funds with the cost, due to the substitution effect, of obtaining the funds internally through the corporate levy rather than obtaining them externally through new debt financing. This, in turn, requires that the real cost to the firm, due to the substitution effect, of obtaining the additional investment funds internally through the corporate levy be converted into an implicit interest rate.

Conceptually it is possible to break down into two parts the probable long-run impact of the rise in price on a megacorp-price leader's realized corporate levy. There is first the anticipated immediate increase in the realized corporate levy, spread over the number of time periods for which the net substitution effect is likely to be negative or zero.[10] If the additional corporate levy likely to be realized in each of these time periods is properly discounted and if the adjusted figures for each of the time periods are then added together, the result is an estimate of the present value of the additional internal funds likely to be obtained through the price increase.[11] This is the equivalent of a principal sum, such as could alternatively be borrowed from external sources.

Besides the anticipated immediate increase, however, there is also the possible eventual decline in the realized corporate levy, beginning with the time period during which the substitution effect is first likely to become positive and continuing thereafter.[12] If the anticipated loss of corporate levy in each of these time periods is properly discounted so that the interval between the rise in price and the positive impact of the substitution effect is, in essence, eliminated and if the adjusted figures for each of the time periods are then averaged, the result is an estimate of the subsequent loss of income per time period to the megacorp-price leader.[13] This is the equivalent of a periodic interest payment on the principal sum likely to be obtained.

Dividing this last estimate by the first produces a ratio, R_1, which may be viewed as an implicit interest charge, due to the substitution effect, on the additional internal funds likely to be obtained through a rise in price.[14] This ratio is, of course, a contrived figure, designed to permit comparison both with the marginal efficiency of investment, r, and with the 'permanent' rate of interest, i, that must be paid on external funds.[15] Nevertheless, R_1 is derived from the real cost likely to be incurred by a megacorp-price leader when it uses the price mechanism to increase the amount of investment funds available to it from internal sources. This real cost, in the sense of forgone income, is the possible decline in the total corporate levy being realized, below the initial level, if the substitution effect should in a subsequent time period become positive.

The implicit interest charge due to the substitution effect, R_1, will be a function not only of time and the increasing price elasticity of demand which time is likely to bring but also of the percentage change in price, n. The greater this percentage change in price, the greater will be the arc elasticity of demand in any given time period, that is, the greater the resulting percentage decline in sales.[16] To assume otherwise would be to imply an industry demand curve considerably more curvilinear than any ever actually observed empirically.[17] The greater the arc elasticity of demand in any given time period, however, the greater will be the arc elasticity of demand in every subsequent time period. At the same time, the greater will be the overall substitution effect. Thus,

$$R_1 = f(n). \tag{3.6}$$

In other words, the greater the percentage increase in price, the greater will be the implicit interest charge due to the substitution effect. This relationship derives from the fact that the arc elasticity of demand in any given time period - a key determinant of R_1 - is itself a function of the percentage increase in price. That is,

$$|e_j| = h_j(n) \tag{3.7}$$

where h_j is the factor by which the absolute value of the arc elasticity of demand in any given time period, $|e_j|$, increases as n increases.[18]

There are a number of reasons why R_1 may not be very significant, at least as a factor inhibiting the megacorp-price leader from raising the industry price. If the available empirical evidence on the elasticity of industry demand curves is to be accepted, the immediate impact of a rise in price is likely to be a substantial increase in the total corporate levy realized. Whether, over time, the substitution effect will become positive and thereby impose any real cost on the megacorp-price leader is by no means certain.[19] Moreover, if the megacorp-price leader underestimates the long-run impact or, alternatively, has reason to assume that the industries supplying substitute goods will raise their prices too, R_1 is likely to be quite small if not actually negligible. But while the substitution effect may not suffice by itself to restrain the megacorp-price leader, it may, when considered together with the other sources of real cost arising from an increase in price, nonetheless be important.

The entry factor. Any increase in absolute price, holding costs constant, will facilitate the entry of new firms into the industry. This is because, as the absolute price rises (and with it the margin between revenue and costs), potential rivals will have a better chance of overcoming the cost disadvantages which constitute the barriers to their entry. If, as a result of a higher absolute price, new firms should succeed in entering the industry, the established enterprises will necessarily find that their own relative shares of the market have been reduced. The resulting decline in the sales of these established firms, including that of the megacorp-price leader, is what is meant by the entry factor.

Whether in fact new firms - or established firms from other industries - will succeed in entering the industry will depend on the size of the barriers they face. In the case of an oligopolistic industry, these barriers, by the very nature of the industry, can be expected to be quite significant. Otherwise, the number of firms is not likely to have remained small over time nor the concomitant interdependence of those firms to have persisted. Following Bain's schema, barriers to entry can be divided into three types, depending on whether they relate to (a) economies of scale, (b) absolute cost advantages, and (c) product differentiation.[20]

The economies of scale barrier reflects the fact that unless the potential entrant is able to attain a certain size it will find itself at a cost disadvantage. This necessary size has two aspects, one related to the scale of the individual plant, the other related to the number of such plants, that is, the scale of the firm itself. To be able to produce with the least direct cost per unit of output, the new firm must enter into production with a plant of minimal optimal size, *m*, where *m* is a certain percentage of total industry sales. The value of *m* will vary from industry to industry, depending on what sorts of technical indivisibilities exist relative to the total volume of sales.[21] This situation presents the potential entrant with two choices. It can, on the one hand, erect a plant of size *m*. If it does, however, it may not be able to capture a sufficiently large share of the market to operate the facility at its most efficient level of output. Alternatively it can choose to build a smaller plant, one which gives rise to slightly higher average variable costs but the least-cost point of which is reached at a lower level of output. In either case the potential entrant will find itself at a disadvantage compared with established firms having plants of minimal optimal size which can be operated, at full capacity, more efficiently.

This disadvantage will be compounded if there are economies of multi-plant operation and if the established firms are of sufficient size to exploit them. The ability to adjust to fluctuations in demand by starting up or shutting down entire plants or plant segments rather than by using any one plant more or less intensively has already been pointed out as one of these economies. Another is the ability to spread over a larger volume of output the overhead costs of managerial personnel. The same benefits of scale are also manifest with respect to what are herein defined as forms of investment but which are more usually classified as additional items of overhead expense. These include expenditures on advertising, research and development, distribution systems and other forms of vertical integration.[22] Again, the importance of these economies of multi-plant operation will vary from industry to industry, but to the extent they do exist, they place the potential entrant at an even greater disadvantage (Bain, 1956, pp. 82-93).

The absolute cost barrier reflects the ability of the established firms, because of their prior existence, to obtain certain of their inputs on more favorable terms than a potential entrant. The established firms may, for example, control superior production techniques through patents or secret processes. If so, a new firm will be forced either to pay royalties or do without the superior techniques (Steele, 1964; O'Brien, 1964). The established firms may, in addition, already employ all the available skilled manpower, including experienced executives. Should this be the case, a new firm will either have to bid away key employees by offering them higher wages and salaries, or suffer the disadvantages of having to operate with a less competent work force. The established firms may also control all the known supplies of a certain raw material. In this case, a new firm will either be forced to develop its own sources of supply at considerable expense, or find itself put in an extremely vulnerable position with regard to a critical input. Finally, the established firms may be able to obtain external investment funds more easily and at lower rates of interest than a potential entrant.[23] This is a reflection not only of the close ties to various financial intermediaries that the established firms are likely to have cultivated over the years but also of the inherently greater risk of a loan to a firm just starting out, especially in an industry dominated by megacorps. Whatever the particular source of the absolute cost advantage enjoyed by the established firms, however, the effect is to add still further to the obstacles which the potential entrant must overcome (Bain, 1956, ch. 5).

The product differentiation barrier reflects the fact that the established firms are likely, over the years, to have created a strong customer loyalty toward their respective brands. The result of advertising and other marketing efforts, this loyalty is likely to be most significant in the case of goods sold to households; but it will exist even in the case of goods sold to other business enterprises. Whether they be households or other business enterprises, buyers can generally be expected, in the absence of any disturbing element, to maintain their habitual purchasing patterns. Thus, to gain a foothold in the industry, a potential entrant will be forced to do one or both of the following: (a) incur promotional expenses even beyond those of the established firms, (b) shave its price. Either recourse will have untoward consequences.

If the new firm attempts to capture a share of the market through extraordinary promotional efforts, it will find that its per unit expenditures for that purpose have placed it at a substantial cost disadvantage - first, because a larger total amount will have to be spent to offset the edge enjoyed by the established firms and, second, because the new firm will have a lower volume of sales over which to spread the cost. The product differentiation and economies of scale barriers thus interact to reinforce one another: unless buyer resistance can be overcome sufficiently to attain *m* per cent of the market, the potential entrant will suffer from higher average variable costs; but the means of overcoming buyer resistance are themselves subject to economies of scale that place the new firm at a disadvantage.

The only alternative is for the new firm to try to capture the necessary share of the market by shaving its price. If it attempts this, however, not only may it invite retaliatory price cutting by the established firms[24] but, more to the point in this context, its own net revenue will be correspondingly reduced. In either case, product differentiation can be expected to make entry even more difficult.

Taken together, all three types of barriers - economies of scale, absolute cost advantages and product differentiation - serve to create a margin between the average variable and fixed costs of the established firms in an industry and those of a potential entrant. The average corporate levy, on the other hand, has the effect of narrowing this margin, and an increase in the absolute price (the equivalent of a rise in both the average and marginal corporate levy) serves to narrow it even further.

While this margin might at first appear to define a precise point at which an increase in price will lead to the entry of a new firm into the industry, as a practical matter it must be taken as little more than a benchmark. Even an established firm like the price leader can be expected to have only a rough notion of how great is the cost disadvantage of a potential entrant; the new firm itself will be still less capable of making a precise estimate. It may consider the barriers to be less than they actually are, or it may consider them to be more. Which will be the case, and to what extent, cannot be known beforehand. Faced with this uncertainty, the megacorp-price leader can at best only estimate the probability of entry following a rise in price, this estimate being based on its own knowledge of how significant are the barriers which a new firm faces. The entry factor, then, must necessarily be probabilistic.

This probability of entry, π, will, like the arc elasticity of demand, e, be a function of time. Following a decision by a new enterprise to enter the industry, plans will have to be formulated, capital funds secured and construction begun. Even then, the gestation period before the plant is actually ready to begin full-scale production may be considerable. This means that, whatever the probability of entry in the time period immediately following an increase in price, it is likely to be even greater in each succeeding time period until finally it attains some maximum value.

While the probability of entry can be expected to increase with time, the loss of sales and thus the real cost incurred by the megacorp-price leader will be the same regardless of when the new entry actually occurs. This real cost will be equal to the marginal corporate levy on the sales of the megacorp-price leader which the new firm displaces. If the new firm is likely to enter the industry with a plant of minimum optimal size, m, and can be expected to find a market for all its output, the sales of the established firms are likely to be reduced by a percentage equal to m, both in the aggregate and, on the average, individually. Given these expectations - and to simplify the exposition these are the expectations which, it will be assumed, are held - the real cost incurred by the megacorp-price leader due to the entry factor will depend on the value of m.[25] Of course, if a new firm is more likely to enter the industry with a suboptimal plant and/or cannot be expected to find a market for its full capacity output, the appropriate percentage will be less than m.

The real cost the megacorp-price leader can expect to incur in any given time period, due to the likelihood of entry, will thus be the product of two factors: (1) the probability of entry, π, in that time period, and (2) the real cost incurred if entry should actually take place, a cost based on the value of m. What this means is that in any given time period following an increase in price, the entry factor can be expected to give rise to two rectangles similar to the rectangles P_1ABP_0 and $BGFE$ in figure 7. In this case, however, the reduction in the quantity of output sold reflects the possibility that a new firm may enter the industry and displace some of the megacorp-price leader's sales. This change in the quantity of output sold will depend, not on the arc elasticity of demand but rather, on the values of π and m; and it will give rise, not to the rectangles P_1ABP_0 and $BGFE$ but rather, to the rectangles $P_1CG'P_0$ and $G'GFF'$ as in figure 8. It should be noted that AR' is the average revenue curve which the megacorp-price leader could expect

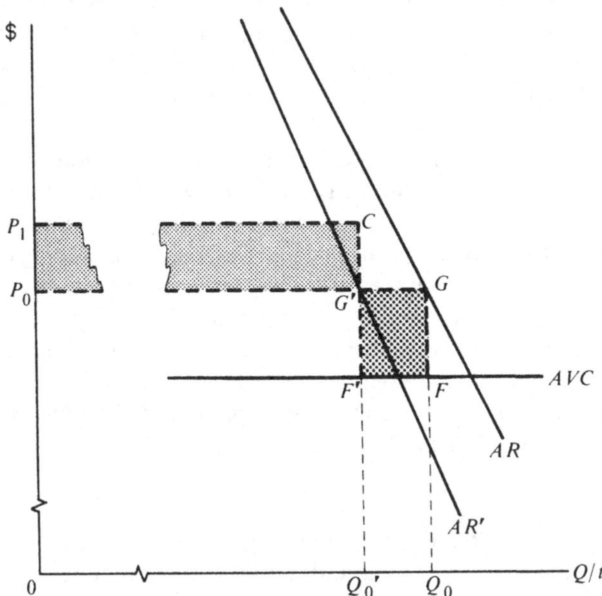

Figure 8

to face following the entry of a new firm of minimum optimal size and that the distance $Q_0 - Q_0'$ is equal to the inroads on the price leader's total sales volume which that new firm could be expected to make ($m \cdot Q_0$) multiplied by the probability of the entry occurring (π).

Again it is likely that over time rectangle $P_1GG'P_0$ will become smaller and rectangle $G'GFF'$ larger – in this case because of the higher probability of entry in each succeeding time period. It is even possible that at some point in time following the rise in price the relative size of the two rectangles may come to be reversed, with the result that the total corporate levy realized by the megacorp-price leader will be less than it was initially. Still, since the internal investment funds being generated will, up to that point, be greater, the megacorp-price leader may be better off to raise the price. Whether in fact it will be better off will depend on how great is the real cost due to the entry factor, relative to the marginal efficiency of investment and the 'permanent' interest rate on external funds. To permit this comparison, it is necessary once more to convert the real cost due to the entry factor into an implicit rate. This can be done by again breaking down into its two parts the long-run impact, due to the entry factor, of the rise in price: first, the more immediate increase in investment funds obtained and, second, the possible eventual decline in the total corporate levy realized.[26] If the latter sum, properly discounted and averaged, is divided by the first, also properly discounted and averaged, the result is a second ratio, R_2, which can be viewed as the implicit interest rate, due to the entry factor, on the additional investment funds likely to be obtained through a rise in price.[27]

This implicit interest rate, R_2, will also be a function, not only of time and the increasing probability of entry which time brings but, in addition, of the percentage change in price, n. The greater this percentage change in price (with average variable and fixed costs remaining constant), the greater will be the average corporate levy and thus the greater will be a new firm's chances of overcoming the barriers to entry which it faces. Assuming that these improved chances will not go unnoticed by a potential entrant, the greater, too, will be the probability of entry in each time period following the rise in price and the more significant will be the overall entry factor. Thus,

$$R_2 = f(n). \tag{3.8}$$

In other words, the greater the percentage increase in price, the greater will be the implicit interest charge due to the entry factor.[28]

Besides the very concrete loss of sales which the entry of a new firm can be expected to cause, there is a less tangible effect. The very ability to coordinate pricing decisions among the various members of the industry may be jeopardized by the intrusion of a new enterprise, one without a vested interest in the price stability of the industry and, indeed, with a real need to undermine that stability if it is to obtain some minimum share of the market. Moreover, once a new firm has been encouraged to attempt entry into an industry, it is not readily dislodged - even if the barriers it faces should turn out to be greater than anticipated. Whatever the returns, the new enterprise is likely to remain in the industry for some time, displacing the sales of the establishment firms and/or making price coordination more difficult.[29] For these reasons, the prevention of new entry into the industry may have come to be viewed as essential to the optimization of a firm's long-run position. It is not possible, of course, to increase the industry price (with average variable and fixed costs remaining unchanged) without running some risk that a new firm will be encouraged to enter the industry. Still, the megacorp-price leader may want to avoid a change in price which has more than a certain probability of entry, π, associated with it in the long run. If so, that percentage increase in price, n_{x_1}, will serve as a ceiling or upper limit on the industry price level. This means that n will be subject to the restraint that the long-run probability of entry, π_t, associated with it not exceed X_1 where X_1 is the maximum acceptable probability of a new firm entering the industry as a result of the attendant increase in price.[30] Even before this upper limit is reached, however, the price leader may be deterred from announcing more than a certain percentage increase in price by the fear of the government's likely reaction. It is this third constraint on pricing discretion that will now be considered.

The possibility of meaningful government intervention. Any increase in industry price, if construed to be contrary to the public interest, may provoke meaningful intervention by the Federal government. What is meant here by the adjective 'meaningful' is that the long-run growth of the megacorp-price leader and/or the other members of the industry is likely to be adversely affected. Meaningful intervention by the Federal government can, at least theoretically, take a number of different forms. These include (a) nationalization, (b) price regulation, (c) taxation, (d) tariff reduction, (e) release of government stockpiles, (f) qualitative restrictions of all types and (g) antitrust prosecution. As a practical matter, however, American political attitudes and precedents effectively preclude most of these alternatives.

Nationalization, for example, is not likely even to be considered seriously by United States political leaders. Aside from the substantial ideological objection to the take-over of private property, there is the feeling on the part of those most likely to advocate such a remedy that nationalization, based on the experience of other countries, simply exacerbates the problem of controlling large-scale enterprise. On the one hand it would seem that too often a change in the nominal owners of the firm does little to alter the behavior of the executive group. A new board of directors may be appointed, its members even chosen from among public officials, but the discretion of the permanent bureaucracy appears to remain unimpaired. On the other hand it would seem that the interjection of politics has sometimes led to the loss of efficiency. Since nationalization has usually been carried out for a complex set of reasons - only one of which may have been the desire to limit pricing power - it may be questioned how relevant is this comparative experience in evaluating the likely effectiveness of that approach in the United States. Still, there can be little doubt as to the lack of significant political support for the nationalization of any part of American industry.[31]

Price regulation of specific industries is somewhat more within the realm of the politically feasible, if only because price regulation is not foreign to the American experience - even in peacetime. Yet the precedents themselves are probably the reason for the lack of enthusiasm which this approach arouses. Aside from the general reluctance to increase still further the government's power to overrule private decisions, there is the widespread feeling that the regulation of public utilities in this country has not brought the results desired. Rather it seems that the industries being regulated have succeeded in capturing the sympathies - if not the independence - of the various regulatory bodies to such an extent that regulation may be said to exist in name only. Some would even argue that regulation serves primarily to give the cover of governmental legitimacy to private cartel arrangements. Meanwhile the elaborate procedures that must be followed by the regulated industries would appear seriously to curtail entrepreneurial initiative.[32] Whatever may be the potential for improving regulatory procedures, it seems fair to conclude that an extention of this approach to the oligopolistic sector on an individual industry basis is not likely to have sufficient public support to make it a realistic possibility. The question of general price regulation - or controls - will be left temporarily to one side.[33]

Taxation of specific industries, selected tariff reduction, release of government stockpiles and qualitative restrictions of various types are forms of government intervention that are far less apt to encounter opposition on ideological grounds alone. They are forms of intervention, however, that can significantly impair the long-run growth of the firms in the industries so affected. Still, the deliberate resort to these remedies as a means of controlling prices in the private sector can hardly be described as an accepted American political practice. Whatever precedents may exist are perhaps best viewed as *ad hoc* measures designed to deal with quite specific, although limited situations.[34] What are lacking are both the legislative authority and the administrative procedures for using these remedies in a systematic way to deal with the problem of private pricing power. This is not to argue that the legislative authority could not one day be obtained and the administrative procedures subsequently developed. So far, however, this has not happened.

In the absence of price controls and the sanctions thereunder provided, the one remedy most generally available to the government when confronted by a price increase considered to be contrary to the public interest is prosecution under the antitrust laws.[35] It is a response by the executive branch which is fully in accord with accepted political and economic beliefs, and a response which does not require prior legislative authorization. It is thus the remedy to which the government, in the absence of price controls, is most likely to resort in any individual situation. This is true despite the inherent limitations of the remedy.

The weakness of the antitrust approach is that, unlike an administrative action under either utility regulation or general price controls, it does not permit the government to intervene directly to countermand a price increase. This lack of authority is intentional, the rationale being that if only the latent market forces can be strengthened by the appropriate means there will be no need for more direct government action.

In practice, the relatively small sums appropriated by Congress for enforcement, together with the lengthy time required to prosecute even a minor case, have meant that only a handful of firms - mostly price leaders - in a handful of industries need fear the possibilities of antitrust prosecution at any given moment in time.[36] Even more critical, the remedies available under the law have proven to be ineffectual against the type of interdependent behavior that militates against price competition in oligopolistic industries. To be effective, antitrust action would have to be capable of significantly altering the structure of those industries. That is, it would have to be able to increase the number of firms to such an extent that interdependent behavior would no longer be possible or - what might produce essentially the same result - lower the barriers to entry until they ceased to be a major obstacle to the entrance of new firms. Yet attempts to increase the number of firms through antitrust action have generally floundered on the fears of judges and Justice Department officials that important economies of scales might be lost as a result;[37] while attempts to lower barriers - insofar as these have been successful - have simply led to the replacement of the proscribed methods by others less vulnerable to direct legal attack.

Antitrust action having proven inadequate as a means of controlling pricing decisions indirectly through the restructuring of oligopolistic industries, it has devolved into an instrument of largely nuisance value.

A firm can be fined or even proscribed from certain behavior by a restraining order, and these penalties will impose a certain cost - that of developing a substitute barrier to entry if not that of the fine alone. What is usually most burdensome, however, is the cost of defending against the antitrust suit itself. The firm's executives may find themselves unable to give their full attention to any other matter for months at a time, with a consequent neglect of the company's long-run interests. Significantly, this cost is incurred whether the government wins its case or not.[38] Whatever the likely result, the suit must be defended against vigorously, for what is at stake is the company's public image. Should that image become seriously damaged, the megacorp and the industry to which it belongs will find themselves increasingly vulnerable to political attack - with the risk of even more restrictive forms of government intervention which that vulnerability carries.

While theoretically it is possible to estimate the cost to the megacorp-price leader of antitrust prosecution or whatever other retaliatory act is the most likely form of meaningful government intervention, as a practical matter this is not necessary. The most likely form of intervention, if meaningful in the sense defined above, will pose such a serious threat to the megacorp-price leader's long-run growth prospects that it will be unwilling to run more than a certain risk of provoking the government to act. That risk, ρ, will depend on the percentage increase in price, n. The greater that percentage increase in price, the more likely it is that the megacorp-price leader will appear to be exploiting its market power, the more likely it is that public criticism will be heard and the more likely it is that the government will feel compelled to respond in some manner.[39] If this percentage increase in price is less than the increase in price associated with the maximum acceptable probability of new entry, it will be this percentage increase in price, n_{x_2}, that will serve as the ceiling or upper limit on the industry price. This means that n will now be subject to the restraint that the probability of meaningful government intervention associated with it, p, not exceed X_2 where X_2 is the maximum acceptable probability of meaningful government intervention.

The supply curve of internally generated funds. By combining the restraints imposed by the substitution effect, the entry factor and the fear of meaningful government intervention, it is possible to derive the megacorp-price leader's supply curve of internally generated funds. This supply curve will reflect the differing amounts of additional investment funds per planning period, $\Delta F/p$, that can be generated internally through the corporate levy at differing implicit interests rates, R.

To obtain R, it is necessary to take into account both the substitution effect and the entry factor, keeping in mind the restraint imposed by the maximum acceptable probability of either new entry of meaningful government intervention. In each time period following a rise in price, the megacorp-price leader can expect its sales to decline by a certain amount, such as $Q_0 - Q_1'$ in figure 9. Part of this decline, such as $Q_0' - Q_1'$, will be due to the substitution effect and part, such as $Q_0 - Q_0'$, will be due to the entry factor. The internal funds being generated in any one of these time periods will thus, on the one hand, be increased by an amount equal to the rectangle $P_1A'B'P_0$ - this representing the additional corporate levy that will be realized, as a result of the higher price, on the quantity of output still being sold. Offsetting this gain, on the other hand, will be both the corporate levy no longer realized due to the substitution effect, an amount equal to the rectangle $B'G'F'E'$, and the corporate levy no longer realized due to the entry factor, an amount equal to the rectangle $G'GFF'$. The net change in the total corporate levy realized in any given time period will, then, be equal to the rectangle $P_1A'B'P_0$ less the rectangle $B'GFE'$. When and if in any subsequent time period the latter comes to exceed the former, the combined impact of the substitution effect and the entry factor may be said to have become positive. By taking this combined impact into account for each of the time periods following the rise in price, it is then possible to derive R.

The denominator of R in this case is the present value of the net

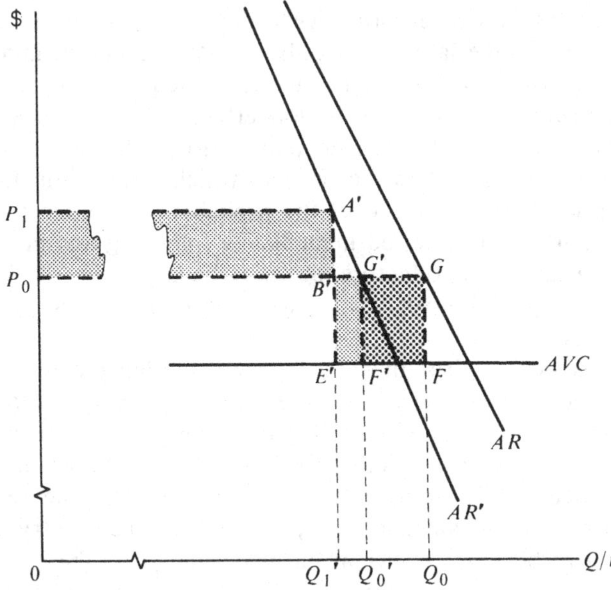

Figure 9

gain in the corporate levy, summed up for all the time periods prior to the one in which the combined substitution effect and entry factor is likely to become positive. It is, then, equal to the present value of the additional funds likely to be obtained through the price increase. The numerator, on the other hand, is the eventual decline in the total corporate levy realized, due to both the substitution effect and the entry factor, properly discounted and averaged for all subsequent time periods. It is, then, similar to the interest that would have to be paid periodically if a sum equal to the denominator were to be obtained from external sources. The resulting ratio, R, may be viewed as the implicit interest rate on the additional investment funds generated internally through an increase in price.[40]

This ratio, R, like the ratios R_1 and R_2 from which it is derived, will depend on the actual percentage change in price, n. The greater that percentage change in price, the greater will be both the substitution effect and the entry factor, and thus the greater will be the value of R. This positive relationship between R and n is depicted in quadrant IV of figure 10.

The slope of the curve $0R$ in quadrant IV reflects the changes likely to occur in both the arc elasticity of demand and the probability of new entry as n varies. A small rise in price, if it still leaves the megacorp-price leader on the inelastic portion of its revenue curve while not significantly compensating for the barriers to entry which a new firm faces, will lead to a value for R which is close to zero. But as n continues to rise, the megacorp-price leader can expect the arc elasticity of demand to become larger, not only in the time period immediately following the rise in price but in all the subsequent time periods as well. This means that the substitution effect will eventually become positive, at least beyond a certain point. Moreover, as n rises, thus providing a greater offset to the barriers which a new firm faces, the megacorp-price leader can expect the probability of entry to become greater, both in the time period immediately following and in each time period thereafter. The two factors together, the larger substitution effect and the greater probability of entry, will lead to an increasingly higher value for R as n rises.

As n continues to rise, the arc elasticity of demand and, with it, the substitution effect can be expected at a certain point to become larger at an increasing rate. This is because, with a negatively sloped linear - or nearly linear - industry demand curve, the absolute value of e_j must necessarily increase at a disproportionate rate relative to the industry price. Meanwhile, the probability of new entry can also be expected to become greater at an increasing rate. This is because, as the barriers to entry are more certainly compensated for by the higher

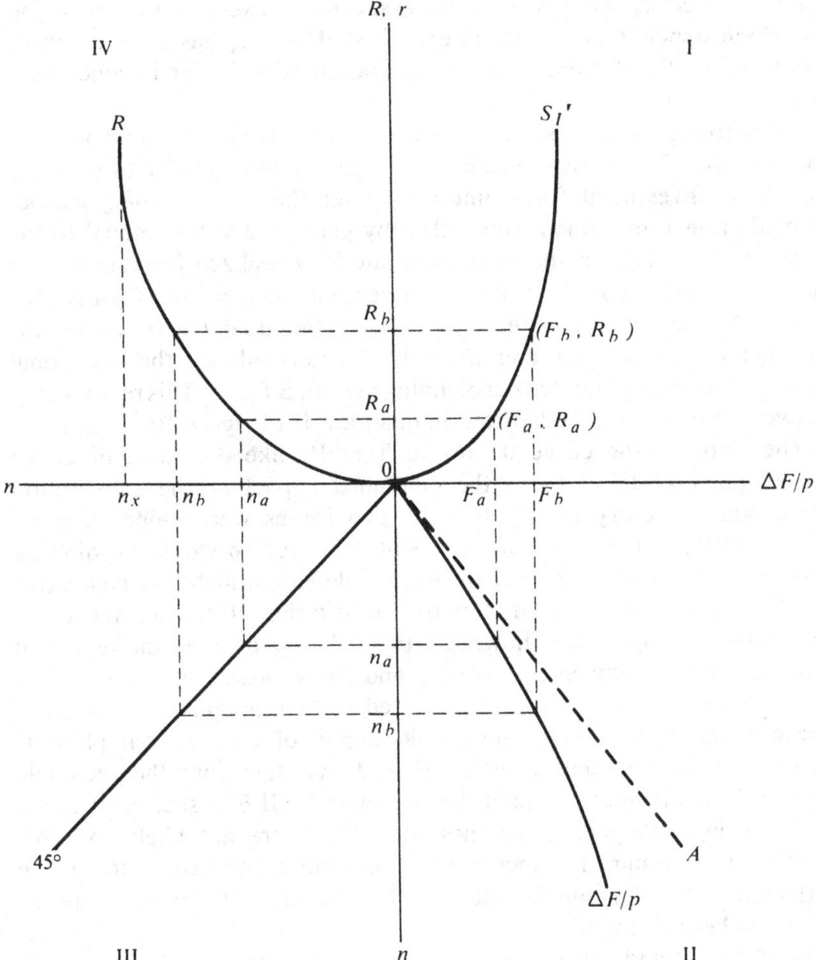

Figure 10

average corporate levy, new firms are increasingly likely to be attracted into the industry. Thus *R*, reflecting both the substitution effect and the entry factor, will at some point begin to rise at a more rapid rate than *n*.

If *n* continues to rise still higher, the megacorp-price leader will finally encounter the ceiling imposed by the maximum acceptable probability of either new entry or meaningful government intervention. This ceiling, n_x in figure 10, is the percentage increase in price for which either the associated π_t exceeds X_1 or the associated p exceeds X_2, depending on which upper limit is encountered first. Once n_x has been reached, the value of R will, insofar as the megacorp-price leader is concerned, become infinitely large.

An increase in the industry price not only gives rise to an implicit interest rate, R, but also enables the megacorp-price leader to generate additional investment funds internally over the next planning period. The additional investment funds thereby generated will be equal to the average net change in the total corporate levy realized for each of the time periods that comprise the subsequent planning period. Clearly, the greater the percentage increase in price, n, the greater will be the new average corporate levy and thus the greater will be the additional investment funds generated per planning period, $\Delta F/p$.[41] This relationship between $\Delta F/p$ and n is depicted in quadrant II of figure 10.

The slope of the curve $0F$ in quadrant II, like the slope of curve $0R$ in quadrant IV, reflects the combined impact of the substitution effect and the entry factor. If these two forces were inoperative or, alternatively, if they were independent of n, $\Delta F/p$ would be directly proportional to n and the curve $0\Delta F/p$ would be a straight line emanating from the origin such as $0A$. For the substitution effect and the entry factor to be inoperative, however, the industry demand curve would have to be perfectly price inelastic and the probability of new entry would have to be completely unaffected by the margin above average variable and fixed costs. This would imply, of course, that point G in figure 9 is the same as point B' and that therefore the rectangle $P_1A'B'P_0$ can increase without the rectangle $B'GFE'$ - such as it exists - also being enlarged. Since these conditions are not likely to hold, $\Delta F/p$ can be assumed to increase at a less rapid rate than n, this being reflected in the diagram by the fact that the curve $0F$ is parabolic to the hypothetical ray, $0A$.

Quadrants I and III in figure 10 are designed to link the curves in quadrant II and IV to one another. Quadrant III, with the aid of a 45° line emanating from the origin, simply measures the percentage change in price, n, along both its axes. Its purpose is to convert what is essentially a three-quadrant diagram into a four-quadrant one. Quadrant I, however, draws upon the relationships depicted in quadrants II and IV to derive an entirely new relationship, one showing the differing amounts of additional investment funds per planning period, $\Delta F/p$, that can be generated internally through the corporate levy at differing implicit interest rates, R. This new relationship is S_I', the supply curve of internally generated investment funds.

If, for example, the contemplated percentage increase in price were n_a, the amount of additional investment funds thereby obtained per planning period would be F_a and the implicit interest rate on these funds, R_a. F_a and R_a would then constitute the coordinates for one point on the supply curve S_I'. If instead the percentage increase in price were n_b, the amount of additional investment funds obtained would be F_b and the implicit interest rate, R_b. F_b and R_b would constitute the coordinates for still another point on the supply curve S_I'. By continuing to vary n in this manner, it is possible to trace out the full supply curve S_I'. This supply curve will indicate, for any given quantity of additional investment funds, $\Delta F/p$, the implicit interest rate, R, thereby incurred. Viewed in conjuction with the other three quadrants, it will also indicate by what percentage, n, the industry price must be increased to provide from internal sources that given quantity of additional investment funds.

It should be noted that the supply curve in quadrant I, like most supply curves, will for the most part be positively sloped. S_I' will also, necessarily be curvilinear, this because of the shape of the $0R$ and $0F$ curves in quadrants IV and II. It will, moreover, be infinitely inelastic beyond a certain point, this reflecting the ceiling on further price increases imposed by the maximum acceptable probability of either new entry or meaningful government intervention. The last point to be noted is that S_I' is predicated on the assumption that all factors except n - in particular, the arc elasticities of demand and the probabilities of new entry over time - are fairly stable. This is not an unreasonable assumption from the viewpoint of a megacorp-price leader trying to decide what change in industry price to announce. Nonetheless, if one of these parameters should change, S_I' will shift accordingly. So, too, may the curves $0R$ and $0F$.

Of some interest is the elasticity of this supply curve, S_I', whether it be measured at a particular point or over a particular interval. Comparison of this elasticity for different firms and/or industries provides one measure of relative pricing or 'monopoly' power. It points to an important truth about pricing power - that the power depends on the existing structure of relative prices, and that as this relative price structure changes, so too will the relative pricing power of different firms and/or industries. Another measure of relative pricing or 'monopoly' power is the size of the average corporate levy, *ACL*. The first of these two measures indicates the firm and/or the industry's potential pricing power, the second their already realized pricing power.

S_I' is merely the supply curve for additional investment funds generated internally through the corporate levy. To derive S_I, the supply curve for all additional investment funds, whatever their source, it is necessary to take into account the cost of external funds to the megacorp-price leader.

The cost of external funds. The megacorp-price leader can obtain additional investment funds externally by floating a new issue of either fixed-interest obligations or equity shares. If it is the former type of security that is to be relied upon, the cost of the additional investment funds will simply be the coupon interest rate on the bonds, adjusted for whatever brokerage fees are to be deducted from the principal sum. If, however, it is a new equity issue that is to be floated, the cost of the additional investment funds will be somewhat more problematical. On the one hand, the principal sum obtained will depend on the price at which the additional shares can be safely marketed, given the current price of the company's shares on the stock exchange. On the other hand, the interest that must be paid on this principal sum will depend, not only on the current level of dividends per share but also on the rate at which those dividends can be expected to increase over time. It is the price-dividend ratio derived from these two adjusted figures that is the equivalent of an interest rate on the new equity issue.

As previously suggested, fixed-interest obligations and equity shares can be viewed as substitutes for one another only in the long run. In the more immediate period, they are more likely to be viewed as complements, with the megacorp first determining its optimum debt-equity ratio based on the attendant risks and other relative disadvantages of the two types of securities, then using that optimum debt-equity ratio as a rule of thumb in its subsequent decision-making.[42] The cost of external funds will thus be an average of the interest rate that must be paid on fixed-interest obligations and on equity shares, weighted by the current debt-equity ratio.[43]

It should be noted, at this point, that the megacorp-price leader, in determining this cost of external funds, need not be significantly affected by current money market conditions. Only a minor portion of its investment expenditures will, in any case, need to be financed externally. Since the planning period for which investment decisions are made encompasses the normal business cycle, the megacorp-price leader can expect to arrange its financing in such a way that it will be able to tap the capital funds market for the marginal sums it may require during those phases of the cycle when the cost of borrowing will be at a minimum. Thus it is only the change in the lowest level of interest rates over successive business cycles, not the change in interest rates during any given business cycle, that is likely to alter the cost of external funds as the megacorp-price leader views that cost *ex ante.* This minimum cost during the most favorable phase in the business cycle is what is meant herein by the 'permanent' interest rate, i, on external funds.[44] To the extent that the megacorp-price leader is able to obtain whatever quantity of additional investment funds it may desire at this rate - and this seems a reasonable assumption as long as the amounts required remain relatively small – the supply curve of external funds will be infinitely elastic. Of course, if at some point further reliance on external funds is likely to lead to an increase in i, the supply curve will from that point on have an upward slope.

Only one last comment needs to be made about the cost of external funds. The megacorp-price leader may be reluctant to resort to outside financing for reasons that are not easily quantified and thus have not yet been taken into account. The reliance on financial intermediaries which the floating of a new securities issue entails will pose a certain risk to the control of the megacorp by the incumbent executive group. Any subsequent failure to meet the additional obligations, implicit as well as explicit, which the megacorp incurs by increasing its outstanding fixed interest and equity debt could lead to the replacement of the executive group. This danger can be avoided if, instead, the megacorp relies upon the corporate levy to obtain its additional investment funds. Thus the permanent interest rate on external funds may, in the eyes of the executive group, be somewhat higher than a simple weighing of the costs to the megacorp itself would suggest.[45]

The total supply curve of additional investment funds, S_I, can be obtained simply by combining the supply curve for additional internal funds, S_I', with the supply curve for external funds, based on the permanent interest rate, i. This is done in figure 11. Up to the point

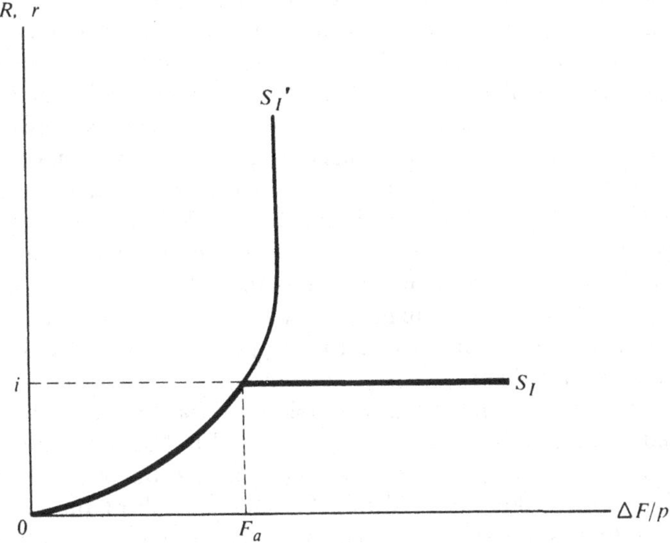

Figure 11

F_a in figure 11, since R is less than i, the megacorp-price leader can be expected to obtain any additional investment funds internally through the corporate levy. Over that interval, therefore, the S_I curve is coextensive with the S_I' curve. Beyond the point F_a, however, since R is greater than i, the megacorp-price leader can be expected to resort to outside financing for any additional investment funds it may need. Over this interval, the S_I' curve runs parallel to the horizontal axis at a height equal to i. The total supply curve for investment funds having been derived in this manner, it is now necessary to consider the megacorp-price leader's demand curve for those same investment funds.

The demand for investment funds. The demand for investment funds by the megacorp-price leader arises from the need to finance those expenditures which, though unrelated to current output, will nonetheless lead to the growth of the corporate levy over time and thus to the growth of the firm itself. The extent to which a particular type of expenditure results in a subsequent increase in the total corporate levy realized relative to the amount of expenditure required is the marginal efficiency of investment, *r*, for that particular type of expenditure.[46]

It should be noted that under oligopolistic conditions, with price competition virtually ruled out because of its potentially destructive effect,[47] a megacorp will grow and prosper depending on how well it allocates the investment funds obtained through the corporate levy. It should also be noted that while the individual firm is constrained by the *ex ante* savings rate which the industry as a whole has chosen - this *ex ante* average savings rate being the margin above costs, or average corporate levy, implicit in whatever price level is currently being maintained by the various members of the industry - it is not so constrained with respect to the rate of investment. The rate of investment for the individual firm may diverge from the industry average,[48] and the capital outlays themselves may take different forms. This greater degree of freedom on the investment side gives rise to the non-price competition so characteristic of oligopoly. Indeed, one can say that, under oligopolistic conditions, competition through investment will replace competition through price. This will be as true for the price leader as for the other megacorps in the industry.

Assuming for the moment that technological change is entirely capital embodied,[49] a megacorp-price leader interested in but a single industry will be faced with a choice among four types of investment expenditures, each of which can be expected to affect the growth of the corporate levy in the long run and each of which will thus have its own marginal efficiency of investment schedule. These four types of investment expenditures can be categorized as follows: (a) the purchase of new plant and equipment, (b) the differentiation of the industry's product more sharply, (c) the erection of higher barriers to entry, or (d) the creation of a more favorable public image.[50] The varying additional amounts, $\Delta F/p$, that can be spent on each of the four categories at varying prospective rates of return, r, is what defines the megacorp-price leader's overall marginal efficiency of investment schedule. This overall MEI schedule, in turn, is what constitutes the megacorp-price leader's total demand curve for investment funds, D_I.

The purchase of new plant and equipment. As previously suggested, the optimization of long-run market share - the prerequisite generally for maximizing the growth of the corporate levy over time in a single industry - requires that a megacorp have sufficient capacity to supply whatever demand for its product is likely, within certain limits, to manifest itself in the foreseeable future. This means that a megacorp, particularly one that is a price leader, must plan ahead. First, it must anticipate what the demand for its product is likely to be at the end of the next planning period, the time required to bring a new plant or plant segment into operation; and second, it must arrange to have the necessary additional capacity built and ready to begin production by that date.

The first part of this planning function is generally the responsibility of the firm's operations research or a similar staff group. This planning body within the megacorp can be expected to have estimated the income and population elasticities for the particular product supplied by the industry. Since an oligopolistic industry is likely to be a relatively mature one with growth determined by aggregate conditions, these elasticities, together with projections of national income and population, should provide the best estimate of total industry demand over the next planning period and perhaps even beyond. The estimates can, of course, be improved upon by taking into account whatever other factors may affect the demand for that particular industry's product - for example, the growth rate of another industry which is a principal customer, the trend of imports, etc.

From these extrapolations of future industry demand with respect to time, the operations research or planning group will attempt to derive the individual megacorp's own growth curve. Since the share of the market which the megacorp is presently supplying is the share it is likely to continue supplying, the industry estimates need only be reduced by that percentage to obtain estimates for the firm. Of course, if there is reason to believe that the megacorp's share of the market will increase in the future, the appropriate percentage will be somewhat larger. However, given the strong interdependence that exists in an oligopolistic industry, any such upward revision is apt to be a relatively minor one, especially if based on a realistic assessment of the possible shift in market shares.

It is in light of the projected growth curve supplied by the operations research or planning body that the megacorp's executive group will decide how much new plant and equipment should be added to the existing capital stock. With this growth curve indicating the most probable level of sales at the end of the current planning period, the executive group can determine how much productive capacity will be required at that point in the future not only to meet the expected demand for the megacorp's product but also to provide an adequate reserve.[51] Comparing this amount with the existing capacity, the executive group can then authorize expenditures for whatever additional plant and equipment will be needed. No precise calculation of probable rates of return will be necessary since, if the firm is to maintain its long-run market position, that level of expenditures is essential. The purchase of new plant and equipment to meet future anticipated increases in industry demand will, therefore, be given first priority in the formulation of an investment strategy by the megacorp's executive group. Of course, once plans have gone forward and subsequent experience reveals that the sales projections have been either overly optimistic or unduly pessimistic, the actual expenditures can be stretched out or speeded up, depending on what the situation calls for.[52]

While the purchase of new plant and equipment to meet future anticipated increases in industry demand is likely to constitute by far the largest proportion of all expenditures on new plant and equipment, still, at the margin, there are apt to be other investment possibilities - to wit, the replacement of some portion of the existing capital stock with more efficient equipment - which provide the executive group with an option. Before a choice can be made among these alternatives, the probable rates of return will have to be determined. It is these marginal investment opportunities, small as they may be relative to the whole, that give the megacorp-price leader's demand curve for new plant and equipment, D_{I_1}, whatever negative slope it may have.

The differentiation of an industry's product more sharply. If the ability to obtain additional investment funds internally through the corporate levy is limited by the fear of losing part of the existing market to substitute products, it may be to a megacorp's advantage to see to it that the industry's product is differentiated more sharply from those of other industries. This can be done in several ways, the most important being advertising and research and development (R & D). The effect of such expenditures will be to reduce the absolute value of the arc elasticities of demand for all subsequent time periods, whatever may be the percentage change in price decided upon. This reduction in the arc elasticities of demand will enable the megacorp-price leader and the other firms in the industry to set a higher price without incurring any additional cost due to the substitution effect. The greater percentage increase in price thus made possible - the equivalent, other things being equal, to a greater percentage increase in the marginal corporate levy - will appear to the megacorp contemplating the increased expenditures on either advertising or R & D as a potential permanent yield of additional investment funds. These additional investment funds, taken as a percentage of the expenditures required to produce the reduction in the arc elasticities of demand, will determine the marginal efficiency of differentiating the industry's product more sharply.

Each of the several ways of differentiating the industry's product more sharply will have a separate marginal efficiency schedule, reflecting the particular characteristic of that type of differentiating mechanism. Advertising expenditures, for example, must be continuous or they soon lose their effectiveness (Eldridge, 1958; Jastrom, 1955; Palda, 1964, 1966). R & D expenditures, on the other hand, lead to returns that are highly uncertain if not entirely unpredictable (Scherer, 1967, pp. 359-63). Each of these separate marginal efficiency schedules, moreover, is likely to display decreasing returns - and even, at some point, at an increasing rate. This is because there is an ultimate limit to which a product can be differentiated, whatever the method chosen. As that limit is approached, further expenditures will be of decreasing efficiency. Thus each of the several ways of differentiating an industry's product more sharply can be expected to give rise to a distinctive marginal efficiency of investment (MEI) schedule, one that is negatively sloped.

Though these MEI schedules will each be different, they can nonetheless be equated at the margin to determine the optimal mix or combination of expenditures to differentiate an industry's product more sharply. If one method should offer a higher rate of return than another, the megacorp can be expected to shift its relative expenditures until the differential is eliminated. In this way, the marginal efficiencies of each of the several differentiating mechanisms are likely to become equalized over time. This, however, will necessarily mean that varying amounts are spent on each of the several differentiating mechanisms, the varying amounts representing the optimal mix or combination of such expenditures at that point in time. Because of the need to economize on decision-making, at least insofar as the executive group is concerned, such an optimal mix, once determined, is likely to persist for some time as a rule of thumb for determining relative expenditures on the several differentiating mechanisms.

Given this optimal mix, it is possible to derive a marginal efficiency of investment schedule for all expenditures to differentiate an industry's product more sharply, this composite MEI schedule being merely the geometric summation of the separate MEI schedules for each of the several differentiating mechanisms. Like any MEI schedule, it will be negatively sloped, thus indicating that as total expenditures to differentiate the industry's product more sharply are increased, the marginal efficiency, *r*, of such investment will decline. This composite MEI schedule is the megacorp's investment demand curve, D_{I_2}, – that is, the demand curve for expenditures to differentiate the industry's product more sharply.

Expenditures by a megacorp to differentiate the industry's product more sharply will, of course, benefit the other firms in the industry as well. However, because of the interdependence which characterizes an oligopolistic industry, the other firms cannot avoid making the same types of expenditures themselves. Advertising and R & D, if undertaken by some but not all of the firms in an industry, will probably lead to a change in relative market shares. To guard against this possibility, all the firms in the industry will be forced to match their rivals' expenditures on differentiating mechanisms, at least to the extent of neutralizing whatever effect those expenditures may have on relative market shares. In this way, the burden of differentiating the industry's product more sharply is shared to some extent by all the firms in the industry.

The erection of higher barriers to entry. If the ability to obtain additional investment funds internally through the corporate levy is also limited by the fear of losing part of the market to potential new firms, it may be to a megacorp's advantage to see to it that the barriers to entry are raised even higher. This can be done not only through advertising and R & D but also through vertical integration or the establishment of dealer-franchise systems (Bain, 1956; O. Williamson, 1963; Comaner, 1967, pp. 652–7; Mueller and Tilton, 1969). The effect of such expenditures will be to reduce the probabilities of entry for all subsequent time periods, whatever may be the percentage change in price decided upon. This reduction in the probabilities of entry will enable the megacorp-price leader and the other firms in the industry to set a higher price without incurring any possible additional cost due to the entry factor. The greater percentage increase in price thus made possible – the equivalent, other things being equal, of a greater percentage increase in the marginal corporate levy – will again appear as a potential permanent yield of additional investment funds to the megacorp contemplating those types of expenditures. These additional investment funds, taken as a percentage of the expenditures required to produce the reduction in the probabilities of entry, will determine the marginal efficiency of erecting higher barriers to entry.

Here, too, each of the several ways of erecting higher barriers to entry will have a separate marginal efficiency of investment schedule, the relative efficiency of each depending on the economies of scale associated with that particular type of expenditure, as well as the applicability of the various barriers to the industry in question. These separate MEI schedules can also be equated at the margin to determine the optimal mix or combination of such expenditures. Given this optimal mix, it is then possible to derive a marginal efficiency of investment schedule for all types of expenditures to erect higher barriers to entry. This composite MEI schedule, also negatively sloped, is the megacorp's investment demand curve, D_{I_3}, - that is, the demand curve for expenditures to erect higher barriers to entry. Again, because of oligopolistic interdependence, it can be assumed that whatever is being spent by one megacorp for this purpose will be matched, *pro rata*, by the other firms in the industry.

The creation of a more favorable public image. If the ability to obtain additional investment funds internally through the corporate levy is, finally, limited by the fear of meaningful government intervention, it may be to a megacorp's advantage to see to it that it creates a more favorable public image. This can be done through 'institutional' advertising as distinct from product advertising, through basic research as distinct from applied research or through the erection of aesthetically pleasing office buildings and similar public relations gestures. The effect of such expenditures will be to reduce the probability of meaningful government intervention, whatever may be the percentage change in price decided upon. This reduction in the probability of meaningful government intervention will enable the megacorp-price leader to set a higher price than it would otherwise be able to do, given the upper limit imposed on the industry price by the fear of such intervention. The greater percentage increase in price thus made possible - the equivalent, other things being equal, to a greater percentage increase in the marginal corporate levy - will in this case, too, appear as a potential permanent yield of additional investment funds to the megacorp contemplating the increased expenditures. These additional investment funds, taken as a percentage of the expenditures required to produce the reduction in the probability of meaningful government intervention, will determine the marginal efficiency of creating a more favorable public image.

Again, each of the several ways of creating a more favorable public image will have a separate marginal efficiency of investment schedule. Again, too, an optimal mix of such methods can be determined and from this optimum mix the marginal efficiency of investment schedule derived for all types of expenditures to create a more favorable public image. This composite MEI schedule, also negatively sloped, is the megacorp's investment demand curve, D_{I_4} - that is, the demand curve for expenditures to create a more favorable public image. However, since expenditures to create a more favorable public image are not likely to affect relative market shares and since the megacorp-price leader is more likely to be vulnerable to meaningful government intervention, one cannot assume that whatever is being spent by one megacorp for this purpose will necessarily be representative of what the other firms in the industry are spending.

The total demand for investment funds by the megacorp, D_I, is simply the sum of the four schedules, D_{I_1}, D_{I_2}, D_{I_3} and D_{I_4}. Alternatively, D_I can be viewed as the sum of the demand curves for new plant and equipment, advertising, R & D and other types of expenditures designed to shift the S_I' curve outward. While the latter taxonomic scheme has the disadvantage of blurring important analytical distinctions, it is based on the categories actually used by business firms and hence on categories that lend themselves more readily to empirical investigation. However formulated - whether on the basis of the types of expenditures to be made, for example, advertising and R & D, or on the basis of the purposes to be served by the expenditures, for example, to differentiate an industry's product more sharply and to erect higher barriers to entry - this composite curve, D_I, indicates the varying amounts of investment funds that can be spent at varying rates of return. As such, it represents the megacorp's overall marginal efficiency of investment schedule.

If the current level of investment is subtracted from this marginal efficiency of investment schedule - each category of current expenditure from its corresponding category of possible investment - one has the megacorp's total demand curve for additional investment funds, $\Delta F/P$. This schedule indicates the differing amounts of additional investment funds, $\Delta F/P$, that can be expended at differing rates of return, r.

Advertising, R & D and the like as investment. While economists have long been accustomed to viewing expenditures on new plant and equipment as part of a firm's investment outlays, expenditures to differentiate the industry's product more sharply, to erect higher barriers to entry and to create a more favorable public image are a different matter. In fact, there is likely to be serious objection to treating them as forms of investment. This questionable inclusion of D_{I_2}, D_{I_3} and D_{I_4} as part of the overall D_I can be defended and reconciled with customary usage, however, once the distinction between investment in a social sense and investment in a private sense is recognized.

The latter can be defined as a decision by some private entity, whether it be a household or a business firm, to allocate resources so that the benefits from the allocation are received by the private group *qua* private group, for a time beyond some arbitrarily defined current period. Under such a definition, the use of funds to increase the barriers to entry, to create a more favorable public image and to differentiate more sharply the industry's product all qualify as private investment decisions.

Economists, however, have generally been unwilling to define as investment those types of allocation decisions which are not also investment in a social sense - that is, which provide benefits to society as a whole. Such allocation, they have felt, represents only a transfer of claims on resources, not new capital formation. This attitude has been predicated, in part, on the assumption that capital formation itself necessarily consists of the accumulation of physical goods capable of facilitating the production process (cf. Bonner and Lees, 1963). With capital formation so defined, it stands to reason that investment in a private, but not a social, sense can take place only by a transfer from one group in society to another of the physical goods that have already been accumulated, that is, the resources that have already been invested in a social sense. The sale of securities on a stock exchange would be an example of such a purely private form of investment, and as already indicated, economists would not regard it as a true case of investment.

Still, it has to be recognized that resources can also be allocated so that benefits are derived over time from non-material sources as well. The use of scientists and engineers to advance a field of technology would certainly be an example of this type of investment. But while it might be recognized that the stock of knowledge was thereby being augmented, providing benefits both to private groups and to society as a whole, economists would nonetheless be troubled by the fact that nothing tangible remained as a physical replica - like a building or a piece of machinery - of the resources that had been allocated. On the one hand, the physical goods involved - the material things required to keep the bodies and souls of the scientists and engineers together - would already have been used up. On the other hand, the benefits from the allocation - the new technology produced - would be extremely difficult to disentangle from the physical goods in which they were embodied, and would thus be extremely difficult to measure. It is for these reasons that economists have been unable - if not unwilling - to include increases in not only technology but also individual skill in their computations of capital formation.[53]

With respect to the definition of investment, it is thus possible to present the matrix shown in the accompanying table. One box still remains to be filled in, this being the type of investment which provides benefits to private groups only, from non-material sources. It is in this box that D_{I_2}, D_{I_3} and D_{I_4} as defined above fall. Insofar as these types of expenditures lead only to a more sharply differentiated product, higher

Types of Investment
Source of benefits

		Material	Non-material
Recipient of benefits	Private groups and society as a whole	I. Purchase of new plant and equipment	III. Development of new technology
	Private groups only	II. Transfer of ownership of plant and equipment	IV.

barriers to entry and a more favorable public image, they will result in benefits to private groups alone, in this case to the members of the oligopolistic industry. The further implications of this distinction will be taken up below, in chapter 8. Suffice it for now to note that these benefits accruing to the members of the oligopolistic industry will be derived in large part from non-material sources.

Which of these four variants of the definition of investment is the 'correct' one will, of course, depend on what is being investigated. To understand the cause of cyclical instability, for example, variant I alone may be sufficient. On the other hand, to delineate the sources of long-run economic growth, it may be necessary to include variant III along with variant I. The point here is that in order to provide a complete description of how prices are determined under oligopolistic conditions, the definition of investment must be broadened to encompass expenditures - such as those to differentiate an industry's product more sharply, to erect higher barriers to entry and to create a more favorable public image - that are non-material in form and benefit only the megacorp itself, not the rest of society. This means that none of the four variants of investment - and certainly not variant IV - should be excluded from the megacorp's overall MEI schedule.[54] Indeed, all four variants constitute investment in the broad sense of discretionary income, the sense in which the term 'investment' will be used in chapters 6 and 7 to analyze the macrodynamic behavior of the economic system as a whole. However, even if all but variant I, the customary definition of investment, are eliminated, the model is not invalidated or even made indeterminate. It is merely less fully specified and gives rise to a slightly different solution.

The determinate solution. By placing the megacorp-price leader's demand curve for investment funds, D_I, on the same set of axes as its supply curve of investment funds, S_I, it is possible to determine what change in price, if any, will optimize the megacorp-price leader's long run market position. Assuming that the other firms in the industry will defer to the price leader's judgment - and if the price leader enjoys a cost advantage or possesses some other form of market power, the other firms will have little choice in the matter - this will be the change in price that will then prevail until at least the next pricing period. Of course, the other firms in the industry can let the price leader know, through the informal channels that are available to them, what change in price they would prefer on the basis of their own D_I and S_I curves. The price leader can then take these views of its fellow oligopolists into account to the extent that it wants or needs to in order to achieve, in Fellner's phrase, joint profit maximization.

Before proceeding with the analysis, one word of caution is necessary. What has been said so far and what now follows is not meant to imply that returns and costs are actually computed with the mathematical exactitude of a geometric curve. It is, in fact, possible that a megacorp, and in particular, a megacorp-price leader, will develop an investment strategy consisting of a variety of projects designed to further its long-range goals with no one project evaluated separately.[55] The returns, or efficiency, of even the overall strategy may be only crudely estimated.[56] Similarly, it is possible that the costs of a price increase will be only dimly perceived and very likely not precisely calculated. Nevertheless, the logic of its position will dictate that the megacorp-price leader act as though it were, indeed, governed by S_I and D_I curves such as those now being discussed. At the very least these curves will define the upper limit of rational behavior.

With this qualification in mind, it is possible to conclude that, as a new pricing period approaches, a megacorp may be confronted by any one of three possible pricing and investment situations, corresponding to the three situations depicted in figures 12 through 14. In the first situation, shown in figure 12, the S_I and D_I curves fail to intersect in the positive quadrant. This does not mean that investment will fall to zero or below. Even at the existing industry price, P_0, a certain amount of investment funds will be forthcoming from the corporate levy - an amount equal to $(ACL_0 \cdot Q_0)$. As long as the return from expending some part of these funds is positive, investment will continue. The failure of the S_I and D_I curves to intersect in the positive quadrant means simply that no additional investment funds will have to be obtained through an increase in the industry price.

Of course, since the demand for investment funds is less than the current supply, it might seem that a reduction in the industry price - or at least the margin above costs - would be called for. While this may well be what happens, it should be pointed out that there are several factors mitigating against a reduction in the price, and thus in the margin above costs, in an oligopolistic industry. First, the benefits of a price reduction are not exactly the opposite of the costs associated with a price increase. The substitution effect and the entry factor may have a different value as well as a different sign when the price adjustment is downward. The fear of meaningful government intervention, meanwhile, is likely to disappear entirely. Second, a price reduction, if soon to be followed by a price increase, is best avoided in the first place since the difficulty of coordinating pricing decisions makes it desirable to hold the number of such price changes to a minimum. Thus, even if a decrease in the demand for investment funds is anticipated, the general inflationary trend of the economy is likely to cause a megacorp-

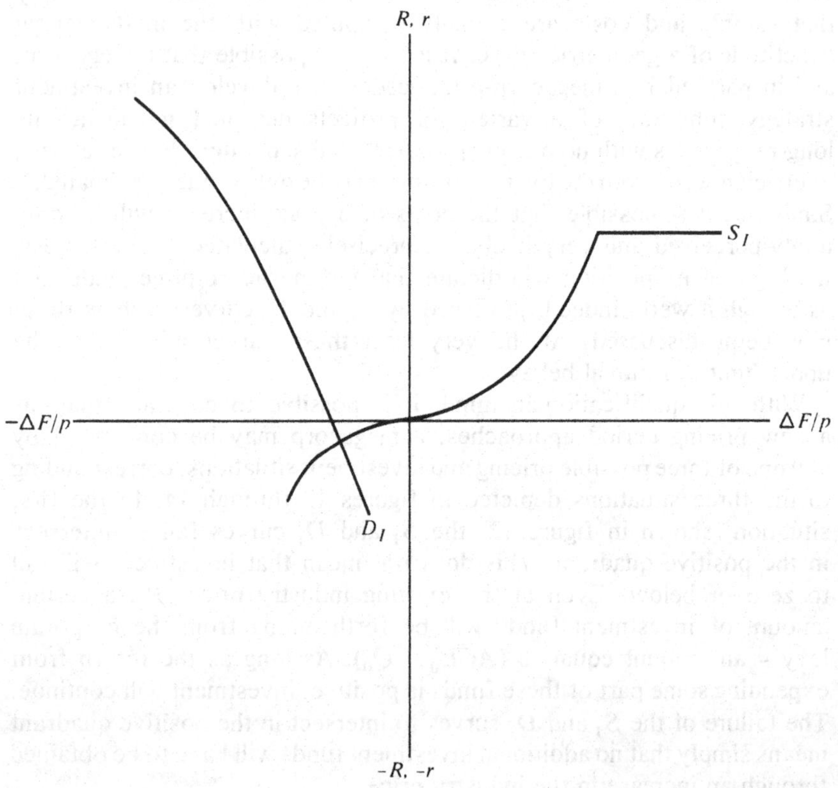

Figure 12

price leader to discount the value of a price reduction.

In the second situation that can be delineated - the one depicted in figure 13 - the D_I curve intersects the S_I curve at a point where the S_I and S_I' curves are coincidental, that is, at a point where R is less than i. Under these circumstances, the demand for investment funds exceeds the amount already being obtained through the corporate levy, and a price increase is necessary. F_a, as determined by the intersection of the D_I and S_I curves, is the amount of additional investment funds required to optimize the megacorp's long-run market position; and n_a, as shown in the other quadrants, is the percentage increase in price that will make it possible to obtain those additional funds internally - at an implicit interest charge equal to R_a. It can thus be inferred that n_a is the percentage increase in price (and, with costs assumed

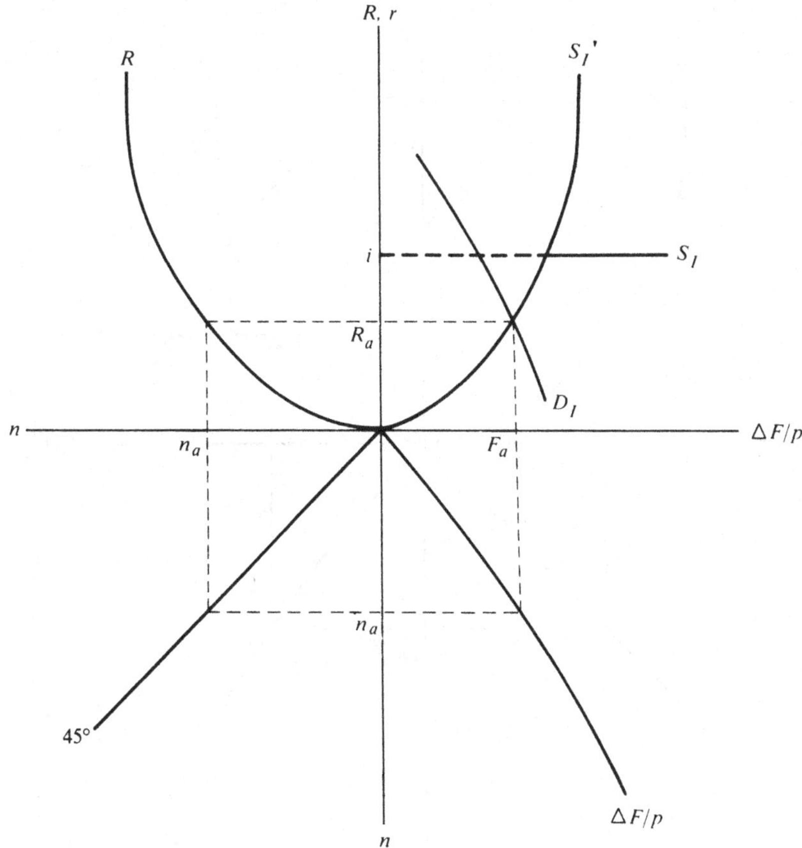

Figure 13

constant, in the margin above costs) which, in this second of the three possible situations, the megacorp-price leader will announce. It should be pointed out that the diagram indicates not the long-run equilibrium position toward which the industry will tend to move in time through trial and error but rather represents a summary of the subjective factors determining the single price adjustment permitted the price leader at the onset of a pricing period.

In the third of the three possible pricing and investment situations - that depicted in figure 14 - the D_I curve intersects the S_I curve at a point where the S_I and S_I' curves diverge from one another, that is, at a point where R exceeds i. Under these circumstances, the demand for investment funds again exceeds the amount already being obtained through the corporate levy, and a price increase is necessary. However, not all the additional funds required to maximize the megacorp's long-run

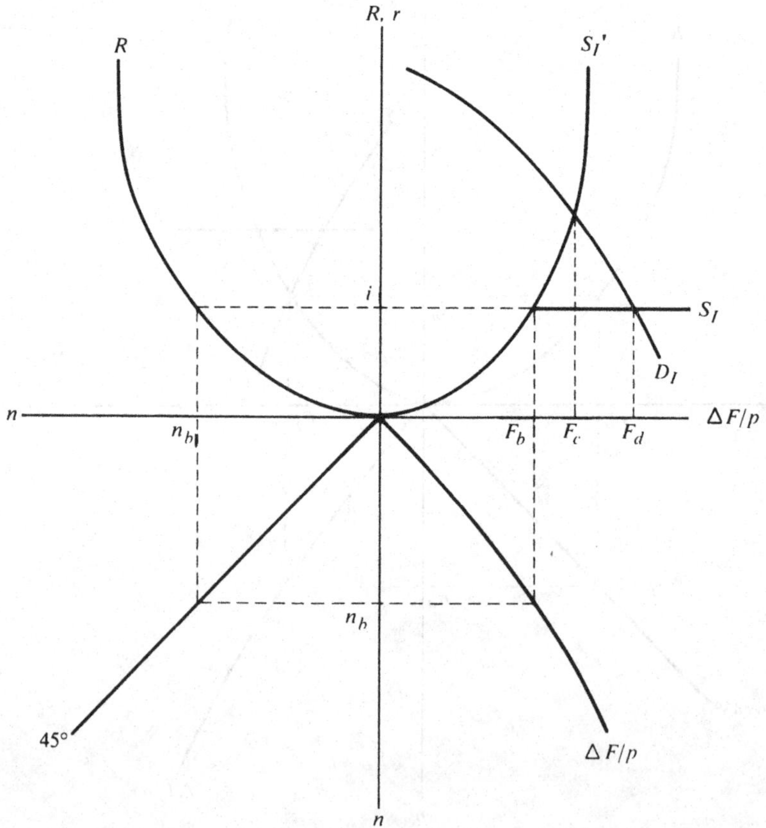

Figure 14

market position, F_d, will be obtained through the price increase. Only F_b, the amount of additional funds for which the implicit interest charge is not greater than the cost of external funds, will be raised internally. The remaining portion, $F_d - F_b$, will be obtained by tapping the capital funds market during the most advantageous phase of the current planning period, the cost of these as well as the other investment funds being equal to the permanent interest rate, *i*. It can thus be inferred that n_b, the percentage increase in price required to obtain F_b investment funds internally, is the percentage increase in price which, in this third of the three possible situations, the megacorp-price leader will announce. It should be noted with respect to this third possible situation that the availability of external funds at a cost equal to *i* enables the megacorp to undertake a larger amount of investment, $F_d - F_c$, than would otherwise be possible.

In summary, then, regardless of where the D_I and S_I curves intersect, the price in an oligopolistic industry is determinate. It is determinate based on the price previously prevailing in the industry and the change in that price necessary to provide the megacorp-price leader with the additional investment funds it needs to optimize its long-run market position - provided that the implicit interest charge on those additional internal funds is not greater than the cost of external funds. These additional investment funds, when added to the investment funds already being generated internally, determine the new value for *CL* in the oligopolistic pricing formula,

$$P = AVC + \frac{FC + CL}{SOR \cdot ERC},$$

and hence the new price level, P_1, in figure 15. For with *AVC, FC, SOR* and *ERC* all held constant, ΔP must necessarily be equal to ΔCL. That is,

$$P_1 = P_0 + \Delta P = AVC + \frac{FC + CL}{SOR \cdot ERC} + \frac{\Delta CL}{SOR \cdot ERC}. \qquad (3.9)$$

The change in industry price is, then, equal to the additional corporate levy planned for or required *ex ante*, divided by the anticipated level of sales ($SOR \cdot ERC$). From this it follows, based on the preceding analysis, that, holding costs constant, any change in the price of an oligopolistic industry must reflect a change in either the marginal efficiency of investment for firms within that industry, the implicit interest charge on internal funds, or the 'permanent' cost of external funds. In other words, the change in price will depend on the demand for and supply cost of additional investment funds.

There are two aspects to this determinate solution - even aside from

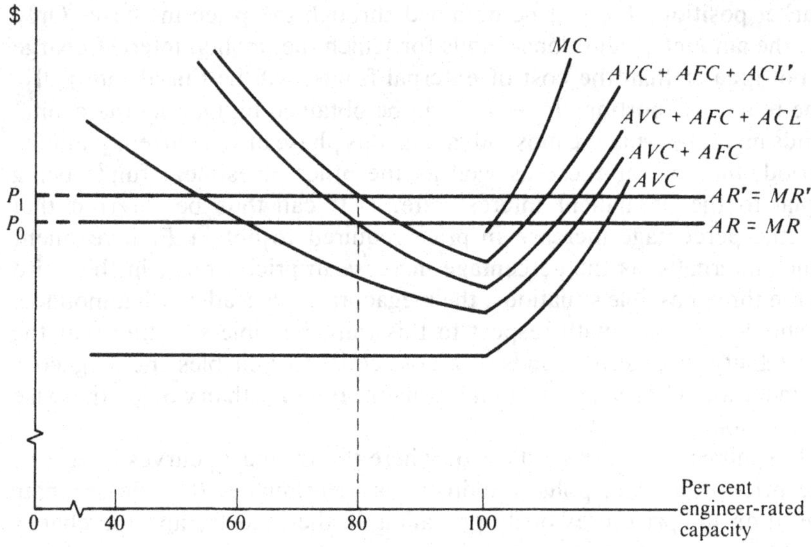

Figure 15

the collusive behavior assumed in and carried over from the preceding chapter - which may well leave some readers restive. The first is that only the change in industry price is explained, so that the price level itself becomes determinate only by taking into account the past pricing history of the industry. Why this aspect of the model should prove troubling to economists - as it has to some who have seen this treatise in earlier drafts - is itself an interesting point to ponder. After all, economists themselves have emphasized the importance of changes at the margin; and as serious social scientists they can hardly deny that the present set of possibilities is necessarily bounded by the past train of events. The disquiet on this point perhaps springs from the fear that, with the model able to explain only the change in price, and not the absolute level, economists may no longer be able to make the types of normative judgments which the more conventional neo-classical model, for all its other shortcomings, permits. That this is an unwarranted fear will be shown in chapter 8 below. Still, while similar types of judgments can be made based on the model of oligopolistic pricing just developed, the specific conclusions to which that model leads are quite different. Indeed, if the model did not lead to different conclusions, there would be little point in making such a fuss over it. One can only hope that it is not the policy implications so at variance with those of the conventional neo-classical analysis that economists find disturbing about a model that explains only the change in, and not the absolute level of, price.

The second aspect of the above model which may well prove troubling to economists is its seeming lack of symmetry. What has been emphasized are the factors which lead to an increase in the average corporate levy - or margin above costs. Little has been said about what causes a decline in that margin. Indeed, it has been pointed out that even if the marginal efficiency of investment should be so low that the expenditure of all the internal funds currently being generated is no longer warranted, the megacorp-price leader may still be reluctant to adjust the industry price downward and thereby reduce the size of the average corporate levy. Yet if the average corporate levy is not lowered - perhaps less frequently but still, over time, to the same extent that it is raised - the margin above costs will necessarily grow larger. This apparent implication of the model is, however, inconsistent with the historical evidence. While the margin above costs has over time varied in oligopolistic industries, there is no reason to believe that it has increased secularly. It is for this reason that any simplistic theory of inflation, based on the argument that megacorps merely exploit their market power to push prices upward, cannot withstand critical scrutiny.

Still, the pricing model developed above is not thereby invalidated. The failure of the average corporate levy to rise over time, despite the fact that the price in an oligopolistic industry is more likely to be raised than lowered, can be attributed to two factors. One, the less significant, is the possibility that at various points in time the community of interest which exists among the members of the industry and which permits the price leader to announce a rise in price confident that its fellow oligopolists will follow suit may break down. This possibility will be discussed in the chapter immediately following as one of the exceptions of the general oligopolistic pricing model. The other, more significant factor is that costs are not likely to remain unchanged over time. Thus the size of the average corporate levy, or margin above costs, may decline even as the price level itself rises. It all depends on the struggle over relative income distribution between the megacorp on the one hand and its several constituencies on the other. The analysis of this struggle must wait, however, until certain extensions of the oligopolistic pricing model have been explored.

Appendix to Chapter 3
Antecedent Formulations of the Entry Factor

As the main body of this chapter has tried to make clear, a determinate theory of oligopolistic pricing requires more than just an analysis of the entry factor - Bhagwati's suggestion (1970) to the contrary notwithstanding. Still, an analysis of the entry factor is a critical element in any fully specified model. Indeed, it is difficult to conceive of any true case of oligopoly without significant barriers to new entry. The purpose of this appendix is to indicate the relationship between previous work on the entry factor and the approach adopted in this treatise.

The importance of barriers to entry has been recognized by a large number of writers following Bain's pioneering work in this area.[1] Bain's approach, since it allows for the substitution effect as well as the entry factor, is more comprehensive than that of most subsequent writers on the subject - the work of Sylos-Labini (1962) and Wenders (1967) being notable exceptions.[2] The first requisite, then, for an adequate treatment of the entry factor is that it be viewed as but one of several determinants (actually three) of the supply curve for internally generated funds, this supply curve in turn being viewed as but one of several determinants (again three) of any change in the industry price level.[3] Not even Bain - and following him, Sylos-Labini and Wenders - employs so comprehensive a model, however.

Although Bain recognizes the importance of the substitution effect in addition to the entry factor, he nonetheless adopts a simple 'stay-out' or 'entry-limiting' theory of oligopolistic pricing. In other words, he assumes that the fear of possible entry by other firms sets only a specific upper limit on the price that can be charged by the megacorp-price leader. This is the equivalent, in the model set forth above, of assuming that R_2 is equal to zero for any percentage change in price below a certain fixed ceiling and that otherwise it is prohibitively large. It implies that the supply curve for internally generated funds, S_I', is perfectly inelastic at a specific point, n_x, as in figure 16a.

The objection to this approach, an approach adopted also by Sylos-Labini (1962), Wenders (1967), Johns (1962) and Lydall (1955), is that it ignores the probabilistic nature of new entry, especially when the percentage increase in price is relatively small. This treatise, by allowing for the possibility that the supply curve for internally generated funds may, because of an unacceptably high risk of new entry, become inelastic beyond a certain percentage increase in price, encompasses that part of the Bain argument which has validity. At the same time, however, by positing that the supply curve for internally generated funds will, up to that percentage change in price (or up to the percentage change in price associated with an unacceptable risk of meaningful government intervention), be somewhat elastic, the model developed above goes beyond a simple 'stay out' approach to oligopolistic pricing. One need only compare figure 16b with figure 16a to see what difference this makes. The second prerequisite, then, for an adequate treatment of the entry factor is a proper recognition of its probabilistic nature.

Sylos-Labini carried Bain's line of analysis one step further by considering the likely effect of conjectural interdependence - that is, by considering what the 'stay-out' price will be if the potential new entrant expects the firms already in the industry to lower their price when entry is attempted. To assume that the firms already in the industry will lower their price if and when entry by a new firm is attempted has, in fact, been termed the Sylos postulate. It is one of several factors which have been suggested by various writers as influencing the probability of entry.

To the extent that the Sylos postulate is valid, it will lead to a smaller value for π and thus to the entry factor imposing less of a restraint on pricing discretion. It is questionable, however, whether a potential entrant need fear that the industry price will be lowered once entry is attempted. For one thing, as Leeman (1956) has pointed out, any reduction in price is likely to prove more deleterious to the established firms, with their greater volume of output, than to the newcomer.

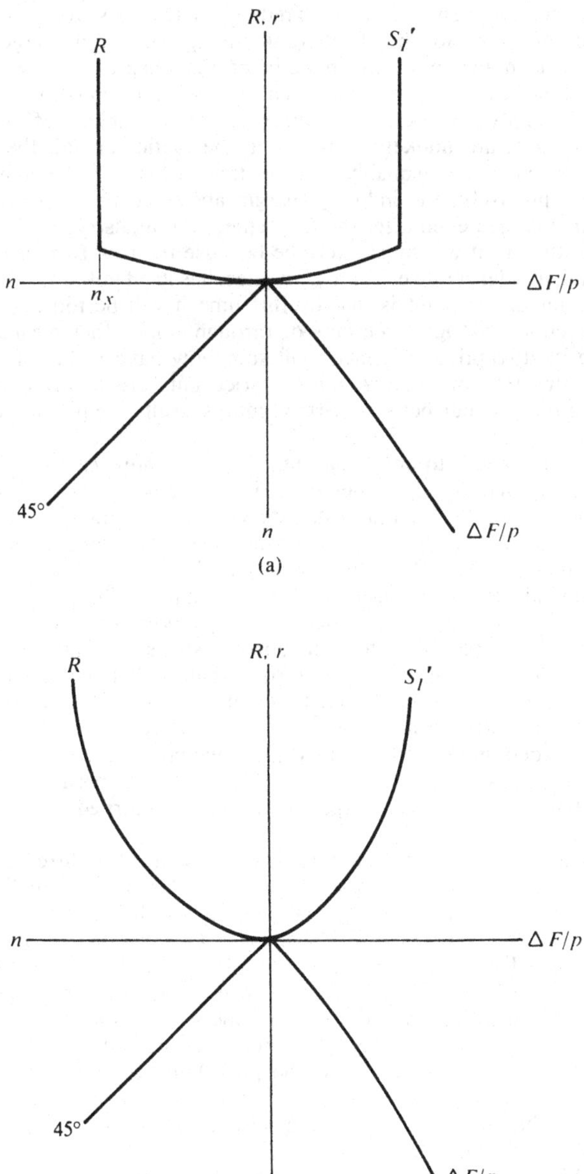
R, r
R
S_I'
n
n_x
$\Delta F/p$
45°
n
$\Delta F/p$
(a)
R, r
R
S_I'
n
$\Delta F/p$
45°
n
$\Delta F/p$
(b)

Figure 16

For another thing, it may bring down the wrath of the Justice Department's Anti-trust Division or even the Federal Trade Commission's Bureau of Competition, especially if the established firms rank among the nation's largest corporations. Finally, as noted in the main body of the chapter, a new firm, once it has committed resources to a particular industry, is unlikely to be driven out of business simply because of lower prices; and the established firms, knowing this to be the case, are unlikely to resort to the tactic. For all these reasons, a potential entrant can reasonably assume that, whatever the industry price level (or more precisely, the industry margin above costs), that price level is likely to be maintained even after the firm enters the industry. Indeed, if prices are subsequently cut, it will most likely be because the new firm has misjudged the market and, in a desperate effort to gain sales, has itself initiated the reductions in price. The important point is that by this time it will be too late to remedy the situation, either through price cuts or through some other means. The new firm, despite its disruptive influence, will somehow have to be integrated into the industry structure or organization. If price cuts are to discourage entry, they must therefore occur before a firm commits itself to entering an industry, and not after.

Whenever the barriers to entry may be, they will more easily be overcome, it has been suggested by a number of writers, including Sylos-Labini (1962, pp. 61-2) and Johns (1962), if industry demand is growing steadily (see also Stigler, 1966a, p; 229; Pyatt, 1971; Gaskins, 1971). The argument, however, is based on the questionable assumption that the firms in the industry will not invest ahead of demand precisely to forestall that possibility. Indeed, investing ahead of demand is standard practice for megacorps - as the existence of substantial reserve capacity within the oligopolistic sector attests. Thus it is only if industry demand is growing more rapidly than could have been anticipated, or more rapidly than the established firms are actually able to expand, that entry will be facilitated. But neither of these two conditions is likely to be approximated except in newer industries, those which have not yet settled down to a stable oligopolistic pattern. This is a point which, because it is central to the analysis of conglomerate expansion, will be returned to soon (chapter 4, pp. 118–22).

Lydall (1955) was among the first to stress a somewhat different offset to the barriers which a new firm might face. An industry is more likely to be entered, he noted, by a firm which is already established in another industry, one which turns out a somewhat similar product (see also Hines, 1957; Kottke, 1966). Two quite different corollaries follow from this line of argument. The first is that the probability of entry, π, will be greater the higher is the cross-elasticity of substitution with other products, there thus being a separate, interactive influence when the entry factor and the substitution effect are combined. The other corollary is that the probability of entry will be greater the fewer are the restrictions placed on the movement by established firms into different industries. This latter point also bears on the analysis below of conglomerate expansion.

The probabilistic nature of the entry factor has been recognized by Dewey (1969, ch. 6), O. Williamson (1963b), and Kamien and Schwartz (1971), among others. For Dewey, the probability of entry depends on whether there is excess capacity in the industry, this probability being close to zero when the established firms have sufficient excess capacity to supply whatever share of the market the potential entrant might hope to capture. In light of what has already been said about the existence of reserve capacity in oligopolistic industries, Dewey's argument collapses to little more than a slight elaboration of the simpler 'entry limiting' model.

Williamson's approach to the entry factor is closer to that adopted in this treatise. He not only treats the entry of a new firm as being probabilistic, he also views the established firms as being able to affect the height of the barriers which the new firm faces by the sums they are willing to spend on advertising. His approach nonetheless differs from that followed in this treatise in two ways: (1) he assumes that advertising is the only means of restricting entry which needs to be taken into account when analyzing pricing behavior, and (2) he assumes that the effects of advertising in restricting entry are felt only during the current pricing period, this making the decision of how much to spend on advertising co-determinate with the decision of what price to charge. A third prerequisite, then, for an adequate treatment of the entry factor is a proper recognition of the intertemporal effects on new entry, both of a change in price and of a change in the levels of expenditures for such activities as research and development, raw material acquisitions and product servicing, as well as for advertising.

Pashigian (1968), on the other hand, though he recognizes the intertemporal effects of new entry, nonetheless ignores its probabilistic character. This permits him to postulate a monopolistic situation in which the firm has no maximally acceptable risk of new entry. The result is that entry occurs continuously for some period of time until a stable oligopolistic market structure develops. Pashigian recognizes that the model explains only the emergence of oligopoly out of monopoly, and not the determination of price once the oligopolistic structure of the industry has stabilized (Pashigan, 1968, p. 177).

For Kamien and Schwartz (1971, p. 19), entry is not only probabilistic, its effects are also intertemporal. Indeed, their model comes closest to the approach adopted in this treatise. Still, there are important differences. For one thing, while Kamien and Schwartz recognize that new entry will cause a decline in revenues over time, they overlook the fact that the probability of entry will itself vary with time. Even more serious, they regard profit as being an end in its own right rather than just a means to a larger goal - that of achieving maximum growth. As a result, they fail to note the relationship between the intertemporal alteration in revenue flows caused by new entry and the implicit interest rate on internally generated investment funds which the alteration in revenue flows gives rise to. The fourth and final prerequisite, then, for an adequate treatment of the entry factor is to show how it relates to both the price and investment decisions.

4. Extensions of the basic model

The model set forth in the preceding chapter pertains to an oligopolistic industry in which the price leader is a member of that one industry alone. As such, it can be used to analyze pricing behavior in a significant portion of the oligopolistic sector. Still, if it is not to be unduly limited in its applicability, the model needs to be modified to encompass other types of industries and other types of firms. This is the task of the present chapter.

The most important of those other types of firms is the conglomerate megacorp - a megacorp that is a member of more than one industry.[1] Such firms are becoming increasingly more common.[2] Indeed, it has been suggested that they represent a higher stage in the evolution of the corporation in the United States.[3] Insofar as one of these conglomerate megacorps is a price leader in one or more industries, its behavior may not be entirely explainable in terms of the model set forth above. At the same time, many firms that might otherwise meet the criteria for being classified as a megacorp are members of regulated industries. Such firms, too, are important - if only because they dominate certain critical sectors of the economy. The question is whether the oligopolistic pricing model set forth above can be applied to these regulated enterprises as well. Each of these two types of firms, the conglomerate megacorp and the regulated monopolist, will be analyzed in turn, beginning with the latter. Once this has been done, it will be seen whether the same basic oligopolistic pricing model can be modified still further to encompass even the polypolistic enterprise as a special case.

The case of monopoly

The unregulated monopolist. Were it not that it occupies such a prominent place in the textbooks, the case of unregulated monopoly - an industry consisting of but a single unregulated firm - would hardly be worth pausing to consider. In the real world, it is a type of market structure rarely encountered. Of course, if an industry is defined sufficiently narrowly, as for example all the firms producing a particular trade mark item, monopoly does emerge as a somewhat general phenomenon. But monopoly of this sort, because of the probable high cross-elasticity of demand with other products, is unlikely to pose a serious social problem. It is monopoly of a broader sort - monopoly in an industry supplying a significant component of aggregate output, one for which there is no close substitute - that provides the challenge to public policy. However, it is precisely monopoly of this sort which is so rare.

There being so few observable examples from the real world, it is difficult to say with certainty what the characteristics of the single firm in such an industry are likely to be. But insofar as these characteristics include the separation of management from ownership and multiple-plant operation, the analysis is but a simple extension of the basic oligopolistic model. The behavioral principle - to maintain an existing market share (in this case 100 per cent) - will remain the same. The cost curves, displaying constant marginal costs over the relevant ranges of output, will be unchanged. The only difference will be in the mechanism for achieving price coordination. Since the firm is the industry, there is no need to rely on price leadership. The monopolist, unlike an oligopolist, can simply set the industry price as it sees fit.

Even so, the monopolist's price decision will be subject to the same restraints suggested previously in connection with the price leader in an oligopolistic industry. On the one hand, the monopolist - if otherwise able to qualify as a megacorp - will want to set the price at a level which, in addition to enabling it to cover its average variable and fixed costs, will make it possible for the firm to finance as much of its desired investment out of internally generated funds as is optimal, given the prospective rates of return from that investment and the cost of external funds. On the other hand, the monopolist will want to set the price at a level which does not entail too great a cost in terms of customers lost to substitute products, of outside firms encouraged to enter the industry and of the government being provoked to intervene in a meaningful manner. The precise nature and influence of these various factors have already been spelled out in the preceding chapter, the replacement of an industry price leader with a monopolist affecting that analysis not at all. In other words, monopoly, when a megacorp is involved, can be analyzed as a special case of the oligopolistic pricing model developed in the preceding chapter.[4] Indeed, with the problem of price coordination among competing firms obviated, it stands as the simplest and most basic variant of that model.[5]

The regulated monopolist. The case of regulated monopoly (and of regulated oligopoly) is perhaps more interesting, and not just for the reason that within the American economy it is far more prevalent than the unregulated variant. The case of regulated monopoly warrants special attention because, while the megacorp under these circumstances still retains the right to initiate a change in price or 'rates', it must obtain approval from the governmental body charged with overseeing its operations before that change can be put into effect; and the regulatory body is likely to be guided by principles that, for the most part, preclude the megacorp from financing a higher level of investment through an increase in the corporate levy. The regulated megacorp, then, is at somewhat of a disadvantage in trying to secure the additional investment funds it may need.

To understand why this is the case, it is necessary to understand the principles which are likely to guide a regulatory body in approving or disapproving a change in rates by a regulated megacorp or, to use the more common term, a public utility. Insofar as its efforts are sincere, the regulatory body will seek to limit the rates charged by the public utility to the current costs of operation plus a 'fair return on reasonably invested capital' (Wilcox, 1966, chs. 12-13; Bonbright, 1961, part 2; Kahn, 1970, I, pp. 1-65). The first part of this formula, the current costs of operation, is the same, with certain important modifications, as the first part of the oligopolistic pricing formula specified in the previous chapter:

$$AVC + \frac{FC + CL}{SOR \cdot ERC}$$

On the one hand, the current costs of operation in the regulatory formula do not include the interest and dividends paid capital debt holders as do the fixed costs, or *FC*, in the oligopolistic pricing formula. On the other hand, the fixed costs in the oligopolistic formula do not include the depreciation allowances as do the current costs of operation in the regulatory formula. Still, since these components appear elsewhere in the formulas, they do not represent the critical difference between the two approaches.

That critical difference emerges when one compares the 'fair rate of return on reasonably invested capital' with the corporate levy. A fair rate of return, though subject to varying interpretations, means most generally a rate of return sufficient both to compensate investors for the capital funds they have already supplied the firm and to attract additional capital funds in the future. To the extent that regulatory bodies accept an opportunity cost theory of compensation, that is, to the extent they act on the presumption that the capital debt holders of public utilities should receive a rate of return equal to that which could be earned on alternative investment opportunities of comparable risk, the two criteria of what constitutes a 'fair' return converge to one. That single standard is a rate of return equal to the current cost of external funds or, in the terminology previously employed, the permanent interest rate for public utilities. Such a rate of return, while not a part of the corporate levy, is nonetheless included among the fixed costs in the oligopolistic pricing formula. Similarly, the depreciation allowance portion of the corporate levy, while not a part of the 'fair' return, is included among the current costs of operation in the regulatory pricing formula. It is the retained earnings portion of the corporate levy that has no counterpart in the fair rate of return provided under regulation.

Of course, a regulated megacorp can legally generate retained earnings simply by reducing the dividend rate, that is, by increasing what is termed the retention ratio (cf. Marris, 1964; J. Williamson, 1966). As a practical matter, however, it can do so only within certain narrow limits. Insofar as the regulatory body has been effective in holding down the public utility's rates to the current costs of operation plus a fair return on reasonably invested capital - that fair return being equal to the current cost of external funds, including projected future increases in the dividend rate - any attempt to generate retained earnings by increasing the retention ratio runs the risk of impairing the megacorp's ability to attract outside funds. This result would not, in itself, be fatal to the utility's survival, provided its executive group were to be assured on two points: (1) that the stockholder could be sufficiently mollified so that they would not exercise their right, acting collectively, to replace the incumbent management; and (2) that the regulatory body could be induced to allow the megacorp to raise its rates sufficiently so that the megacorp could instead finance its future investment expenditures primarily from internal sources. On the first point, the executive group may be reasonably safe, especially if other regulated firms are being forced to pursue essentially the same dividend policy and public utilities are recognized as offering a greater regularity of return which offsets, in part, their lower rate of growth in dividends. It is on the second point that the executive group is unlikely to receive sufficient assurances - in fact, any assurances whatsoever. Were a regulatory body willing to grant approval for what in effect would be a corporate levy that encompasses more than just depreciation allowances, the very principle of a 'fair' return would be violated.[6] And this points to the quite different perceptions of how investment funds ought to be accumulated and allocated which are implicit in public utility regulation on the one hand and in oligopolistic pricing on the other as they are separately practiced in the United States.

Alternative accumulation models. For the regulatory body and those who concur with the principles upon which it 'ideally' bases its decisions, the appropriate capital accumulation and allocation model is the pre-megacorp one in which savings flow from numerous households to a single capital funds market, thence to be apportioned among different firms on the basis of which enterprise is able to employ those funds with the highest prospective rate of return. The salient point about this model is that, assuming all firms to have equal access to the capital funds market,[7] savings which could be put to better use by one group of firms will not fall into the possession of some other group. It is this feature of the model - its putative tendency to allocate capital funds optimally - that recommends it so highly to regulatory bodies. What is less clearly perceived is that the model limits the total volume of savings that are available for investment to the amount which various financial intermediaries - banks, insurance companies, pension funds, etc. - are able to attract from the household sector.

In sharp contrast to this first conceptualization stands the megacorp model in which savings, bypassing the capital funds market, flow directly from households to those firms which, as members of oligopolistic (or unregulated monopolistic) industries, possess sufficient market power to exact a corporate levy. Under this model, whatever savings are accumulated need not necessarily be allocated optimally among different firms; for the amount of investment funds a firm can obtain will depend, not on its ability to utilize those savings more effectively than other firms but rather, on the elasticity of demand, the barriers to entry and the likelihood of government intervention in the various industries to which it belongs. Of course, to the extent that conglomerate expansion provides, as suggested in the section that follows, a means of transferring to newer, more rapidly growing industries the corporate levy obtained in older, less dynamic sectors, the rate of return to investment even in the second model may still be equalized. But since it is unrealistic to assume that such an adjustment mechanism will function perfectly - though perhaps not more unrealistic than to assume that the capital funds market itself will function perfectly - it must be granted that, in an economy populated by megacorps, investment funds are likely to come into the possession of some firms unable to put them to as good a use as other firms with less market power.

Even conceding this last point, however, the important question - from the perspective of the individual firm, if not from that of the society as a whole - may well be which model, the conventional one or the megacorp alternative, will make available the larger volume of savings for capital formation. The answer will, of course, depend on the willingness of the household sector to restrict its consumption expenditures relative to the ability of business firms to exact a corporate levy, that is, to generate internal funds. *A priori,* there would appear to be no reason to assume that the one factor is likely to be stronger than the other. Yet in view of the evidence already cited as to the relative importance of external and internal financing in the manufacturing sector (where the choice between the two alternatives is unaffected by regulation), it is difficult not to conclude that the megacorp model is capable of generating a far larger volume of savings for capital formation (see note 17 to chapter 1).

This relatively greater capacity for generating savings is not the whole of the matter, however. The two models, it must be noted, are complementary rather than mutually exclusive. As indicated in the preceding chapter, the unregulated megacorp, in addition to relying on the corporate levy, always has the option of resorting to the capital funds market when this is preferable. With this added degree of freedom, the megacorp can either obtain a larger amount of investment funds at the same cost or the same amount of investment funds at a lower cost than if it were restricted to the corporate levy alone. The insistence of regulatory bodies that public utilities follow only the first model of the capital accumulation and allocation process means therefore that the regulated megacorp is at a considerable disadvantage, compared to its unregulated counterpart, in obtaining additional investment funds.

The effect that this disability will have both on the regulated megacorp's rate of growth and on the price level in its industry will depend, in part, on the elasticity of its demand curve for additional investment funds, D_I, and, in part, on the elasticity of its supply curve for additional investment funds, S_I, including the hypothetical supply curve for additional internally generated funds, S_I'. If the demand curve for additional investment funds is perfectly inelastic, that is, if no additional investment will be undertaken even if the cost of investment funds were lower, the amount of capital formation will be no different even if the regulated monopolist were free to obtain additional investment funds internally through the corporate levy by raising its price. The regulated monopolist will simply be able to finance that same amount of additional investment, $\Delta F/p$, at a lower implicit interest rate. How much lower will depend on the value of R associated with $\Delta F/p$ relative to the permanent interest rate on external funds, i. This differential between R and i will, in turn, reflect the elasticity of the supply curve for internally generated funds, S_I'.

By its very nature, a regulated monopolist can be expected to have a supply curve for internally generated funds which is even more elastic than that of an unregulated megacorp. To the extent that regulation is accompanied by an absolute barrier to entry - and in most cases it is[8] - the cost, due to the entry factor, of raising funds internally through an increase in price will approach zero. R_2 will thus necessarily also be close to zero. The upper limit to any price increase set by the fear of meaningful government intervention is a somewhat different matter. The fact of regulation will, in effect, already have placed a ceiling on the industry price, limiting the corporate levy to little more than a depreciation allowance. Yet if a regulatory body could be persuaded to approve an increase in rates so that some agreed upon amount of additional investment could be financed internally, the monopolist would be able to exact its corporate levy without fear of further government intervention. In this case, ρ, too, would approach zero - as long as the rates were not increased by more than the approved percentage.

For a regulated firm, then, the sole restraint on raising funds internally through the corporate levy would come from the substitution effect. In other words, R would be equal to R_1 alone. But even R_1 is likely to have a lower value - and thus the supply curve for internally generated funds is likely to be that much more elastic - for a regulated megacorp than for its unregulated counterpart. This is because the value of R_1 depends on the elasticity of industry demand; and as empirical studies have shown,[9] the demand curves faced by regulated industries are even more inelastic, and therefore have a lower absolute value, than those faced by other types of industries.

The import of the above argument is that, if a regulated monopolist were free to resort to the corporate levy, its cost of obtaining additional investment funds would be substantially reduced. What the effect will be on the price or rate level within the industry is more problematical. The fact is that whether the additional investment funds are obtained internally through the corporate levy or externally from the capital funds market, higher rates will have to be charged. If it is the corporate levy that is to be relied upon for the additional funds, the rate level will have to be increased by the percentage, n, associated with the desired amount of additional investment funds, for example, the percentage n_a associated with F_a in figure 13 above. Alternatively, if it is the capital funds market that is to be relied upon, the rate level will again have to be increased, in this case to cover the cost of the additional interest and dividends that will have to be paid out to the capital debt holders. This cost, the additional debt service, ΔD, will be equal to the additional investment funds, ΔF, multiplied by the permanent interest rate, i. How much the rate level will have to be increased to cover this additional debt service will depend on three ratios: (a) the ratio of the additional debt service to the prior debt service, $\Delta D/D$; (b) the prior ratio of debt service to fixed costs, D/FC, and (c) the prior ratio of fixed costs to price, FC/P_0. In other words,

$$n' = \frac{\Delta D}{D} \cdot \frac{D}{FC} \cdot \frac{FC}{P_0} = \frac{\Delta D}{P_0}$$

where

n' = percentage change in price necessary to cover an increase in debt service, and

D = amount of debt service, encompassing both dividends and interest.

It should be noted that n' will reflect an increase in fixed costs, or ΔFC, while n will reflect an increase in the corporate levy, or ΔCL.

Whether resort to the corporate levy by a regulated monopolist would lead to a higher or a lower level of rates in that industry will thus depend on whether, for a given amount of additional investment funds, $\Delta F/p$, n is greater or less than n'. *A priori* it is not possible to say which will be the case, since it will depend on the conditions, peculiar to each industry, which determine the values of n and n' respectively as $\Delta F/p$ varies. Still, the question is an important one, since the greater the percentage increase in rates, the greater the loss of real income by the consuming public. At the same time it should be noted that the basis for judging whether the regulated monopolist's customers will be better off if funds are obtained internally through the corporate levy or externally from the capital funds market, that is, whether n or n' is greater, is not the same as the basis for judging whether the regulated monopolist itself will be better off. The latter will depend on whether R or i is greater. Thus the possibility exists that in reducing its own cost of obtaining additional investment funds the regulated monopolist may contribute to a lowering of real income - at least in the short run. But then this is not an unusual consequence of the capital accumulation process.

Up to this point, in order to reveal more clearly the influences on the supply side, the demand for additional investment funds has been assumed to be perfectly inelastic. This, of course, is not entirely realistic. In fact, on the basis of the empirical evidence, it would appear that the investment demand schedule of regulated firms is quite elastic with respect to interest rates (Evans, 1967, especially pp. 160–2). Not only are public utilities more likely to be affected by monetary conditions because, due to regulation, they are more dependent on the capital funds market (Kuh and Meyer, 1963, pp. 410–20), but, in addition, their very prominence in that market gives rise to a separate effect on interest rates. Accounting as they do for approximately 40 percent of all new security issues,[10] public utilities must recognize that their decision to enter the capital funds market may well push up the cost of funds, especially in a period of tight credit.[11] For that very reason, the more stringent overall monetary conditions are, the more hesitant these regulated firms are likely to be to resort to new external financing. Since changes in interest rates are closely correlated with changes in overall monetary conditions, this effect shows up as part of the interest elasticity of investment by public utilities.

Whatever the source of the interest elasticity, it means that a lowering of the cost of obtaining additional investment funds, such as would be the case if resort could be had to the corporate levy as well as to the capital funds market, will likely lead to a higher rate of capital formation. Investment projects which now have to be abandoned or delayed because funds are either unavailable or too expensive might well, under the circumstances, be carried out. Of course, some would argue that regulation already provides too great an incentive for investment because capital expenditures, unlike expenditures on other types of inputs, can be included in the rate base.[12] But this simply means that the choice of production technique is biased by regulation in favor of more capital intensive methods. It does not mean that all the socially worthwhile investment opportunities are necessarily taken hold of by the regulated firm. In fact, given the bias toward capital intensive methods of production, the shortage of funds for socially worthwhile investment projects is likely to be all the greater (cf. Weintraub, 1968).

Here an important distinction arises between a regulated monopolist and a regulated oligopolist. The regulated monopolist is protected against competition both with respect to price and with respect to investment, but the regulated oligopolist is protected only with respect to the former. In the area of investment, it faces the competition of its fellow oligopolists, and this means that if it fails to seize a worthwhile investment opportunity, no matter how serious the problem of obtaining additional funds may be, it risks losing part of its long-run share of the market to its rivals.[13] For this reason, the investment demand curve of a regulated oligopolist can be expected to be somewhat less interest elastic than that of a regulated monopolist. This, of course, means that the regulated oligopolist, in contrast to the regulated monopolist, is likely to incur a higher cost for investment funds but that the amount of investment it undertakes will be less sensitive to monetary conditions.

It seems probable, then, in summary, that the effect of regulation as presently practiced in the United States is to slow down the rate of capital formation and thus the rate of growth in those sectors where regulation prevails, particularly in those sectors characterized by regulated monopoly. This is because of the insistence by regulatory bodies that the pre-megacorp model of the capital accumulation and allocation process be followed. Whether such a slowing down of the growth rate is undesirable is a question still to be considered. It will be taken up after the problems of income distribution and macro-micro theory integration have first been dealt with. For now it will suffice to note that the pricing behavior of a regulated monopolist - not to mention a regulated oligopolist and an unregulated monopolist - can best be understood by extending to that somewhat different case the basic model of oligopolistic pricing developed in the preceding chapter. The same is true, it will now be domonstrated, of the pricing behavior of an unregulated oligopolistic operating in more than one industry. This is the case of the conglomerate megacorp, next to be explored.

The conglomerate firm

Megacorp as a conglomerate. The conglomerate megacorp, as an ideal type, consists of various quasi-independent operating divisions, each of which belongs to a different industry and each of which might well, if allowed to stand alone, qualify as a megacorp in its own right. The various divisions are likely to enjoy virtual autonomy - with two crucial exceptions. Both the selection of men to fill the top executive positions in each division and the choice of major investment projects to be funded can be expected to rest with the central management, that is, with the executive group for the megacorp as a whole. It is this control over the critical factors of capital expenditures and executive personnel that gives the conglomerate megacorp its essential unity as an economic organization.

The conglomerate firm, then, must be viewed - conceptually if not historically - as a centrally directed coalition of megacorp equivalents. But while it may represent a more complex and highly evolved form of business organization than the simple megacorp from which it has probably grown, the conglomerate firm can nevertheless be expected to follow essentially the same behavioral pattern. Its executive group, still exercising *de facto* final authority by virtue of its position at the head of the bureaucracy which runs the firm on a day-to-day basis, will want to see the firm grow at a maximum rate. The only difference in the case of a conglomerate megacorp is that its own growth rate will no longer be bounded by the growth rate of any particular industry.

How rapidly the firm can grow will depend on the total corporate levy it is able to exact. The greater the amount of investment funds thereby obtained, the greater will be the megacorp's ability to command the resources necessary for further expansion. The corporate levy is thus the means by which a conglomerate enterprise is able to exploit the opportunities available to it for increasing the scale of its operations *vis-à-vis* either other firms or the economy as a whole. It is for this reason that the behavioral pattern of a conglomerate megacorp may be said to be, more specifically, to maximize the rate of growth of the corporate levy. Success in this respect is, as already noted, the prerequisite for maximizing the growth either of sales or of assets (see above, chapter 2, pp. 23-4).

A megacorp-price leader that is a member of but a single industry is able to achieve this goal simply by setting its price and then allocating the investment funds obtained through the corporate levy so as to optimize its long-run share of that one market. For the megacorp-price leader that is a member of more than one industry, the task is more complicated. Setting a price and allocating investment funds so as to optimize the market share in one industry may make it impossible to optimize the market share in another. The conglomerate firm's task is made all the more difficult by the fact that it may be a member of many different industries and, at least theoretically, a potential member of all the others.

Still, as a practical matter, the number of industries in which a megacorp can be interested will be limited, at any given moment in time, by its managerial resources.[14] Because of the demands continuously being made on the time and energies of the executive group, it can be assumed that a megacorp will in fact be able to contemplate seriously expansion into only one other industry besides those to which it already belongs. This premise, if accepted, has two implications. The first is that any investment funds obtained through the corporate levy need be allocated only among $X + 1$ industries where X is the number of industries in which the megacorp is presently involved.[15] The second implication is that these internal funds can be derived from only X industries. With these limitations in mind, it then becomes possible to set forth the principles governing both the allocation of the corporate levy and its derivation.

Allocation of the corporate levy. The principle for allocating the investment funds obtained through the corporate levy in an optimal manner is a relatively simple one. The funds should be apportioned among the $X + 1$ industries so that the rate of return to the megacorp - measured by the present discounted value of the expected future increases in the corporate levy - is equalized among all the industries. In other words, the megacorp will want to allocate its investment funds so that

$$r_a = r_b = r_c = \dots = r_x = r_{x+1}$$

where $r_a, r_b, r_c, \dots, r_x, r_{x+1}$ are the marginal efficiencies of investment in industries $A, B, C, \dots, X, X + 1$.

Clearly, if the rate of return is higher in one industry than in another, the megacorp will find that it can improve its long-run position by allocating relatively more investment funds to the first rather than the second - up to the point where the respective rates of return are equalized.

Two corollary points can be derived from this general principle. The first is that the equalized rate of return among all the industries can itself become a guide for evaluating investment decisions. Any opportunity that may have arisen in the past to achieve a higher rate of return, it can be assumed, will have already been exploited. If so, the conglomerate firm should be in, or close to, a position where the rate of return from investment is the same in each of the industries with which it is presently involved. Expressed in the more easily understood form of the payoff period - that is, the number of years required before the costs of any investment project are likely to be recovered[16] - this benchmark rate of return can then be used as a rule-of-thumb against which to measure the expected rate of return from any new investment opportunity that may subsequently arise. Unless the project offers the hope of an equally short or shorter pay-out period, it is not likely to be undertaken. In fact, by allowing for somewhat longer payoff periods than the present minimum cut-off one, the conglomerate megacorp will be able to establish standards for screening investment projects at successively lower levels of management, a necessary means of decentralizing the investment decision process in a large bureaucratic enterprise.

The second corollary point is that expansion into a new industry - whether by merger, construction of new facilities or a combination of the two - will be undertaken only if the expected rate of return from doing so is greater than the present minimum cut-off rate of return. The rule-of-thumb governing diversification is thus but a special case of that governing investment in general[17] - even though the diversification decision, because of the substantial fixed commitment which it entails, is likely to be more carefully considered and the probabilities more cautiously estimated.

Indeed, it would be a mistake to equate the expansion by a megacorp into a new industry with the mere commitment of investment funds. The megacorp, if it decides to enter the industry, will be transferring something far more valuable than funds alone. That something is its organizational and managerial capacity. It is this additional input which gives rise to part of the differential between the return which an investment banker could expect to earn by investing in the industry and the return which the megacorp itself can expect to earn. This differential, in turn, explains why the megacorp will be unwilling merely to turn its funds over to some other enterprise to invest on its behalf.

The fact is that, if the megacorp has not lost its entrepreneurial capacity, the return from investing funds within the firm, including funds invested as part of a diversification move, should always be higher. The megacorp may, of course, lend out funds to others for strategic reasons - to secure the loyalty of an important customer, for example. It may also lend out funds to others on a short-term basis - this as a means of better managing its liquid assets. But lending out funds to others on a long-term basis solely for the financial reward to be gained is inconsistent with the megacorp's goal of maximizing its own rate of growth over time, for the megacorp's growth rate is almost certain to be higher if the funds are used by the megacorp itself.

The discrepancy in the perceived value of r when funds are to be lent out to others rather than being invested directly has, then, two sources: (a) the greater risk associated with lending out funds to others because of the uncertainty as to their managerial competence, and (b) the opportunity lost by the megacorp's executive group to utilize its own entrepreneurial talents. This discrepancy in the perceived value of *r* is in addition to the greater risk of a successful take-over bid which an executive group incurs when it adds to the megacorp's investment portfolio (see below, chapter 5, pp. 165-6). Together, they explain why the price in an oligopolistic industry is not likely to be increased simply to finance outside investment or to supply in some other way funds to the capital market. The conglomerate megacorp, in other words, is not to be confused with an investment banking firm - unless investment banking is an industry into which the firm chooses to expand, developing the special managerial competence which that industry requires.

At the same time, it is the very ability of the megacorp to expand into new industries offering a higher rate of return on investment than those in which it is presently involved that enables the megacorp to maintain a certain rate of return over time.[18] The conglomerate firm must, therefore, be seen as a supra-industry mechanism for allocating investment funds, one that is perhaps less comprehensive in its purview than the idealized capital funds market but nonetheless broader in its reach than the megacorp limited to but a single industry.

What is being suggested here is that in the larger arena of inter-industry competition there exist powerful economic forces tending to push all megacorps toward a single rate of return on investment and, *pari passu,* a single rate of growth in terms of the corporate levy. The form which this competition takes is a contest to invest the funds obtained through the corporate levy in a manner that will best contribute to the firm's long-run growth. Those firms which lose out in this competition, that is, fail to grow at the same rate as other megacorps, will find themselves increasingly handicapped by their inability to command vital inputs such as capital funds and technical-managerial manpower. Even though these firms may survive in the sense of not being forced out of business, they are likely to find themselves caught in a process of cumulative decline, the failure to grow sufficiently rapidly and thus to attract critical resources serving to place a further brake on their expansion over time until finally they cease to be significant elements in the economy.

To avoid this process of cumulative decline, megacorps must continually seek out and take advantage of new investment opportunities. But this very seeking out and taking advantage of new investment opportunities should, by forcing a shift of resources from less to more rapidly expanding industries, lead to the equalization of the growth rate among all megacorps - or at least among all megacorps which still remain vibrant. On the one hand, those megacorps which, because they belong to less rapidly expanding industries, anticipate growing more slowly than the others will be under the greatest pressure to expand into new industries; and assuming diversification is begun before the slowdown in the rate of growth seriously affects the ability to obtain investment funds, they will be in the best position to finance that new entry. This is because the demand for investment funds in the industries to which they already belong will be less than the funds currently being generated internally. On the other hand, those megacorps which, because they belong to more rapidly expanding industries, are growing at a faster pace than the others will be under less pressure to expand into new industries. Not only are they likely to find the industries to which they already belong absorbing all the capital funds they are able to obtain, they are also likely to face a greater threat of other firms invading their markets. As a result, they are apt to grow at a less rapid rate than the industries to which they belong. The combined effect of these several tendencies, insofar as they produce a differential shift of megacorps into newer, more rapidly expanding industries, should over the long run tend to bring about an equalization of the growth rate for all vibrant megacorps.

Of course, for a number of reasons, this equalization of the growth rate will never actually occur. Scientific and technological breakthroughs will continually lead to the creation of new industries, and different megacorps will be in different positions to exploit the resulting opportunities. Moreover, the different industries in which megacorps are already involved will be continually subject to different exogenous forces affecting their rate of growth. Finally, the management of different megacorps will perceive and respond differently to the changes in their external environment. Yet, though the equalization of the growth rate may never actually occur, the tendencies in that direction will be quite strong – so strong, in fact, that it is possible to speak, at least conceptually, of a single growth rate for all megacorps, $\overset{*}{G}_0$. This single growth rate, in turn, implies the equalization of the marginal efficiency of investment so that it is possible to speak of a single value for r as well. It is this equalization both of the growth rate and of the marginal efficiency of investment which serves in this dynamic framework as the alternative to the equalization of the rate of return on capital generally assumed in static analysis.[19]

To recapitulate briefly, it has been argued that the conglomerate megacorp will, in order to maximize its long-run rate of growth, allocate its investment funds among the $X + 1$ industries in which it is interested so that the marginal efficiency of investment, r, in each industry – measured by the present discounted value of future expected increases in the corporate levy – is eventually equalized. Moreover, it is the possibility of being able to expand into a new industry, the $+1$ or marginal industry as it may be termed - an industry that promises a higher rate of return on investment than the industries to which the megacorp already belongs - that enables it and all the other megacorps to maintain the same rate of growth *vis-à-vis* each other over the long run. But while the marginal rate of return to investment will tend to be the same among the various industries in which the megacorp is involved, the actual amount of investment undertaken in each of the industries will almost certainly not be the same. That is, the rate of return from investment in the $X + 1$ industries can be equalized only by allocating differing amounts of investment funds to each industry, just as the rate of return from investment in D_{I_1}, D_{I_2}, D_{I_3} and D_{I_4} within a single industry can be equalized only by allocating differing sums to each of those four types of investment.

Taking the analysis one step further, the amount of investment undertaken in any one of the $X + 1$ industries need not be exactly equal to the amount of corporate levy derived from that industry. The mere fact that expansion into a new industry can be financed through the corporate levy means that this must necessarily be the case. More to the point, it is the very ability of the conglomerate megacorp to take the corporate levy derived from one industry with a lower growth potential and use it to finance investment in another industry with a higher growth potential that makes the conglomerate megacorp such a vital, dynamic force in the economy. While the principle governing the allocation of investment funds among the $X + 1$ industries has been spelled out, the principle governing its derivation from the X industries still needs to be made clear.

Derivation of the corporate levy. If the megacorp had control over the price level in each of the X industries to which it belongs - that is, if it were either a monopolist or a price leader in each of those industries - the principle governing the derivation of the corporate levy in an optimal manner would also be a relatively simple one. Given the need to finance a new level of desired investment in the $X + 1$ industries, the megacorp would want to raise prices in each of the X industries in which it is involved, and thus increase the average corporate levy being realized therein, so that the value of R associated with each percentage increase in price, n, would be equalized among all the industries. In other words, the megacorp will want to set the various prices so that

$$R_a = R_b = R_c = \ldots = R_x$$

where R_a, R_b, R_c, ..., R_x are the implicit interest rates associated with percentage changes in price, n_a, n_b, n_c, ..., n_x.

Clearly, if the value of R associated with the percentage increase in price in one industry were less than the value of R associated with the percentage increase in price in another industry, the megacorp would be able to reduce its overall cost of obtaining investment funds internally by raising the price by a larger percentage in the first industry and by a smaller percentage in the second - up to the point where the two Rs were equalized.

Still assuming the megacorp to have control over the price level in each of the industries to which it belongs, it would follow, as a corollary to the above principle, that in order to equalize R the price level would have to be increased by a different percentage, n, in each industry. This is because the values of $|e_j|$, m, k_j and ρ - the underlying determinants of the relationship between R and n - are likely to vary with the industry. For the same reason, the actual amount of additional investment funds, $\Delta F/p$, obtained in each of the industries would also be different. In other words, if a conglomerate megacorp is to minimize the overall cost of obtaining additional investment funds internally, it must necessarily set a different price in, and derive through the corporate levy a different amount of investment funds from, each of the X industries.

Of course, it is not entirely realistic to assume that the megacorp will have complete control over the price level in each of the industries to which it belongs. In at least some of those industries it is likely to be a price follower - acquiescing to whatever change in price is announced by the price leader. While it may attempt to influence the price leader's decision through public statements made by its chief executive officer as well as in other ways, its control over the industry price level will nonetheless be at best only slight. And even in those industries in which the megacorp is the price leader, it will still be somewhat limited in its discretion by the need to take into account the views of its fellow oligopolists. To the extent, then, that the megacorp does not have complete control over the price level in each of the industries to which it belongs, it may well find itself unable to equalize R between industries. In particular, it may find that it could reduce its overall cost of obtaining additional investment funds internally if prices were to be raised by a larger percentage in those industries in which it is not the price leader.[20]

This point notwithstanding, it may still be reasonable to assume that R will at least tend toward equality, if not actually be equalized, among the various industries to which the conglomerate megacorp belongs. As long as the megacorp can reduce the overall cost of obtaining internal funds by raising prices relatively more in one industry than in another, it can be expected, even if it is not the price leader, to press for a higher price in that industry. Moreover, to the extent that all megacorps are striving to maintain the same long-run growth rate, a firm which is a price leader can be expected to have as much of a need for additional investment funds as any of the other firms in its industry. While the price leader may find that it can generate those additional funds at a lower implicit interest because it belongs to a different set of industries, one in which the value of $|e_j|$, m, k_j, and ρ are less, the differential is not likely to be that great. Thus, even though R may be lower in an industry in which the conglomerate megacorp is not the price leader, it is not apt to be so much lower that one cannot simply assume, as is done in the analysis that follows, that R will, in fact, be equalized between industries.

The conglomerate firm's pricing decision. On the assumption that both r and R will be equalized - the first among $X + 1$ industries and the second among X industries alone - it is possible to determine, in the case of a conglomerate megacorp, both an overall supply curve and an overall demand curve for additional investment funds. Given these supply and demand curves, it is then possible to indicate what change in price, if any, the conglomerate megacorp will seek in each of the industries to which it belongs.

The overall supply curve of additional investment funds depends both on the supply curve for additional internally generated funds and the permanent interest rate that must be paid on external funds. The former simply indicates the total amount of additional investment funds that can be generated internally, through the corporate levy, in the X industries to which the megacorp belongs as R is varied equally within all those industries. As the price level in each industry is increased by a different percentage, n, in order to vary R equally, different amounts of additional investment funds, $\Delta F/p$, will be realized in each industry. The total amount of additional investment funds that can be generated internally by the conglomerate megacorp is the sum of these different amounts generated in each separate industry, and the relationship between this overall figure and R is what is meant by the supply curve of additional internal investment funds.

Geometrically, the conglomerate megacorp's supply curve for internally generated funds is the aggregate of the individual supply curves in each of the industries to which the firm belongs - these individual supply curves being similar to the supply curve depicted in the top right quadrant of figure 10 above. Due to the peculiarities of geometric addition, this supply curve for the firm as a whole will also be similar to the one depicted in figure 10 above. Since the conglomerate megacorp, like the single industry enterprise, should be in a position to obtain externally whatever additional investment funds it may require at the permanent interest rate, *i*, the overall supply curve of additional investment funds will be similar to the one depicted in figure 11 above. In other words, the fact that a megacorp is a member of more than one industry may change the scale, but not the general nature, of its supply curve for additional investment funds.

The overall demand curve for additional investment funds simply indicates the total amount of expenditures that can be undertaken by the megacorp in $X + 1$ industries as the marginal efficiency of investment, *r*, is varied equally among each of those industries. At the same marginal efficiency of investment, different amounts of expenditures can, of course, be undertaken in each of those industries. The total amount of expenditures that can be undertaken at a given value of *r* is the sum of these different amounts that can be undertaken in each separate industry, and the relationship between this overall figure and *r* is what is meant by the demand curve for additional investment funds. It is the intersection of this overall demand curve with the conglomerate megacorp's overall supply curve of additional investment funds that will determine not only the amount of additional investment undertaken in each of the $X + 1$ industries but also by how much prices will have to be raised, if at all, in the *X* industries to which the megacorp belongs and whether these internally generated funds will have to be supplemented through external financing.

As in the earlier analysis of a single industry firm, the conglomerate megacorp should be willing to increase its investment expenditures as long as the expected rate of return is not less than the cost of capital funds, whether internally or externally obtained. The actual amount of additional investment undertaken, then, will be that amount, $\Delta F/p$, associated with the point at which the S_I curve intersects the D_I curve. If, as shown in figure 13 above, the implicit interest rate on internally generated funds, *R*, is less at that point than the permanent cost of external funds, *i*, all of $\Delta F/p$ will be financed internally - at an implicit interest rate equal to R_a. If, however, as shown in figure 14, *R* exceeds *i* at that point, only part of the additional investment, F_b, will be financed internally. The rest, $F_d - F_b$, will be financed by resort to the capital funds market - the cost for both types of funds being equal to *i*. Of course, if D_I should intersect S_I outside the top right quadrant, as in figure 12, the existing corporate level will be sufficient to finance the desired level of investment and no increase in price levels will be necessary.

Once the total amount of additional investment funds to be obtained internally through an increase in the corporate levy has been decided upon, the conglomerate megacorp will seek to push up prices in each of the *X* industries to which it belongs to a level for which the implicit interest rate on internal funds is equal to either R_0 or i, whichever rate happens to govern. In the industries for which the conglomerate megacorp is the price leader, this will, of course, be easier than in the industries for which it is not; but even in the latter the megacorp will bring to bear whatever pressure it can to achieve the desired higher price.

The pricing decision of a conglomerate megacorp, then, while somewhat more complicated and difficult to analyze, is nonetheless understandable within the same theoretical framework as that developed in the previous chapter to handle the case of a single industry oligopolist. What is perhaps even more important, given the evolutionary trend previously cited with regard to such firms, the pricing decision of a conglomerate megacorp, it would appear from the above discussion, can be understood *only* within that framework. What will now be demonstrated is that the same theoretical framework can be used to throw a somewhat different light on the polypolistic model which occupies such a prominent place in the theoretical literature.

Polypoly

Polypoly, within the framework of the oligopolistic model developed previously, is perhaps best described as the type of industry in which, due solely to market forces, the corporate levy is restricted in the long run to a depreciation allowance alone. But this is polypoly only in a Marshallian sense. For there to be polypoly in the Walrasian sense - the sense in which the terms 'competition' and 'competitive model' have suffused the thinking of economists - a more stringent condition must hold, one which assumes even more of a restraint on the firm than just the inability to obtain over the long run any residual income in the form of a margin above costs. That more stringent condition is that the firm itself be a price taker, powerless to influence the industry price.[21] Since polypoly in the Walrasian sense is thus an extreme case of polypoly in the Marshallian sense, the discussion will proceed from the latter to the former.

The question being posed here is what modifications in the structural characteristics of oligopoly are necessary if market forces alone are to limit the corporate levy to little more than a depreciation allowance and, going beyond that, transform the firm into a price taker. To answer this question, each of the assumptions underlying the oligopolistic model will, in turn, be relaxed and the effect which this has on the margin above costs, or average corporate levy, then assessed. In this way, it will be possible to indicate what departures from the oligopolistic model are required to produce polypolistic pricing behavior on the part of the neo-classical proprietorship, both in the Marshallian sense and the more extreme Walrasian sense.

The congruence of management and ownership. It is the separation of management from ownership, and the establishment of a self-perpetuating business bureaucracy which this presumes, that gives rise to the long-run time perspective associated with the megacorp. To the extent, then, that management and ownership are combined in the personality of one or more owner-entrepreneurs, the firm's time horizon can be expected to be somewhat shorter. Unless sons (or sons-in-law) can be brought into the business and trained to take over, the life of the firm is likely to end with that of its principal partners - and if serious disagreement should arise among them, the existence of the firm may terminate even sooner. Its limited life expectancy, is not, however, the only cause of the neo-classical proprietorship's shorter time perspective. Its owner-entrepreneurs, unlike the megacorp's executive group, benefit immediately and directly from any increase in net revenue. They do not have to wait for higher earnings to be translated into organizational growth for their own incomes to be augmented. For this reason, it is the prospective short-run personal gain rather than the possible long-run detrimental effect on the firm itself that is likely to weigh more heavily on the minds of the owner-entrepreneurs. The more uncertain the future of the firm, the greater will be this tendency to discount the long-run impact of decisions.

Thus, at one extreme, it can be assumed that the time horizon of the neo-classical proprietorship extends only through the current pricing period.[22] What this means, in the framework of the oligopolistic model previously developed, is that the substitution effect is likely to be the only restraint in the firm's pricing discretion. Both the entry factor and the possibility of meaningful government intervention can be ignored, the first because of the time required for a new firm to organize itself and construct adequate facilities, the second because of the laissez-faire political philosophy implicit in a neo-classical world. With the substitution effect as the only constraint on pricing discretion, and even that effect taken into account for only a single time period, the pricing situation corresponds to that depicted in figure 17, a variant of that in figure 5 in chapter 2. With the firm still assumed to have multiple plants or plant segments, all equally efficient and each operated with fixed technical coefficients, its marginal cost curve will continue to be constant over the relevant ranges of output. With the firm still assumed to be either the only member of its industry or the member whose price the other firms all follow, its average revenue curve will continue to have the same elasticity as the industry demand curve. The only difference

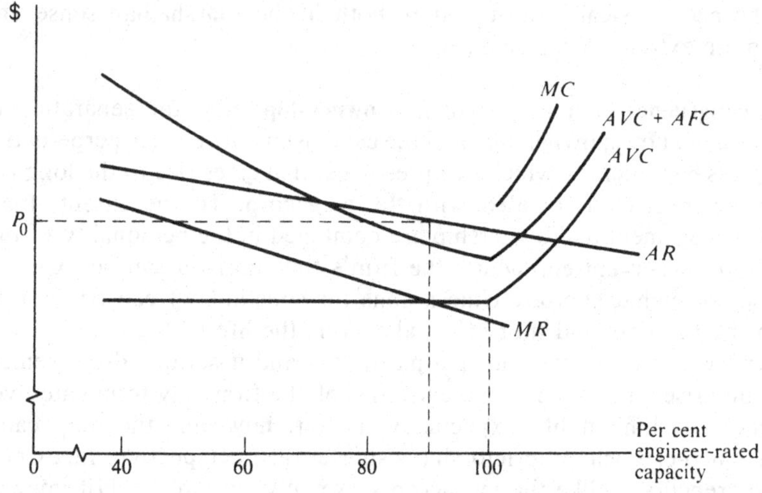

Figure 17

is that, if the marginal revenue curve associated with that average revenue curve is to intersect the marginal cost curve so that net revenue can be maximized in that one time period, the price level will have to be pushed up to the point where the firm finds itself somewhere on the elastic portion of its own and the industry demand curve.

To assume, however, that the time horizon of any firm, even a neo-classical proprietorship, extends only through the current pricing period is clearly unrealistic. It implies that the owner-entrepreneurs are so short-sighted as to virtually preclude their ever having risen to the status of property owners or, if that status has been inherited, to virtually preclude their remaining property owners for long. It is far more reasonable to assume that the time horizon of the neo-classical proprietorship extends beyond the current pricing period - though falling short of the planning period itself.[23] This means that the substitution effect will be determined by the arc elasticity of industry demand, not in the time period immediately following any change in price but rather, in the time period which marks the outer limit of the owner-entrepreneurs' time horizon.[24] Since the arc elasticity of demand in that later time period is likely to be higher, the substitution effect will be greater and the price set to maximize net revenue within the relevant time frame correspondingly lower. Still, the substitution effect will not be as great nor the price as low as it would be if the neo-classical proprietorship's time horizon were as long as the megacorp's.

From the above line of argument it can be seen that dropping the assumption that there exists a separation of management from ownership does little to transform the previously developed oligopolistic pricing model into the polypolistic model of conventional analysis. In fact, the shorter time horizon implicit when that assumption is dropped is likely to lead to a higher, rather than a lower, industry price and thus to what is generally taken to be the monopolistic, rather than the polypolistic result. The next step is to examine what happens when the assumption of multiple plants and fixed technical coefficients is also dropped.

Coextensiveness of the firm with the plant. It is the existence of multiple plants or plant segments, each of which is operated either at its least cost point or not at all, that gives the megacorp constant marginal and average variable costs over the relevant ranges of output. If, then, the neo-classical proprietorship consists of but a single plant so that the firm is coextensive with the plant, it will instead be governed by the traditional U-shaped cost curves, with marginal and average variable costs first declining and then, after reaching their respective minima, rising. This presumes, of course, that the firm has the ability to vary the technical coefficients in the short run, with differing quantities of other inputs being combined with the fixed plant or fixed managerial resources to produce differing quantities of output.

By itself, the existence of the U-shaped cost curves does little to alter the pricing situation. As long as the other conditions underlying the oligopolistic model still hold - a long-run time perspective and interdependent behavior - the only change produced is that the firm can no longer assume that its costs in the short run are independent of its actual operating ratio. Both marginal and average variable costs will vary with the rate of capacity utilization, and this, in turn, means that both the average and marginal corporate levy associated with any given price level will also vary. This, however, is not a new complication. In the earlier discussion of a megacorp with multiple plants or plant segments it was pointed out that, with technological progress over time embodied in replacement capital, the various plants or plant segments are not all likely to be capable of operating with equal efficiency. Thus, as plants are either shut down or started up again in order to adjust output to fluctuating sales, the megacorp will find that its average variable and marginal costs will vary discretely. It was merely to simplify the ensuing analysis that this complication was ignored - by implicitly assuming that the discrete changes in marginal costs were so small as to be analytically insignificant.

In the case of a firm with but a single plant, the variability of marginal costs cannot, however, be so easily ignored. The fact that additional output can be obtained only by using a given facility more intensively implies a greater discrepancy between marginal and average variable costs than when a somewhat obsolescent plant or plant segment is pressed back into service to provide reserve capacity. Still, it is only a complication. That it does not fundamentally alter the oligopolistic pricing situation can be seen when, as in figure 18, the constant marginal and average

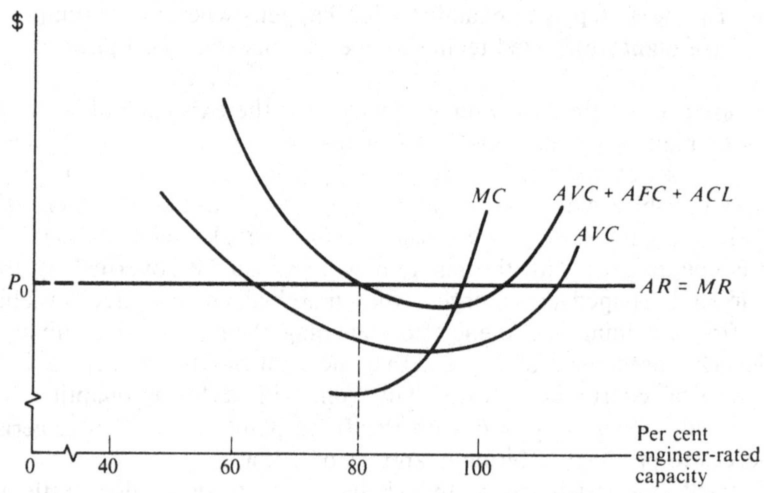

Figure 18

variable cost curves are replaced by the more traditional U-shaped ones. As long as the price is set and then maintained so as to cover, over the long run, average variable and fixed costs plus the corporate levy necessary to finance an optimal level of investment, the price will be determinate based on the same factors analyzed in connection with oligopoly. Under those circumstances, with given average variable and fixed cost curves, the price will still depend on the demand for and supply of additional investment. The only difference is that the corporate levy realized will be even more sensitive to the actual operating ratio since average variable costs, as well as average fixed costs and the average corporate levy, will decline as the rate of capacity utilization increases. But this is a difference of degree, not of kind.

The U-shaped cost curves become significant only when considered in conjunction with the shorter time horizon of the neo-classical proprietorship. With additional net revenue desired only because it immediately and directly increases the personal income of the owner-entrepreneurs and with marginal costs varying with the level of output, the price situation resembles the conventional monopolistic model. The firm's marginal revenue curve will be equated with its marginal cost curve to maximize net revenue within the neo-classical proprietorship's relevant time frame; and since marginal costs will vary with the level of output, an increase in industry demand will necessarily give rise to an increase in the industry price. What thus emerges is the positively sloped industry supply curve of conventional analysis. The significance of this result is that, with the industry supply curve positively sloped, fiscal and monetary policy can be used with some degree of effectiveness to control the aggregate price level.

So far, then, relaxing the assumptions of the oligopolistic model has led, not to polypoly but rather, to the conventional model of monopoly. The next step is to examine what happens when the third and final assumption of the oligopolistic model - membership in an industry characterized by interdependent behavior - is dropped. This assumption has already been relaxed by positing in an earlier section of this chapter the case of a firm which, though the only member of its industry, is still marked by a separation of management from ownership and by multiple plant operation. This megacorp model of monopoly, as distinguished from the conventional model just discussed, was seen to be but a special case of oligopoly in which the problem of price coordination was merely obviated. Now the assumption of interdependent behavior among two or more firms is to be dropped, not by stipulating the existence of only a single firm in the industry but rather, by stipulating that the two or more firms behave independently of one another.

Independence of pricing behavior. It is the interdependence of pricing behavior and the approximation to joint profit maximization which this leads to once the practice of price leadership has been accepted that makes it possible for the price in an oligopolistic industry to be maintained, even in the face of declining demand. To the extent, then, that the firms in an industry act independently of one another - that is, to the extent they are willing to engage in price cutting - the industry price can be expected to fall whenever the rate of capacity utilization itself falls. This decline in the industry price is the equivalent of a decline in the average corporate levy being realized and thus a decline in the amount of savings being generated within the business sector. If the firms in the industry persist in cutting the price whenever it seems to their immediate advantage to do so, the entire corporate levy, including even any depreciation allowance, may well be eliminated.

While the pursuit of an independent pricing policy will not suffice by itself to transform the neo-classical proprietorship into a price taker, the fact is that, unless the firms in the industry are prepared to cut the industry price whenever it is to their advantage to do so, there cannot be polypoly in the Walrasian sense. As pointed out above in chapter 2, the difference between the perfectly elastic average revenue curve which the neo-classical proprietorship faces as a price taker in the Walrasian model and the perfectly elastic average revenue curve which the megacorp faces once a new industry price has been announced by the price leader is that the former is likely to be undermined by the willingness of at least some firms in the industry to accept a lower price when industry demand softens. Moreover, even if the price cutting by the other firms in the industry is not so certain or so automatic that the neo-classical proprietorship is for all practical purposes a price taker, the price cutting may still be severe enough to eliminate any counterpart to the corporate levy and thereby produce the same result as when only polypoly in the more limited Marshallian sense prevails. What needs to be brought out, then, are the factors likely to induce the neo-classical proprietorship to pursue an independent pricing policy rather than act in concert with the other members of the industry.

One of these factors is the number of firms in the industry and their relative size. The larger the number of firms, the more difficult it will be to pinpoint exactly which firm is responsible for cutting the price. This greater assurance of anonymity, by protecting a firm against possible censure or retaliation by other members of the industry, will encourage the firm to pursue an independent pricing policy. At the same time the more equal in size are the firms in the industry, the more evenly distributed will be the loss of sales suffered by the other members of the industry when one firm shaves the price. With the impact on any one of these other firms thus minimized, they will have less incentive to find out which firm is responsible for the price cutting and less incentive to retaliate against it. Also, the more equal in size are the firms in the industry, the less capable any one of them will be of invoking sanction against another. This lesser chance of provoking an adverse reaction will further encourage the firm to pursue an independent pricing policy. The obverse of this argument is that, as the number of firms is reduced and/or some firms become larger than others, an industry price, once established, is more likely to be maintained.[25]

The greater tendency of firms in an industry to pursue an independent pricing policy the more numerous and the more equal in size they are is reinforced when those firms are also neo-classical proprietorships with a relatively limited time horizon. The gains from shaving the industry price are usually a short-run phenomenon; it is only over time that the untoward consequences of this behavior pattern will become evident. If, because of a sudden drop in industry demand, a firm should find itself with excess inventory, it can always improve its financial position, at least for the moment, by shaving its price. This is because the firm is better off if it obtains a lower price for its unsold output than no price at all. Knowing that if it fails to act in accordance with the change in the industry's economic situation it may lose any opportunity to dispose of its excess inventory, the firm cannot hold back hoping that the other firms in the industry will exercise similar forbearance. Since no firm can count on all the other firms to avoid shaving the industry price, every firm must be prepared to act unilaterally. As a result, the price is almost certain to be cut by some member of the industry and, assuming the industry demand to be price inelastic, every firm will be made worse off - with lower net revenue and lower levels of output. In the short run, then, the firms in the industry will find themselves caught in the classic prisoners' dilemma: what is the most rational course of action for any one of them is irrational for the group as a whole (Luce and Raiffa, 1957, pp. 95-6; Rapoport and Chammah, 1965). It is only in the long run, with cumulative learning experience, that the firms in the industry can be expected to perceive the common interest in escaping from the dilemma through the establishment of some mechanism for achieving joint profit maximization. As long as the firms retain their short-run perspective, however, maximizing their own position as best they can within that time horizon, they are likely to remain in the grip of larger market forces.

The existence, then, of many firms, each roughly equal in size to its rivals and each a neo-classical proprietorship with the shortened time horizon associated with that type of firm, implies a high probability that the various members of the industry will pursue an independent pricing policy (cf. Stigler, 1964; see also McKinnon, 1966). The pursuit of an independent pricing policy will, in turn, lead to a high probability that any margin above costs - the counterpart outside the oligopolistic sector of the corporate levy - will be eliminated if the industry should experience a sufficient decline in the demand for its product. The minimum condition which must therefore be met if there is to be polypoly in the Marshallian sense, with firms still able to exercise some control over the price variable but nonetheless unable to maintain the margin above costs over the long run, is that the industry consist of numerous, similarly small neo-classical proprietorships. To go beyond just the elimination of any counterpart to the corporate levy and assume, more boldly, that the firms in the industry have no control over the price variable - to assume, in other words, that they are price takers as implied both in the Walrasian model and by the perfectly elastic revenue curve attributed to the polypolistic firm in all the economics textbooks - two further conditions must be met. One of these pertains to the type of buyer which the firms face in the market place, the other pertains to the likelihood of new entry into the industry. Indeed, if these two additional conditions are not met, the stability over time of polypoly even in the more limited Marshallian sense is suspect.

Type of buyer faced in the market place. If the pursuit of an independent pricing policy is to be the rule rather than the exception, more than a certain industry structure and more than a certain type of seller firm is required. The other side of the market must also have certain characteristics. Buyers must have continuity in the market, they must be of a certain minimum size relative to the sellers and they must be indifferent as to the sources of supply as long as the price being charged is the best obtainable. In other words, the buyers must be capable of speculating – increasing their purchases when they have reason to believe that the current market price is low relative to the long-run expected price and holding off, using the accumulated inventories, when they have reason to believe the current industry price is high. Unless the buyers have continuity in the market, they will be unable to judge whether the current industry price is low or high; unless they are of a certain minimum size relative to the sellers, they will be unable to hold sufficient inventories to speculate effectively; and unless they are indifferent as to the sources of supply, they will be unable to bring effective pressure on suppliers by switching their orders to other firms. The above conditions assume, of course, that price quotations, if reported, are not identified with any particular seller.[26]

In the past these conditions were generally met by a network of middlemen, encompassing brokers, commission merchants, wholesalers and the like, which was likely to have arisen with the polypolistic industry itself (Porter, 1970; Porter and Livesay, 1971). It was these middlemen who, by their speculative activities, served to keep the industry price 'honest', that is, close to the long-run equilibrium or 'normal' price described by Marshall (1920, Book V, ch. 3). Even today the presence of this middleman network is one of the surest indications that an industry is polypolistic. Still, in many other industries, particularly those which have at some point in their history been consolidated, this middleman network is missing; and, as a result, the market characteristics necessary to assure independent pricing behavior on a regular basis are, at best, only approximated.

If the buyers are monopsonists or, what is more likely, oligopsonists dealing with large numbers of suppliers, the result may be little different from what they would be if a middleman network still existed. In fact, these are precisely the conditions to be found in a large number of industries where the principal customer consists of one or more megacorps. In these satellite industries the pricing situation closely approximates the polypolistic model - at least on the sellers' side. Indeed, it even approximates the extreme Walrasian form of polypoly, with the sellers having so little control over the price variable that they are, for all practical purposes, price takers. Together with the suppliers of certain commodities traded on a world-wide basis, the members of these satellite industries represent the last vestiges of what was the typical nineteenth-century manufacturing firm and upon which example the textbook analysis of polypoly is based.[27]

When, however, the buyers are not megacorps, the absence of a middleman network makes a critical difference. First, it increases the probability that factors other than price - for example, styling, servicing, geographical proximity, etc. - will determine the choice of supplier, and that as a result buyers will be constrained from shifting their business in response to a price differential. This probability is especially strong when the buyers are households and the industry's product a consumer good. Second, the absence of a middleman network increases the probability that buyers will have little day-to-day contact in the market and that they will therefore be less capable of judging whether the price is high or low relative to the 'normal' price. Again, this probability is especially strong when the buyers are households and the industry's product a consumer good. Finally the absence of a middleman network increases the probability that buyers, if small relative to sellers, will lack the resources to speculate effectively and thus will be less able to bring pressure to bear on suppliers. The more closely these several conditions are approximated, the greater is the likelihood that an industry price, once established, will be maintained. In the absence, then, either of a middleman network or of an oligopsonist as the principal customer, it is likely that selling firms will pursue, not an independent but rather, an interdependent pricing policy. This, in turn, makes the oligopolistic pricing model previously developed, and not the textbook model of polypoly, the relevant one for understanding the industry's behavior.

It is not enough, however, just to take note of the type of buyer. The type of seller is also crucial. If an industry consists of numerous, similarly small neo-classical proprietorships, then the absence of a middleman network or oligopsonists as buyers need not preclude independent pricing behavior. Still, the type of independent pricing behavior likely to be observed will not be that of a polypolistic firm. With a group of neo-classical proprietorships selling to a large number of small buyers, each of which is active in the market only occasionally and each of which is more interested in factors other than the price being charged, it is the monopolistically competitive model developed by Chamberlin - rather than either the textbook model of polypoly or the oligopolistic pricing model developed herein - which then becomes the relevant one.[28] Alternatively, when the selling firms are megacorps, then even if the market is characterized by oligopsony, with other megacorps as the principal buyers, independent pricing behavior can no longer be counted on. Indeed, in that case, a bilateral monopoly model, with room for discretion on both sides, will be the appropriate one.[29]

While taking into account the type of buyer which the firm faces in the market place may seem to blur somewhat any distinction between the oligopolistic and non-oligopolistic sectors, the line separating the two is actually quite sharp. The critical point is whether the price, once set, is maintained by the industry as a whole for the rest of the pricing period, or whether, alternatively, the firms in the industry pursue an independent pricing policy, with at least some members of the industry likely to accept a lower price when it appears to be in their interest to do so. In the first instance, the industry - even if the buyers are themselves primarily megacorps - falls within the oligopolistic sector. In the second instance, it does not. On these grounds, the monopolistically competitive firm, though it does not face either a middleman network or a group of oligopsonistic megacorps, is clearly part of the non-oligopolistic sector.[30] It is just that, with its average revenue curve having a downward slope to it, the monopolistically competitive firm cannot be considered a price taker. Being a price taker, however, is not essential for a firm's being within the non-oligopolistic sector. All that is required is that the firm, along with whatever other firms may comprise the industry, pursues an independent pricing policy.

The line separating the oligopolistic and the non-oligopolistic sectors becomes even sharper if one takes into account the second further condition which is required before there can be polypoly in the extreme Walrasian sense, with every firm a price taker. That second further condition pertains to the likelihood of new entry.

Ease of entry. If industry demand is expanding rather than contracting, the tendency of firms to act independently of one another will not necessarily lead to the elimination of any margin above costs. In fact, the margin will most probably rise as the various members of the industry take advantage of the stronger market to push up the price level. The higher price means that each and every firm will experience an increase in income relative to its costs, with a consequent rise in net revenue. This will be true even if the firms in the industry are neo-classical proprietorships, with but a single plant each and with the goal of maximizing their net revenue in the short run. Under these circumstances, the industry price will be pushed up to a level dictated by the marginal cost curve of the least efficient firm; and since a firm's marginal cost curve rises more steeply than its average total cost curve, the net revenue obtained by each and every firm in the industry can be expected to increase - not just at the same rate as sales but in fact - at a more rapid rate.

This disproportionate gain in the amount of residual income accruing to the firm is critically important. It provides the savings necessary to finance - either directly through retained earnings or indirectly through the distributed profits returned via the capital funds market - any subsequent growth by the industry. Without such an expansion of the industry's capacity, the increase in demand cannot long continue to be met. Yet, paradoxically, the polypolistic model posits the eventual elimination of any such residual income. This is an aspect of the microeconomic theory underlying the neo-classical growth analysis which is frequently overlooked; and for that reason it is especially instructive to examine how, in the face of rising demand, the elimination of the residual income is presumed to occur.

Any residual income accruing to the firm - the counterpart to the corporate levy within the non-oligopolistic sector - can be eliminated during a period of general economic expansion only if the industry's productive capacity is increased at a sufficiently rapid rate relative to the growth of demand for the industry's product. This is so whether the firms in the industry are price takers or not. An increase in the industry's productive capacity can, in turn, occur in only one of two ways: (a) through the replication of plant by the existing firms in the industry, or (b) through the entry of new firms.

To the extent that single-plant operation is intrinsic to polypoly - and to monopolistic competition as well - the first alternative is precluded in the case of the non-oligopolistic sector. Expansion must necessarily occur through the entry of new firms. There is, in fact, good reason to believe that, within the non-oligopolistic sector, firms will operate with but a single plant. It is not just that the neo-classical proprietorship - the representative firm both in polypoly and in monopolistic competition - is defined in terms of single-plant operation. It is, more importantly, that the neo-classical proprietorship is likely to encounter diseconomies of scale if it tries to expand beyond a single plant. With the firm's management limited to a small number of owner-entrepreneurs, the addition of another plant may impose such a strain on the company's top officials that the firm will be unable to maintain the same level of efficiency as when only one plant was being operated. It is precisely this limitation on the managerial capability of the neo-classical proprietorship which militates against its growing internally to encompass more than one plant.[31] While this one plant could conceivably be enlarged, the firm runs a considerable risk in doing so if, given the existing state of technology, that facility is already of optimal size. Should industry demand subsequently contract, the firm may find itself unable to compete on an equal footing because of its cost disadvantage (see above, chapter 3, pp. 71-2). The neo-classical proprietorship, then, is likely to be limited to a single production facility, one that is no larger than a plant of minimal optimal size.

The megacorp, of course, is relatively free of this constraint. It is already accustomed to operating more than one plant, and will necessarily have developed an appropriate managerial structure. With a professional group of executives to which new members are continuously being recruited, even if they make no financial contribution to the firm, the megacorp can usually add another plant without serious diseconomies of management. Indeed, the addition of a new plant, by opening up opportunities for advancement within the executive hierarchy, is likely to improve the overall quality of management. For this reason, expansion by the existing firms is not precluded in the case of an oligopolistic industry. On the contrary, it is the principal means by which, in that sector, productive capacity is increased - the desire to avoid new entry strongly inducing individual megacorps to expand their plant and equipment at the same rate as the growth of industry demand.

The situation with respect to expansion is, then, quite different in a polypolistic industry, and even in a monopolistically competitive industry, from that in the oligopolistic sector. In the former, expansion is most likely to take place through the entry of new firms; in the latter, it is most likely to occur through the internal growth of the existing firms. This manner in which expansion occurs in the non-oligopolistic sector has important implications for whether or not any residual income - the equivalent of a corporate levy - will be eliminated in the face of rising demand. With the entry of new firms the only means by which productive capacity can be increased in the non-oligopolistic sector, the elimination of any residual income will depend on the probability of entry, π, over time. If that probability is equal to one in the time period immediately following the expansion of industry demand and hence immediately following the rise in industry price, the residual income will be eliminated at once. If, as is more likely, the probability of entry does not reach one until some subsequent time period, it will be eliminated only after the corresponding time lag. But eliminated it will ultimately be - as long as π has a value equal to one in the long run.

Under these circumstances, any residual income accruing to the firm will be only a temporary windfall and thus cannot serve as the basis for the long-run planning which is a distinguishing feature of the megacorp. Of course, industry demand may continue to expand and, if the entry of new firms into the industry should lag behind, the windfall may persist for quite some time. Still, unless entry into the industry is in some manner effectively impeded, the excess returns will be only temporary. In the long run - that is, when industry capacity has finally been brought back into line with industry demand - the price will approximate the 'normal' level described by Marshall, with long-run average revenue equal to long-run average variable and average fixed costs.

With any residual income certain to be eliminated in the long run through the entry of new firms, the existing members of the industry are more likely to pursue an independent pricing policy. For to maintain the industry price at a fixed level, regardless of short-run demand conditions, imposes a certain cost on the members of an industry. If they are to have the benefit of the higher industry price that is being maintained, they must each be prepared to give up their independence of action - in particular, to forgo any opportunity for increasing their sales at the expense of the other firms in the industry by shaving their price. Yet, if the eventual entry of new firms into the industry will, in any case, prevent the price from exceeding the 'normal' level, there is little incentive for the firms to make that sacrifice. They might just as well set their prices independently of one another, cutting the price whenever it appears to their advantage to do so. Thus, of the two conditions essential for assuring the elimination of the corporate levy - independent pricing behavior and unrestricted entry - the first depends in part on the second.

The polypolistic model. From the preceeding discussion it should be evident that, by assigning the proper values to certain of the key variables, the oligopolistic pricing model developed in the last chapter can be transformed into the polypolistic model of conventional analysis. It is not possible, however, to reverse this procedure - that is, assign certain values to the conventional model of polypoly and thereby explain oligopolistic pricing behavior. This is because the conventional model of polypoly makes no allowance for a corporate levy linked to investment planning. On these grounds, an argument can be made for treating the conventional model of polypoly as a special case within the general oligopolistic pricing framework set forth in chapter 3.

If the probability of entry, π, in some subsequent time period is equal to one, any residual income accruing to the firm as a result of a secular rise in demand - the equivalent of a corporate levy - will be eliminated. The number of time periods required for the entry of the new firms to take place, and thus for the industry's productive capacity to be brought back into line with the demand for its product, simply measures the length of the long-run period. The first prerequisite, then, of the polypolistic model is a value for π in some subsequent time period equal to one, if and when the industry price exceeds average variable and average fixed costs. If, on the other hand, entry into the industry can in some manner be permanently impeded, the residual income accruing to the firm will be more than a temporary windfall and, manifesting itself as a corporate levy, will form the basis for the long-run planning that distinguishes oligopoly from polypoly.

With π equal to one in some subsequent time period, the probability of the firms in the industry pursuing an independent pricing policy will also approach one. That probability is enhanced when both of the following conditions are met: (1) the firms in the industry are neo-classical proprietorships; and (2) the firms are numerous and relatively equal in size. The second prerequisite of the polypolistic model, then, is that the assumption of price maintenance be dropped, to be replaced by the assumption of independent pricing behavior.

With both the probability of independent price behavior and the probability of new entry equal to one, the value of *CL* will be equal to zero in the oligopolistic pricing formula:

$$P = AVC + \frac{FC + CL}{SOR \cdot ERC}.$$

This is because the independent pricing behavior assures the elimination of any corporate levy when industry demand is contracting and the entry of new firms assures the elimination of any corporate levy, at least ultimately, when industry demand is expanding. To the extent that the absence of a corporate levy is the only important result to be inferred from the polypolistic model, the above two conditions - independent pricing behavior and unrestricted entry - are sufficient; and both are subsumed by setting *CL* in the oligopolistic pricing formula equal to zero.

The absence of a corporate levy, however, implies only the existence of polypoly in the Marshallian sense. It does not assure that the industry supply curve will be positively sloped or that the individual members of the industry will be price takers - two conclusions which are usually drawn from the textbook analysis of polypoly. To obtain these results, still further assumptions must be made.

The first of these is that the firms in the industry are subject to some type of significant supply constraint in the short run - in other words, that one of the critical inputs required in the production process is fixed in quantity and cannot be increased even if output must be expanded. When this is the case, production can be increased in the short run, only by utilizing the fixed input more intensively; and this, in turn, as pointed out above (pp. 30-31), will lead beyond a certain point to rising average variable and marginal costs. Assuming independent pricing and short-run profit maximizing behavior - conditions already subsumed by setting the corporate levy equal in the long run to zero - it then follows that the price insisted upon by the firms in the industry will vary as the quantity of output being supplied varies, thereby giving rise to a supply curve that is positively sloped. A third prerequisite, then, for polypoly in the more limited Marshallian sense is that, over the relevant range of output, the firms in the industry be subject to a significant supply constraint so that average variable costs are a positive function of the rate of capacity utilization. It should be noted that this condition will almost certainly be met if the firms in the industry each consist of but a single plant with variable technical coefficients.

Pursuing an independent pricing policy and having a positively sloped supply curve are still not sufficient conditions by themselves, however, to assure that a firm is a price taker. One further condition must be met. This is that the firm must confront a certain type of buyer in the market place, one that is able to engage in effective speculation in the commodity being sold, increasing its purchases when it has reason to believe that the current market price is low relative to the long-run 'normal' price and holding off, using the accumulated inventories, when it has reason to believe that the current industry price is high.[32] This, in turn, means that the buyer must either be part of a middleman network or, alternatively, be a megacorp. Indeed, the existence of one or the other type of buyer as a significant factor in the market is the fourth and final prerequisite of polypoly in the Walrasian sense, and when that condition is not satisfied, it seems unlikely that any firm will remain a price taker for long (cf. Jenner, 1966). This is especially true if the polypolistic industry to which the firm belongs is experiencing rapid growth.

As already pointed out, the only way that a polypolistic industry characterized by single-plant firms can meet a rising demand for its product while still eliminating any margin above costs in the long run is through the entry of new firms. There is no mechanism, however, for regulating the entry of these firms so that the expansion of capacity keeps pace with the rise in demand. Initially, due to the lack of information by outsiders, the entry of new firms may lag. But at some point in time, as the profit opportunities within the industry become more apparent, new firms can be expected to come flooding into the industry, creating an excess supply capacity relative to demand. The depressed prices which will then follow, with revenues falling short of total costs, are precisely the conditions which can be expected to persuade the various members of the industry to eschew their independent pricing policy and seek instead some form of joint profit maximization. It is at this point that the type of buyer faced in the market place becomes critical, for only the speculative activities of middlemen or powerful megacorp customers can thwart the resultant price fixing arrangement, forcing the members of the industry to revert to the previous pattern of each firm making the best 'deal' possible on its own.

What this suggests is that for an industry without a middleman network or megacorps as buyers - especially if the industry is expanding rapidly - polypoly in the extreme Walrasian sense is not a stable form of industrial organization. If the industry does not evolve into oligopoly, it is likely to remain polypolistic only in the more limited Marshallian sense, with firms no longer price takers (Haynes, 1964). Somehow, either through informal meetings or other quasi-legal means, they will attempt to gain control over the price level. In other words, the firms will become price setters, even though the price which is decided upon and then announced is likely to be undermined before not too long by firms shaving the price. The industry will then be characterized by imperfect collusion, the inability to enforce whatever price has been decided upon being the reason why any residual income, the equivalent of a corporate levy, will tend to be eliminated over time.

The more probable result, however, is that the industry experiencing the rapid growth will evolve into oligopoly, either as a result of consolidation from within (see Eichner, 1969, Stigler, 1950) or through conglomerate expansion by megacorps seeking to maintain a certain minimum rate of growth for themselves. The transformation from polypoly to oligopoly means that the industry will have the ability both to assure maintenance of whatever price has been decided upon at the industry level and to limit the entry of new firms into the industry. That is, it will be able to exercise some degree of control over the price level. This control over price is, in turn, what distinguishes oligopoly from polypoly in the limited Marshallian sense.[33]

It should be noted that the same factor which leads to the instability of a polypolistic market structure - namely, the impossibility of regulating the entry of new firms into the industry so that the expansion of capacity keeps pace with the growth of demand - is also the factor which leads to the instability of investment in what may be termed the non-oligopolistic subsector and thus to the instability of income and employment in the economy as a whole when or if that subsector is the sole or dominant portion of the business sector. This is a point which will be picked up in chapter 6. For now let it simply be recognized that a steady state neo-classical growth model, based as it is on the presumed existence of polypoly in the extreme Walrasian sense, involves more than one inherent contradiction. Not only is the growth of the economy likely to be erratic due to the manner in which expansion occurs - that is, through the uncoordinated entry of new firms - but, even more significant, the growth is likely to be limited by the lack of residual income, or savings, being generated internally by firms over the long run, this being a second effect of the unrestricted entry which is presumed to exist. Where, it may be asked, are the savings to come from to finance the ever higher level of investment which a steady-state growth model implies? There are, to be sure, theoretical answers to this question. But even aside from the socio-political implications of those answers,[34] one must face up to the fact that in the American economy the expansion of the business sector is financed for the most part from internal sources (see chapter 1, note 17). This calls into further question the relevance of any macrodynamic model based on the assumption that the micro-economic units within the business sector are polypolistic price takers.

Despite its limited relevance, the textbook model of Walrasian polypoly can still be derived from the oligopolistic pricing model developed in the preceding chapter. All that is necessary is that one (a) assign the value of one to the probability of entry in the long run; (b) drop the assumption that the industry price, once set, will be maintained by all the firms in the industry for the duration of the current pricing period; (c) posit that, over the relevant range of output, average variable costs are an increasing function of the rate of capacity utilization, and (d) assume the existence of a middleman network or a similar type of buyer able to engage in effective speculation against the firms which are sellers in the market. The first two modifications lead to the elimination of any corporate levy in the long run, and thus are sufficient by themselves to establish the existence of polypoly in the more limited Marshallian sense. The third modification results in a short-run supply curve that is positively sloped. Together with the first two modifications, it serves to distinguish the non-oligopolistic subsector from the oligopolistic.[35] The fourth modification is necessary only to assure that the firms in the industry are price takers and thus that the industry is polypolistic in the extreme Walrasian sense. What has thus been demonstrated is that both oligopoly and polypoly - not to mention monopoly, monopolistic competition and conglomerate enterprises - can all be encompassed within the general theoretical framework developed in the preceding chapter.

5. The distribution of income

Up to this point, average variable and fixed costs have been held constant so that a change in price could be analyzed in terms of a change in the margin above costs, or average corporate levy. Now the procedure is to be reversed. The average corporate levy will be held constant so that a change in price can be analyzed in terms of a change in average variable and fixed costs.

This shift in focus bears on more than just the pricing policies of the megacorp. It touches on the distribution of income, for the change in average variable and fixed costs which is to be emphasized in this chapter is the change that occurs when the rates of compensation paid by the megacorp to those who supply it with essential inputs or otherwise have a claim to a portion of its revenues are revised, usually upward. Any such increase in the rates of compensation received by certain of the megacorp's constituencies will be one element in the ongoing dynamic that characterizes pricing behavior in the oligopolistic sector of the economy. The other element, at least insofar as costs are concerned, pertains to the secular growth of output per worker. This windfall from technological progress is not to be confused with the change in productivity which occurs when various inputs are used in different combinations. The latter is essentially a short-run phenomenon, and is precluded, in the present analysis, by the assumption of fixed technical coefficients.[1] What is to be taken into account here is rather the change in productivity which occurs when technological progress makes it possible to achieve greater output over the long run with the same, or a similar, fixed combination of inputs. Normally this increase in output per worker serves to offset, at least in part, the increase in the rates of compensation paid by the megacorp to its several constituencies, and for this reason it is an integral part of the pricing dynamic. Indeed, as will subsequently be brought out, the increase in the rates of compensation which the megacorp is required to pay will, to some extent, depend on the secular rise in output per worker. The precise nature of this interrelationship and its impact on the cost structure of the megacorp are the principal subject matter of this chapter and the next two.

Thus, while chapter 3 sought to determine the amount of residual income which the megacorp would attempt to gain for itself as an organization, this chapter will take up the question of how, independently of that sum, the megacorp's revenue is apportioned among certain of its constituencies, in particular, the laboring manpower force and the equity debt holders. It is thus concerned with the distribution of income within the megacorp and, on a larger scale, with the distribution of the income originating in the oligopolistic sector of the American economy.

The chapter will take up, in turn, each of the major theories of income distribution which have at one time or another found favor among social scientists, this with the aim of accertaining the extent to which they pertain to the megacorp. These major theories are (1) the marginal productivity theory of conventional, neo-classical analysis; (2) the power-focused theory of the institutionalists; (3) the normative theory of the medieval scholastics and latter day sociologists; (4) the surplus value theory of Marx, and (5) the aggregate demand-related theory that has emerged in the wake of the Keynesian revolution in economics.[2] From these various theories an eclectic model will be developed to explain changes in the rate of compensation received, first, by the megacorp's laboring manpower force and, second, by its equity debt holders. It is the change in these two rates of compensation which, with a fixed rate of growth of output per worker, will determine the change in the megacorp-price leader's average variable and fixed costs from one pricing period to the next and hence, with the corporate levy held constant, the change in the industry price level over that interval.

Marginal productivity theory

The most widely taught, if not the most widely held, theory of income distribution in the Western world is the marginal productivity theory developed by the neo-classical economists (Ferguson, 1969; Schumpeter, 1955, pp. 909-24; Stigler, 1941; Kaldor, 1955-6). According to this, the conventional theory, each factor of production will receive as compensation for its services the value of its marginal product. More specifically, it will receive the market value of the increment of output made possible by the employment of the last additional unit of that factor in the production process.

The marginal productivity theory, it should be noted, has several characteristics that particularly recommend it to economists, both those with purely academic interests and those with certain political proclivities. First, it can be applied to any factor of production, whether it be a member of the laboring manpower force, a piece of capital equipment or even a natural resource such as land. No matter what the input may be, its rate of compensation will, according to the theory, be equal to the value of its marginal product. This, by eliminating the need for separate theories to explain different factor shares, greatly simplifies the analysis of income distribution (cf. Tobin, 1960; see also Kaldor, 1960b). Second, the marginal productivity theory readily lends itself to mathematical treatment using calculus. Assuming that all of the firm's revenue can be accounted for by the value of each factor's marginal product,[3] partial differentials can be derived to delineate the relative contribution of each input. This, aside from permitting the powerful tools of mathematics to be used, is essential to any empirical research on factor productivity. Finally, since the marginal product of any factor is determined solely by technological considerations interacting with factor endowments, the theory provides a strong argument against conscious efforts to redistribute income within the firm. To do so, it can be argued on the basis of the theory, will have an adverse effect on either output, employment or efficiency. This provides powerful intellectual support for certain political stances.

The marginal productivity theory nonetheless has a serious defect. Its usefulness in analyzing the distribution of income in a modern, technologically sophisticated society such as that of the United States is, to say the least, questionable. This is a point which has been made many times before - most recently by the Cambridge, England, critics of neo-classical growth models[4] - and there is no need to repeat all of those arguments here. What perhaps does need to be brought out is the precise way in which the special characteristics of the megacorp limit the relevance of marginal productivity theory, at least insofar as the oligopolistic sector is concerned - why, in fact, the theory cannot be used to explain (a) the relative rates of compensation received by different members of the laboring manpower force; (b) the relative rates of compensation received by different capital debt holders, and (c) the relative rates of compensation received on the one hand by the laboring manpower force as a whole and on the other hand by the capital debt holders *en masse*. These very considerable shortcomings of marginal productivity theory, it will be shown, can be traced to (1) the bureaucratic nature of the megacorp; (2) the distinction between the marginal efficiency of investment and the value of a capital good's marginal product, and (3) the fixed nature of the technical coefficients governing production by the megacorp in the short run.

The laboring manpower force attached to a megacorp is not simply an undifferentiated mass, as is generally assumed in the conventional analysis, but in fact consists of individuals with quite numerous and varied skills. The division of labor which such a heterogeneous work force makes possible is a major source of the megacorp's manifest productivity. If individuals so numerous and varied in their skills are to work together effectively, however, they must be governed by a set of rules and relationships. It is the latter, defining who are each employee's superiors and subordinates - that is, the persons from whom he takes direction and the persons to whom he gives direction - that constitute the megacorp's bureaucratic structure.

Once established, a bureaucratic structure can be expected to set rather narrow limits within which may vary the relative rates of compensation received by different members of the laboring manpower force. If organizational morale is to be maintained, employees must be paid a wage or salary that is at the same time both higher than that received by their subordinates and lower than that received by their superiors. Of course, if two individuals are both supervised by the same person (or by two different persons of equal rank) and thus are peers within the bureaucratic structure, the higher wage or salary will most likely go to the individual whose job requires the greater skill, physical exertion, responsibility or risk to his health (cf. Reynolds, 1964, pp. 503-8, especially p. 504 fn7; Sibson, 1960). Similarly, if two individuals perform functions which are essentially identical and thus fall within the same job classification, the higher wage or salary will most likely go to the individual with more years of service to the company. But these are only qualifications to the more general rule governing relative rates of compensation within a bureaucratic structure. The distribution of income among the laboring manpower force depends, then, not on marginal contributions to the firm's overall revenue - contributions which, due to the group nature of most work activity, cannot in any case be ascertained - but rather, on relative position within the corporate hierarchy. It is the differential rates of compensation thus determined that constitute what is referred to as the internal wage structure of the laboring manpower force (Livernash, 1957). This internal wage structure, in turn, is what makes it possible to speak of *the* rate of compensation received by the laboring manpower force as a whole - for an increase in that overall rate of compensation simply means an increase in each of the separate rates that make up the internal wage structure.[5]

The inability of marginal productivity theory to explain the relative rates of compensation received by various capital debt holders derives from a somewhat different source - the generally ignored distinction between the marginal efficiency of capital and the value of the marginal product of capital goods. The capital debt holders, it should be kept in mind, do not themselves contribute anything directly to the production process but rather simply provide funds so that certain types of physical resources can be purchased and used by the firm. These capital goods are as heterogeneous as the skills of the laboring manpower force (Sraffa, 1960; Lachman, 1956). What makes it possible to treat the capital debt holders as a homogeneous body is the presumption that the funds they supply, when used to purchase capital goods, will all add the same increment to the firm's total revenue. In other words, it can be assumed that a dollar provided by one capital debt holder will, at the margin, have the same value to the firm as a dollar provided by another capital debt holder - or even a dollar provided by the firm itself from internal sources. This being the case, the firm should be willing to pay each and every capital debt holder a rate of compensation equal to that increment in total revenue - or, in other words, a rate of compensation equal to the marginal efficiency of investment.

Superficially, this might seem to be but an application of marginal productivity theory. The marginal efficiency of investment, however, is not the same as the value of the marginal product of capital goods. The latter represents the change in the firm's total revenue that occurs as the quantity of capital goods is varied, holding all other inputs constant. It thus reflects the greater physical productivity of that factor - it being possible to determine how much of the additional output is to be attributed to the capital goods alone only because the influence of the other inputs has, in effect, been neutralized by holding them constant. The marginal efficiency of investment, however, need not imply that the quantity of other inputs remains unchanged. In fact, the amount of capital goods and the amount of other inputs used in the production process may both be increased together - the marginal efficiency of investment, in this case, simply reflecting the anticipated growth in the firm's total revenue after the cost of those other inputs has been taken into account. It is for this reason that it is possible to specify a marginal efficiency of investment even if, as will soon be pointed out, the factor coefficients are fixed and the value of the marginal product of capital goods cannot therefore be separately determined.

The megacorp's capital debt holders, it should also be kept in mind, comprise two major classes. On the one hand there are those whose debt holdings consist of fixed-interest obligations. In return for supplying the firm with investment funds, they become contractually entitled to an unvarying amount of compensation equal to the marginal efficiency of investment at the time the commitment of funds is made, less the cost of brokerage services and the premium required, if any, to offset the risk to the executive group from an increase in fixed-interest obligations (see above, pp. 86-7). Since the marginal efficiency of investment can be expected to vary over time - even if new long-term debt is entered into only infrequently - different groups of fixed-interest debt holders will, as viewed from the perspective of the megacorp, be receiving different rates of compensation, depending on the dates at which they have provided the firm with investment funds.[6]

On the other hand, there are those whose debt holdings consist of equity shares. In return for supplying the firm with investment funds, they become implicitly entitled to a rate of compensation in the form of dividends which, though initially less than that received by the fixed-interest debt holders, can nonetheless be expected to increase over time. Precisely what determines the growth of the dividend rate from one year to the next will be discussed at some length later in this chapter. All that need be noted at this point is that the upper limit will depend on whether previously projected returns from investment are being realized, the lower limit on the non-economic pressure which the equity debt holders are able to bring to bear on the executive group through their right, acting collectively, to depose the incumbent management. If the megacorp were managed entirely in the interest of its putative owners, the equity debt holders could, of course, be confident that all of the increment in revenue would accrue to them - eventually, if not in the short run - and the lower limit would, in that case, be the same as the upper limit (see above, pp. 25-7, 52-4, as well as the discussion below in this chapter, pp. 164-72).

The distribution of income among the capital debt holders depends, then, not on the marginal productivities of the capital goods which their funds have enabled the megacorp to purchase at various points in time but rather on the marginal efficiency of investment over the years, both *ex ante* and ex post, as well as the non-economic power of the equity debt holders *vis-à-vis* the executive group. It is the relative rates of compensation thus determined that constitute what may be termed the megacorp's capital cost or external debt structure. However, since the fixed obligations, once entered into, are invariate, only the equity portion of this capital cost structure need be taken into account in considering changes in relative income shares. An increase in *the* rate of compensation received by the capital debt holders means therefore an increase in the dividend rate.

Though marginal productivity theory has been shown to be inapplicable to both the laboring manpower force and the capital debt holders as separate entities, the theory may nonetheless be capable of explaining the division of the firm's total revenue between these two principal constituencies. In other words, if the assumption is made that production is carried out with only two composite inputs, one supplied by the laboring manpower force and the other by the capital debt holders, it may then be possible to determine the value of the marginal product of each of those two inputs on the basis of marginal productivity theory, the respective rates of compensation being equal to the value of the two marginal products. This possibility is precluded, however, by one of the characteristics of the megacorp already emphasized - the fixed nature of the technical coefficients governing production in the short run (see above, pp. 28-30). As Stigler (1939) pointed out many years ago, the marginal productivity theory of income distribution becomes inoperative if these coefficients are invariate, 'since it is not [then] possible, by incremental analysis, to impute productivities'.[7] The same point applies, of course, even to the distribution of income among the members of the laboring manpower force, insofar as men of different skills must be used in fixed combinations, and to the distribution of income among the capital debt holders, insofar as machines of different types must also be used in fixed combinations (Finkel and Tarascio, 1969). It thus reinforces the earlier arguments about the inapplicability of marginal productivity to the short-run determination of relative rates of compensation within each of the megacorp's two principal constituencies.

Granted, marginal productivity theory may not be so inapplicable to the longer run situation. As already stressed, the megacorp will be in the process of continually adding new plant and equipment, both to replace existing facilities which have become obsolescent and to make it possible to meet any likely increase in future industry demand. This new plant and equipment will embody the technology compatible with current trends in relative factor prices. Thus, if the price of labor has been growing relative to the cost of capital - as has been the recent historical experience in the Western world for reasons which, as will eventually be pointed out, are inherent in a progressing economy - the demand will be for capital equipment which is labor saving. While the evolution of technology is subject to laws other than economic, a general tendency will nonetheless be discernible for the new equipment being developed by the manufacturers of capital goods to involve the substitution of capital for labor in the manner suggested by marginal productivity theory.[8] However, what the marginal productivity theory purports to explain in this long-run situation is not the distribution of income among the various factors of production but rather, given certain trends in relative factor prices, the combination of inputs that will be used in the production process (Dunlop, 1957). To pretend that it is more than simply a theory of factor proportions is to place more intellectual weight on marginal productivity analysis than the theory is capable of holding. If one wishes to understand the distribution of income, in the long run as well as for shorter periods of time, it is necessary to turn to other explanations.

Power theory

The distribution of income being indeterminate on the economic grounds stressed by marginal productivity theory, it might seem reasonable to conclude that the division of the megacorp's revenue will be decided, as certain of the institutional economists have suggested, by the power - non-economic as well as economic - which the various claimants can bring to bear in a bargaining process. As the lawyer Robert Hale has put it,

> All incomes, in the last analysis, whether derived from ownership of property or from personal services, are not products created by the recipients; they are payments derived from the rest of the community by the exertion of some sort of pressure. To say this is not to condemn the exertion of such pressure; it is the only means a man has, under present arrangements, and perhaps under any workable scheme of things, for keeping alive . . . The justification of each income must rest on some other ground than that the recipient has produced it. (Tugwell, 1924, quoted in Gambs, 1946, p. 12.)

The view of the institutional economists is that this struggle over who will receive what share of the available income is waged, not by atomistic individuals in the market place but rather, by organized social groups operating within an institutional framework that includes value systems, political mechanisms and the law. To pursue this line of inquiry it is therefore necessary to specify the organized social groups and the institutional framework relevant to the distribution of the megacorp's revenue.

Actually, only one additional organization, aside from the megacorp itself, need be introduced at this point. This is the industrial trade union which is likely to represent a substantial portion of the megacorp's production work force[9] - that is, the workers who are directly involved in the production process and who are generally paid on an hourly basis. As an organization, the trade union can be expected to have goals of its own, separate and distinct from those of its members. Still, if it is to retain the loyalty and support of the rank and file, and thus remain a viable entity, it must take as its primary function the pressing of those workers' claims against the megacorp. This it can be expected to do through a process of collective bargaining, with the trade union leadership periodically sitting as an equal across the table from the representatives of the company to work out mutually acceptable arrangements. While the trade union cannot be said to speak for all of the megacorp's laboring manpower force - and perhaps not even for all of its production workers - it will nonetheless be the key social agent, together with the megacorp itself, for determining the compensation to be paid employees. This is because the bargain reached between the union and the megacorp will set the wage standard for the entire laboring manpower force. Indeed, whatever gains are won by the trade union for its members are likely to be extended, almost as a matter of course, to all other employees since any other policy would lead to greater disaffection, higher turnover rates and, eventually, an increase in the percentage of the laboring manpower force represented by a trade union.

The same argument applies to megacorps whose employees, for some reason, have not yet been organized by any trade union. These megacorps, too, in order to keep the trade unions out of their plants, can be expected to extend to their employees whatever wage gains are won by the organized workers in their branch of industry or in similar skill categories (see, for example, Rosen, 1969). It is for this reason that the assumption made implicitly throughout the rest of this treatise, thai every megacorp faces a trade union in collective bargaining, is not an unreasonable one to make even though there are a number of exceptions within the oligopolistic sector.

The capital debt holders, on the other hand, are not likely to be as highly organized as the unionized portion of the laboring manpower force - except in unusual circumstances, as for example when the megacorp defaults on its fixed-interest obligations and a bondholders committee is formed.[10] There are two reasons for this lesser reliance on formal associations. One is the existence of a well-organized capital funds market which enables capital debt holders, especially those owning stock, to sell out and obtain some other financial asset instead when they are dissatisfied with their treatment by the megacorp. The other reason is the close identification with the capital debt holders that the megacorp's executive group is likely to have - a point which will be elaborated on shortly. The megacorp's other constituencies are even less formally structured - with several notable exceptions. For example, the automobile and retail gasoline dealers, virtual satellites of the megacorps from which they must obtain their products, have in certain cases set up associations in order to increase their bargaining power. However, these associations are generally more concerned about the terms of the franchise agreements than the prices they must pay for the product. Conspicuous is the absence of any formal organization to represent the interests of the general consuming public, that is, the household sector.

Thus the analysis of the power relationships determining the distribution of the megacorp's revenue - once the cost of material inputs and of future investments have been met - need only be concerned with the process of collective bargaining between two organized social groups, the industrial trade union representing a significant portion of the laboring force and the megacorp itself. It is the agreement reached/between these two contending parties that is the single most important factor determining the apportionment of the megacorp's revenue. Again, in examining a particular industry, it is sufficient to focus on the price leader alone, since the settlement reached between it and the trade union will in most cases set the pattern for the industry as a whole.[11]

While there is no generally accepted theory of bargaining comparable to the marginal productivity theory of income distribution, there is wide agreement that such a theory must indicate, first, the objective market forces which set the limits within which bargaining will take place and, second, the subjective factors (or states of minds of the negotiators) which will determine the actual agreement that is reached.[12] In the case of contract negotiations between a megacorp-price leader and an industrial trade union, the range of possible agreement is bounded, on the one hand, by how low the megacorp can push wage rates without losing the labor services it needs and, on the other hand, by how high the trade union can push those same wage rates without jeopardizing the employment of its members. These objective constraints on the bargaining process - or 'competition limits on the contract zone', as Pen (1959, p. 61) terms them - still leave considerable room for discretion, however.

Even if the trade union were so weak that the megacorp-price leader could impose whatever settlement terms it wished, the wages received by the members of the trade union could not fall below what those workers could earn from alternative employment outside the industry. Were the rate of compensation to be set below this floor, the megacorp would find itself losing at least part of its manpower laboring force and, insofar as the technical coefficients are fixed, forced to cut back proportionately on production. The objective lower limit on the rate of compensation that is to be negotiated will therefore be determined by conditions in the labor markets outside the oligopolistic industry.

This floor on wages will be considerably below the current rate of compensation, both because of the specialized knowledge which the trade union's members are able to exploit on their current jobs and because of the past gains won by the trade union. This means that, unless the megacorp's management is prepared to insist on substantial wage cuts, the floor set by market forces will have no influence on the actual negotiations. Yet the historical experience indicates that a megacorp's management is unlikely to insist on a wage cut - even a small one - except under the same depressed business conditions that lead to substantial price cutting. For this reason it is perhaps more useful to regard the lower limit on the negotiations as being the current rate of compensation, a limit determined by subjective factors still to be explained rather than by objective market forces.

At the same time, if the megacorp-price leader were so weak that the trade union could impose whatever settlement terms it wished, the wages received by its members could not rise above the point where either at existing price levels no revenue was left to meet other contractual obligations or, alternatively, the amortized cost of obtaining and training a new work force was less than the cost of the settlement. If wages were to be pushed up to the point where no revenue was left to meet other contractual obligations, the megacorp would be forced into receivership, thereby nullifying the trade union's claims to a larger share of the revenue. On the other hand, if the amortized cost of obtaining and training a new labor force were less than the cost of the settlement, the megacorp could simply dismiss or lock out its present organized labor force, thereby eliminating the need for further collective bargaining. Which of these two conditions will impose the ceiling on negotiations will, of course, depend on which is encountered first.

No matter what the ceiling is, however, the trade union will still be able, within that objective upper limit, to secure a substantial increase in the rate of compensation for its members. On the one hand, the cost of obtaining and training a new work force to replace the organized one will be considerable - if not prohibitive. While the American economy usually operates with somewhat more slack than that of most Western European countries (cf. Shonfield, 1965, pp. 11-18; Sorrentino, 1972), it is nonetheless doubtful whether the large number of organized workers employed in a typical oligopolistic industry could be immediately replaced *en masse* at existing rates of compensation. Moreover, even if the replacements could be found, it is doubtful whether they could be brought up to the skill and efficiency level of the old work force without a long period of on-the-job training. On the other hand, the portion of the megacorp's revenue currently earmarked for investment and the payment of dividends could all be diverted to increased compensation for the manpower laboring force - or for the organized work force alone - without immediately endangering the company's solvency.

What is more - and it is this condition which uniquely characterizes the bargaining environment of the megacorp - the trade union will be able to secure a substantial increase in wages without any offsetting loss of employment, at least in the short run. For insofar as the megacorp operates with fixed technical coefficients, employment after the increase in compensation will be the same as it was before. Of course, in the long run, when the existing plants and equipment have been scrapped in favor of new machinery embodying more capital intensive methods of production, the effect of the higher wages on employment will be felt. But if in the long run not all union members are dead, some will have retired and others will have moved on to other jobs. Even if the goal is to maintain a stable union membership and thus to protect the viability of the organization, union officials will find that the jobs lost through the adoption of labor-saving technology may be more than made up for by the jobs created through the coincidental growth of demand as a result of population and real income trends (Finkel and Terascio, 1969). While it can be argued that union membership will still be less than it would have been had the increase in wages not stimulated the development of more capital intensive production methods, it is questionable whether this long-run consideration is one which does and ought to influence the union's bargaining position.[13]

The significance of the fact that an increase in the rate of compensation leaves employment unaffected, at least in the short run, is that it removes what has sometimes been thought to be the principal restraint on trade union demands. For whatever it is that the trade union is assumed to want to maximize - whether it be individual wages, short-term employment, the total wage bill or some variant of these three (cf. Dunlop, 1950, pp. 32-50) - the goal is consistent with a rate of compensation equal to the objective upper limit specified above, provided that factor coefficients are fixed.

That upper limit, together with the lower limit previously discussed, provide such a wide range within which the actual rate of compensation can fall that is questionable whether, by themselves, they explain very much about the outcome of the negotiations between the megacorp and the trade union. Given this wide range, it is necessary to focus on the non-market factors influencing the collective bargaining process.

Within the competition limits of the contract zone the power relationships emphasized by the institutional economists might at first seem to be determining. The economic strength of the two parties (the resources they can draw upon in the event of a strike), their political strength (the support they can expect to receive both from government and various social groups), their psychological state (the degree of internal cohesion and fastness to bargaining goals), the individual bargaining skill of the respective negotiators and - most important - how the negotiators evaluate these factors subjectively would appear to be crucial to the outcome of the bargaining. Yet, even when all these elements of power have been taken into account, the fact remains that, as the system of collective bargaining has developed in the United States, neither of the two parties can be compelled to agree to any particular rate of compensation.

Both the typical megacorp and the typical union have such ample resources at their command that, except for an improbably long strike, they need take little account of the debilitating effect that an extended struggle may have on their respective strengths. Indeed, they are likely to carefully marshal their resources before the negotiations so as not to be limited by that consideration. The support which the two parties can expect to receive from government and various social groups is, meanwhile, best regarded as a supervening element in the bargaining situation, this factor historically determining the legal climate in which negotiations are conducted. Currently, the legal climate dictates that - with certain notable exceptions - neither government representatives nor any third party intervene directly to force a settlement on one of the parties. In other words, compulsory arbitration of the differences between the megacorp and the trade union over the rate of compensation is at present precluded by law.[14] Finally, the psychological states of the parties, the individual bargaining skill of their respective negotiators and the subjective evaluation of these factors would appear to be little more than random factors which cancel themselves out over time and across sample populations. Thus, while the power relationships pointed out by the institutional economists will not be absent, they are more properly treated as parameters of the collective bargaining process (cf. Pen, 1959, pp. 98-112; Coddington, 1968, pp. 68-70, 77-80). This means that still another theory must be invoked, at least as a complement, to explain the share of the megacorp's revenue received by the laboring manpower force - not to mention the share received by the megacorp's other principal constituency, the capital debt holders.

Normative theory

It being impossible to erect a model on the power relationships alone, one must ask whether there is some additional element in the collective bargaining situation which determines the nature of the settlement reached between the two parties and thus helps to explain the division of the megacorp's revenue among its principal constituencies. Such an element would be the existence of an external standard of compensation to which both the megacorp and the trade union could be expected to give obeisance, even if they could not be compelled to accept it. This would imply a normative theory of income distribution similar to that propounded by the medieval scholastics with their notion of a 'just' or 'fair' price. To pursue this line of inquiry it is necessary, first, to specify what that external standard of compensation might be and, second, to indicate the extent to which it is likely to be consistent with the divergent goals which both the megacorp and the trade union carry with them into collective bargaining. The point at which to begin this task is with a consideration of the latter, the goals which the megacorp and trade union are likely to pursue in collective bargaining.

These particular goals will, of course, depend on the more general goals which the megacorp-price leader and the industrial trade union pursue as ongoing institutions. The previous chapters have already argued that, insofar as the megacorp-price leader is concerned, its objective within a given industry will be to maintain and perhaps even increase its relative share of the market. This can be viewed as the derivative of a larger goal common to all such institutions, to grow at the maximum rate and, if nothing else is possible, at least to preserve the organization as a functioning entity. The trade union can be presumed to pursue the same general goal, with the particular objective of maintaining and perhaps even increasing the proportion of the laboring manpower force - or rather the proportion of the production work force - which it represents.[15] The leaders of the trade union will seek first and foremost to preserve their organization as a functioning entity for the same reason that the meggacorp's executives will seek to preserve theirs: whatever status they have in the larger community will be but a reflection of the power and prestige enjoyed by the trade union they head. And while it is even more difficult to determine empirically the behavioral pattern of the trade union than it is to determine that of the megacorp, the logical connection between the proportion of the production work force which the trade union represents and the ability of the trade union to survive as a functioning entity can be well demonstrated.

For one thing, the income which the trade union receives, that is, the economic resources which it can potentially command, will be a function of the number of persons included in the various collective bargaining units it represents. The more workers it covers, whether formally enrolled in the union or not,[16] the larger will be the amount of dues which it collects. Second, and perhaps even more crucial, the trade union must be able to count on the loyalty of a certain minimum number of workers, that is, be assured they will follow its orders to stay off the job, if it is to have effective bargaining power. Unless this critical degree of response by the workers can be assured, the trade union will be unable to bring a halt to production by the megacorp and will therefore lack the *quid pro quo* to exact an agreement from the megacorp's management.

Of course, the response of the workers to the trade union's strike call will depend, at least in part, on the trade union's past success in achieving gains for its members. It will thus be a complex set of interdependent factors that will have historically determined the degree of 'solidarity', as the trade union officials themselves term it, which the labor organization currently enjoys. The points to be noted here are that the trade unions which typically represent the production work force in oligopolistic industries will already have achieved sufficient solidarity to be able to bring production to a halt, and that given the importance of this solidarity, they will insist on obtaining through collective bargaining a contract which does not endanger or diminish the loyalty of their members. In other words, as the trade union officials themselves express it, they want a contract they can 'live with'.

The question still remains, however, as to what kind of contract trade union officials can live with. Such a contract, it should first be pointed out, will contain many provisions, only a small number of which will pertain to the rate of compensation (defined to include fringe benefits and other labor cost items). This chapter will ignore all the other provisions - though much the same type of analysis could be applied to them. Thus it is only one part of the contract, and a minor part at that, with which this chapter will be concerned. So delimited, the contract which trade union officials can live with is a contract containing satisfactory provisions affecting the rate of compensation. In the words of trade union officials, it is a contract which provides an 'equitable' wage.

The concept of equity is a sociological rather than an economic one. That is, it reflects the normative values of a society or a particular subgroup within the society, these values resulting from the social interaction of its members rather than from the balancing of objective market forces. A theory of income distribution based on the concept of equity has not been fashionable among economists since certain of the mercantilist writers began to question the usefulness of the medieval notion of a 'just' price (Roll, 1942, pp. 99-107; Schumpeter, 1955, ch. 2). A normative theory based on traditional values was, of course, hardly likely to prove useful in a society starting to undergo rapid economic development, a process which in itself tends to undermine established norms. Still, the fact that social philosophers once paid too little attention to the forces of supply and demand is no reason why economists should in turn ignore the role played by social values, whether traditional or otherwise, in the market process.

Economists have been able to close their eyes to this factor because they have implicitly assumed that most of the important markets were of such wide scope, covering so large a territory or so many disparate individuals, that the social interaction necessary to develop a consensus on values would be lacking, particularly in view of the rapid changes likely to be occurring in the underlying material endowment. Of course, the more thoughtful members of the profession have recognized that where markets were narrowly circumscribed, social values - or 'custom' - might play a prominent role. This was particularly likely to be true, they realized, with regard to labor markets, these tending to be essentially local in character. (cf. Mill, 1965, Book II, ch. 4; Marshall, 1920, Book I, chs. 2 and 3).

Important as this acknowledgement of the role played by social values may be, it would seem to have little relevance to the problem at hand - namely, the determination of a rate of compensation through collective bargaining. For the large number of megacorps and trade union officials involved in such negotiations, their dissimilar interests and their lack of continuing personal contact with each other would seem to preclude the type of social interaction necessary if a general consensus as to what constitutes an 'equitable' wage is to develop. Indeed, under the circumstances, it would seem that social values would be able to play a role in the determination of wages through collective bargaining only if there were an institutional arrangement to make up for the lack of continuing personal contact among the parties to the negotiations. Yet in the United States no formal arrangement of this sort exists. There is no meeting 'at the top', such as there is in Sweden, between the trade union organization representing all blue-collar workers and the management organization representing all employers to determine, in accordance with nationally planned economic objectives, a wage pattern for the country as a whole. Nor is there a system of compulsory arbitration enforced by the courts, such as there is in Australia, to accomplish the same end (Roberts, 1958, ch. 6; A. Weber, 1963; Turner and Zoeteweij, 1966, ch. 5). In the absence of any such formal arrangement, it has been necessary in the United States to fall back on an informal system, one that is based on the national incremental wage pattern established in certain 'bellwether' industries through a 'key' bargain.

The remainder of this chapter will explain how power and normative factors together determine the rate of growth of compensation for the megacorp's two principal constituencies, the laboring manpower force and the equity debt holders, through the intervening mechanism of the national incremental wage pattern. First the nature of the national incremental wage pattern and its influence on wage rates within the oligopolistic sector will be described. Next the effect which acceptance of the wage pattern is likely to have on the megacorp's cost structure, including dividends, will be analyzed. Finally, the extent to which those higher costs can be passed on to customers through a rise in price will be brought out. While two additional theories, the Marxian and the Keynesian, still remain to be woven into the argument before the explanation can be considered complete, an appreciation of the role played by the national incremental wage pattern is the critical first step in understanding the distribution of income within the megacorp.

The national incremental wage pattern. The norm as to what constitutes a 'fair and equitable' increase in wages is, under ordinary circumstances, established through the collective bargaining agreement reached in one of the 'bellwether' industries. Since the end of World War II, a period in which trade unions in the United States have been able to demonstrate their enduring nature and a period in which therefore the informal system has emerged, these 'bellwether' industries have at various times been automobiles and steel. The choice of these two industries reflects the fact that the parties to collective bargaining - both the industrial trade unions and the megacorp-price leaders in automobiles and steel - are at the same time among the strongest economically of their kind and the most evenly matched. It is as though the two sides to the historic class struggle between labor and capital (or rather, in the modern context, between labor and management) have each selected their most powerful member to act as champion in the periodic jousting over the division of the national income. While the industrial trade unions and the megacorp-price leaders in automobiles and steel are perhaps best equipped to don the colors of labor and management at present, changing economic fortunes could in the future bring the industrial trade union and megacorp-price leader of some other industry into the lists.

Several factors serve to convert the wage settlement reached in the bellwether industry - the so-called 'key' bargain - into a national standard of what constitutes a 'fair' or 'equitable' percentage increase in the rate of compensation for the organized laboring manpower force. This percentage increase in compensation, W_p, is what is meant by the national incremental wage pattern. One of the factors which serves to convert the 'key' bargain into a national standard is the existence of what Dunlop (1957, pp. 17-20) has called 'wage contours' - groups of industries 'linked together (a) by similarity of product markets, (b) by resort to similar sources for a labor force, or (c) by common labor market organization and/or the recognition that they have common wage-making characteristics'.

The most important of these wage contours in the United States is the group of capital intensive, mass production industries which Soffer (1959) has labeled the 'auto-steel orbit'. It includes, in addition to automobiles and steel, the aluminum, agricultural implements, electrical equipment, rubber and flat glass industries. Besides the features already mentioned, these industries share in common certain important input-output relationships and a similar geographical concentration in the Midwest. To the above list could be added the air frame, petroleum refining, meatpacking, shipbuilding, and copper industries. These have many of the same characteristics as the members of the auto-steel orbit including, most important, the fact that they are oligopolistically structured with a large proportion of their production work force organized into powerful industrial trade unions.

Because of the national base of comparison which these common features provide, it is difficult for the firms in one industry not to grant the same percentage increase in the rage of compensation, W_p, which has already been obtained from firms in another industry within this enlarged auto-steel orbit. The invidious distinctions which would otherwise be created would serve as a constant source of worker grievances, and the trade union leadership could not fail to respond to resentment over the issue. In the absence of any objective guide as to how high wages should be set, trade union leaders can be expected to seize upon any such 'inequity', making the elimination of that inequity their prime goal in collective bargaining. In this way, the pattern which is established in the bellwether industry - whether automobiles or steel - eventually comes to be adopted by all the members of the group (Maher, 1961; Eckstein and Wilson, 1962; Eckstein, 1968; Ripley, 1966).

Since the industries forming this principal wage contour employ nearly half of all production workers in oligopolistic industries,[17] the wage settlement reached in the bellwether industry is, for this reason alone, quite likely to become the national norm as to what constitutes an 'equitable' percentage increase in the rate of compensation received by workers. In addition to this private obeisance, however, there is the further recognition often given the bellwether industry's wage settlement by the Federal government itself.

Because of the responsibility which it has assumed for the orderly functioning of the economy, the Federal government frequently finds itself forced to intervene in the labor disputes that arise in either of the two bellwether industries. On the one hand, if the parties remain deadlocked so that a strike ensues and production within the industry comes to a halt, the aggregate output of goods and services may be seriously impaired. On the other hand, since a change in the rate of compensation in the bellwether industry is likely, as will soon be argued, to affect the price level in all oligopolistic industries, a settlement may have significant inflationary consequences. Since neither of these two possibilities are without their disruptive effect on the economy, the Federal government will be forced by political considerations to try to influence the outcome of the collective bargaining in the bellwether industry. But by so intervening - whether by the threat to issue a Taft-Hartley injunction, by the release of statements to the public, or by one of the other methods that are used to sway the positions of the two parties - the Federal government acknowledges that what is being established is a national norm as to what constitutes an 'equitable' percentage increase in the rate of compensation for members of the organized laboring manpower force throughout the economy.

The time that elapses between the setting of a wage pattern in the bellwether industry, as described above, and its replacement by a new wage pattern is sometimes referred to as a 'wage round'. It may consist of one or more contract renewals, a new wage round occurring only when a different basis for determining the rate of compensation in the bellwether industry has been agreed to. Thus, if the pattern of settlement in two consecutive negotiations has been an increase in wages and other benefits of 4 per cent each year, the signing of a new contract in the bellwether industry calling for an increase in wages and other benefits of 5.5 per cent each year thereafter over the life of the contract will mark the beginning of a new wage round with W_p equal to 5.5. A number of such wage rounds can be clearly discerned in the post World War II period from the available data.[18]

What has been said so far has been intended simply to point out how a national norm for wages most typically emerges; it has not been intended to show how the actual wages in a particular oligopolistic industry are determined. In this connection, it should be noted that because of the unique role accorded the contract negotiations in the automobile and steel industries, those deliberations cannot be taken as being typical of collective bargaining in the United States. Since it is by means of those negotiations that a national incremental wage pattern is usually established, the contract negotiations in one of those two industries will ordinarily have to be conducted without the aid of any wage norm. Moreover, since what is in effect being determined is the distribution of the nominal increment in the national income between the laboring manpower force (and, indirectly, as will soon be brought out, the equity debt holders as well) on the one hand and all megacorps on the other hand, it is particularly difficult for a settlement to be reached - unless, of course, a wage norm has already been established through some other means, for example, through government action. On what basis the key bargain will, in fact, be struck in the absence of such an exogenously determined wage norm will be brought out later. All that need be noted here is that collective bargaining in the automobile and steel industries is unrepresentative of the process whereby the rate of compensation is determined in other oligopolistic industries.

These other industries begin with the point of reference provided by the national incremental wage pattern, W_p. Insofar as this increase in the rate of compensation is viewed by the leaders of the trade union in a particular oligopolistic industry as being 'fair and equitable', and thus compatible with the continued existence and growth of their organization, it is likely to constitute the minimum wage terms to which they will, in the absence of a strike, agree. But will it also constitute the maximum wage terms to which the megacorp-price leader's management will agree? This will depend on how, in the eyes of the executive group, the increase in the rate of compensation will - if granted - affect the megacorp's ability to achieve its own long-run goals. The answer, it can be shown, will depend on (a) the impact of the increase in the rate of compensation on the megacorp's cost structure, and (b) whether the resulting increase in costs can be offset by an increase in the industry price level.

Impact on the cost structure. In considering the impact which acceptance of the national incremental wage pattern will have on the megacorp's cost structure, it is necessary to focus separately on the average variable costs and on the fixed costs. With respect to the former, the task of developing an estimate is somewhat simplified if the megacorp has a policy of automatically granting to the rest of the production work force the same percentage increase in compensation as that obtained by the trade union for its members - and there is good reason to believe that, even aside from the need to forestall further trade union inroads, this will, in fact, generally be the case (see Zeman, 1966, especially p. 1252). Under the policy of automatically granting the rest of the production work force whatever gains have been obtained by the trade union for its members, it is necessary to know only the ratio of labor compensation to total direct costs. This ratio, applied to the percentage increase in compensation established as the norm by the national incremental wage pattern, will indicate the percentage by which the megacorp's average variable costs will increase, from labor expenses alone, if it follows the lead of the bellwether industry.[19]

Wages, however, are not the only item of direct expense. Acceptance of the national incremental wage pattern may also have an impact on the cost of the megacorp's material inputs. This is especially likely if wages in the industries supplying the megacorp with its material inputs are keyed to those in the megacorp's own industry or are otherwise subject to the same general influences. In other words, an increase in the rate of compensation received by the megacorp's laboring manpower force may well lead to an increase in the firm's other direct costs. While the precise amount of this related effect cannot be known in advance - it being dependent on the prices set in other industries - certain estimates of the probable rise in material costs, based on past experience, can nonetheless be made. From what has happened on previous occasions when the trade union representing the oligopolistic industry's production work force has obtained an increase in the rate of compensation, it should be possible to estimate statistically the relationship between a rise in industry wages and the resulting change, if any, in other direct costs.[20] The full increase in average variable costs resulting from acceptance of the national incremental wage pattern will, then, reflect both the direct increase in labor costs experienced by the megacorp itself and the indirect increase in labor costs experienced through the rise in the price of material inputs.[21]

As for the impact on the fixed cost component of the overall cost structure, it should first be noted that only those indirect costs which are not fixed with respect to time - more specifically, those indirect costs which are renegotiable before the end of the next planning period - are likely to be affected. These costs consist primarily of the compensation paid overhead personnel and the dividends paid stockholders. Each will be discussed in turn.

The megacorp, again to avoid the type of disaffection which leads eventually to trade union inroads among the unorganized, can be expected to extend to most of its overhead personnel the terms of any new contract covering the organized portion of its production work force. While not all salaries paid members of the overhead work force will thus be directly keyed to the trade union agreement, a significant portion will. Two ratios, then, are needed to transform the projected increase in the rate of compensation for those covered by the agreement into a projected increase in overhead labor costs. There are (a) the ratio of the compensation paid that part of the overhead work force whose wages are keyed to the trade union agreement to total labor compensation, and (b) the ratio of overhead labor compensation to total fixed costs. These two ratios, applied to the percentage increase in compensation established as the norm by the national incremental wage pattern, will indicate the percentage by which the megacorp's total fixed costs will increase from labor expenses alone, should the megacorp follow the lead of the bellwether industry.[22] This leaves only any consequent rise in the dividend rate to be taken into account. To what extent will an increase in the rate of compensation received by the laboring manpower force lead to an increase in the dividend rate? To answer this it is necessary to face up to a crucial question which has so far been avoided - namely, what are the factors which determine the rate of compensation paid the equity debt holders?

The firm's dividend rate. The equity debt holders, though not formally organized like some segments of the laboring manpower force, are nonetheless not without recourse if they feel dissatisfied with their current and projected rates of compensation. They can, as already noted, dispose of their claims against the megacorp's revenue through one of the established stock exchanges, using the proceeds to purchase some other, presumably higher yielding asset. This response, aside from protecting the equity debt holders against the loss of their wealth, can be expected to give the megacorp's executive group pause. For if, as a result of selling pressure, the market value of the company's shares should decline, the price-dividend ratio will be lowered and thus the cost of external funds will be increased (see above pp. 86-8). Even more serious, since the megacorp is likely to be forced to resort to equity financing only rarely, the fall in the value of the company's shares will enhance the chances of a successful take-over bid by some outside party. It is this last possibility, raising as it does the spectre of a fall from power, that can be expected to weigh most heavily on the minds of those who form the executive group. At the very least, therefore, they are likely to follow a policy with respect to the growth of dividends over time that effectively protects them against the possibility of a successful take-over by some outside party. If the members of the executive group anticipate having soon to float a new equity issue, they may then be willing to exceed, at least temporarily, that minimum rate of growth in the dividend payment so as to reduce the cost of external financing.

While an outside group can seek to capture control of a megacorp through a proxy battle, that is, by persuading a majority of the equity debt holders to temporarily turn over to the outside group its voting rights, the far more practical and thus the far more prevalent method is the take-over bid.[23] This involves an announcement by the outside party that it is prepared to purchase some percentage of the company's outstanding stock, usually more than 50 per cent, at a price well above the current market quotation. Even if a proxy battle is contemplated, a take-over bid, as the only means of acquiring a sufficiently large block of stock to wage a successful campaign, may well be the necessary first step. The willingness of the outside party to pay a premium over and above the current market price presumes, however, that the group has some reason for valuing the company's outstanding shares more highly than do the current holders of those shares. The voting rights which go with the stock cannot be the reason since they are merely the means to the end - the acquisition of control. The reason must be in the control itself.

The pay-off may, of course, come in the ability of the outside party, once it acquires majority or near majority control, to replace the incumbent management group with men of its own choosing. This motivation would seem to be most applicable in the case of a conglomerate megacorp attempting to acquire by merger another established firm in an unrelated line of business.

However, given the considerable financial outlays required if a take-over bid is to be successful, it follows that the payoff must, to a considerable extent, be financial. In particular, the outside group, be it another corporation or a financier and his associates, must be able, once it acquires control, to increase the rate of growth in the dividend payment sufficiently to compensate for the price it will have to pay for the company's stock. Unless the outside group is simply seeking short-run speculative gains, it must be able to do this without reducing the rate of investment necessary to maintain the firm's growth rate in the long run and hence the higher rate of growth in dividends. The chances of the outside group being able to achieve its goals in this respect will depend on two factors: (1) whether the company is being managed as efficiently as it could be by the incumbent executive group, and (2) whether the rate of growth in dividends is as great as that of other megacorps. The two factors are not necessarily unrelated.

Managerial incompetence may be of several types. Perhaps the most generally recognized is what Harvey Leibeinstein (1966) has referred to as 'X-inefficiency' - that is, the failure to exploit all the currently available managerial techniques to achieve the highest possible output with a given set of inputs.[24] This type of incompetence is, however, particularly difficult for an outside group, especially one consisting of financiers, to discern. As long as reported net earnings, taken as a percentage of sales, do not differ significantly from those of other firms in the same industry, the X-inefficiency is virtually impossible for an outsider to detect. What is likely to be far more apparent is the failure to exploit the megacorp's investment potential - as evidenced by the continued growth of liquid assets beyond any reasonable need for a contingency reserve. The accumulated cash and other financial assets will show up prominently in the balance sheet, and there attract the attention of an outside group. Here the source of the incompetence is not inefficiency in any narrow sense but rather the inability to find a profitable outlet for the megacorp's investment funds - even if the funds are used for no better purpose than simply to purchase the company's stock in the open market.[25] When the funds invested by the megacorp, for whatever purpose, fail to bring a return sufficient to maintain the firm's long-run growth - as evidenced by a fall in the requisite rate of growth in net revenue - the underlying cause is likely to be some combination of the above two types of managerial incompetence. Whatever its precise nature, however, the existence of the incompetence offers the possibility that an outside party, by adopting better management techniques, will be able to increase the rate of compensation received by the equity debt holders without having to reduce either investment or the rates of compensation received by other constituencies. In this sense, then, the existence of managerial incompetence increases the probability of a successful take-over bid.

Alternatively, the chances of a successful take-over bid will be enhanced by the failure of the executive group to maintain the same rate of growth in dividends as other megacorps. Of course, this failure to increase dividends sufficiently might simply be an indication of managerial incompetence, especially if there is the corroborating evidence of a low rate of growth in net earnings or a low ratio of net earnings to sales. Whether it be an indication of managerial incompetence or not, however, the very fact that dividends are not growing apace with those of other megacorps will facilitate a take-over bid. When a megacorp fails to increase dividends sufficiently, it can expect to be abandoned by its equity debt holders for more promising income-earning assets. The resultant selling pressure, by depressing the price of the equity shares, will not only serve to bring about an equalization of expected future yields, it will also lower the market value of the megacorp itself. This, in turn, will enable an outside group to purchase a controlling interest in the company with a smaller financial outlay of its own. Thus, whatever the prospects of the executive group's performance being improved upon, the megacorp's failure to maintain the same rate of growth in dividends as other firms will increase the probability of a successful take-over bid (cf. Marris, 1964, ch. 1; J. Williamson, 1966).

Whether the obverse is true - that maintaining the same rate of growth in dividends as other firms will preclude the possibility of a successful take-over bid - depends on a further set of considerations. If it were true, as is commonly believed, that most other megacorps pursue policies designed to maximize the rate of growth of dividends over time, that is, if they are equity maximizers,[26] then for any one megacorp to maintain the same rate of growth in dividends as other megacorps would suffice to preclude the possibility of a successful take-over bid. An outside group, taking over control of the firm, would have no way of increasing the rate of growth of dividends over the long run and thereby make possible the permanent capital gain which is necessary if the take-over bid is to have more than just a short-run financial pay-off. But if, as has been suggested earlier in this treatise, most other megacorps in fact seek to maximize their own rates of growth *qua* organizations, that is, if they are growth maximizers, then any one megacorp may still find itself threatened by a take-over bid even though it maintains the same rate of growth in dividends as other firms. An outside group, once it gained control, would have only to shift from a growth maximizing to an equity maximizing policy to achieve a permanent increase in the capital value of the firm.

Nonetheless, there are several factors which are likely to keep the probability of a successful take-over bid below the acceptable risk level. First there are the points stressed by Marris (1964, ch. 1, especially pp. 39-40) - that the difficulty of mounting a successful take-over bid increases with the size of the firm to be taken over, and that the number of persons able to organize a successful take-over bid is in any case quite limited. Then there is the question of why any one firm, as long as it maintains the same rate of growth in dividends as other megacorps, should be singled out for attack by an outside group seeking control.[27] These arguments, by themselves, suggest that the larger the megacorp (as measured by the value of its outstanding equity shares), the greater the impunity with which it can pursue a growth maximizing policy.

In addition, however, there is the widespread belief, whether correct or not, that megacorps are actually equity maximizers. This belief, to the extent that it is shared by the small number of persons able to organize a successful take-over bid, will tend to deflect attention from any megacorp which is increasing its dividends at the same rate as other firms. And the same belief, to the extent that it is held by the great majority of equity debt holders, will cause any take-over bid which might nonetheless be mounted to be viewed with suspicion. Shareholders will be hard to convince, in light of the dividend record, that the take-over bid is not simply a speculative flier, one which will leave them holding the short end of the stick when the organizers of the take-over bid subsequently sell out and take for themselves whatever short-run capital gains are to be had.

The dividend policy necessary, then, if the executive group is to be effectively protected against being deposed is quite simple. Assuming it is able to report both a growth of net earnings and a ratio of net earnings to sales which is no lower than those of comparable firms and assuming, moreover, it has not allowed financial assets to accumulate excessively, it need only maintain a rate of growth of dividends equal to that of other megacorps.[28] Generally, this will also suffice to assure it of external borrowing costs no greater than those of other firms. However, if the executive group anticipates a particular need to resort to new equity financing in the near future, it can reduce the cost of those funds even further by announcing a dividend payment which falls above the previously established long-run growth rate. Even if this higher growth rate in dividends is not subsequently maintained, it may well give rise to expectations that will bring about a temporary bidding up of the price of the company's shares and hence lead to a more favorable price-dividend ratio.[29]

The above argument - that a megacorp's executive group will be reasonably well protected *vis-à-vis* the equity debt holders as long as it maintains a rate of growth in dividends which is not less than that established by other megacorps - still leaves unanswered, however, the question of what, aside from the desire to reduce its external borrowing costs, might induce any significant number of executive groups to initiate a change in the rate of growth in compensation for the equity debt holders. Since the rate of growth in dividends established by one group of megacorps is likely to influence the rate of growth decided upon by others, at issue here really is what determines the rate of growth in dividends paid by megacorps in general. In other words, while the need to be protected against the dangers of a take-over bid can be expected to exert strong pressure toward the equalization of the growth rate in dividends among all megacorps, other forces will be exerting pressure of their own to determine what that single growth rate will be. The nature of those other forces is the next topic to be taken up.

The overall rate of growth in dividends. Two factors can be expected to influence whether a megacorp will increase its own dividend payments above the trend already established by other megacorps. They are (1) the extent to which the executive group is in empathy with the equity debt holders, and (2) the rate of growth in compensation received by the members of the laboring manpower force. Each of these two factors will be discussed in turn.

The megacorp's executive group has several reasons to be empathetic toward the equity debt holders, even aside from the voting rights which the latter exercise. In the first place, the members of the executive group are likely to identify themselves more closely with the equity debt holders than with any of the megacorp's other constitutencies. They form part of the same social class, meeting frequently not only on business but also during leisure hours (C. Mills, 1959, chs. 6-7). As a result of this substantial interaction on a personal level, they are likely to share a common world view. This close identification which the members of the executive group have with the equity debt holders is further reinforced through stock option plans and, even more important, since shares acquired through those plans are likely to be disposed of as soon as possible in order to permit portfolio diversification, through the holdings which the members of the executive group have in other megacorps. As equity debt holders themselves, though not necessarily in their own company, the members of the executive group have good reason to be empathetic toward that constituency - even if it does not outweigh their first loyalty to the megacorp itself.

Secondly, the members of the executive group are likely to subscribe themselves, at least in some degree, to the myth that the megacorp actually 'belongs' to the equity debt holders. In part, this belief derives from the world view which the two groups both share. But it is also an important element in the group norms by which the behavior of the executive group itself is regulated. According to that code, the salaried officers of the megacorp occupy a position of trust which requires that they act in the best interests of the company and, indirectly, in the best interests of the stockholders as the group in whom the legal property rights reside. It is from fulfilling this fiduciary role that the authority of the executive group is said to be derived (Sutton *et al.*, 1956, pp. 64-6). Indeed, on these grounds, the members of the executive group are able to argue that they are responsible to the stockholders, and to them alone. This position, as long as it remains convincing both to the members of the executive group and to others, serves two useful functions. In a socio-economic system that stresses either property rights or democratic election as the source of all authority, it satisfies a deeply felt need for legitimacy (Berle, 1959, especially pp. 98ff; Rostow, 1959); and in a democratic age which abhors unchecked power, it helps fend off demands for increased social control over the megacorp. These benefits are in addition, of course, to the protection against a take-over bid which comes from the feeling by stockholders that the members of the executive group themselves subscribe to the myth. While the self-serving aspect is clearly evident, this does not preclude the members of the executive group from actually believing the myth of stockholder supremacy – at least to the extent that such a belief does not threaten either the executive group's prerogatives or the megacorp's ability to survive. This means that the equity debt holders are likely to be viewed with greater favor than any of the megacorp's other constituencies, though not with greater favor than the megacorp itself. Still, to this limited degree, the myth of stockholder supremacy will further contribute to the empathy which the members of the executive group feel toward the equity debt holders.

How strong that empathy is will be put to the test whenever the rate of compensation received by the laboring manpower force is increased. On the one hand, there is no other factor, aside from the fear of being deposed, which is as likely to induce the members of the executive group to increase the rate of compensation being paid the equity debt holders. On the other hand, the higher wages and salaries obtained by the members of the laboring manpower force will provide a basis for invidious comparison between the treatment of the two constituencies. What may be postulated here is that the empathy felt by the members of the executive group toward the stockholders will be sufficiently great to assure that, whenever wages and salaries are increased, the dividend rate will be increased as well. This does not mean that dividends will necessarily rise immediately following any increase in wages and salaries, or even that the rate of growth of dividends will be a smooth one. It is only to point out that acceptance of the national incremental wage pattern by a megacorp will necessitate a certain percentage increase in the rate of compensation received by the equity debt holders, this increase to occur at some point in the future.[30]

Whether the percentage rise in dividends will exactly match the percentage rise in wages and salaries cannot be stated with any certainty *a priori*. One of the points which this chapter hopes to make clear is that the dividend rate, like the national incremental wage pattern to which it is at least partially linked, is indeterminate on economic grounds alone. This fact has two implications. The first is that, insofar as any theoretical model of the economy is concerned, the rate of growth of dividiends, like the rate of growth of wages and salaries, is at least partially an exogenously determined variable; and that with certain changes in the socio-political environment it could even become an instrumental variable entirely subject to policy control by the government. The second implication is that, with institutional arrangements as they now are, the precise functional relationship between the percentage rise in wages and the percentage rise in dividends can only be determined with certainty through empirical investigation.

The hypothesis may nonetheless be tentatively advanced that, whatever the percentage increase in compensation granted the members of the trade union - and through them the rest of the laboring manpower force - the equity debt holders will receive at least an equal percentage increase in dividends. A certain theoretical argument can be made on behalf of this hypothesis. To treat the equity debt holders any less generously would surely leave the members of the executive group open to the charge - a serious one in the social milieu they inhabit - that they were favoring the workers at the expense of the company's legal owners. There is even some empirical evidence consistent with the hypothesis.[31] In any case, it is a workable hypothesis, one which states in its boldest form the more fundamental point - to wit, that an increase in wages and salaries will necessarily lead to a rise in dividends, and that indeed this is the critical relationship.

It is, of course, possible that the empathy which the members of the executive group feel toward the stockholders will be sufficient to bring about a more than equivalent increase in the dividend rate. Several factors, however, can be expected to militate against the executive group's generosity extending that far. On the one hand, any increase in the dividend rate represents a compromise of the megacorp's primary goal - that of maximizing its own rate of growth over the long run. This is because the higher dividend payments will require either a rise in the price level or a reduction in the average corporate levy, a choice which, however made, is likely to place the megacorp at a competitive disadvantage.[32] On the other hand, while an increase in the dividend rate at least equal to the growth of labor compensation may be essential to avoid the charge that the 'workers' are being favored at the expense of the 'owners', any further increase in the dividend rate beyond that point, assuming the possible threat of a take-over bid has already been sufficiently eliminated, offers no particular benefit to the members of the executive group. On this basis, that the empathy felt by the members of the executive group will be completely expended once the percentage increase in compensation obtained by the trade union for its members has been matched, it can be argued that an equivalent increase in the dividend rate is all that is likely to be received by the equity debt holders. This will, in fact, be the assumption made throughout the rest of this treatise.[33] From such an assumption it follows that, upon acceptance of the national incremental wage pattern by a megacorp, not only the labor component but also the dividend portion of fixed costs will rise by the same percentage, W_p.[34] It should be added, however, that the assumption is made largely for expositional convenience and that none of the arguments which follow depend on it. Indeed, those arguments would still largely hold true if, instead, the dividend portion of fixed costs were to rise by less than W_p or, alternatively, by some multiple of W_p.

In summary then, acceptance of the national incremental wage pattern by a megacorp foretells a substantial increase in costs, going even beyond the higher wages obtained by the trade union for its rank-and-file. Both the salaries received by other members of the laboring manpower force and the dividends received by the equity debt holders are likely to have to be increased by an equal percentage, the precise impact that this will have on the megacorp's cost structure depending on the relative importance of all three types of compensation.[35] Whether the megacorp will be willing to accept this substantial increase in costs will depend on what the effect is likely to be on the megacorp's ability to survive and grow. This, in turn, will depend on whether the megacorp is able to pass along the added costs in the form of higher prices or, alternatively, must absorb the added costs out of the existing corporate levy. Although chapter 3 has already discussed the factors determining the ability of a megacorp-price leader, acting as the surrogate for its fellow oligopolists, to increase the industry price, that analysis was predicated on the assumption that average variable and fixed costs remained constant. Now that the corporate levy is to be held constant as average variable and fixed costs are increased, the analysis needs to be modified accordingly.

A cost-compensating price increase. The restraints on pricing discretion, it will be recalled from the earlier chapters, are threefold. They derive from (1) the substitution effect, (2) the entry factor, and (3) the fear of meaningful government intervention. Each of these three restraints will be discussed in turn, as it bears on the megacorp-price leader's ability, acting as the surrogate for the industry as a whole, to pass along in the form of a higher price level the increase in average variable and fixed costs resulting from acceptance of the national incremental wage pattern.

The substitution effect, not very powerful to begin with in an oligopolistic industry, is likely to be further weakened in the case of a rise in price made necessary by increased claims against the megacorp's revenue in the form of higher wages, salaries and dividends. This is because the industries which produce the closest substitutes for the industry's product will themselves probably be forced to follow the national incremental wage pattern and will thus experience a comparable increase in average variable and fixed costs. This interdependence is most clearly evident for those industries which form the auto-steel orbit, but it will also hold true for those oligopolies which are part of some other wage contour. While different industries can be expected to have different labor-output (and different dividend-output) ratios, thereby necessitating different percentage increases to offset the higher costs, all will be subject to the same general pressure to raise their price levels. In this manner the substitution effect of a price increase in any one industry will be significantly reduced - if not completely neutralized - when the purpose of the price increase is to match the higher costs induced by a trade union agreement. Only when there is significant competition from imports is the substitution effect likely to loom large, but even then rising labor costs in the same industry abroad may tend to mitigate its restraining influence.

The entry factor, should the industry price be increased to offset higher costs, will be almost totally inoperative. This is because an industrial trade union, before it can demand significant wage concessions from the megacorps which comprise the industry, must have the organizational power to impose the cost-affecting terms of any settlement it reaches, not only on the firms already in the industry but also on any firms which might in the future try to gain entry. Once assured that the trade union has this prerequisite power, the megacorps - and in particular, the price leader - can be certain that any concessions they make will not give some other firm, even a new one, a competitive advantage in labor costs. Thus a potential entrant will find that an increase in price made necessary by the existing firms' acceptance of the national wage pattern will not lower the barriers to entry by increasing the margin between its own average variable and fixed costs relative to those of the established firms in the industry - except insofar as the new firm may be able to avoid matching any ensuing increase in the dividend rate. This last qualification should not be overemphasized, however, since the ultimate effect will be to make an equity interest in the new firm less attractive.

This leaves only the fear of meaningful government intervention as a possibly significant restraint on the megacorp-price leader's ability to raise the industry price following an increase in costs stemming from acceptance of the national incremental wage pattern. This fear, it will be recalled, imposes not a calculable cost but rather an upper limit on the percentage increase in price, n, which the megacorp-price leader is willing to announce, this upper limit being the price leader's estimate of the value for n which has associated with it a more than acceptable risk of government retaliation in some effective manner. The very fact that the price increase follows acceptance by the megacorp of the national incremental wage pattern will, however, make it extremely difficult for the government to intervene successfully. For the national incremental wage pattern, as the norm of what constitutes a 'fair and equitable' increase in the compensation of labor, reflects a social decision which the government must respect; this is particularly true since the government itself will ordinarily have given its tacit approval to the wage agreement in the bellwether industry by which the pattern was established.

The government - and in the American context at the present time this almost necessarily means the executive branch - will be able to muster the political support necessary for meaningful intervention only if it can be demonstrated that one of two conditions exists: (a) that the increase in price, *n*, is greater than the increase in the firm's total costs resulting from acceptance of the national incremental wage pattern,[36] or (b) that the industry is presently generating excessive earnings, that is, that net revenue has increased sufficiently so that the industry can absorb part or all of the increased costs without being forced to cut back on investment outlays. To demonstrate the existence of either condition for any large number of industries is, however, extremely difficult for the government at the present time, with its limited access to confidential business data. In any case it suffices for now to point out that an increase in price limited to the amount necessary to offset the increase in costs brought about by acceptance of the national incremental wage pattern will be most unlikely to provoke meaningful government intervention.

In summary, then, the three restraints on pricing discretion, even when taken together, will ordinarily be insufficent to prevent an increase in average variable and fixed costs from being passed along to customers in the form of a higher price level. The value of *R*, under those circumstances, is likely to be close to, if not actually equal to, zero, while the probability of meaningful government intervention can generally be discounted completely. It can thus be seen that while, on the one hand, the megacorp-price leader conducting contract negotiations faces a complete shutdown of its production facilities if it refuses to grant the trade union members an increase in compensation consistent with the national incremental wage pattern, it will, on the other hand, by raising its price, be able to grant that increase in compensation without incurring any substantial cost or penalty itself. This is not to argue that a strike will always be avoided. To the megacorp-price leader, a brief walkout by the trade union's members may be the least expensive way to cut back on production temporarily. Similarly, to the industrial trade union, a brief work stoppage may be the best means of reviving a flagging sense of worker solidarity, that is, loyalty to the trade union. A strike may even ensue for other than wage-related issues. The point is that, strike or no strike, the wage provisions of the contract finally agreed to by the megacorp-price leader and the industrial trade union will almost certainly be those called for under the national incremental wage pattern. The higher rates of compensation which a settlement along those lines implies for the trade union's rank-and-file members will, almost as certainly, for reasons already mentioned, be extended both to the unorganized portion of the laboring manpower force and to the equity debt holders. It is thus the national incremental wage pattern which determines the increases in compensation, at least in nominal terms, received over time by the megacorp's two principal constituencies - acceptance of the pattern being due both to the power relationships stressed by institutional economists and to the normative factors emphasized by contemporary sociologists.[37] What still remains to be explained are the factors which determine the value of W_p, that is, the percentage by which rates of compensation are to be increased under the national incremental wage pattern. This, in turn, means being able to explain the cost provisions in the key bargain reached in the bellwether industry. As a preliminary step, however, it is necessary to introduce still another theory of income distribution, that associated with Marx.

The surplus value theory

The relative value of any two goods, according to Marx, is determined by the relative amounts of 'socially necessary' labor required to produce them - including the labor embodied in the means of production. Thus if it takes twice as much labor to produce the one as the other by the best known method, a single unit of the first will, under competitive conditions, tend to exchange for two units of the second. This was the labor theory of value which Marx borrowed almost unaltered from the English classical tradition.[38] To the extent that labor costs are the only costs of production - that is, to the extent that all other necessary inputs are free to society - this theory has considerable plausibility. Even today, with proper allowance for the time-related capital costs incurred in the development of human competences, it provides perhaps the best explanation of prices in the personal services sectors of the economy, although, like all cost-of-production theories of value, it slights the demand blade of Marshall's famous scissors analogy.

Marx's point of departure from the classical tradition was his insistence that the relative value of labor - or to use his own term for the physical and mental effort put forth by a worker on the job, the relative value of laboring power - is also determined by the amount of socially necessary labor required to produce it. In the case of laboring power, this socially necessary labor is by definition equal to the subsistence level of wages. Thus in a society in which the growth of knowledge and technique is making labor increasingly more productive, there develops an ever widening gap between the value of what laboring power is responsible for creating and the value of laboring power itself. This gap, which is manifested in every commodity produced by modern methods, was called 'surplus value' by Marx (1935, chapters 7-8).

What Marx was primarily interested in demonstrating was the exploitation of labor by the owners of capital (cf. J. Robinson, 1962d). By assuming that labor was generally limited to subsistence wages and that the owners of capital, while contributing little or nothing to the production process, were nonetheless strategically situated to control it, Marx could quite logically argue that all of the surplus value went to the latter group in society. Although the validity of the two crucial assumptions would now be doubtful, at least for the United States, the usefulness of the general Marxian framework should nonetheless be recognized (cf. Samuelson, 1971). For what is being determined through the 'key' bargain which sets the national incremental wage pattern is the division of the surplus value or - when taken in the aggregate, the social surplus - between conflicting claimants to the megacorp's revenue. The term 'social surplus' in this context is meant to connote the total quantity of goods and services still remaining and available for other purposes after the subsistence needs of society have been met. (Subsistence is, of course, something largely determined by social values.)

In the conventional view, the conflict over the disposition of the surplus value, social surplus or however else it may be termed is usually seen as being between the 'workers', as represented by the trade union, on the one hand and the 'owners of capital', as represented by the megacorp's management, on the other. The extent to which the rates of compensation received by those two constituencies of the megacorp are inextricably linked has, however, already been pointed out. In a real sense the trade union, when sitting down at the bargaining table to negotiate a new contract, is setting forth the claims of the unorganized portion of the laboring manpower force and of the equity debt holders no less than the claims of its own rank-and-file members. The conflict, then, is actually between those constituencies with an understandable desire for increased current income, whether in the form of higher wages, salaries or dividends, and the megacorp itself with an inherent need for additional investment funds to finance future growth. This is especially true of the collective bargaining in the bellwether industry - even though a certain confusion on these points is likely to be found on both sides, complicating the task of reaching an agreement. The confusion derives, in part, from the continuing adherence by both the megacorp's executive group and the trade union leadership to the myth that the company actually belongs to the stockholders in some real sense and that therefore the retained earnings should be counted as part of the equity debt holders' returns.[39] But the confusion is also due to the difficulty of determining precisely what is the amount of surplus value available within the firm - or, alternatively, the amount of social surplus available throughout the oligopolistic sector - for distribution among the competing claimants (cf. Dye, 1967).

Fortunately, at least for the prospects of reaching an agreement, collective bargaining in the bellwether industry and in every other industry begins with a past history that has resulted in the present level of wages, salaries, dividends and corporate levy. As a consequence, the participants in the bargaining process need be concerned, not with the division of any total surplus value - assuming that the total surplus value could, in some meaningful manner, even be measured[40] - but rather, only with the division of any new or incremental surplus value that may have arisen since the previous contract negotiations. This is similar to the executive group's having to determine only an optimum change in the price level, not the optimum price level itself. Still, even the amount of incremental surplus value, as distinct from the total surplus value, will be difficult to determine precisely. This is because, while it is closely approximated by the increase in net earnings over time holding wages, salaries, dividends and investment constant, it is not the same as the increase in net earnings at any given moment. (This increase in net earnings is the equivalent of an increase in savings, or discretionary income, within the firm and the counterpart on the income side of the secular growth of output per workers taking place on the product side.) To explain why this is the case, it is necessary to introduce the final theory of income distribution to be considered in this chapter, that developed by certain of the Cambridge, England, economists as an extension of the Keynesian insights.

Keynesian and post-Keynesian theory

From the Keynesian division of the national income into two parts - the one representing the claims used to purchase consumption goods and the other the claims which, by not being so exercised, constitute the aggregate level of savings - it is possible to develop two separate, though related, macroeconomic theories of income distribution. All that is necessary is to make the not unreasonable assumption that the aggregate level of savings, whatever it may be, derives entirely from the net revenue, or profits, earned by business firms. This means that the national income can also be divided into those claims which, on the one hand, accrue to workers in the form of wages (and salaries) and which are then used entirely to command the available consumption goods and, on the other hand, those claims which accrue to property owners, or capitalists, in the form of profits (and rents) and which are then the sole source of societal savings.

The first of the two macroeconomic theories focuses on the cyclical, or intermediate-run, behavior of relative income shares, and it is the version most directly traceable to Keynes himself. Keynes' own way of putting it was that any increase in aggregate demand would lead to a rise in the price level relative to nominal wages, with the result that real wages would decline. Even in the oligopolistic sector, although the price level might not rise, profits could still be expected to increase as output expanded and average total costs simultaneously fell. Either way, with a rise in aggregate demand, there would be an increase in the proportion of national income accruing to the property-owning class in the form of profits. Conversely, with a decline in aggregate demand, there would be, where competitive conditions prevailed, a fall in the price level, an increase in real wages and a reduction in the share of national income represented by profits. Even if, because of oligopolistic market structures, the price level did not fall, a decline in aggregate demand, by lowering sales volume and thereby pushing up per unit costs, would still reduce the relative share of profits. These ideas, found only in embryonic form in Keynes' own writings,[41] have since been worked out with some care by a number of economists.[42]

The second of the two macroeconomic theories emphasizes the secular, or long-run behavior, of relative income shares. It is a theory implicit more in Harrod's dynamic extension of Keynesian theory than in the Keynesian analysis itself, and for this reason it is best regarded as post-Keynesian theory. The model depends, not on the rate at which a given amount of capacity is presently being utilized but instead, on the rate of accumulation, or investment, taking place continuously while the rate of capacity utilization is held constant. The important distinction - one which converts the static analysis of Keynes into a dynamic one - is between the effect of an increase in investment as an event at a single moment in time and the effect of having a high *rate* of accumulation taking place steadily over time. As the post-Keynesian theory of income distribution points out, the more capitalists as the property-owning class invest, the larger will be the share of the national income they command in the form of profits. This is because the higher the rate of accumulation, the greater will be the proportion of total output that must be made unavailable to workers for consumption - the curtailment of consumption being reflected in the relative increase of profits, or savings.[43] If it can be assumed that workers save nothing out of their wages, or that the amount they save is equal to the expenditure on new residences and similar household durables, the relationship between investment and profits is even more direct. Then, as in Kalecki's pithy saying: 'Capitalists get what they spend and workers spend what they get'.[44]

The preceding discussion of the megacorp and its oligopolistic milieu suggests the need for certain refinements in both the Keynesian cyclical and the post-Keynesian secular theories of income distribution. In the first place, as has been emphasized throughout this work, the owner-entrepreneur, or capitalist, of the nineteenth century has been replaced, insofar as effective control is concerned, by the executive group representing the megacorp *qua* organization. The capitalist's direct descendants as the legal owners of the properties involved have become mere *rentiers*, receiving dividend payments as a sort of pension. To the extent that these dividends simply constitute part of the income available to the household sector to finance consumption expenditures, they are no different, at least insofar as the macrodynamic behavior of the economic system is concerned, from the wages and salaries received by the laboring manpower force. The effect which dividends have on the relative distribution of income is, of course, another matter, but that is a point which will be taken up later.[45] What does make a difference, in terms of the macrodynamics of the economy, is the remaining portion of what is commonly regarded as the profits, or net revenue, of the megacorp. This remaining portion, the retained earnings, taken together with the depreciation allowances plus whatever sums are devoted to advertising, R & D and the like, comprises the total corporate levy used to finance investment expenditures within the oligopolistic sector. It is equal to the gross savings generated within that sub-component of the business sector.[46]

The more significant distinction, therefore, is not between wages and profits but rather, between the compensation received by the megacorp's two principal constituencies - both the laboring manpower force and the equity debt holders - and the residual income accruing to the firm itself in the form of the corporate levy. Where the post-Keynesian literature sometimes refers to the portion of national income represented by profits, it is perhaps more appropriate to speak of the portion represented by the corporate levy - keeping in mind that the respective rates of compensation received by the megacorp's two principal constituencies may not vary together, that the marginal propensities to save out of the resulting wages and dividends may not be identical, and that the total amount of savings thus generated within the household sector may not be equal to the demand by the business sector for external funds.[47] These latter qualifications are necessary if the subsuming of dividends within household income is not to conceal certain potentially significant consequences of the pattern of income distribution within the megacorp itself.[48]

Secondly, as also emphasized in the previous discussion, the profit margin - or rather the average corporate levy - is not likely to be adjusted in response to short-run changes in industry and aggregate demand. The usual procedure in an oligopolistic industry is for the price leader to announce a new price level based on the consideration of certain long-run factors, then for all the firms in that industry to maintain the new price level for the remainder of the current pricing period, regardless of short-run fluctuations in demand. Of course, wage rates are likely to be adjusted even more slowly than the average corporate levy, especially given the prevalance in the United States of multiple-year labor contracts. This means that the intermediate-run redistributive effect emphasized in the cyclical Keynesian model depends not on changes in the margin above costs, but rather on changes in the megacorp's actual operating ratio.

As previously noted, the amount of corporate levy being realized is quite sensitive to changes in that ratio. Since the corporate levy being realized at the margin is greater than the corporate levy being realized on the average, the megacorp's total residual income - whether viewed as net revenue, cash flow or a corporate levy - will rise, and fall, at a more rapid rate than the actual operating ratio itself. The latter, in turn, is quite sensitive to changes in industry sales and, as the force behind that statistic, to changes in aggregate demand. While fluctuations in final goods inventory provide something of a cushion between industry sales and the actual operating ratio, the two can be expected to vary quite closely together over the intermediate run, that is, over the planning period.

An increase in aggregate demand, because of its effect on the actual operating ratio, will therefore lead to a disproportionate increase in the corporate levy, even if the industry price level remains unchanged (Moyer, 1968). It will also, because of the additional labor inputs required to produce the greater output, lead to an increase in the total compensation received by the laboring manpower force - whether because previously laid-off workers will have to be recalled or the existing labor force will have to be paid overtime - but this increase in labor compensation is more likely to be only proportional to the higher operating ratio. Similarly, a decrease in aggregate demand will lead to a disproportionate decline in the total corporate levy being realized, though more likely to only a proportional decrease in the compensation received by the laboring manpower force. The compensation received by the capital debt holders, including even those with equity shares, will, of course, remain the same whatever the actual operating ratio.

This impact which short-run changes in aggregate demand have on the amount of corporate levy realized will, it is true, tend to be neutralized over the business cycle. The standard operating ratio, as the part of the oligopolistic pricing formula which takes into account the likely fluctuations in industry sales, is specifically designed to accomplish that purpose. It is for this reason that the redistributive effect suggested by the Keynesian cyclical model is not likely to influence industry price levels directly. This does not mean, however, that the effect is unimportant or can be ignored. Indeed, it is the failure to take into account this cyclical effect, controlling for its influence and focusing instead on the secular pattern of income distribution emphasized in post-Keynesian theory, that explains why the key bargain in the bellwether industry often leaves the executives of megacorps with the feeling that they have no choice but to raise their prices. To understand this point, it is necessary to consider the dynamic by which the key bargain, and thus the national incremental wage pattern, is determined.

The size of the key bargain. As already noted, the megacorp and the trade union involved in negotiating the key bargain are, in effect, trying to determine what proportion of the incremental surplus value which has emerged in that firm or industry in the form of increased net earnings should be distributed to the megacorp's two principal constituencies. This amount of incremental surplus value is more or less typical of the incremental surplus value available throughout the oligopolistic sector. The surplus value, it should be noted, has two sources: (1) the gains from technological progress, as manifest by a secular decline in average variable and fixed costs, that is, by the secular rise of output per worker, and (2) the growth of the firm itself, as manifest by the secular increase in engineer-rated capacity. Each warrants a brief discussion.

Though it is investment by the megacorp in new plant and equipment which makes it possible for emergent technological possibilities to be exploited, the developments themselves are more likely to come from other industries - in particular, from the industries in the capital goods sector which supply the megacorp with the various means of production it requires.[49] Whether or not the firms in these other industries are themselves megacorps is beside the point. As part of their non-price competitive strategy, they will vie to supply the megacorp with those capital goods that will lead to the greatest possible reduction in costs. In the competition to put the most efficient plants and equipment on the market, these firms will be able to draw on the basic scientific knowledge which has been accumulated by men the world over ever since an unknown hominid took stone in hand and fashioned the first tool. This knowledge, before being applied, however, will have to be adapted along lines determined by the relative price of labor and capital inputs, a constraint imposed by the cumulative impact of past decisions as to how the megacorp's available revenue should be apportioned. In the most general terms, then, a decline in the megacorp's average variable and fixed costs will reflect the growth of scientific knowledge through historical time, the past success of the trade union movement in increasing the relative cost of labor inputs, the rapidity with which the capital goods industry develops better products, and the rate at which the megacorp itself adds new plant and equipment. What this overview suggests is that technological change is, for the most part, capital embodied[50] and that the individual megacorp's own contribution to the process does not go much beyond the role it plays in determining its own growth rate.[51] This brings us to the second source of surplus value, the secular increase in engineer-rated capacity.

Even when it comes to determing its own growth rate, the individual megacorp's contribution is somewhat limited. Certainly without the executive group's ability to manage material and human resources effectively, survival - let alone growth - would not be possible. By this token, the very fact that the megacorp has succeeded in growing over time is evidence of the critical role played by those responsible for directing its fortunes. Yet as essential as effective management may be, it is not by itself sufficient to explain a megacorp's movement along a particular growth path. The earlier discussion of the demand for investment funds to purchase new plant and equipment stressed the importance of population and income trends. These, as well as most of the other factors likely to affect the fortunes of any particular industry, reflect forces beyond the control of any single firm and, to a large extent, even beyond the control of the industry itself. It is this dependence of the megacorp's growth rate and, *a fortiori*, of technological change on larger social determinants which justifies the treatment of the resulting increase in net earnings - and the corresponding growth of output per worker - as part of the surplus value created by the entire society, both past and present, and not as something produced by just one segment of that society contemporaneously.

Still, the surplus value - or at least the incremental portion of it - has to be apportioned in some manner. Toward this end, the trade union involved in negotiating the key bargain can be expected to insist that some 'fair' or customary share go to those whom it represents. What that 'fair' share is construed to be is likely to depend on the past history of collective bargaining within the bellwether industry. It reflects still another way in which normative judgments, backed by effective institutional power, help determine the distribution of income within the oligopolistic sector. For in the absence of any other standard, the share of the increase in net earnings which has customarily gone to the laboring manpower force, or at least the organized portion of it, takes on, through the precedent thereby established, a validity of its own - certainly in the eyes of the trade union leadership, if in no other.

It is the willingness of a particular trade union to press its claim to this 'fair' share of the incremental surplus value steadfastly and determinedly, even to the point of undergoing a long and costly strike, that enables it to enter the lists as labor's champion (and indirectly, as the pensioned-off capitalists' champion, too). At the same time, it is the success of the trade union in having its claim met that determines the distribution of income, ostensibly between the megacorp's two principal constituencies but actually, as it turns out, for both constituencies together *vis-à-vis* the megacorp. With distribution of the surplus value through a reduction in price levels virtually precluded by the lack of any advantage to the megacorp from doing so, a strong and vigorous assault by that one trade union upon the megacorp's revenue as the spearhead of similar forays by other trade unions is the only alternative - at least under present arrangements.[52] Besides, as already noted, it brings the leadership of that one trade union power and prestige, both within the ranks of labor and within the larger community.

In setting forth its demands, the trade union involved in negotiating the key bargain can be assumed to be guided by two considerations. The first is that its members should suffer no loss in real income. Toward this end the trade union can be expected to insist upon an increase in wage rates at least equal to the rise in the cost of living since the last contract settlement. This can be regarded as a minimal demand, one which ties the national incremental wage pattern to the rise in price levels throughout the economy. The second consideration is that the trade union's members should receive their 'fair' or customary share of any incremental surplus value - either that which has already emerged in the industry or that which is likely to emerge in the future. Toward this end, the trade union can be expected to insist upon an increase in wages equal to what it considers the secular growth rate of net revenue within the industry; it is this further demand which, however imperfectly, links the national incremental wage pattern, W_p, to the secular rate of growth of output per worker in the oligopolistic sector, $\overset{*}{Z}_s$. As a first approximation to that secular growth rate, the trade union may well seize upon the percentage by which net revenue has increased since the last contract settlement. If the growth of net revenue has been greater than the rise in the cost of living, maintaining 'labor's' customary share in this manner will be all that the trade union need be concerned about. It is only if the rise in the cost of living has exceeded the growth of net revenue within the industry that the trade union will be forced to focus instead on maintaining real wage rates. In general, then, the trade union involved in negotiating the key bargain can be expected to insist upon the establishment of a wage pattern equal either to (a) the percentage increase in the cost of living or (b) the percentage increase in reported net earnings since the last contract settlement, whichever figure is higher.[53] Yet for a number of reasons the megacorp-price leader and the other megacorps in the bellwether industry may find that figure unacceptable.

In the first place, if the growth of net revenue has been less than the rise in price levels, particularly for capital goods, these megacorps will already be faced with a decline in the purchasing power represented by the average corporate levy. The establishment of a new wage pattern, even if it represents a lower figure than the previous wage pattern, will, because of its effect on average variable and fixed costs, most likely further impair the ability of these firms to maintain their desired levels of investment with the industry price unchanged. While of course the industry price could be increased, this expedient may seem less desirable to the megacorp-price leader and the other members of the bellwether industry than trying to hold down wage rates. As a final comment, it should be noted that the rise in the cost of living is likely to exceed the growth of net revenue only when the economy has taken a sudden downturn just prior to the beginning of a new wage round.

More typically, the growth of net revenue can be expected to exceed the rise in the cost of living. Even in this case, however, two obstacles to the contract settlement may arise. One is that the increase in reported net earnings may reflect, not just the increment in surplus value due to technological change and the growth of the firm itself but, in addition, the redistributive effect produced by cyclically high levels of aggregate demand. That is, it may reflect the short-run Keynesian effect. Focusing exclusively on the amount of reported net earnings may therefore lead to an exaggerated notion of how much surplus value is actually available for apportionment.

It might seem that any controversy over this point would be relatively easy to resolve. All that is necessary is for the two parties to agree on the extent to which the actual operating ratio has exceeded the standard operating ratio since the last contract negotiations and then to make due allowance for that factor. The effect of this would be to shift from a Keynesian to a post-Keynesian framework. The problem is more complicated than that, however. One can never be entirely certain whether the past pattern of cyclical fluctuations still holds. The high levels of aggregate demand may well be consistent with previously experienced deviations from the established trend, but then on the other hand they may presage an entirely new trend. This complication would not, in itself, be so serious were it not for a second factor – the asymmetrical bargaining positions which the two parties often take. The megacorp's executive group has, of course, good reason to insist, when the actual operating ratio has been running above average, that any increase in the rates of compensation be limited to the more modest secular growth rate of net earnings; but it is generally unwilling to accept the argument in reverse. When the actual operating ratio has been running below average, it is likely to urge, citing the threat of insolvency, that increases in the rates of compensation be limited to the even more modest growth in reported net earnings since the last contract negotiations. Needless to say, the trade union is often guilty of taking the same asymmetrical bargaining position, it being generally unwilling to accept a reduction in the rates of labor compensation even though the megacorp's net revenue may actually have declined. At the root of the conflict is the uncertainty over what proportion of any increase in net earnings represents incremental surplus value and what proportion represents the temporary redistributive effect produced by a cyclical change in aggregate demand.

This obstacle to a settlement in the bellwether industry is a minor one, however, compared to a second - the megacorp's frequent desire to increase the proportion of the incremental surplus value accruing to itself. The megacorp's motive in seeking this larger share is to obtain the investment funds deemed essential to its future growth and survival. Indeed, the industry price level may well have been raised at a prior point in time with this objective specifically in mind. To the megacorp's executive group, the resulting increase in reported net earnings is simply part of the corporate levy, and thus is unavailable for distribution among the firm's principal constituencies. But to the trade union it is part of the returns to 'capital', and as such represents a reduction in 'labor's' customary share of the incremental surplus value. At the root of this even more fundamental conflict is the confusion, partially shared by members of the executive group, over whether the residual income belongs to the equity debt holders as nominal owners or to the megacorp itself *qua* organization.

The impasse in collective bargaining likely to result from either or both of these two types of conflict would seem to preclude a settlement in the bellwether industry - except under the unusual circumstances when industry sales, the demand for investment funds and reported net earnings were all growing at the same rate and price levels were holding steady. The fact that an agreement is nonetheless always reached can be explained in terms of the intervention likely to occur from without and of the safety valve available from within.

The source of the probable intervention is the Federal government, concerned that an impasse may lead to a prolonged shutdown of a critical industry. While the nature and tenor of this intervention will vary, depending on which party controls the executive branch and what are the current political considerations, in general the Federal government can be expected to take a position more in line with that of the trade union than that of the megacorp. This reflects, not just the greater voting strength of the trade union but, perhaps even more important, the greater tractability of the megacorp. The latter can more easily be persuaded to accept the government's suggested basis for a settlement because it knows that, whatever the increase in labor compensation and other costs it may have to absorb, it will be able to largely offset them through a subsequent increase in the industry price level. In this respect, the megacorp responsible for negotiating the national incremental wage pattern has the same additional degree of freedom as do the other megacorps which will be forced to follow its lead. It is the ability of these firms to raise their prices, following the acceptance of a contract granting higher wages, which serves as an essential safety valve, dissipating social tensions which might otherwise burst the seams of society.[54]

In summary, then, the trade union involved in working out the key bargain can be expected to insist that its members receive their customary share of whatever increase in net earnings has occurred since the last contract negotiations - as long as the increase in wage rates is not less than the rise in the cost of living. Indirectly, of course, the trade union is putting forward a similar claim on behalf of both the unorganized workers in its own industry and the union members in other oligopolistic industries. Given the nature of the political forces shaping government intervention once the contract talks have reached their almost inevitable deadlock, the trade union is likely to be largely successful in achieving its goal - even if this means an increase in the rate of compensation for the oligopolistic sector's laboring manpower force that is greater than the increase in compensation projected for the equity debt holders under the present rate of growth of dividends. In that case, assuming the executive group's empathy with the stockholders is sufficiently strong, the dividend rate will also have to be increased so as to match the gains won by the trade union. Alternatively, if for some reason the increase in the rate of compensation obtained by the laboring manpower force falls short of the rate of growth of dividends, or even of the rate of growth of net revenue, the trade union can be expected to try, with increased determination, to make up the difference at the next wage round.

The point made earlier in connection with the determinants of the dividend rate applies here as well. The national incremental wage pattern, like the rate of growth of dividends which is linked to it, does not depend solely on economic factors. Indeed, economic factors merely set certain limits on the value which the national incremental wage pattern,

W_p, can take - at least in real terms. To explain the actual size of the wage pattern, even in nominal terms, it is necessary to posit the salient features of the larger socio-political environment.

Thus the arguments made in this section about the economic determinants of the national incremental wage pattern are based on the assumption of a certain institutional framework - the one which has existed throughout most of the post World War II period, with the wage pattern left to be determined through the key bargain reached in the bellwether industry. The arguments are based also on the assumption of a certain behavioral pattern on the part of trade union leaders, especially those in the bellwether industry. If that institutional framework or that behavioral pattern were to change, as could easily be the case in the future, the same economic relationships would not necessarily still apply. In fact, if the measures recommended in the final chapter of this treatise were to be adopted, W_p would become an instrumental variable whose value would depend, not on the consumer price index and/or reported net earnings in the bellwether industry but rather on the planned growth of aggregate disposable income. That the basis for establishing the national incremental wage pattern, and thus the basis for determining the growth of wages, can be altered in this or some other equally significant manner because neither the wage pattern nor the growth of wages depends solely on economic factors is one of the principal points which this treatise hopes to demonstrate.

Possible changes in the socio-political environment pertain, however, to what might be. Returning to the institutional framework which has existed for most of the post World War II period and which for the most part is still intact, the national incremental wage pattern depends on the collective bargaining agreements worked out in the bellwether industry. Presidential guideposts and pay boards notwithstanding, the key to the distribution of income within the oligopolistic sector continues to be the determination of the trade union setting the national pattern to obtain for its members an increase in wages equal to the percentage by which either prices for consumer goods or net earnings within the bellwether industry have risen since the last wage round. Its very success in doing so, however, together with the likelihood that any gains obtained by the trade union for its members will be matched by an equivalent increase in the dividend rate, means that, with the need to maintain a certain rate of growth for the corporate levy, the megacorp will be confronted by more claims against its revenue than it can meet at the existing price level. In the face of this type of pressure, it is generally the price level which, not surprisingly, gives way.

This suggests a distinction between nominal increases in the rates of compensation obtained by the megacorp's principal constituencies as a result of a higher value for W_p and what those increases in compensation actually come to represent in real terms once the effects of any ensuing rise in prices within the oligopolistic sector have been taken into account. To develop this point further, however, it is necessary to place the microeconomic variables dealt with so far into a post-Keynesian macrodynamic framework, such as the one provided in the next two chapters.

6. Micro and macro

One of the striking aspects of present economic theory is its disjointed nature. The two major bodies of theory, micro and macro, have only a slight relationship to one another; and it is possible, as the current practice in introductory economics courses demonstrates, to learn the one with but a passing reference to the other - or to master both, equally as well, in either of the two possible sequences. Price and quantity relationships, the heart of the micro theory, can be incorporated into macro analysis only by adding additional equations to the basic Keynesian model, and then the equations are likely to have an *ad hoc* empirical flavor detached from the ordinarily solid theoretical underpinnings of micro theory. The consumption and investment aggregates, on the other hand, the core of the macro theory, can be approached from a micro starting point only by derogating or ignoring the importance of many of the usual variables, and in that case the aesthetic balance of the general equilibrium system is likely to be lost. From a partial equilibrium model, the consumption and investment aggregates cannot even be derived. Micro and macro theory, then, stand as two separate bodies of analysis, with little in the way of a common perspective or a common set of variables to bind them together.

The reason for this dichotomous state of economic theory can be traced to the original Keynesian formulation. In *The General Theory*, Keynes (1936, especially ch. 2) was concerned primarily with destroying a belief in the efficacy of Say's Law, the intellectual foundations of what then passed for a theory of aggregate income and employment. But Say's Law was not fundamental to the work of Marshall, Keynes' mentor. Indeed, it is conspicuously absent from Marshall's published writings, particularly the *Principles* (1920; see also 1923). More generally, there was little in the Marshallian system to stand in the way of the propositions which Keynes wished to demonstrate.[1] And so, in propounding his macro analysis, Keynes could remain a loyal disciple, taking over unchanged whatever elements of Marshall's synthesis of neo-classical theory he required for his own purposes. If this led to an uncritical acceptance of competitively determined prices and marginal productivity-related income shares, the lapse can be excused on the grounds that Keynes already had battle enough to wage.

Still, it must be conceded that the updating of economic theory as a belated response to the evolution of economic institutions was incomplete. If the emergence of organized capital markets to supply corporations with investment funds raised the possibility that *ex ante* savings and investment might diverge, the rise of the oligopolistic megacorp itself called into question the very elements of the Marshallian system which Keynes uncritically incorporated into his own analysis. In truth, as will soon be pointed out, it even called into question the savings-investment adjustment process upon which Keynes based his arguments. The result was a job only half done, with Keynesian theory resting on a micro foundation which had not itself been revised to take into account the same structural changes which necessitated the writing of *The General Theory*.

That this grafting of the new upon the old - despite the many points of incongruity between them - remains the fundamental weakness of macroeconomic theory should not prove a startling thesis to economists who have witnessed, for all their success in controlling excessive unemployment, the persistence over the last several decades of stubborn cost-push inflation. Indeed, if this attempt to develop a determinate model of oligopolistic pricing has been intended to serve any useful purpose, it is to provide the basis for a reconstruction of micro theory which will at the same time be more congenial to the Keynesian aggregate analysis and better able to explain the post World War II inflation. The major elements required for that reconstruction of micro theory have already been introduced in the preceding chapters. All that remains to be done is to fit them into a Keynesian - or more accurately, a post-Keynesian macrodynamic - framework.

A common bond between the micro model set forth above and post-Keynesian macroeconomic theory should already be apparent. This is the emphasis which they both place on *ex ante* investment as the critical factor. In the Keynesian system it is this variable which, holding monetary conditions constant and ignoring both the government and rest-of-the-world sectors, determines aggregate demand and, hence, the level of national income. In the micro model developed above it is the same variable which, holding costs constant and ignoring changes in the supply conditions of investment funds, determines the industry price level and, hence, the price level in the oligopolistic sector of the economy. Yet merely to establish this common bond is not enough. The two bodies of theory must be made truly compatible so that the implications to be derived from the one are not inconsistent with the deductions made from the other. As we shall see, this will require certain modifications or refinements in the conventional macroeconomic analysis. Nor is it sufficient merely to adjust micro theory to the comparative statics of *The General Theory*. If the long-run consequences of public policies are to be fully traced out, it is necessary to conduct the aggregate analysis within a macrodynamic framework. Thus it is a dynamic version of the Keynesian model, such as that worked out by Joan Robinson, Nicholas Kaldor and certain other Cambridge, England, economists, with which the reconstruction of microeconomic theory must be made compatible.[2]

The agenda for this chapter is, then, as follows: first the rate of growth of investment, then the rate of growth of savings are to be discussed from the perspective of the oligopolistic sector alone. Investment demand and savings functions, with the rate of growth of aggregate output as the independent variable, will then be developed, first for that one sector alone and then for the remaining portion of the business sector as well as for the household, government and rest-of-the-world sectors. Finally, with the aid of these various investment demand and savings functions, derived from the microeconomic base developed in the earlier chapters, it will be possible to explain the macrodynamic properties of an economy like that of the United States with a significant oligopolistic sector.

The rate of growth of investment

An investment demand function for the oligopolistic sector has already been specified as an integral part of the pricing model developed in chapters 3 and 4. This investment demand function is based on two independent variables: (1) the marginal efficiency of investment and (2) the expected growth rate of industry sales. Which of the two variables is the more significant depends both on the type of investment being undertaken and on the context in which the investment demand function is being viewed.

The various categories of investment previously considered can be broken down into two broad groupings. The first of these groupings is limited to investment outlays which have as their object an incremental increase in the corporate levy over the long run. They consist of expenditures on advertising, research and development, or any other activity which will enable the megacorp to differentiate its product more sharply, erect higher barriers to entry and/or create a more favorable public image. This first broad grouping even encompasses the purchase of cost-reducing equipment and the initial expansion into a new industry. For all these types of investment, the key determinant is the estimated marginal efficiency or, as a more readily determined approximation, the inverse of the pay-off period.

What is significant about this first broad category is that it gives rise to the downward sloping investment demand schedule which lies at the heart of both the original Keynesian analysis and the pricing model set forth in chapter 3 above. By ranking each of the possible investment projects in the descending order of their expected return over cost, whether measured in terms of the increment in net revenue or the increment in the realized corporate levy, it is possible to indicate how the total amount of investment that can profitably be undertaken will vary as the marginal efficiency itself varies. An explicit treatment of this relationship is essential if the amount of investment being undertaken is to be explained in terms of some other variable, such as the permanent interest rate or the price level, and that other variable in turn is to be explained by the amount of investment being undertaken. It is for this reason that it has been necessary to incorporate a negatively sloped investment demand schedule into both the original Keynesian analysis and the pricing model developed above - even though the amount of investment involved in this first broad grouping is only a small portion of the total investment likely to be undertaken at any given point in time.

Most investment, then, falls within the second broad grouping, limited to investment outlays which have as their object the maintenance of the existing market share within each of the industries to which the megacorp belongs. These investment outlays consist entirely of expenditures on new plant and equipment, and are intended to provide the megacorp with sufficient capacity to meet whatever demand for its various products is likely to manifest itself. Only if the megacorp is assured on this point can it expect to hold on its historical share of whatever markets it serves. For this type of investment, the key determinant is the expected growth rate of industry sales.

This expected growth rate is based on the past trend of industry sales, not because the past is necessarily thought to repeat itself but because it is the only guide to the future. What the megacorp must assume is that there exists a strong secular trend in the growth of industry sales, reflecting the influence of population, income and similar long-run factors. The megacorp's problem is to determine what that secular trend is so it can increase its productive capacity accordingly. The past pattern of industry sales is perhaps the best indication of what that secular growth path may be. At the same time, however, in extrapolating forward the past trend of industry sales, the megacorp must be careful not to preclude the possibility that the industry's secular growth path has changed. It will allow for this contingency by giving considerably greater weight to its more recent sales experience. What this means is that as long as the past trend of industry sales continues to be maintained, the individual firm's rate of growth of investment will hold steady; but if industry sales should begin to follow an erratic path, the rate growth of investment will vary as a lagged response to changes in that underlying factor. Since most of the investment undertaken in the oligopolistic sector - if not throughout the rest of the economy - falls into this second broad category, it is the expected growth rate of individual industries, estimated in the above manner, which is the more significant explanatory variable underlying investment. This conclusion is reinforced by the fact that, over the long run, the marginal efficiency of investment can be expected to fluctuate only within certain narrow limits.

It should be emphasized that the variable under discussion here is the rate of growth of investment, $\overset{*}{I}$, and not just the level of investment, I. To focus on the latter, as is usually done, is to restrict the analysis to a static mold. The fact is that the purchase of new plant and equipment by a megacorp is not a discrete act taking place intermittently but rather a continuous process occurring over time, one which involves an increasing *level* of expenditures as the size of the firm itself increases. It is therefore necessary to speak of the rate of growth of investment, not only with respect to the individual megacorp but with the respect to the industry as well and, indeed, with respect to the entire oligopolistic sector. This, in turn, converts the static analysis of Keynes into the dynamic analysis of the post-Keynesians. The last-mentioned rate of growth of investment, that for the oligopolistic sector as a whole, will depend primarily on the rate of growth of sales in each of the industries comprising the oligopolistic sector. In other words, the determinants of the aggregate investment function are the same as those for the individual firm and industry functions.

Thus, while the marginal efficiency of investment must be brought into the analysis if adequate links to the capital funds market and to the price level are to be established, the expected growth rate of industry sales is, for the most part, sufficient by itself to explain the rate of growth of investment, $\overset{*}{I}_O$, within the oligopolistic sector. An investment demand function formulated in this manner has several important macro-dynamic implications. First of all, since the rate of growth of industry sales is likely to reflect the rate of growth of aggregate investment - a significant part of which will derive from the growth of investment within the oligopolistic sector as a result of the secular rise in industry sales - the basis has been established for the continuous expansion of the economy as a whole, once growth has been initiated. Second, because of the lag in adjusting investment expenditures to the change in industry sales, investment in the oligopolistic sector can be expected to exert an overall stabilizing influence. No matter how much industry sales may vary in any given year due to exogenous forces, the change in investment in the oligopolistic sector will be considerably more moderate. There will thus be a powerful endogenous force at work, at least within the oligopolistic sector from the investment demand side, to dampen any fluctuations in aggregate demand and national income.[3]

It should be noted that an investment demand function of this type is consistent with the current econometric emphasis on accelerator models of investment. In fact, this investment demand function and recent empirical research reinforce one another - the latter helping to provide quantitative verification of the micro theory[4] and the former making it possible to choose not only between the accelerator model and alternative formulations but also among different versions of the accelerator model itself.

For many years the accelerator model - regardless of how formulated - fared less well under empirical testing than an investment model based on other variables.[5] But then Eisner (1960), building on earlier work by others, began to develop an accelerator model that was different from previous formulations in two important respects. First he argued - with empirical data to support his contention - that an investment demand function properly specified would depend on changes in aggregate demand not in any one previous year but rather distributed over several years previously.[6] Second he asserted - again with empirical data to support his contention - that changes in investment were related less to changes in aggregate demand than to changes in the demand experienced by individual industries, these changes being reflected in past sales figures (Eisner, 1963). As finally set forth, then, the Eisner version of the accelerator model related changes in the demand for investment by individual industries to changes in sales over the previous seven-year period, the aggregate investment demand function being simply the sum of these individual industry demand schedules.

An investment demand function of this form not only better fits the empirical data Eisner examined but, by that very fact, also tends to confirm the validity of the investment demand function which is so integral a part of the oligopolistic pricing model developed in chapter 3. The difference between that investment demand function and the estimating equation used by Eisner is relatively insignificant.[7] At the same time, the earlier analysis of oligopolistic pricing behavior provides a strong theoretical argument in support of Eisner's empirical findings. As that analysis sought to make clear, the demand for investment based on past sales experience derives from the megacorp's fundamental goal of maintaining, and perhaps even increasing, its share of whatever market it supplies. In the light of that underlying motivation, it is hardly surprising that investment by firms in the aggregate should be geared to what Eisner has termed the 'permanent' sales of various industries.

The oligopolistic pricing model also helps to explain why a capacity utilization variable, which in some ways is much closer than the past sales variables to the original spirit of the acceleration principle, performs less satisfactorily in some of the econometric models. As has already been emphasized, the megacorp's management will always seek to have a certain amount of excess capacity available to meet any unexpected increase in demand. To do otherwise would be to jeopardize the company's relative market position. Typically, therefore, the megacorp's management will act to increase the company's plant and equipment before the limits of capacity have been reached. Variations in capacity utilization, then, are merely a reflection of the cyclical volatility of demand, a phenomenon which is most likely to have already been taken into account in the past planning of investment expenditures. They will not, except under unusual circumstances, be the direct signal for further outlays on new plant and equipment.

The oligopolistic pricing model developed in chapter 3 helps to explain, moreover, why an interest rate variable, if included in the accelerator model, accounts for such a small part of the total variation in investment expenditures.[8] The fact that only certain marginal projects, representing but a minor portion of all investment expenditures, depend on the marginal efficiency of investment, and hence on changes in the cost of external funds, has already been pointed out. What must also be kept in mind is the relationship between this cost of external funds, the 'permanent' interest rate as it has been termed, and the market rate of interest observed at any given moment in time. That permanent interest rate reflects only the expected minimum rate of interest expected to prevail over the business cycle - so that a change in the actual market rate of interest observed at any given point in time is likely to have an effect on investment only insofar as it is taken as evidence of what the minimum rate of interest will be in the future. Even then, as already pointed out, the cost of fixed debt obligations is merely one of two elements that must be taken into account in determining the permanent interest rate on external funds. In light of these theoretical arguments it is hardly surprising that for many years econometric studies failed to disclose any significant relationship between short-run changes in interest rates and changes in the level of investment in new plant and equipment, such as a highly simplified model based on *The General Theory* would suggest exists.[9] Nor is it surprising that, in order to reveal at last the relatively minor influence on investment exerted by conditions in the capital funds market, more recent econometric studies have found it necessary to employ a lagged, long-term interest rate variable.[10] As is implicit in the oligopolistic pricing model, a change on the monetary side of the economy can be expected to affect investment decisions on the real side only slightly, and even then only over the long run.[11]

Finally, the oligopolistic pricing model provides strong theoretical support for rejecting an investment demand function based on the past profits variable. For a long time, after the initial empirical studies failed to reveal any significant relationship between interest rates and investment, econometricians were content simply to base their investment demand function on the amount of profits previously earned (cf. Tinbergen, 1968, Klein and Goldberger, 1955; Suits, 1962). It was difficult to justify this expedient on theoretical grounds - unless one assumed that businessmen were so irrational as to confuse past profits with future anticipated gains, or that past profits were a measure of liquidity and hence an indication of the ability to finance subsequent capital outlays. In the latter case, of course, one had a theory not of investment demand but rather of investment funds supply. Still, econometricians continued to fall back on the past profits variable because, until Eisner and others began to refine the accelerator model, it was the only variable that could be used with any success to predict investment.

The oligopolistic pricing model helps to explain why, when a lagged accelerator model is employed, the past profits variable loses virtually all of its explanatory power (Eisner, 1963, pp. 241, 243, 246; see also Jorgenson, 1971, p. 1133). It will be recalled that, rather than the level of investment being determined by the amount of net revenue, or corporate levy, available to finance investment, the price level in an oligopolistic industry is under ordinary circumstances set so as to yield sufficient net revenue, or corporate levy, over the planning period to finance the level of desired investment. In other words, assuming that the restraints on pricing discretion are not so great as to preclude any further increase in prices, the availability of funds, or liquidity, will not set a limit on the amount of investment expenditures undertaken. Even if the restraints on pricing discretion are momentarily prohibitive, investment will depend on the amount of net revenue, or corporate levy, realized not in any single year but rather over the entire planning period. It is only because net revenue is highly sensitive to changes in sales that the past profits variable can be used with such success to predict subsequent investment. However, the past trend of sales is an even better predictor. For while the past profits variable, as will soon be brought out more clearly, simply measures *ex post* savings, the past trend of industry sales is the basis for estimating the expected growth rate of industry sales and hence is the best proxy variable for desired investment.[12]

From the oligopolistic model it is possible, then, to extract an investment demand function based, to some degree, on the marginal efficiency of investment, *r*, and, to a far greater extent, on the expected growth rate of industry sales, the latter being approximated in the aggregate by the secular trend of the growth of total output, $\overset{*}{G}_s$.[13] That is,

$$\overset{*}{I}_O = f(r, \overset{*}{G}_s). \tag{6.1}$$

The investment demand function, in this form, is based on the assumption that the actual growth rate is equal to the secular, and thus to the expected, growth rate. When that condition does not hold - which is almost always the case - the rate of growth of investment within the oligopolistic sector, $\overset{*}{I}_O$, must be taken to be a function, more generally, of the difference between the actual and the secular growth rates, $\overset{*}{G}-\overset{*}{G}_s$. With expectations thus being disappointed, that additional factor - along with every other carry-over from the past into the present - needs to be taken explicitly into account. This can be done through the inclusion of a shift variable, $\overset{*}{I}_{O_a}$, in the investment demand function, indicating the rate of growth of investment which will occur independently of any current conditions. Both lag effects from the past as well as expectations about the future are encompassed by this shift variable, which serves as a separate parameter of the oligopolistic sector's investment demand function. That is,

$$\overset{*}{I}_O = \overset{*}{I}_{O_a} + f(r, \overset{*}{G}-\overset{*}{G}_s). \tag{6.2}$$

An investment demand function of this type is not only consistent with recent econometric investigations of expenditures on new plant and equipment, it also lends strong theoretical support to those very same empirical studies.

The rate of growth of savings

Just as an investment demand function was implicit in the oligopolistic pricing model developed in chapters 3 and 4, so a savings function was implicit in the income distribution model sketched out in chapter 5. Unlike the savings function found in *The General Theory* and employed in virtually all the macroeconomic textbooks, this function emphasizes the savings generated in the business sector through the corporate levy. Indeed, the corporate levy is what is meant by savings in the oligopolistic sector and, to the extent that other industries approximate the oligopolistic model as discussed in chapter 4, throughout the rest of the business sector as well. This savings function is based on the following variables: (1) the industry price level; (2) the national incremental wage pattern; (3) corporate and/or *ad valorem* tax rates, and (4) the rate of growth of aggregate output. Each of these variables will be discussed in turn.

As has frequently been emphasized in this treatise, the price level in an oligopolistic industry will ordinarily be set so as to yield a margin above costs, or average corporate levy, sufficient to finance the anticipated level of investment over the current planning period. The revenues thereby obtained, over and above the sums set aside for payment to the various constituencies, constitute the residual income, or savings, of the megacorps in that industry. The higher the price level, holding wages and tax rates constant, the greater will be the rate of growth of savings.

Again here, as in the earlier discussion of investment, it is not enough to speak merely in terms of levels. If the investment financed from internal savings brings the increments in the realized corporate levy that were projected at the time the capital funds were committed - largely because the added capacity has enabled the megacorps in the industry to increase their sales - the savings being generated within the industry should also increase over time. For this reason it is better to speak of the rate of growth, and not just the level, of savings. An increase in the price level will lead to an increase in the rate of growth of savings within the industry, and what is true of one oligopolistic industry will be true of the oligopolistic sector as a whole. One can therefore specify a rate of growth of savings for the oligopolistic sector. $\overset{*}{S}_O$, this rate of growth of savings being a function, among other things, of the average price level within the sector, $\bar{P}_O$.

The rate of growth of savings will also be a function of the national incremental wage pattern, W_p - and, in particular, of any difference between that rate of growth of wages and the secular rate of growth of output per worker in the oligopolistic sector, $\overset{*}{Z}_s$. An increase in the national incremental wage pattern relative to the growth of output per worker will, as described in the preceding chapter, lead to an increase in average variable and fixed costs within the oligopolistic sector; and this increase in costs, holding the price level and tax rates constant, will in turn lead to a decrease in the rate of growth of the corporate levy, or savings, within that sector. There is thus a negative relationship between $W_p - \overset{*}{Z}_s$ on the one hand and $\overset{*}{S}_O$ on the other, just as there is between W_p alone and $\overset{*}{S}_O$. The rate of growth of output per worker, reflecting as it does the marginal social surplus being created in the oligopolistic sector, will, of course, vary positively with the rate of growth of savings.

There is a similar negative relationship between the rate of growth of savings within the oligopolistic sector and the various tax rates to which the megacorp is subject. This is because, so far as the megacorp is concerned, the taxes paid the government are no less of a drain on its discretionary income than the wages paid the laboring manpower force. At present the megacorp is subject to two major types of taxes: (a) *ad valorem* taxes, either specific excise taxes or general sales taxes, levied as a percentage of the industry price, and (b) the corporate income tax levied as a percentage of reported net earnings. The imposition of, or an increase in, the first type of tax has the effect, with the price level remaining unchanged, of reducing the megacorp's average revenue by an amount equal to the price multiplied by the difference between the old and new tax rates, that is, by an amount equal to $P(\Delta t_e)$, where Δt_e is the change in the *ad valorem* tax rate. The imposition of, or an increase in, the corporate income tax has the effect, with the price level remaining unchanged, of also reducing the megacorp's average revenue. In this case, however, since the tax is levied only on the firm's reported net earnings, the effect is somewhat muted. Average revenue will decline by an amount equal, not to the price multiplied by the difference between the old and new tax rates but rather, by the proportion of that amount represented by the ratio of net income to total income. That is, it will decline by an amount equal to $Net \cdot P(\Delta t_y)$, where Δt_y is the change in the corporate income tax rate and *Net* is the ratio of net income to total income.[14] In either case, with the price level remaining unchanged, the imposition of or an increase in the tax will lead to a decline in the amount of savings being generated within the oligopolistic sector. Thus there is a negative relationship between the various tax rates which apply to the megacorp and the rate of growth of savings, $\overset{*}{S}_O$.

What is interesting about the three determinants of the rate of growth of savings in the oligopolistic sector considered so far is that each involves a certain degree of discretion by a different group in society. The national incremental wage pattern, W_p, depends largely on the will of the trade union setting the key bargain in the bellwether industry. The corporate income tax rate, t_y, and the *ad valorem* tax rate, t_e, depend entirely on the fiscal policies of the Federal government. Finally, the average price level in the oligopolistic sector, $\bar{P}_O$, holding W_p, t_y and t_e constant, depends on the pricing decisions of megacorps. The autonomous nature of at least the first two of these variables contrasts sharply with the purely endogenous nature of the variables determining the rate of growth of investment in the oligopolistic sector, $\overset{*}{I}_O$.

Of course, the various determinants of the rate of growth of savings in the oligopolistic sector are not necessarily independent of one another. As pointed out in the preceding chapter, an increase in the national incremental wage pattern, W_p, may well be followed by an increase in the price level for the oligopolistic sector, $\bar{P}_O$. As will be argued later in this chapter, an increase in either of the two tax rates, t_y or t_e, is also likely to have the same effect. On the other hand, an increase in $\bar{P}_O$ will, under some circumstances, lead to an increase in W_p. Thus a change of a certain sort in one or more of these independent variables may initiate the dynamic sequence of events known as the wage-price spiral, with a subsequent decline in the aggregate growth rate, engineered by the government itself, the most probable outcome. Still, it is only certain changes in these variables which are likely to have such an effect. As long as the new wage pattern and/or tax rates do nothing to impair the ability of megacorps to generate sufficient investment funds from internal sources to finance their desired rate of growth of investment, a wage-price spiral is not likely to be initiated. The condition which must therefore be satisfied if there is to be macrodynamic stability is that, following the change in the wage pattern and/or tax rates, the rate of growth of savings in the oligopolistic sector, $\overset{*}{S}_O$, must be equal to the rate of growth of investment, $\overset{*}{I}_O$, without the price level in the oligopolistic sector, $\bar{P}_O$, having first had to be adjusted. It is clear, then, that a delicate balance is required for macrodynamic stability.[15]

The argument so far has been predicated on the assumption that prices in the oligopolistic sector are set so as to enable the megacorps in that sector to finance during the current planning period all of their desired investment by means of the corporate levy - or, in other words, that the amount of planned savings likely to result from the prices that have been set is equal to the amount of planned investment over the intermediate run. To the extent that the demand for investment funds is so great relative to the cost of obtaining them internally that megacorps are forced to resort to external financing, this assumption is no longer entirely valid. The gap between planned savings and planned investment in the oligopolistic sector must, under the circumstances, be filled by tapping the savings of the household sector. Still, since megacorps rely primarily on internal financing, this is not a serious qualification (see note 17 to chapter 1). There is thus good reason for assuming, as the argument which follows starts out by doing, that planned savings within the oligopolistic sector will be equal to planned investment.[16] And this assumption, in turn, insofar as it holds true, requires an important modification of the savings-investment adjustment process formulated by Keynes in *The General Theory*.

The critical difference between Keynes and those whom he referred to as the classical economists was Keynes' gradual awareness that since the decisions of how much to save and how much to invest were made by different groups in society - the one by households and the other by business firms - savings and investment were unlikely to be equal to each other, at least before the decisions were acted on, that is, *ex ante*. In erecting his theory on this insight, the author of *The General Theory* was merely giving belated recognition to a significant change that had occurred in the institutional character of the economy. The increased use of the corporate form of business organization, enabling firms to obtain their investment funds through well-organized capital markets, meant that the decision to save could no longer be assumed to be the equivalent of the decision to invest as it had been when an extrepreneurial class was forced to finance plant, equipment and inventory expansion largely out of its own pockets. The existence of a monetary system capable both of expanding the money supply in response to business firms' credit needs and of sterilizing any increase in personal savings by households now made it possible for the one type of decision to be undertaken independently of the other - at least initially.[17] Yet the further evolution of the economic system has led to a situation which, in some ways, is closer to that implicit in the pre-Keynesian understanding of the savings-investment process. This newer reality reflects the megacorp's ability to finance most of its desired level of investment internally by means of the corporate levy. In other words, the decisions to save and invest - at least in the oligopolistic sector of the economy - are once again joined in a single entity, even if that entity is a social organization rather than any single person (see above, pp. 21-7).

Despite this fact, it is still possible for savings and investment to diverge - though not in the usually stated *ex ante* sense. To understand how this can be the case, it is necessary to introduce into the analysis the fourth and final factor determining the rate of growth of savings in the oligopolistic sector. This variable is the rate of growth of aggregate output, $\overset{*}{G}$. What is of particular significance here, in discussing the rate of growth of savings over the intermediate run, that is, during the planning period of the typical megacorp, is the difference between this growth rate and the secular growth rate, $\overset{*}{G}_s$, upon which the standard operating ratio is based, for this difference is a measure of the cyclical level of aggregate demand.[18] This same factor, $\overset{*}{G}-\overset{*}{G}_s$, has already been encountered in the preceding chapter where the Keynesian theory of income distribution was discussed. As was then pointed out, the distribution of income between the megacorp's two principal constituencies on the one hand and the megacorp itself on the other depends on aggregate economic conditions - that is, on the difference between the standard operating ratio and the actual operating ratio which, in a dynamic context, is the same as the difference between the secular growth rate, $\overset{*}{G}_s$, and the current aggregate growth rate, $\overset{*}{G}$. Now, in a slightly different context, it will be argued that the divergence between *ex ante* savings (and investment) on the one hand and *ex post* savings on the other can be explained in precisely the same terms.

As planned by the megacorp, savings will almost certainly be equal to investment, for it can be assumed that, ignoring any need for external financing, the price level will be set so as to provide sufficient funds for whatever investment expenditures are contemplated during the current planning period. The amount of funds actually obtained at any given point in time will depend, however, on the level of aggregate demand, for as noted in the earlier discussion of pricing and income distribution, the greater the current operating ratio, the larger will be the amount of corporate levy accruing to the firm (see above, p. 180). Thus, while the amount of savings and investment planned may be equal to one another, the amount of savings and investment actually realized will, to the extent that the current aggregate growth rate differs from the secular growth rate, necessarily diverge. As a measure of this discrepancy, one can look, not only at the gap between actual operating ratios and the standard operating ratio but also, at the change in the liquid asset position of megacorps, holding outlays constant.[19]

During that portion of the planning period which falls within an expansionary phase of the cycle, the actual rate of capacity utilization is likely to be greater than the standard operating ratio, and the savings realized by the megacorp will exceed those originally planned. This means that the megacorp's holdings of short-term liquid assets will tend to increase.[20] During that portion of the planning period which falls within a contractionary phase of the cycle, the opposite will be true and the megacorp's holdings of short-term liquid assets will tend to decrease. Moreover, since the marginal corporate levy is greater than the average corporate levy, the gap between planned and realized savings will be an increasing function of the difference between the current aggregate growth rate and the secular growth rate for the economy as a whole.

Of course, the secular growth rate itself may change. To the extent that this is recognized by megacorps, they will simply adjust their price levels, causing a shift in the price level for the oligopolistic sector as a whole. But to the extent that the change in the secular growth rate goes unrecognized - and, as was pointed out above, in chapter 5, this type of change is extremely difficult to distinguish from the normal cyclical pattern of fluctuations in aggregate demand - it will lead to an even greater difference between the current aggregate growth rate and the secular growth rate as presently perceived.

It should be added that the rate of growth of output per worker in the oligopolistic sector, because of its close correspondence to the rate of growth of savings within the sector, will be subject to the same cyclical fluctuations. Thus to avoid encompassing that intermediate-run effect more than once in the savings function for the oligopolistic sector, it is necessary to take as the base against which to compare the national incremental wage pattern, not $\overset{*}{Z}_O$, the current growth rate of output per worker in the oligopolistic sector but rather $\overset{*}{Z}_s$, the secular growth rate of output per worker, that is, the growth rate of output per worker when the economy is expanding at its secular rate and megacorps are therefore producing at their standard operating ratio.

In summary, then, the rate of growth of savings within the oligopolistic sector, $\overset{*}{S}_O$, will be a function of the price level within the oligopolistic sector, the difference between the secular growth rate of output per worker and the national incremental wage pattern, the several tax rates to which the megacorp is subject, and the divergence between the secular growth rate and the current growth rate. Moreover, it will be affected by any change in the shift variable, $\overset{*}{S}_{O_a}$, which, like the similar shift variable for the rate of growth of investment, is a parameter of the overall function. In this case, $\overset{*}{S}_{O_a}$ indicates the rate of growth of savings within the oligopolistic sector which will occur independently of current conditions. It reflects primarily the lag effect of past decisions about the desired level of savings. That is,

$$\overset{*}{S}_O = \overset{*}{S}_{O_a} + f(\bar{P}_O, W_p - \overset{*}{Z}_s, t_y, t_e, \overset{*}{G} - \overset{*}{G}_s). \tag{6.3}$$

A savings function of this type is quite different from that usually specified in macroeconomic analysis.[21] In the conventional treatment, the savings function pertains only to the household sector. To the extent that the sole interest is in explaining short-run changes in consumption expenditures - these consumption expenditures being the largest component of national income - this exclusive focus on the household sector may be justified. But it should be recognized that, by implicitly ignoring the savings being generated in the business sector, the conventional treatment fails to explain the larger part of aggregate private savings. This is not an argument for abandoning the Keynesian savings function but rather an argument for making it more comprehensive and more fully specified. Instead of being viewed as simply a linear function of aggregate income, and as the obverse of consumption within the household sector, savings must be seen as both an increasing function of the rate of growth of national income - reflecting the disproportionate influence which a higher aggregate growth rate has on the realized corporate levy - and as a linear function of the price level within the oligopolistic sector,[22] with the national incremental wage pattern, the secular growth of output per worker and the several tax rates which apply directly to the megacorp as additional parameters. While a savings function of this sort has not yet been specifically tested empirically, it is nonetheless consistent with the evidence from studies of the cylical distribution of income.[23]

A savings function based on the rate of growth of aggregate output, among other variables, has a number of important dynamic implications, especially when considered in conjunction with an investment demand function based on the expected growth rate of industry sales. It is these dynamic implications, centering on the investment-savings adjustment process appropriate to the oligopolistic sector, that will presently be examined. First, however, it is necessary to take up a minor point, the extent to which the savings and investment functions just defined exist independently of one another.

The rate of growth of aggregate output, $\overset{*}{G}$, is, to be sure, a key determinant of both functions. A change in this variable, to the extent that it is taken as evidence of a change in the secular growth of sales within the oligopolistic sector, will lead to a change in the rate of growth of investment within the sector, $\overset{*}{I}_O$. The same change in $\overset{*}{G}$, to the extent that it marks a change in the differential between the current aggregate growth rate and the secular growth rate, will at the same time lead to a change in the rate of growth of savings, $\overset{*}{S}_O$. However, the fact that both functions are based, at least in part, on the same variable no more precludes them from behaving independently of one another than the joint dependence of conventional supply and demand curves on the price variable precludes them from behaving independently.

It can, of course, be argued that a change in the price level within the oligopolistic sector, since the sector includes many capital goods industries, will affect the marginal efficiency of investment. In that case, since the price level is also a determinant of the rate of growth of savings within the oligopolistic sector, the savings and investment functions would have another independent variable which they share in common. But since most purchases of new plant and equipment depend, not on the marginal efficiency of investment but rather, on the expected growth rate of industry sales, this possible complication can all but be ignored. The effect of a change in the price level of capital goods on the rate of growth of investment will, if anything, be slight.[24] Much the same can be said about the likely effect on capital expenditures of a change either in the wage pattern or in tax rates. With this point covered, it is possible to move on and consider the dynamic adjustment of investment and savings.

The dynamic adjustment of investment and savings

What is of concern here is the process by which investment and savings in the oligopolistic sector, though apt to diverge from one another in the short run, nonetheless give rise to economic forces which tend to bring the two flows back into balance over the intermediate run. Why investment and savings are apt to diverge from one another in the short run should now be clear. While investment expenditures, based as they are on the expected growth rate of industry sales, are likely to remain relatively stable, the amount of savings actually realized will vary considerably depending on the current operating ratio. This is not to suggest that investment expenditures are likely to remain absolutely fixed no matter what the current level of sales may be. It is rather to point out that the expected growth rate of industry sales, which is derived by extrapolating forward the past trend of industry sales, will be only slightly affected by the sales experience at any single point in time. To the extent that the fluctuations in industry sales are consistent with the anticipated cyclical pattern, they may even occasion no substantial revision of the megacorp's investment plans. This is in contrast to the considerable variation in the realized corporate levy, and hence in the amount of savings generated by the megacorp, as a result of those same fluctuations in industry sales.

The fact that investment and savings are apt to diverge in the short run is not the end of the matter, however. The divergence itself will set in motion self-correcting economic forces. To the extent that the amount of savings being generated exceeds the level of investment expenditures, the megacorp will be withdrawing a larger amount of claims from the income stream than it is returning through its purchase of new plant and equipment, as well as through its purchase of other types of investment goods and services. The dampening effect that this will have on aggregate income flows will then tend to reduce the level of sales which has given rise to the excess of savings over investment. Conversely, to the extent that the amount of savings being generated falls short of the level of investment expenditures, the megacorp will be withdrawing a smaller amount of claims from the income stream than it is returning. The stimulative effect that this will have on aggregate income flows will tend to expand the level of sales so as to eliminate the deficiency of savings.

Since aggregate economic conditions are the operative factor here, what is true of one megacorp is likely to be true of all megacorps; and thus the oligopolistic sector of the economy can be expected to exert a contracyclical influence similar to that of the Federal government itself through its tax and transfer programs. In other words, because of the way it is exacted, the corporate levy acts as an automatic stabilizer over the intermediate run. In an expansionary phase of the cycle, the savings realized by the megacorp through the corporate levy are likely to be greater than the current level of investment and thus will have a restrictive effect on the economy in general. In the contractionary phase of the cycle, the reverse will be the case, the excess of investment over savings giving rise to a stimulative effect. Over the intermediate run, however, to the extent that the fluctuations in industry sales are consistent with the anticipated cyclical pattern, the two effects should offset one another, with the result that investment can be expected to equal savings over the business cycle, both *ex post* and *ex ante*, even though they will not necessarily be equal to each other at any particular point in time.

The savings-investment adjustment process just described differs significantly from that found in *The General Theory* and in most of the subsequent elaborations of that static macroeconomic model. In the usual Keynesian formulation, it is the ability of business firms to undertake investment expenditures independently of the savings decisions reached by households that permits savings and investment to diverge, at least *ex ante*; and it is the resulting effect of those investment expenditures on household income which then brings the two flows back into equilibrium. The burden of the preceding argument is not to deny that an adjustment process of this type exists. It is rather to point out that only a minor portion of business investment is financed from external sources and that therefore the more significant adjustment process is that which takes place within the business sector itself, and, in particular, within the oligopolistic component of that sector (see note 17 to chapter 1). As brought out above, it is the sensitivity of the realized corporate levy to aggregate economic conditions that permits savings and investment to diverge, not *ex ante* but rather, *ex post* in the short run; and it is the contracyclical effect of the fluctuations in the realized corporate levy which then tends to bring the two flows back into equilibrium over the intermediate run. Despite these differences, both adjustment processes are alike in emphasizing the role of the monetary system in enabling savings and investment to diverge in the first place; and alike in emphasizing the preponderant influence of investment in determining a new macrodynamic balance.

What has just been said about savings and investment being equal to one another, *ex post*, over the planning period is predicated, however, on the assumption that the past secular growth rate of individual oligopolistic industries and of the economy as a whole will continue to be maintained. Otherwise, the standard operating ratio, upon which is based the average corporate levy and, *pari passu*, the industry price level, will be incorrectly estimated. If there has been an increase in the secular growth rate so that the actual rate of capacity utilization within the oligopolistic sector consistently exceeds the standard operating ratio, the rate of growth of savings will be greater than planned when the price level was set. Similarly, if there has been a decrease in the secular growth rate so that the oligopolistic sector continually finds itself producing below its standard operating ratio, the rate of growth of savings will be lower than anticipated.

Of course, the rate of growth of investment is likely to be adjusted accordingly. If, for example, the secular growth of aggregate demand has been greater than previously anticipated, the megacorp will need to expand its plant and equipment at a more rapid rate. Similarly, if the secular growth has been smaller than anticipated, the megacorp will be likely to expand its plant and equipment more slowly. Still, because of the long lead time required to bring a new plant into operation, or even to modernize the equipment in an old one, any change in investment is likely to lag behind, and be smaller than, the change in savings due to a difference between the average rate of capacity utilization over the current planning period and the standard operating ratio. This gives rise to a somewhat different investment-savings adjustment process over the long run, one that is inherent in combining an investment demand function based on the trend of past sales - as a proxy for the expected future growth of the industry - with a savings function highly sensitive to current sales alone. How this adjustment process works is perhaps best explained with the aid of figure 19.

The diagram, by measuring both the rate of growth of investment - or, to use Joan Robinson's phrase, the rate of accumulation - and the rate of growth of savings along the vertical axis, shows each of these two variables as a function of the aggregate growth rate, $\overset{*}{G}$, measured along the horizontal axis (cf. J. Robinson, 1962a, pp. 34-48). For the moment it will simplify the exposition to assume that the aggregate growth rate is the same as the growth rate within the oligopolistic sector. Later, when the non-oligopolistic subsector and the household, foreign

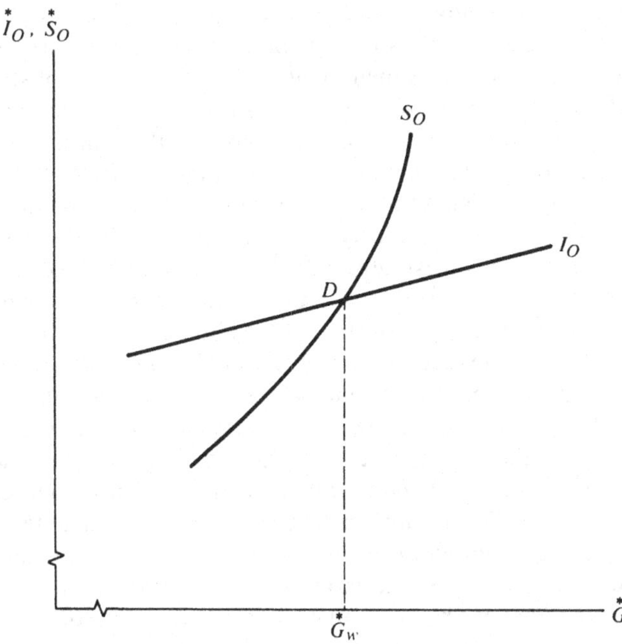

Figure 19

and government sectors are brought into the analysis, this assumption will be dropped. In the diagram, curve I_O is the investment demand curve, indicating the effect that an increase in the aggregate growth rate will have on the rate of growth of investment, holding the marginal efficiency of investment, *r*, constant. It is a straight line with a slope of less than one, reflecting the fact that an increase in the aggregate growth rate will, within a single time period or even over the entire planning period, lead to only a partial increase in the rate of growth of investment. If an increase in the aggregate growth rate were to lead immediately to a proportionate increase in the capital stock, the slope would be equal to one; if it had no effect whatsoever on investment expenditures, the slope would be equal to zero and curve I_O would be horizontal.[25] Curve S_O is the savings curve, indicating the effect that an increase in the aggregate growth rate will have on the rate of growth of savings. It bows upward, reflecting the fact that an increase in the aggregate growth rate, both in the short run and over the intermediate, or planning, period, will lead to a disproportionate increase in the rate of growth of savings.

Point *D* is the one point at which, under the conditions presumed in figure 19, the rate of growth of investment, $\overset{*}{I}_O$, is equal to the rate of growth of savings, $\overset{*}{S}_O$. Ignoring for the moment the possibility of a divergence between investment and savings in some other part of the economic system, it is thus the one point at which the corresponding growth rate, $\overset{*}{G}$, can be maintained indefinitely. If the oligopolistic sector should find itself at a point above *D* - as it will if the secular growth rate, due to exogenous factors, has been greater than anticipated - the rate of growth of investment over the planning period, that is, the intermediate run, will fall short of the rate of growth of savings. With savings and investment previously equal to one another, the resulting excess of savings over investment will then act as a drag on the growth rate until it has been slowed down to the rate associated with point *D*. Alternatively, if the oligopolistic sector should find itself at a point below *D* - as it will if the secular growth rate has been less than anticipated - the rate of growth of investment will exceed the rate of growth of savings. In this case, the excess of investment over savings will act as a stimulant on the aggregate growth rate until it has been increased to the rate associated with point *D*. It is in this sense that $\overset{*}{G}_w$, the rate of growth associated with point *D*, is the only warranted growth rate, that is, the only growth rate for the oligopolistic sector (and, since all the other sectors are for the moment being ignored, for the overall economy as well) that can be maintained indefinitely, given the investment and savings functions represented by curves I_O and S_O.[26]

Of course, since the variables employed in this analysis are rates of growth, and not levels, once the growth path defined by the warranted growth rate has been deviated from, differing rates of growth both of savings and of investment will be required to bring the economic system back on to that track. These interceding values for $\overset{*}{I}_O$ and $\overset{*}{S}_O$ respectively can be ignored, however, and the analysis focused solely on the value of $\overset{*}{I}_O$ and $\overset{*}{S}_O$ at point D as the limit toward which both the rate of growth of investment and the rate of growth of savings will approach, whether monotonically or not, as the economic system returns to the growth path defined by the warranted growth rate. It should be noted that this warranted growth rate is not the same as the secular growth rate. The former is simply a theoretical construct. It refers to a rate of expansion which can be maintained indefinitely once certain conditions have been met - in this case $\overset{*}{I}_O$ being equal to $\overset{*}{S}_O$. Such a warranted growth rate is unlikely ever to be actually observed, however, since various factors will continually make their influence felt, causing the economy to deviate from the steady-state rate of expansion defined by the warranted growth rate. The secular growth rate, obtained by averaging out these deviations over time, is in fact the closest that it is possible to come to measuring the warranted growth rate, and it is thus the secular growth rate upon which expectations about the future are based. The distinction between the warranted growth rate and the secular growth rate is a crucial one. Indeed, it is essential for understanding how a macrodynamic disequilibrium can occur. Before taking up that point, however, it is necessary to make more explicit the interaction between the oligopolistic sector and the other parts of the economic system.

Intersectoral effects

The growth rate of the oligopolistic sector cannot be understood simply in terms of the forces operating within that one part of the economic system alone. The very fact that the secular growth rate can change points to this conclusion, for the inherent tendency of the oligopolistic sector, as just explained, is to maintain a single warranted growth rate. What must then be examined is the extent to which other parts of the economic system are capable of generating on their own a change in the rate of growth either of savings or of investment, thereby offsetting any divergence between those two flows within the oligopolistic sector. The other parts of the economic system which need to be examined in this connection are: (1) the non-oligopolistic subsector of the business sector, consisting of both polypolistic and monopolistically competitive industries; (2) the household sector in its entirety; (3) the foreign sector, and (4) the government sector. For each of these sectors or subsectors, a savings and investment demand curve similar to that already derived for the oligopolistic subsector will have to be developed and two questions then posed. (a) Which curve, the savings or the investment demand curve, is more sensitive to the aggregate growth rate, $\overset{*}{G}$, that is, which curve has the greater slope? (b) Is either curve capable of shifting autonomously, thereby initiating a change in the aggregate growth rate?

The non-oligopolistic subsector. It is the absence of a corporate levy which, as explained above in chapter 4, characterizes the non-oligopolistic subsector of the economy. This condition does not preclude, however, an increase in the amount of savings being generated within that subsector as aggregate demand rises. Quite the opposite. As aggregate demand rises, shifting industry demand curves outward, the price level within the non-oligopolistic sector will also rise, reflecting, if not the increasing marginal costs of production as the theoretical models would suggest, then at least the greater willingness of customers to surrender their monetary claims. Since in any case the average total costs of production can be expected to rise less rapidly than the marginal costs, the neo-classical proprietorship which is the representative firm within the non-oligopolistic subsector will experience a disproportionate gain in net revenue. These higher profits when the economy is expanding are, of course, matched by the disproportionate losses suffered when the economy is contracting. Thus, over the normal business cycle, the gains and losses in net revenue can be expected to offset one another for the most part, just as they do in the oligopolistic subsector. The distinction, as will soon be brought out more clearly, is that in the non-oligopolistic subsector the fluctuations in net revenue are accompanied by fluctuations in the price level while in the oligopolistic subsector they are not.

Again, perhaps the more interesting question is what happens when the cyclical pattern of demand changes, that is, when the secular growth rate varies. If the expansion of the economy has been greater than one would have anticipated on the basis of past trends, the owner-entrepreneurs who control the neo-classical proprietorships in the non-oligopolistic subsector will be encouraged to treat the increased net revenue as a windfall, withdrawing an ever greater proportion of the profits to enhance their own personal income, confident that they will still have an adequate reserve for whatever less prosperous times may follow. In other words, as the secular growth rate rises, the savings being generated within the non-oligopolistic subsector are likely to be transferred at an increasing rate to the household sector. Alternatively, when the expansion of the economy has been less than one would have anticipated on the basis of the past trends, the owner-entrepreneurs will be forced to slow down the rate at which they are withdrawing income from their businesses, and indeed may even be forced, beyond a certain point, to reverse the flow (Ferber, 1962, pp. 126-8 and the sources cited there). In view of these several factors - the tendency of average total costs to rise and fall with the level of output and the tendency of the savings being generated in the form of profits to be siphoned off, above a certain reserve, into personal income with these savings to be returned to the firm if needed - it seems only reasonable to conclude that the savings curve for the non-oligopolistic subsector will rise less sharply than that for the oligopolistic and regulated industries, and may, in fact, even be linear.[27]

Single-plant operation, though not so basic as the absence of a corporate levy, is nonetheless another important distinguishing feature of the non-oligopolistic subsector. It has particular significance insofar as the investment demand function is concerned. To the extent that the neo-classical proprietorship is limited by managerial resources to the operation of but a single plant or some other finite number of facilities, it cannot be expected, like the megacorp, to expand its own capacity smoothly and continuously as the economy itself grows (see above, p. 142). Instead, as pointed out in chapter 4 above, a secular rise in industry demand will lead to an even greater gap between the price level and average total costs. The growing profit margin will, in turn, encourage the entry into the industry of new firms, each with its own separate plant and equipment.

This process by which new capacity is added in the polypolistic and monopolistically competitive industries is muted, however, by two offsetting factors. The first is the likelihood that such industries will be growing at a less rapid rate than the oligopolistic subsector. Were this not the case, they would soon be invaded by conglomerate megacorps on the alert for investment opportunities promising above average rates of return. The non-oligopolistic sector thus represents, in the main, the less rapidly expanding parts of the economic system. The exception consists of those industries which are still relatively new and which offer the prospect of greater than average growth in the future. Over the long run, however, these more dynamic industries can be expected to shift over into the oligopolistic subsector, either through the emergence of megacorps from within or through the invasion of megacorps from without.

The second offsetting factor, limiting the expansion of capacity through new entry, is the effect of technological change in permitting a greater rate of output for the individual production facility at its least cost point (see Scherer, 1970, pp. 88-90). This means that the size of the neo-classical proprietorship can be expected to increase somewhat over time even if the firm is limited by managerial resources to the operation of but a single plant. All the same, if the industry's secular growth has been sufficiently great so that the increased demand cannot be met through the output of the larger plants coming into use as the worn-out capacity is replaced, the profit margin will rise. And even if the existing firms should somehow find a means of overcoming the limitation of managerial resources and are thus able to increase the number of their plants, outside firms can still be expected to enter the industry in growing numbers as it becomes clear that the rise in demand is not simply temporary. In fact, with no way to coordinate or even limit this type of expansion it may well be that, beyond a certain point, the growth of capacity will exceed the growth of industry demand as more and more entrepreneurs rush to take advantage of the seemingly attractive investment opportunity. Alternatively, if the industry's secular growth should begin to slow down, the growth of investment can be expected to come to a halt - especially if the industry is already showing signs of excess capacity.

What the above line of argument suggests is that the rate of growth of investment in the non-oligopolistic subsector will be largely a function of the profit level over the intermediate run, the latter in turn reflecting the secular growth rate of the polypolistic and monopolistically competitive industries which comprise that subsector. Initially, the rate of growth of investment will increase less rapidly than the secular growth rate as owner-entrepreneurs wait to make sure that the rise in demand is more than cyclical. In the meantime, of course, the increased demand will be met, partly through the larger size plants which the improved technology has made possible and partly by using the existing capacity more intensively. As profit margins continue to rise, however, new firms will be encouraged to enter the subsector in increasing numbers, thereby giving rise to a disproportionate increase in the rate of growth of investment. This implies an investment demand curve for the non-oligopolistic subsector which, though less sensitive at low levels to the growth rate than is the investment demand function for the oligopolistic and regulated industries, nonetheless bows upward as the growth rate increases until it has a slope which is even greater than that of the savings function previously postulated for the non-oligopolistic subsector.[28]

Figure 20 shows an investment demand function of this type, together with a savings function appropriate to the polypolistic and monopolistically competitive industries. The two functions, when considered together, suggest a savings-investment adjustment process which is the opposite of that already indicated as applying to the rest of the business sector. To the extent that the rate of growth of investment,

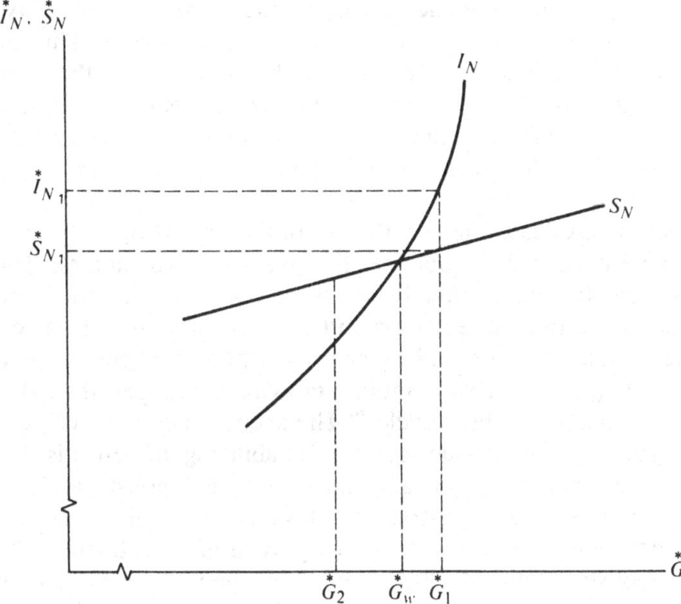

Figure 20

$\overset{*}{I}_N$, is more sensitive to the aggregate growth rate, $\overset{*}{G}$, than is the rate of growth of savings, $\overset{*}{S}_N$, the subsector will be dynamically unstable. Any displacement from the warranted growth rate, $\overset{*}{G}_w$, will lead to an even greater displacement.

For example, if the secular growth rate were to increase to $\overset{*}{G}_1$, the rate of growth of investment would rise to $\overset{*}{I}_{N_1}$, thereby exceeding the rate of growth of savings, $\overset{*}{S}_{N_1}$. This excess of investment over savings (assuming investment and savings were initially equal to one another at the warranted growth rate, $\overset{*}{G}_w$) would in turn lead to a further increase in the aggregate growth rate, this producing an even greater gap between the rate of growth of investment and the rate of growth of savings. The resulting explosive growth would come a halt only when supply constraints in the capital goods industry finally placed a ceiling on the amount of new plant and equipment which could be added or - what is the more probable alternative - when an excess of capacity relative to demand finally led to a collapse of the investment boom.

On the other hand, if the secular growth rate were to fall to $\overset{*}{G}_2$, the rate of growth of investment would be less than the rate of growth of savings, and the aggregate growth rate would decline, this leading to a further drop in the rate of growth of investment. The resulting downward spiral in economic activity would come to a halt only when the rate of growth of investment finally reached zero. This process of cumulative decline may, of course, be a sequel to the period of explosive growth. What emerges from the analysis is the picture of a sector subject to alternating booms and busts. This is in sharp contrast to the stabilizing effect which the oligopolistic subsector can be expected to have.[29]

The potentially destabilizing influence of the non-oligopolistic subsector tends to be mitigated in practice, however, by two factors. The first follows from the point already stressed, that many of the industries which comprise the subsector are either stagnant or in secular decline. This means that only a certain segment of the non-oligopolistic sector, that consisting of the newer, rapidly growing industries, is likely to go through the boom-and-bust cycle.[30] The second factor which serves to mitigate the non-oligopolistic sector's destabilizing influence is the small percentage of total investment accounted for by polypolistic and monopolistically competitive industries.[31] This means that, whatever the disproportionate change in the rate of growth of investment within the non-oligopolistic sector resulting from a change in the aggregate growth rate, it will be more than offset by the less than proportional change in the rate of growth of investment within the oligopolistic sector. The crucial question, then, insofar as aggregate stability is concerned, is whether the other sectors - household, foreign and government - more closely approximate the oligopolistic portion of the business sector, where the rate of investment is less responsive to a change in the aggregate growth rate than is the rate of growth of savings, or whether they more closely approximate the non-oligopolistic subsector, where the opposite is true.

The other sectors. Traditionally, the term savings has been restricted in economics to that portion of household income not used to command consumption goods, while the term investment has been limited to physical capital formulation in the business sector. Already, in order to describe the pricing behavior of oligopolistic industries in more realistic terms it has been necessary to broaden the meaning of both terms, to extend the concept to the business sector in the case of savings and to encompass expenditures on items that subsequently bring non-material benefits, even if those benefits accrue only to private parties, in the case of investment. Now, in order to carry through this analysis of the macrodynamics of a modern, technologically progressive economy such as that of the United States, it is necessary to extend the concepts even further.

What is about to be argued is that savings and investment demand functions can be derived for the household, foreign and government sectors no less readily than for the two parts of the business sector itself. If the terms savings and investment seem inapplicable to some of these other sectors, one need only recall the most general definition of the two words - income not otherwise required to meet ongoing needs in the case of savings and the present commitment of physical resources in order to derive benefits beyond the current period in the case of investment. If the terms savings and investment still seem inapplicable, then one can substitute the phrases discretionary income and discretionary expenditures while keeping the definitions themselves the same (see Eichner and Kregel, 1974; Eichner, 1975).

Insofar as the household sector alone is concerned, the term savings presents no problem, of course. It is only with respect to investment, or discretionary expenditures, by the household sector that a demurrer is likely to be heard. It seems not at all unreasonable, however, to equate the latter with the purchase of consumer durables as well as of those services, such as education, whose benefits lie primarily in the future. In any case, the separation of durable goods from other consumer purchases has been found to be essential in econometric investigations.[32] Residential construction presents a more difficult problem. The convention, at least in the United States national income and products accounts, is to treat this type of expenditure as part of business investment, with home owners, both new and old, viewed as being in the business of renting their properties to themselves. Yet it seems clear that residential construction reflects the derived demand for additional shelter by households in the same way that business fixed investment reflects, not simply the output of the capital goods sector but, more basically, the derived demand for additional plant and equipment by the business sector as a whole. For this reason it would appear best to include new housing as part of the discretionary expenditures by the household sector. While there is no problem, theoretically, in treating residential construction along with consumer durables and certain services as part of household investment, empirically it has been shown to have quite different determinants and to behave quite unlike what are usually classified as consumer durable expenditures. The practice followed here will be to include residential construction as part of the household sector's discretionary expenditures but then to note its distinctive behavioral characteristics. With the definitional problem thus resolved, the question becomes how do the rates of growth both of savings and of investment within the household sector vary as the aggregate growth rate itself varies.

The rate of growth of savings within the household sector and the rate of growth of expenditures on consumer durables depend, of course, on the rate of growth of disposable income, $\overset{*}{Y}_D$. Were this to be a full exposition of the macrodynamic model in its entirety, it would be necessary to dwell at some length on the short-run relationship between $\overset{*}{G}$ and $\overset{*}{Y}_D$. But since what concerns us here is simply the relative slopes of the savings and investment curves for the household sector and whether they suggest a destabilizing influence similar to that of the non-oligopolistic sector, the argument can be abridged somewhat.

In order for the household sector to be destabilizing, the individual family units within the sector would have to vary their own rate of growth of investment, that is, their purchase of consumer durables and certain services, more rapidly than their rate of growth of savings. This would, in turn, imply an increasing marginal propensity to consume (actually to invest in) household durables and discretionary services as the secular growth rate rises. Yet such a relationship is contrary to the observed evidence. The overall marginal propensity to consume is likely, if anything, to decline as income levels increase - especially if, as is more appropriate to the situation under consideration, it is the growth of transitory income rather than of permanent income which is being measured. In other words, savings are the more volatile part of household income.[33] Since this proportionately greater change in the rate of growth of savings within the household sector is, in part, but the obverse of the proportionately smaller change in the rate of growth of savings occurring within the non-oligopolistic subsector - it being owner-entrepreneurs whose incomes within the household sector are likely to fluctuate most widely - this result is hardly a surprising one. Nonetheless, it suggests that the household sector, rather than being destabilizing, serves to reinforce the short-run dynamic impact of the oligopolistic subsector. Adding residential construction to consumer durable purchases merely makes the household sector even more of a stabilizing factor, for while the countercyclical pattern of new housing starts may be more supply than demand related, it nonetheless gives further evidence of an investment demand curve for the household sector with a slope which is less than that of the sector's savings curve (see Evans, 1965, ch. 7, especially section 5).

In the foreign or rest-of-the-world sector, not even the concept of savings is usually applied. Yet it should be clear, if one views the situation from the perspective of other nations, that the dollar credits (or whatever else may serve as a local or international currency) which must be surrendered to pay for imports represent, for those other countries, discretionary income. The larger the volume of their goods imported into this country or dollar credits otherwise earned, the greater will be the income of the United States' trading partners available for meeting other than their ongoing needs in international markets. Similarly, the larger the volume of American exports, including the transfer overseas of managerial skills, the greater will be the amount of capital formation abroad. Thus the rate of growth of savings and the rate of growth of investment within the foreign sector can be identified approximately with the rate of growth of imports and the rate of growth of exports respectively.

Again, the main question that is of concern here is whether the slope of the investment demand curve relative to the slope of the savings curve makes the foreign sector destabilizing insofar as the domestic American economy is concerned, holding all factors except the aggregate growth rate constant. For the foreign sector to be destabilizing in this sense, its rate of growth of investment, that is, the purchase of goods and services in this country by other nations, would have to vary more sharply in response to a change in the level of aggregate demand than the rate of growth of dollar flows overseas. This would, in turn, imply a rate of growth of exports which is more sensitive to the aggregate growth rate in this country than is the rate of growth of imports. Once more, the conditions necessary for the sector to be destabilizing are contrary to what has been observed. It is the rate of growth of imports and, more broadly, the rate of growth of dollar outflows, which depends more directly on the level of domestic economic activity. In fact, the rate of growth of exports is likely to be somewhat insensitive to the domestic growth rate (cf. Rhomberg and Boissoneualt, 1965; Evans and Klein, 1967; Evans, 1969, ch. 9, section 7; Suits, 1962).

Important as the household and foreign sectors may be in determining whether the savings-investment adjustment process associated with the oligopolistic subsector will prevail in the aggregate, the government sector, because of the large amount of discretionary income which it generates, is even more important. By now, one should have little trouble in identifying the rate of growth of savings in the government sector with the rate of growth of tax revenue, and the rate of growth of investment with the rate of growth of government outlays. Clearly, taxes represent the discretionary income of government, and the outlays by the various sovereign entities, the public sector's discretionary expenditures. By now, too, it should be understood that the critical question is whether the slope of the investment demand curve relative to the slope of the savings curve makes the government sector destabilizing.

On this point, one cannot help but conclude that, rather than counteracting the stabilizing effect which the oligopolistic subsector is likely to have, the government sector will reinforce that tendency. On the one hand, the rate of growth of savings, in the form of taxes, will be highly sensitive to the aggregate growth rate. Given a progressive income tax and, even more important, a corporate income tax geared to the rate of growth of savings in the oligopolistic sector, government revenues can be expected to rise, and fall, at an increasing rate as the aggregate growth rate itself varies. The savings curve for the government sector is thus similar to that for the oligopolistic subsector.[34] On the other hand, the rate of growth of investment, in the form of expenditures, will be only partially sensitive to the aggregate growth rate. Some government outlays will, of course, be entirely independent of economic considerations. More will be said of them soon. The rest, representing in varying proportions public goods and quasi-public goods, can be expected to increase over time as population and income grow. Still, over the intermediate run, any change in the secular growth rate is likely to have only a muted impact on these expenditures. The investment demand function for the government sector is thus similar to the lagged accelerator model already postulated for the oligopolistic subsector (cf. Ando, Brown and Adams, 1965; Evans and Klein, 1967; Suits, 1962).

In summary, then, it can be presumed that the savings-investment adjustment process applicable to the economy as a whole is not significantly different from that analyzed in the case of the oligopolistic subsector alone. While the non-oligopolistic subsector may well have an offsetting influence, this impact is more than outweighed by that of the household, foreign and government sectors. The latter, in particular, can be expected to experience a disproportionate change in the rate of growth of savings as the aggregate growth rate itself varies. This means that one can postulate aggregate savings and aggregate investment demand functions such as those shown in figure 21. S_O is the savings curve for the oligopolistic subsector and S, the savings curve for the economy as a whole; while I_O and I are the corresponding investment demand curves. These aggregate savings and investment curves make it possible to analyze the larger dynamic of which the interrelationship between the oligopolistic subsector and the economy as a whole is but a part.

The larger dynamic

As shown in figure 21, I, the investment demand curve for the economy as a whole, lies below I_O, the investment demand curve for the oligopolistic subsector, and has a lesser slope. The lower rate of growth of aggregate investment which this presumes for a given value of $\overset{*}{G}$ reflects the inability of the government sector and, even more, of the non-oligopolistic subsector to match the rate of capital formation occurring within the oligopolistic subsector. At the same time, the lesser sensitivity of aggregate investment which this positioning also implies derives from

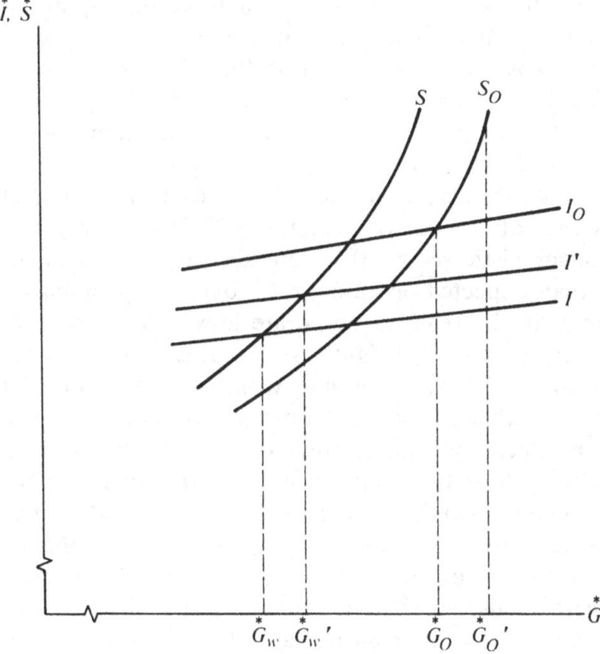

Figure 21

the dampening effect exerted by the lack of responsiveness of government expenditures to changing income levels in the short run. Both factors, as reflected by the position of I relative to I_O in the diagram, assure that the warranted growth rate for the economy as a whole, $\overset{*}{G}_w$, will be less than the warranted growth rate for the oligopolistic subsector alone, whether S lies slightly to the right of S_O or - as is more likely to be the case, given the high marginal tax rates that presently prevail in the United States - somewhere to the left of S_O.

From the diagram it can be seen that, once the other sectors besides the oligopolistic one have been taken into account, a change in the warranted growth rate for the economy as a whole is possible even without a shift in either the oligopolistic sector's savings curve or its investment demand curve. If, for example, the investment demand curve for one of the other sectors should shift upward, the investment demand curve for the economy as a whole will shift upward as well. This, as can be seen from figure 21, will lead to a new warranted growth rate, $\overset{*}{G}_w$, for the economy as a whole, even though the savings and investment demand curves for the oligopolistic sector remain unchanged.

The significant point here is that the new warranted growth rate will be consistent with a rate of growth of savings for the oligopolistic sector that is no longer equal to the rate of growth of investment - or, to put it another way, the intersection of the S_O and I_O curves will no longer define the warranted growth rate for the oligopolistic sector. The upward shift in the investment demand function for one of the other sectors will necessarily push the oligopolistic sector up further along on its own savings curve so that its rate of growth of savings exceeds its rate of growth of investment.[35] This simply means that, within the oligopolistic sector, the increased levels of demand will lead to a higher than expected operating ratio over the planning period and that consequently the realized corporate levy will be greater than the planned investment outlays. This excess of savings over investment within the oligopolistic sector, and possibly within one or more of the other sectors, will be balanced by the excess of investment over savings in the sector in which the autonomous shift in the investment demand curve initially occurred. In all, it will be the same as though the oligopolistic sector's own investment demand curve had shifted upward.

What has just been said about an upward shift in the investment demand curve for one of the other sectors applies, of course, in reverse if instead there should be either a downward shift in that other sector's investment demand curve or an upward shift in its savings curve. No matter what the direction of the shift or the curve involved, the result will be a divergence between savings and investment within the oligopolistic sector. As will soon be explained more fully, any such divergence is apt to set off a wage-price spiral throughout the economy. At this point, however, we are concerned only with the possible initiating cause of the divergence. This means turning our attention, at least briefly, to the second of the two questions posed at the beginning of this section, whether it is possible for either the savings or investment demand curves for one of the other sectors of the economy to shift autonomously, that is, for some reason other than a change in the secular growth rate.

While it is possible to stipulate conditions under which the savings curve in one of the sectors might shift autonomously, it is questionable whether the change in the rate of growth of savings - holding the growth rate for the economy as a whole constant - will be more than a temporary one. For example, the savings curve for the non-oligopolistic sector will shift autonomously if, because of a sudden change in economic prospects arising from non-economic events, owner-entrepreneurs decide to alter the rate at which they have been withdrawing income from their businesses. The savings function for the household sector will shift autonomously if, following a similar sequence of events, family units decide to alter the rate at which they have been purchasing consumer goods. But at some point expectations will necessarily have to be brought back into line with reality so that the rate of growth of savings will once more depend on the secular growth rate for the economy as a whole. The savings curve for the government sector, while capable of shifting autonomously in a way that is not simply temporary, nonetheless poses a special problem to be brought out later.

It is thus the investment demand function - and, even more specifically, the investment demand curve in three of the four other sectors - which is most likely to shift in such a way as to initiate on its own, independently of other factors, a permanent change in the secular growth rate. Such a shift can occur in the investment demand curve for the foreign sector through autonomous developments abroad. It can occur in the investment demand curve for the non-oligopolistic sector through the impact of a Schumpeterian grand invention or even some lesser technological breakthrough. Finally such a shift can occur in the investment demand curve for the government sector through the addition of new programs or through the liberalization of existing programs. Of these several possible shifts, only the latter two warrant a more extended discussion.

A Schumpeterian grand invention, like, for example, the automobile in the early decades of the twentieth century, can be expected to generate a major expansion of aggregate demand. As the new technology becomes commercially exploitable, significantly altering consumption patterns, the secular growth rate for the business sector as a whole will increase even without any stimulus from the government and foreign sectors. While the oligopolistic subsector will experience some increase in its own growth rate, the more dramatic result will be the birth of entirely new industries within the non-oligopolistic subsector. Over time, of course, these industries will tend to become oligopolistic as a result of the evolutionary process already described. Concurrently, as the portion of total income which the new product can command approaches some asymptotic limit, the growth rate of these industries will tend to slow down until it approaches that for the oligopolistic subsector as a whole, this slowing down of the growth rate corresponding to the contractionary phase of that particular Kondratieff cycle (Schumpeter, 1939, vol. 1). Still, in the meantime, the overall economy will have experienced a period of vigorous expansion as a result of the investment demand curve for the non-oligopolistic subsector having shifted outward. Lesser technological breakthroughs will simply have a lesser stimulative effect. The key point to be noted here is that this continued birth of new industries within the non-oligopolistic subsector through the impact of Schumpeterian grand inventions and even somewhat paler imitations is the primary source of autonomous growth within the business sector as a whole.

A Schumpeterian grand invention, like autonomous developments abroad, reflects forces over which the society itself has little control. It is precisely the opposite characteristic of government expenditures which makes them of such critical importance. Whatever the existing growth rate for the economy as a whole may be, the society can consciously choose to raise or lower it by varying the rate of growth of government expenditures, thereby autonomously shifting the investment demand curve for the government sector. It might seem that the same result could be achieved by manipulating the various tax rates, thereby autonomously shifting the saving curve for the government sector as well. But as the next chapter will bring out, this alternative approach, since each tax rate is also a parameter of some other sector's savings function, may not have the full effect intended. For this reason, the most certain means of controlling the aggregate growth rate is by shifting the investment demand curve for the government sector.[36]

What is being suggested here is that the society, through its political system, can choose the secular growth rate it wishes - as long as that growth rate does not exceed what is defined in the next chapter as the potential growth rate. If the current growth rate is $\overset{*}{G}_w$, as depicted in figure 21, but the society prefers a higher growth rate, say one closer to $\overset{*}{G}'_w$, the government need only increase its rate of growth of expenditures relative to the rate of growth of tax revenue. Should this excess of investment over savings in the government sector be maintained on the average over the interval which encompasses the normal cyclical pattern of fluctuating aggregate output, the investment demand curve for the economy as a whole will shift secularly from I toward I'. Whether all the intersectoral effects can be fully spelled out in advance is not the issue.[37] The fact is that the government, by maintaining a rate of growth of expenditures, or investment, that on balance exceeds the rate of growth of tax revenue, or savings, over the intermediate run, will assure that a higher secular growth rate for the economy as a whole, one approximating $\overset{*}{G}'_w$, is achieved. Similarly, the government, by allowing the rate of growth of expenditures to fall below the rate of growth of tax revenue, can see to it that a lower secular growth rate is realized.

While the society can, through the intermediary device of its political system, choose the secular growth rate it prefers within certain limits, what must be understood is that the growth rate so selected is unlikely to be a sustainable one - given the economic institutions which presently exist in a country like the United States. The reason is not, as is often supposed, that the growth rate chosen is apt to be different from the so-called natural growth rate. It is rather that the very process by which the secular growth rate is manipulated - in the main, by an autonomous shift in the investment demand curve for the government sector but also, to a lesser extent, by a shift in the savings curve as well - will necessarily lead to a discrepancy between the rate of growth of savings and the rate of growth of investment within the oligopolistic sector. This divergence between the two growth rates, the obverse of the divergence within the government sector, will give rise to a redistributive effect which, together with the nature of the supply curve in the non-oligopolistic sector, is almost certain to touch off a wage-price inflationary spiral. Indeed, this is likely to be the result whether the shift in the government's investment demand and/or savings curve is intentional or not. Why any such change in the secular growth rate will tend to be destabilizing is the subject matter of the chapter which follows.

7. Conventional policy instruments

The previous chapter, in pointing out the macrodynamic properties of an economy like that of the United States, has suggested that it is possible for a society to exercise some choice, through its political system, as to the rate at which the economy will expand. But is that choice unbounded? This is the question which this chapter starts off by exploring. The concept of a potential growth rate is introduced, with the factors which may determine that potential growth rate - the availability of manpower and the rate of technological change - then analyzed. The conclusion reached is that while the potential growth rate may well exist as an asymptotic limit which the economy can only approach, this is not the reason why the rate of economic expansion is usually held in check by the political authorities. Their reluctance to use the control they have to achieve a higher secular growth rate is due instead to the difficulty of getting the economy off the dead center established by the existing secular growth rate. Indeed, any change in the aggregate growth rate - if it is to lead to a new secular rate of expansion and not just represent another cyclical movement - will require a carefully orchestrated series of adjustments, not only on the part of government but in the other sectors of the economy as well. The adjustments required in the oligopolistic sector, involving a shift of its savings curve without leaving the megacorps in that sector short of the investment funds they need, are particularly difficult to achieve; and the inadvertent result, more often than not, is a wage-price inflationary spiral. Here the conventional policy instruments available to the government, whether fiscal or monetary, only serve to exacerbate the problem. The principal theme of this chapter, therefore, is the limited usefulness of the conventional policy instruments in trying to manage an economy with a significant oligopolistic sector.

The chapter has four main sections. The first deals with the potential growth rate and its determinants. The second section explains the adjustments required if any new rate of economic expansion established through government policy is to become a sustainable one, particularly the adjustments required in the oligopolistic sector's savings curve. The third section takes up, in turn, monetary and fiscal policy, pointing out the counter-productive effect they are likely to have when applied to the oligopolistic sector. Finally, the fourth section reviews the economic history of the 1960s as it bears on these points.

The limits on expansion

There are usually two answers given to the question of why those with the political responsibility for the economy's performance do not use the power they have to achieve more rapid economic expansion. The first is an assertion that a higher growth rate is possible only if the society is prepared to sacrifice some other objective. This presumes that there is an inherent conflict between at least two of society's goals, with any success in achieving one necessarily being at the expense of the other. The discussion which follows will indicate that there is some truth to this argument. The conflict, however, is not the one generally presumed to exist between a higher aggregate growth rate and price stability. If such a Phillipsian dilemma exists, it has to do instead with the second reason usually advanced as to why a higher aggregate growth rate is neither possible nor desirable. This is the argument that, beyond a certain point, further economic expansion is not possible because the resources the economy must obtain from without, as distinct from those produced from within, will simply not be forthcoming. In other words, the rate at which the economy can potentially expand may be limited by the availability of externally supplied inputs. If this is true, then the availability of those externally supplied inputs will determine what is the maximally achievable growth rate for the economy, this maximally achievable growth rate being what is meant by the 'potential' growth rate.[1] What precisely the limiting factor is upon which the potential growth rate is based is the subject matter of this section. First the availability of manpower and the employment effects to which an increase in the secular growth rate gives rise will be explored. Then the limits set by technological progress, both in subduing nature and in harnessing human energies, will be taken into account.

Manpower factors. Ever since Keynes identified the potential growth rate with the 'full employment' level of income, manpower has been seen as the limiting factor in economic expansion. In the static terminology of *The General Theory*, it is 'full employment' which, moreover, serves as the benchmark for evaluating public policy. While full employment might not have been an inappropriate target viewed from the depths of the 1930s Depression, the ambiguity of the phrase, now that massive unemployment has been virtually eliminated, is an increasingly serious matter. In dynamic analysis, the definitional difficulties have been skirted by introducing the concept of a 'natural' growth rate, equal to the growth rate of the labor force itself (Harrod, 1948, p. 87; Hahn and Matthews, 1964, pp. 5-6). With the demand for labor assumed to increase at the same rate as output, this 'natural' growth rate can be compared with the aggregate growth rate, $\overset{*}{G}$, to see whether, as a result of any discrepancy, there will be increasing unemployment or, alternatively, an increasing shortage of workers. In this way, while manpower is still viewed as the limiting factor in economic expansion, there is no need to define precisely what is meant by 'full employment'. Whatever it may mean, it is possible to determine whether the economy is moving further away from or closer to that goal, and that may be all that it is necessary to know.

Even so, there are difficulties in substituting the 'natural' growth rate for 'full employment', and they have to do with the implicit treatment of the labor force as an undifferentiated mass. In refining the concept of a 'natural' growth rate, it is necessary to draw on elements from the theory of human resource development (Ginzberg, 1976; Eichner, 1973c; in this connection see Brody, 1966). This theory points to the existence of a major societal system, separate and distinct from the economic system. The system is the anthropogenic system, and it produces not physical commodities but rather human skills, or competences. Just as the output of the economic system can be pictured as a basket of goods, so the output of the anthropogenic system can be described as a vector of skills, indicating the number of persons emerging both from school and on-the-job training with each of the myriad competences required for the functioning of a modern society. Of course, if these skills are to be consolidated and further developed, then the individuals who have acquired them must be able to find employment within the economic system. There is thus an interaction between the supply of and demand for manpower. But just as it is an oversimplification to regard the output of the anthropogenic system, or supply of manpower, as a homogeneous mass, so too it is an oversimplification to view the demand for manpower in the same undifferentiated terms. In considering the potential for meeting this demand, the simple growth rate of population, even that of the working-age segment, is too crude a guide. It may suffice for the non-oligopolistic, or more traditional, part of the economy where the technology demands little more than willing and trustworthy hands. In the oligopolistic sector, however, the specialized and variegated skill requirements of the production process must be taken into account, for untrained and inexperienced labor cannot be used in conjunction with sophisticated equipment - not if the ongoing efficiency of the megacorp is to be maintained. For these reasons, it is the growth rate of the society's skill vector, reflecting the diverse output of the anthropogenic system, rather than any 'natural' growth rate of the population, which, if anything, sets the manpower limits on the rate of economic expansion.

To the extent, then, that manpower is the limiting factor of economic expansion, it is the rate of growth of society's skill vector which constitutes the potential growth rate for the economy as a whole. It is questionable, however, whether manpower is the limiting factor in economic expansion which economists since the publication of *The General Theory* have assumed it to be. In arguing this point, the remainder of this section will take up (a) the differential ability of the oligopolistic sector to obtain manpower, (b) the strain thereby placed on the non-oligopolistic sector in meeting its manpower needs, (c) the considerable elasticity which nonetheless exists insofar as the supply of manpower is concerned, and (d) the mistaken notion that it is rising wage rates in both the oligopolistic and non-oligopolistic sectors, stemming from labor or manpower 'shortages', which is the root cause of inflationary pressures throughout the economy. In dealing with these matters, the paragraphs that follow will cover all the ways in which manpower factors influence the secular growth rate. With that issue out of the way, it will then be possible to take up the question of what, if not the availability of manpower, does determine the potential growth rate.

It should first be noted that the oligopolistic sector is likely to experience little difficulty in expanding the size of its laboring manpower force. This reflects the ability of the oligopolistic sector, because of more generous rates of compensation and the greater security of employment which it affords, continually to attract workers from the non-oligopolistic sector (Kuhn, 1959; Reynolds, 1960, pp. 199-200). The long-term movement of workers from the one sector to the other is simply part of the normal pattern of economic development. It is in this way that the laboring manpower force within the oligopolistic sector is steadily expanded, providing larger numbers of persons with relatively well paying, secure jobs. Any increase in the secular growth rate will merely hasten the process.

While it may be true that the expansion of the oligopolistic sector is not likely to be curtailed for lack of workers, the concomitant effect on the non-oligopolistic sector cannot be ignored. If it is the non-oligopolistic sector from which workers are at least in part being attracted, then it is in that sector that any manpower pinch is likely to be felt. Indeed, with workers being drained off by the oligopolistic sector, it would seem that the rest of the economy would have difficulty maintaining production at its current level, let alone responding to any rise in demand. But this ignores some of the most important features of the developmental process.

To stem the drain on manpower resources, wage rates in the non-oligopolistic sector can be expected to rise as the growth rate of the oligopolistic sector itself increases. Some industries within the non-oligopolistic sector, those which are technologically backward and/or supply goods and services which are only marginally desirable, will, of course, be unable to protect themselves in this manner. Any increase in wage rates, necessitating as it will an increase in prices, will simply speed up their demise. For these industries, the loss of workers and the concomitant decline in output - at least in relative terms - cannot be avoided. But for the other industries within the non-oligopolistic sector it is merely a matter of adjusting wage rates upward.[2] By drawing upon the workers released from the declining industries as well as by tapping any surplus manpower available in the countryside, they should even be able to expand their labor force as needed.

Although wage rates in the non-oligopolistic sector will thus rise, they will at most only approach those prevailing in the oligopolistic sector. This is in part because any narrowing of the gap between wage rates in the two sectors will weaken the very factor tending to pull up wage rates in the non-oligopolistic sector. But it is also because wage rates in the oligopolistic sector will themselves rise - not because additional workers cannot be obtained at prevailing wage rates but rather because the trade unions will insist, as the secular growth rate increases, that their members obtain a 'fair' share of any ensuing increment in the social surplus.

These several effects on the non-oligopolistic sector can hardly be viewed as untoward social developments. The higher wage rates, whether occurring indirectly as a result of the upward pull exerted by the oligopolistic sector or directly as a result of persons finding employment outside the non-oligopolistic sector, will lead to increased household income. The more rapid demise of certain industries, on the other hand, simply means that a class of marginally desirable goods and services will be cast beyond the pale of what is economically feasible sooner than would otherwise be the case. What needs to be viewed with concern are not these consequences of the higher secular growth rate but rather the possibility that the ultimate source of manpower reserves for both the oligopolistic and non-oligopolistic sectors, the underutilized human resources in the countryside, will eventually run out, creating an absolute barrier to a further rise in the secular growth rate in real terms.

While it may be comforting to note the stimulative effect on technological progress that any manpower shortage is likely to have, the more salient point is that there is a substantial labor reserve throughout the countryside of the world, and that given the size of this pool of underutilized human resources, it will be quite some time before it is eliminated entirely. Even after all the disguised unemployment has been sopped up in the United States and in the other technologically advanced nations, a substantial labor reserve will continue to exist over much of the globe for at least decades to come. This is because social institutions in the less developed countries of the world cannot be expected to change to the extent necessary to create a single modern sector any more quickly. Thus, whether production is transferred to less developed parts of the world or persons from those areas are brought to the technologically advanced nations to supplement the labor force, the oligopolistic sector will continue to have, at least within the foreseeable future, a virtually unlimited pool of surplus manpower upon which to draw.[3]

To be sure, it takes some time for a rural peasant to become acculturated to an urban, industrial setting, and usually the transition can only be accomplished intergenerationally. Still, at any given point in time, there will be large numbers of persons proceeding through each of the several stages. At most, therefore, should the long-run rate of economic expansion within the more advanced nations of the world be increased, it may require a certain interval of time before the movement of persons from the countryside into industrial types of employment, both at home and abroad, can be adjusted accordingly.

This suggested limitation on any *acceleration* of the secular growth rate, stemming from manpower constraints at the lower end of the skill vector, has a counterpart at the upper end. If the secular growth rate is increased too rapidly, the result may be to swamp the ability of high-level business executives to expand the size of their organizations. The megacorp, as already pointed out, has a much greater elasticity in this respect than the neo-classical proprietorship. Even so, there is a limit to the rate at which new operating divisions, and even new production facilities, can be set up, staffed and brought to peak efficiency. Indeed, the rate at which new organizations or parts thereof can be created is probably the most significant constraint which exists on the supply side in the intermediate run. However, like the ability of rural peasants to make the transition to an urban, industrial setting, it merely determines how quickly the secular growth rate can be increased. It does not set the limit on how rapidly the economy can grow secularly. In other words, the manpower constraints, whatever they may be, affect only the first derivative with respect to time and not the secular growth rate itself.

The import of the above argument is that the rate of growth of a society's skill vector, rather than being a razor's edge delineating too high a rate of economic expansion from too low a rate, is actually an asymptotic limit. The secular growth rate may approach the growth rate of the skill vector, but it cannot exceed it. The reason is that an increase in the secular growth rate, because of the response it is likely to elicit in time from the anthropogenic system, will lead to an increase in the rate of growth of that skill vector. As a corollary, it can be stated that an increase in the secular growth rate is unlikely to exhaust manpower resources, putting a brake on further expansion. It will simply mean a change in the rate of growth of employment. Indeed, there is no such thing as 'full' employment. There are only higher rates of growth of employment, and still higher rates of growth of employment, with the potential growth rate, insofar as it depends on the availability of manpower resources, being always somewhat greater.[4] Finally, while prices may rise as the secular growth rate increases, the explanation will have little, if anything, to do with the rate of growth of employment or any putative labor 'shortage'. This is because, insofar as the oligopolistic and non-oligopolistic sectors are concerned, there is a break in the causal link between the rate of growth of employment and wage rates in the one case and between wage and the price level in the other.

Any change in the rate of growth of employment will, by itself, have no effect on wage rates within the oligopolistic sector. This is because wage rates within the oligopolistic sector, as explained in chapter 5, depend entirely on the national incremental wage pattern. While it is true that a change in the secular growth rate is likely to lead to a change in the national incremental wage pattern, one should keep in mind that the operative mechanism is not the effect of the growth rate on employment but rather the dependence of the national incremental wage pattern on reported net earnings, or savings, within the oligopolistic sector, and especially the bellwether industry – these reported net earnings depending, in turn, as matters now stand, on the secular growth rate. The distinction is a crucial one, because it opens up the possibility that the national incremental wage pattern can be manipulated in such a way that a rise in price levels is avoided. In other words, an increase in the rate of growth of employment, at least within the oligopolistic sector, need not be inflationary.

Wage rates outside the oligopolistic sector, particularly in those industries which trade unions have been unable to organize, will admittedly be affected by the rate of growth of aggregate employment. As pointed out above, the firms in those industries will be forced to offer higher wage rates if they are to attract, or even retain, a sufficient labor force in the face of the increased drain on manpower resources being exerted by the oligopolistic sector. The higher the rate of growth of employment throughout the economy, the greater the increase in wage rates will have to be.[5] Still, upward pressure on wage rates will diminish as wage rates within the unorganized industries approximate those prevailing in the oligopolistic sector. Even more to the point, the higher wage rates are likely to be an insignificant factor in any concurrent rise of the price level within the non-oligopolistic sector. This is because prices in polypolistic and monopolistically competitive industries are influenced more by demand conditions than by labor costs.[6] The upward drift of wage rates within the non-oligopolistic sector is, in fact, significant only because it places a higher floor under prices in that sector when and if the secular growth rate subsequently declines.

In summary, then, it is not the supply of manpower as reflected in the skill vector of society which is the limiting factor in economic expansion - despite the inference usually drawn from the fact of rising wage rates. Indeed, an increase in the secular growth rate should always be possible without a shortage of manpower developing to make that higher growth rate unsustainable.[7] But if it is not the supply of manpower which is the limiting factor in economic expansion, then what is? In answering this question, it is necessary to take up somewhat more explicitly the role played by technological progress.

Technological progress and the potential growth rate. If a higher secular growth rate is to lead to an improvement in the economic position of the representative household as measured by real per capita disposable income, and not simply to make it possible to sustain a larger working population, then it must be accomplished by an increase in output per worker. The mere expansion of output is not enough. Unless there is also an increase in what each worker is able to produce, there will be no additional resources available for distribution to the representative household. The household sector can, of course, be made better off if resources are diverted to it from some other sector. But except for the case in which those resources have previously been less than optimally allocated, the gains of the household sector will almost certainly prove to be short-lived or illusory - as, for example, when wage gains in excess of improvements in productivity are offset by higher prices, leaving disposable income in real terms unchanged.[8] Thus the prerequisite for an improvement in the economic position of the representative household is a secular increase in output per worker, hopefully throughout the economy as a whole but at least within the oligopolistic sector.

But this is only one side of the coin. The increase in output per worker, indicating as it does greater productive power on the part of the labor force, also extends whatever is the limit placed on the rate of economic expansion by the supply of manpower. As a further step in defining what is meant by the potential growth rate, one can therefore say that it will not be less than the rate of growth of the society's skill vector, compounded by the secular increase in output per worker.

What emerges from the data as a secular increase in output per worker is, however, only the contrived result of controlling for increments in the labor force when the gain in aggregate output is measured. Behind this statistic lies the far more fundamental fact of technological progress. Indeed, it is the rate of technological progress, reflected in rising output per worker, which transforms economic growth from the mere ability to support a growing population at a certain fixed level into the capacity to provide that same population with an increasingly better standard of living.

Of all economic phenomena, the rate of technological progress is probably the least well understood. This undoubtedly accounts for the tendency in economic model-building to treat it as being entirely exogenous - a windfall from social processes outside the economic system. To the extent that technological progress depends ultimately, as explained above (p. 181-2), on the growth of scientific knowledge, there is perhaps some justification for this approach - even though the ability of a society to support some of its members while they pursue their idle curiosity is not entirely independent of the margin above subsistence which that society is capable of generating nor of the pattern in which the surplus itself is distributed. The rate of technological progress is, however, even more directly related to the secular growth rate. As already indicated, the sort of improvement in production methods reflected in higher output per worker is to a large extent capital embodied. That is, the laboring manpower force, whatever its skill composition, is able to produce more only because of the improved equipment with which it works. This means that the higher the secular growth rate, and thus the more rapidly the capital stock is being replaced and augmented by better types of plant and equipment, the greater will be the rate of technological progress. Indeed, this is the point of the technical progress function postulated by Kaldor (Kaldor and Mirrlees, 1962; see also Kregel, 1971, ch. 9).

The possibilities for exploiting the best production techniques presently known by the more rapid replacement of the capital stock are, of course, not unlimited. This is why the technical progress function, beyond a certain point, bows downward. Still, the possibilities are almost certain to be greater than what might be inferred from the actual observed rate of technological progress. This is especially true as the time horizon is extended beyond the intermediate run. All the factors which are likely to serve as the most immediate constraints on the rate of technological progress - the still not fully depreciated older capital stock, the learning curve associated with the introduction of new technology, the need to adjust the size and skill composition of the laboring manpower force to match the new plant and equipment - can be expected to wane with the passage of time. What this implies is that, with technological progress as with the growth of the skill vector, it is more the speed at which the rate can be adjusted than the rate itself which is limited. Since it is the two together - the rate of growth of the skill vector and, through its effect of output per worker, the rate of technological progress - which determine the potential growth rate, it follows that the latter will itself be somewhat open-ended, an increase in the secular growth rate leading to an increase in the potential growth rate. Indeed, this is the reason for using the term 'potential' to describe the upper limit on the rate at which the economy can expand. What can only be surmised, because of how little is actually known about technological change and the meager experience there has been with high secular growth rates, is whether the increase in the potential growth rate will match, and thus keep pace with, the increase in the secular growth rate (J. Robinson, 1956, ch. 9, especially the last paragraph).

Perhaps a word should be entered here about a third factor which might seem to limit the sustainable secular growth rate. This is the availability of natural resources, including the most basic of all such resources, energy (cf. Georgescu-Roegen, 1971, ch. 10; Forrester, 1971; Lapp, 1973). In a certain sense, this has been the problem of man from his earliest beginnings. Indeed, what is meant by technological progress is simply the ability of man, by employing better techniques, sometimes derived from a scientific understanding of physical phenomena but more frequently not, to wring a better standard of living from his natural environment. Thus the question as to the availability of natural resources is actually the question of whether the rate of technological progress experienced in the past can even be maintained, let alone increased, in the face of the fixed mineral resources found on earth and the fixed quantity of energy coming from the sun. The failure to deal with this question is not meant to depreciate its importance. It is rather to recognize the complexity of the issues involved, a complexity which precludes adequate treatment of the question in this treatise (cf. Nordhaus, 1973).

The sources of inflation

The import of the above argument is that there is no reason to posit a maximally attainable secular growth rate which, if exceeded, will lead to inflation because of the supply constraints encountered. Yet it is an undeniable fact, readily observable from the American experience, that an increase in the growth rate is often followed by a rise in the aggregate price level, thereby forcing the government to take measures restricting the expansion of the economy. To understand the source of this inflationary pressure - pressure which is likely to make the higher secular growth rate unsustainable, at least politically - it is necessary to understand two antecedent points: (1) why, if the higher secular growth rate is to be maintained, the oligopolistic sector's savings curve will almost certainly have to be shifted, and (2) why it is difficult to do this in such a way that a wage-price inflationary spiral is not touched off. The discussion begins with the first of these two points.

The need to shift the savings curve. A higher warranted, or secular, growth rate for the economy as a whole is possible, as explained in chapter 6, only if the savings or investment demand curve for some sector other than the oligopolistic one shifts in the appropriate manner. For a combination of reasons - the fact that its investment demand function depends primarily on endogenous factors while its savings function contains no parameter that can be manipulated so as to stimulate aggregate demand - the oligopolistic sector is unlikely to provide the intial thrust needed to place the economy on a higher growth path. As already indicated, the oligopolistic sector serves primarily to reinforce whatever secular growth rate already prevails. Thus, to move the economy on to a higher growth path, the investment demand or savings curve for some other sector must shift.

Moreover, the curve must shift so as to produce a deficit, or excess of discretionary expenditures over discretionary income, within that sector. Dynamically, this means that the rate of growth of discretionary expenditures, $\overset{*}{I}$, within the sector must exceed the rate of growth of discretionary income, $\overset{*}{S}$, for some minimal period of time. Unless some sector is prepared to take on this role, thereby adding to its debt burden, the economy cannot escape from the built-in forces tending to push it back toward the secular growth rate. Any sector can, of course, be the one to go into deficit. But it is the government which, most realistically, is likely to do so in order to provide a forward thrust to the rate of economic expansion. It is, on the one hand, the sector which can most readily accept a zero rate of return on expenditures financed through borrowing and, on the other hand, the sector most likely to receive the support of the central bank for whatever funds it wishes to borrow. Perhaps most important of all, it is the only sector with an overall perspective and a political mandate. For these reasons it is the sector which, in the situation about to be analyzed, will be assumed to initiate the change in the secular growth rate. Still, if any other sector should, for the moment, have good grounds for going into debt further, and can arrange for the existing set of financial institutions to finance that deficit, it too can play the role of nudging the economy off the dead center established by the secular growth rate.

Let it be assumed, therefore, as shown in figure 22, that the economy is expanding at a rate equal to the secular rate, $\overset{*}{G}_s$. As long as the

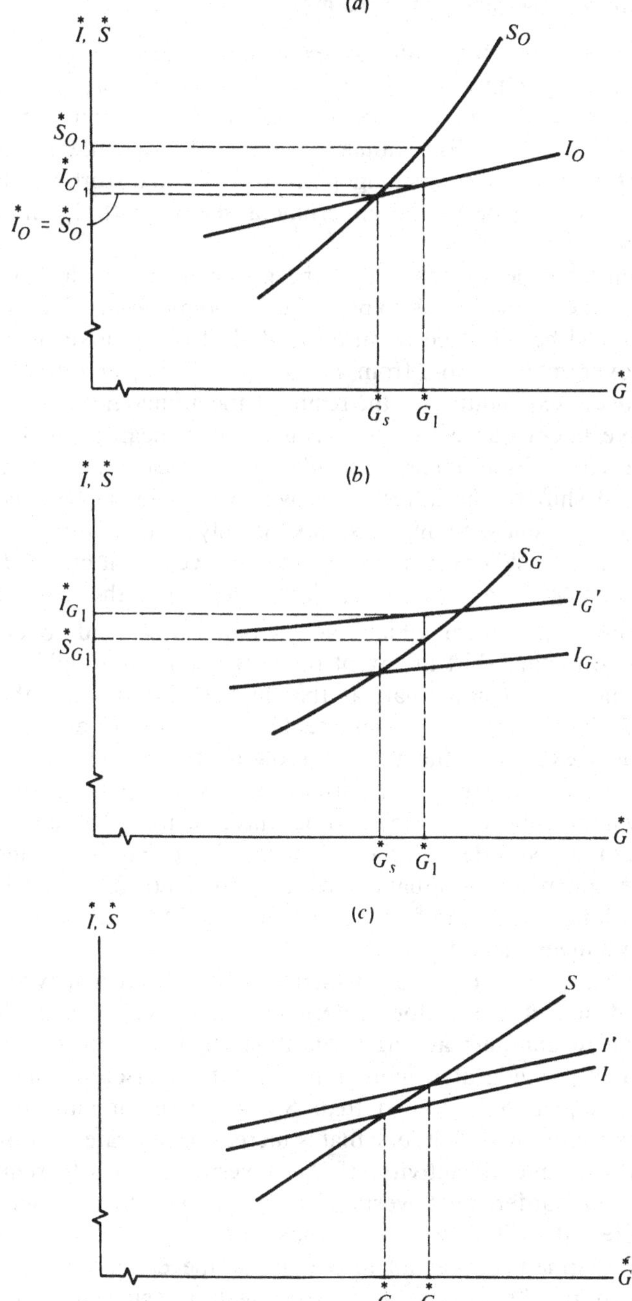

Figure 22. (a) Oligopolistic sector. (b) Government sector. (c) Economy as a whole

economy maintains that rate of expansion, the rate of growth of discretionary expenditures within the oligopolistic sector, $\overset{*}{I}_O$, will, given the initial macrodynamic balance assumed in the diagram, be equal to the rate of growth of discretionary income, $\overset{*}{S}_O$; and there will be no forces arising from within the oligopolistic sector to disturb that balance. The same will be true of the government sector, with $\overset{*}{I}_G$ there being equal to $\overset{*}{S}_G$.[9]

But then let it be supposed that the government decides to step up its rate of expenditures so as to push the economy on to a higher growth path. This will be reflected in an upward shift of the investment curve for the government sector, from I_G to I_G'. The higher rate of growth of government expenditures - the result of the autonomous shift upward of the investment curve for that sector - will mean a similar higher rate of growth of discretionary expenditures for the economy as a whole. The upward shift of the latter curve will be somewhat less, however, because government spending accounts for only a part of total discretionary expenditures. Where this new aggregate investment curve, I', intersects the aggregate savings curve, S, will determine the new aggregate growth rate, $\overset{*}{G}_1$, toward which the economy will tend to converge, assuming no further shift in any of the sectoral savings and investment curves. One should note that, at that higher growth rate, there is a growing deficit in the government sector - with the rate of growth of expenditures exceeding the rate of growth of tax revenues - that is offset in part by the growing surplus in the oligopolistic sector and in part by a growing surplus in the other three sectors. These imbalances at the sectoral level, despite the balance which exists in the aggregate, are the reason why the situation depicted in figure 22 is not likely to persist for long without, in fact, some further shift in one of the sectoral savings and investment curves.

The higher growth rate, $\overset{*}{G}_1$, which has thus been achieved can be maintained only if the sector in deficit - the government in this case - is willing to continue adding to its debt. Indeed, with discretionary expenditures growing at a more rapid rate than discretionary income - at a rate equal to I_{G_1} rather than S_{G_1} - the sector must be willing to accept a mounting deficit, one that is increasing at a rate disproportionate to its own level of activity. If the government tries to reduce this growing debt burden by lowering its rate of growth of discretionary expenditures, the effect will be to cause a downward shift in not only its own investment curve but also that for the economy as a whole. The growth of the deficit, it is true, will be slowed under these circumstances but it will not be ended. Moreover, the aggregate growth rate, $\overset{*}{G}_1$, will be reduced as well. It is only if the investment curves are allowed to fall all the way back to their original positions, I_G and

I respectively, that the deficit will be eliminated altogether. But in that event the hope of getting the economy out of the rut established by the secular growth rate will be frustrated. A mounting deficit in the sector initiating the stepped-up rate of expansion would seem, therefore, essential to maintaining the higher aggregate growth rate thereby achieved. That even the government will be willing to accept a disproportionate increase in its debts burden as a permanent condition seems doubtful, however, and it is for this reason that the situation depicted in figure 22 is not likely to persist for long. Fortunately, there is another way to maintain the higher aggregate growth rate.

The upward shift of the investment curve in the government sector depicted in figure 22 will produce, not only a deficit in that sector but, in addition, surpluses in at least one other sector. This will certainly be true of the oligopolistic sector. The high levels of aggregate demand will lead to high rates of capacity utilization and a disproportionate increase in cash flow. If the oligopolistic sector were to respond to this mounting surplus by stepping up its own rate of discretionary spending, the problem of how to maintain the higher aggregate growth rate without the government or some other sector having to incur a mounting deficit would be solved. The downward shift of I_G' would be matched by the upward shift of I_O, with I' remaining unchanged. The oligopolistic sector, however, cannot be counted on to respond in so convenient a fashion - at least not immediately. True, the higher aggregate growth rate, $\overset{*}{G}_2$, will lead to a higher rate of growth of discretionary expenditures, $\overset{*}{I}_{O_1}$, within the sector as the corporations involved revise their capital spending upward as a hedge against a possibly higher secular growth of sales. But this is merely the endogenous response of investment within the sector - a movement along the investment curve rather than a shift of the curve itself. And it is the latter, a shift in I_O, which is required.

In time, if the government succeeds in maintaining the higher aggregate growth rate, the necessary upward shift of I_O may well occur - at least in part. As corporations become convinced that the higher growth rate is the new secular rate with its attendant effect on the growth of their own sales, they are likely to revise their capital spending plans accordingly. The train of causation thus runs from expectations to a higher value for the shift variable in the investment curve for the oligopolistic sector. What this means is that, with growing confidence that the higher aggregate growth rate will be maintained, the corporations in the oligopolistic sector will gradually move toward a higher rate of growth of discretionary expenditures irrespective of other factors. This upward shift in I_O will reduce the need for the government or whatever other sector has initiated the higher rate of economic expansion to continue adding to its debt. Of course, and this is a key point, the timing is most important. If the government or the other sector acts precipitously to put an end to its mounting deficit, the economy will be brought back down to the previously prevailing secular growth rate, $\overset{*}{G}_s$.

Moreover, even if the investment curve for the oligopolistic sector does eventually shift upward as the megacorps within the sector become convinced that a higher secular growth rate has been established, it cannot be expected to rise sufficiently so that it then intersects the savings curve for the oligopolistic sector at the new secular growth rate, $\overset{*}{G}_1$. This is because the rate of growth of discretionary expenditures within the oligopolistic sector will, at most, only increase proportionately to match the higher aggregate growth rate while the rate of growth of discretionary income will, because of the upwardly bowing savings curve, increase disproportionately. Yet it is precisely that condition - $\overset{*}{I}_o$ being equal to $\overset{*}{S}_0$ at the new secular growth rate $\overset{*}{G}_1$ as shown in figure 23 - which must be met if the oligopolistic sector is no longer to exert a contractionary influence on the growth rate, generating a higher rate of growth of savings relative to investment that must be offset, if the higher growth rate is to be maintained, by a deficit in some other sector such as the government. Indeed, unless the rate of growth of discretionary expenditures for each of the five sectors can be brought into line with the rate of growth of discretionary expenditures within the same sector, $\overset{*}{G}_1$ is unlikely to be maintained for long. It is for this reason that, if the government's efforts to place the economy on a higher warranted, or secular, growth rate are to be successful, there must also be a shift in the savings curve for the oligopolistic sector. Yet this is anything but an easy matter to arrange, as will now be pointed out.

Shifting the oligopolistic sector's savings curve. As previously noted, the savings function for the oligopolistic sector depends, not only on the divergence of the current growth rate from the secular but on three other sets of variables as well, in addition to the shift variable encompassing lagged effects and future expectations. The sets of variables are: (a) the average price level within the oligopolistic sector, $\bar{P}_O$, (b) the difference between the national incremental wage pattern, W_p, and the secular growth rate of output per worker in the oligopolistic sector, $\overset{*}{Z}_s$, and (c) the corporate income tax rate, t_y (and, in the industries to which one applies, the *ad valorem* tax rate, t_e). A change in any one of these three sets of parameters will cause a shift in the savings curve for the oligopolistic sector.[10]

By now it should be clear as to why the necessary shift in the savings

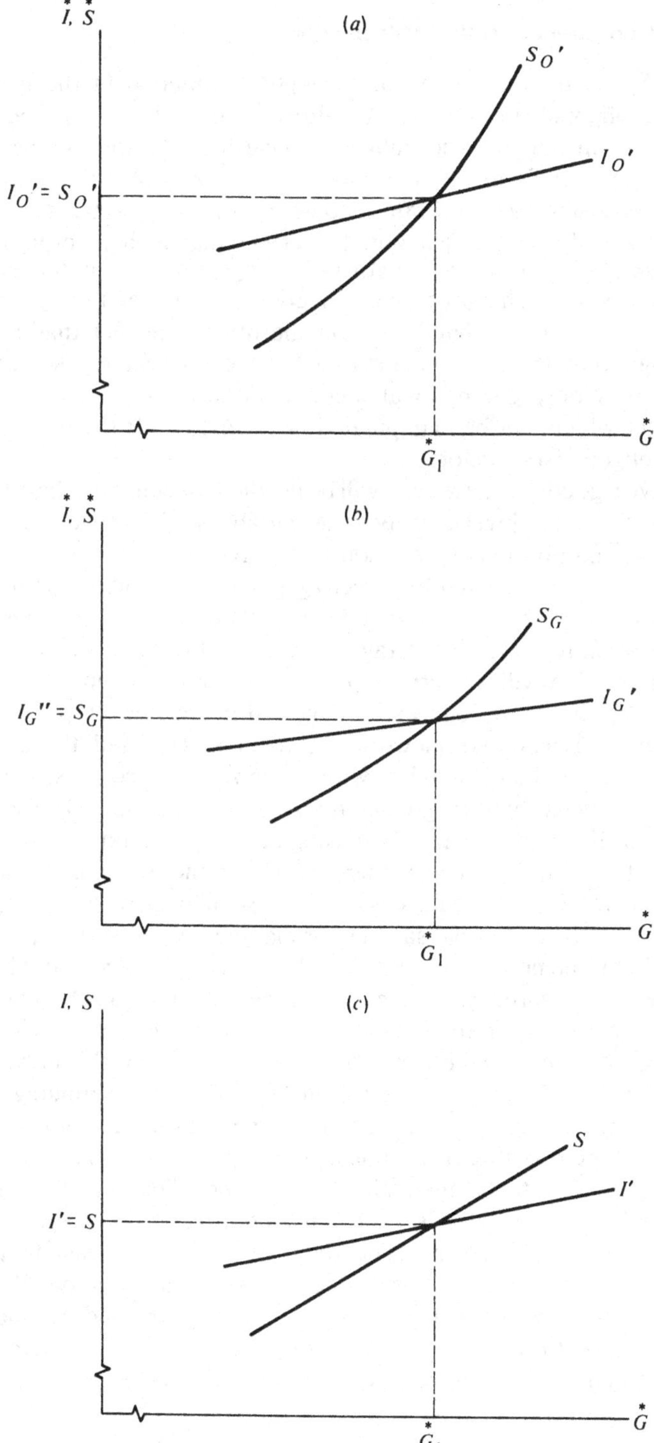

Figure 23. (a) Oligopolistic sector. (b) Government sector. (c) Economy as a whole

curve S_O, is unlikely to occur through a reduction in the price level for the oligopolistic sector. As already pointed out (pp. 98-9), the megacorps in oligopolistic industries have little reason, acting on their own, to lower their prices. Similarly, the possibility of shifting the savings curve by raising the corporate income tax rate can all but be excluded. As will shortly be brought out, the effect that higher corporate taxes will have on the rate of growth of savings throughout the economy as a whole is somewhat problematical, given the interrelationship between $\bar{P}_O$ and t_y on the one hand and, on the other, the fact that t_y is also a parameter of the savings function for the government sector. This, then, leaves only the national incremental wage pattern, W_p, as the parameter which can be manipulated in order to shift the savings curve for the oligopolistic sector.

The average corporate levy, it will be recalled, depends on the difference between the price level and average variable and fixed costs. Thus if the average corporate levy, the source of savings within the oligopolistic sector, cannot be reduced by lowering price levels (or, for that matter, tax rates), the same result can be achieved by raising the rates of compensation reflected in average variable and fixed costs. These rates of compensation will, in turn, depend on the national incremental wage pattern, W_p, in the various ways suggested in chapter 5 (pp. 162-72).

The macrodynamic framework set forth in this and the preceding chapter helps make clear why, with technological progress, a national incremental wage pattern greater than zero is essential. The effect of technological progress - the increasing returns over time as one might refer to it - is to shift the savings curve for the economy as a whole upward to the left at a rate equal to the secular growth of output per worker, with the additional savings, or marginal social surplus, emerging both as increased net income within the business sector and, since business tax rates are geared to business income, as increased government revenues. Were wage rates and the compensation of households in general (ignoring entrepreneurial income) to remain unchanged, this upward drift of the aggregate savings curve would lead to a corresponding decline in the warranted growth rate. It is only the national incremental wage pattern and the resulting rise in household income which enables a certain growth rate, $\overset{*}{G}_s$, to be maintained over time. The fact that the rate of technological progress is itself a function of the aggregate growth rate, the increasing returns depending as they do at least in part on the rate of growth of investment, does not alter the situation. Whatever the relationship between the aggregate growth rate and technological progress, it is still possible, by means of the national incremental wage pattern, to convert the higher output per worker into higher real income for the household sector, thereby enabling the economic expansion to continue undiminished.

Not just any national incremental wage pattern will do, however. There is, in fact, but one value for W_p which, given the other determinants of the macrodynamic system, will be consistent with a particular warranted growth rate at existing price levels. Of course, if one is willing to allow price levels to rise, the choice becomes somewhat more open; but this not only concedes a certain rate of inflation, it also leads to other problems soon to be elaborated on. While there is just one value for W_p which will enable the warranted growth rate to be maintained - holding other factors, including price levels, constant - there is little to assure that this one wage pattern is the one which will in fact be established. For one thing, the national incremental wage pattern is merely constrained by economic variables, it is not controlled by them. This means that there is no endogenous dynamic which can be counted upon to produce the 'right' value for W_p. Within the limits set by economic factors, it all depends on the socio-political forces which shape the national incremental wage pattern. But even if, by some chance, the 'right' value were to be chosen so that the expansion could continue unabated without any attendant rise in price levels, the whole delicate balance would be destroyed as soon as any exogenous disturbance produced a change in the aggregate growth rate.

This, then, is the most significant point of all: any change in the aggregate growth rate will have a redistributive effect, creating strong pressure for a change in the national incremental wage pattern, with little to assure that the new value for W_p will be the 'right' one under the circumstances. The new wage pattern may be too low - in which case there will be an excess of savings within the oligopolistic sector acting, in the manner already pointed out, as a brake on the further expansion of the economy. Or it may be too high - in which case the dynamic sequence known as a wage-price spiral will be initiated. In other words, given the present mechanism for determining the national incremental wage pattern, any change in the warranted growth rate is likely to place the economic system on an erratic growth path. Why too low a wage pattern will serve as a drag on the growth rate should be clear from what has already been said. What still remains to be explained is why too high a wage pattern will touch off a wage-price spiral. To illuminate this point, the effects of an increase in the aggregate growth rate will be traced out.

An increase in the aggregate growth rate, as reflected in higher levels of aggregate demand, will cause megacorps to operate on the average in excess of their standard ratio. It is this higher rate of capacity utilization that will enable the rate of growth of savings to exceed the rate of growth of investment within the oligopolistic sector, the divergence between the two flows being manifest through a disproportionate increase in reported net earnings. To the trade union in the bellwether industry, the disproportionate increase in reported net earnings will be a signal that the division of income has changed to the disadvantage of the workers whom it represents. This feeling that its rank-and-file members have fallen behind in the apportionment of the social surplus will be strengthened by what is likely to be a concurrent rise in the price level outside the oligopolistic sector - for reasons shortly to be made explicit - with the resulting increase in the cost of living signifying a decline in the real value of the wage rates previously negotiated. As pointed out in chapter 5, the trade union in the bellwether industry can be expected to try to counteract this relative decline in the position of its members by insisting upon and then obtaining a higher national incremental wage pattern at the next contract round.

The higher wage pattern, by increasing the compensation received by the megacorp's principal constituencies, will have the effect of shifting the savings curve for the oligopolistic sector outward to the right. As wages, salaries and dividends all increase by a larger percentage, leading to a higher rate of growth of average variable and fixed costs, the residual income accruing to individual megacorps will necessarily be reduced. This outward shift of the oligopolistic sector's savings curve will, it should be noted, tend to eliminate the excess of savings over investment which, in the face of some other sector's unwillingness to continue incurring debt at the same rate, would otherwise make the higher warranted growth rate unsustainable. But it is also possible that the savings curve will shift outward too far, leaving some megacorp-price leaders with insufficient internal funds to finance their desired rate of growth of investment. In that case, a rise in the price level within the oligopolistic sector can be expected to follow. The question is how likely this possibility is.

There are several reasons why, following the establishment of a higher national incremental wage pattern, the megacorp-price leaders in some industries may feel they have been left with too small an average corporate levy. For one thing, the parameters of the pricing decision within the bellwether industry may be atypical of those prevailing throughout the oligopolistic sector. The bellwether industry's cost structure may be unrepresentative, reflecting proportionately lower labor, material or dividend costs, or those costs may respond less directly to a change in the national incremental wage pattern. For any of these reasons, the rise in average variable and fixed costs following acceptance of the national pattern may be greater in some significant portion of industries than that experienced in the bellwether industry itself, this greater rise in average variable and fixed costs necessarily being at the expense of the average corporate levy. Similarly, the bellwether industry's demand for or supply of investment funds may also be unrepresentative. On the demand side, the bellwether industry may be experiencing a lower rate of growth. Or it may just have fewer investment opportunities open to it, managerial attitudes meanwhile limiting the possibility of diversification. On the supply side, it may be operating at a higher rate of capacity utilization, this enabling it to generate a larger volume of internal funds. Whatever the underlying cause, other industries may find that, given their own demand for and supply of investment funds, they simply require a higher average corporate levy.

This first source of difficulty, that conditions in the bellwether industry may be atypical of those prevailing throughout the oligopolistic sector, can be attributed to the specific mechanism by which the national incremental wage pattern is established in the United States - and in particular to the national pattern's dependence on circumstances within a single industry.[11] A second source of difficulty, that the megacorp and trade union responsible for establishing the key bargain may differ on the extent to which they view the change in the warranted growth rate as being secular rather than cyclical, would arise even if the bellwether industry were entirely representative of the oligopolistic sector.

The virtual impossibility of distinguishing an increase in the secular growth rate from an unusually large rise in cyclical demand has already been dwelt on at some length. The evidence for both is the same - a rate of capacity utilization which, over a given interval, has exceeded the standard operating ratio, together with a disproportionate increase in reported net earnings. Only the passage of time will reveal whether the new trend will continue or, alternatively, give way to the contractionary phase of the normal business cycle. Difficult as it may be to answer, however, the question of whether the increase in the aggregate growth rate is secular or cyclical is absolutely critical for both the megacorp and trade union. If the increase is, in fact, secular, both the rates of compensation paid the megacorp's two principal constituencies and the funds retained by the firm itself can be expected to increase by a percentage equal to the higher growth rate without price levels having to be raised. This is because, in this case, the disproportionate increase in reported net earnings will reflect the growth of the social surplus. But if the increase in the aggregate growth rate is merely cyclical, any rise in the rates of compensation paid the laboring manpower force and the equity debt holders will be at the expense of the average corporate levy. This is because, in this case, the disproportionate increase in reported net earnings will reflect only a temporary redistribution of income.

To the extent, then, that megacorps believe that the higher operating ratios they are currently experiencing portend an actual rise in the secular growth rate, they are less likely to feel compelled to raise their prices following acceptance of the national incremental wage pattern. While the increase in the secular growth rate will require a higher rate of growth of investment, both to match the rate of growth of industry sales and to provide sufficient reserve capacity, the concurrent increase in the rate of growth of the realized corporate levy may, even in the face of the higher wage pattern, be adequate for whatever internal funds are required. It all depends, of course, on whether, after making allowance for the rise in average variable and fixed costs, megacorps feel that the current rate at which internal funds are being generated will be sufficient, given the marginal efficiency of investment, even without a rise in price levels. That is, it depends on whether, as analyzed in chapter 3, the investment demand curve, D_I, for most megacorp-price leaders intersects the supply curve for additional investment funds, S_I, where $n = 0$, even after the higher costs implicit in the national incremental wage pattern have been absorbed. On the other hand, to the extent that megacorps believe that the higher operating ratios will shortly be followed by lower ones as part of the normal cyclical pattern of demand, a rise in the oligopolistic sector's price level is all but certain. For while trade unions are likely to view the disproportionate increase in reported net earnings as justifying a more rapid growth of wages, megacorps are likely to view it as simply a temporary windfall, one which will be offset by the disproportionate decline in reported net earnings during the next phase of the current planning period.

What is interesting about the latter expectation on the part of megacorps is that it is likely to be largely self-fulfilling. If megacorps decide to raise their prices following acceptance of the national incremental wage pattern because they feel that a subsequent decline in aggregate demand will leave them with insufficient internally generated investment funds, this very fact, together with the rise in the non-oligopolistic sector's price level resulting from the higher warranted growth rate, is likely to induce the government to take steps to curtail aggregate demand. Before pursuing this point any further, however, it is necessary to pause and analyze government contracyclical policy in light of the micro and macro models previously developed.

Government contracyclical policy

Efforts by the government to control the aggregate growth rate are limited, at least at the present time in the United States, to monetary and fiscal policy.[12] The former involves changes in the money supply and interest rates; the latter, a shift in the government's own savings or investment demand curve through a change in either tax rates or discretionary expenditures. Each of these alternatives will be discussed in turn, with special emphasis on the implications for the oligopolistic sector.

Monetary policy. The efficacy of monetary policy will depend on the effect which a change in either interest rates or the money supply is likely to have on the willingness of decision-making units within the oligopolistic, non-oligopolistic, government and household sectors to incur further debt.[13] The willingness to incur further debt will, in turn, govern the extent to which the rate of growth of investment in any of those sectors can exceed the rate of growth of savings. The discussion of this point will begin with the oligopolistic sector.

A number of reasons have already been suggested as to why investment demand in the oligopolistic sector will, in fact, tend to be interest inelastic. First, it had been pointed out that the expansion of plant and equipment, to the extent that this is indispensable to maintaining a megacorp's existing market shares, is likely under most circumstances to be undertaken regardless of what the prevailing interest rate happens to be. Put another way, the return from such investment, it can be assumed, will almost certainly exceed the cost of borrowing external funds, given the historical limits on interest rates. The same is true of any investment to increase barriers to entry, create a more favorable public image or differentiate the product more sharply which is similarly vital to the preservation of the megacorp's market position. Second, it has been pointed out that the megacorp is able to finance most of its investment by means of the corporate levy, to that extent being able to bypass the capital funds market entirely. This ability to generate internal funds is the very source of the megacorp's economic strength, for it means that the megacorp is one step removed from the direct control of market forces.

Third, even though some small portion of the megacorp's total investment plans may still be subject to the marginal calculation of returns and costs, it has been pointed out that the decision to resort to outside financing is based on what has been termed the permanent interest rate, and not the actual interest rate currently prevailing in the capital funds market. This permanent interest rate, it will be recalled, is the minimal cost of borrowing external funds over the business cycle; and as such it will depend not only on secular changes in long-term interest rates (insofar as new fixed interest debt is concerned), but also on the state of expectations reflected in stock market conditions (insofar as new equity debt is concerned).

It can thus be seen why the action of the Federal Reserve Board in altering the reserves of member banks is likely to have little or no effect on investment in the oligopolistic sector, at least via interest rates. The resulting change in short-term interest rates must first lead to a corresponding change in long-term interest rates, or, more specifically, to a change in the cost to the megacorp of fixed-interest debt financing.[14] This is a process dependent both on time and on the effectiveness of arbitrage in the money markets.[15] Meanwhile, the change in long-term interest rates may be outweighed by a change in the expectations of those active in the stock market.[16] Even if this is not the case, the change in long-term interest rates will have to persist for a sufficiently long period of time to affect the permanent interest rate as perceived, and reacted to, by the megacorp.[17] In that event, however, it is not the cyclical timing but rather the actual amount of investment in the long run that will be affected. For all these reasons, as shown by the empirical evidence, investment by the megacorp will tend to be interest inelastic over the planning period; and monetary policy, insofar as it influences the oligopolistic sector of the economy via interest rates, is likely to be, at best, ineffectual as a short-run policy tool.[18]

Monetary policy, however, can also affect the level of investment through the sheer availability of funds. While the interest inelasticity of investment has been recognized for some time, many economists would nonetheless argue that the Federal Reserve Board, by regulating the overall flow of bank credit, can still influence the level of aggregate investment. If business firms are unable to obtain loans, at any interest rate, because commercial banks are short on reserves, they will have no choice, it is said, but to cut back on those expenditures which involve the least fixed commitment, that is, on their investment expenditures. In other words, the contention is that monetary policy can operate with success via the transactions demand for money.[19]

While the ability of the megacorp to finance investment largely out of the corporate levy might at first seem to refute this line of argument, the point cannot be dismissed so lightly. The fact is that the megacorp, in the course of carrying on its day-to-day activities, may be heavily dependent on short-term commercial credit (Anderson, 1964, ch.2; Christian and Mazek, 1964; Bosworth, 1971). Of course, as a large, important customer, the megacorp can expect its credit needs to receive first priority from banks. Still, if the Federal Reserve Board persists with a tight money policy long and hard enough, even a megacorp will feel the pressure. Unable to obtain all the short-term credit it needs, the megacorp will be forced to divert funds from investment in order to satisfy its more immediate obligations. Though the rate of capital formation may in the long run be unaffected, the cyclical pattern of investment will nonetheless be altered.[20] It should be noted, however, that the ability of the Federal Reserve Board to stimulate investment in the short run via the transactions demand for money is not likely to be as great as the ability to curtail investment. As long as the megacorp is able to obtain all the short-term credit it requires, a further easing of monetary policy is unlikely to result in increased investment - except insofar as the megacorp may be encouraged to borrow short-term funds to make up a temporary deficit in the corporate levy and/or avoid having to borrow long-term funds when market conditions are unfavorable. Thus monetary policy is not fully reversible in its effect on the oligopolistic sector.

Moreover, while it cannot be denied that the Federal Reserve System may ultimately succeed in curtailing megacorp investment through a tight money policy, the consequences of its regulating aggregate demand in this manner should at the same time be kept clearly in mind. Because the typical megacorp has both an internal source of long-term investment funds and a more favored access to short-term credit, the brunt of monetary policy tends to fall on other sectors of the economy. Of course, the regulated industries, because resort to a corporate levy is for the most part denied them, will be more directly affected, both by a change in interest rates and by a change in the availability of funds, than the rest of the oligopolistic sector (see above, p. 115). Still, the major impact of any shift in monetary policy will be felt in the non-oligopolistic sector. This is because the non-classical proprietorships which predominate in that sector not only are likely to lack sufficient market power to exact much in the way of a corporate levy, they also have the least favored access of all business firms to the financial intermediaries which supply long-term credit.[21]

Outside the business sector, it is households which will be most directly affected by a change in monetary policy. Although the purchase of other consumer durables may continue to be financed, by the megacorps which supply them if not by financial intermediaries themselves, residential dwellings are a different matter. Their purchase requires particularly long-term financing which the builders of homes, being dependent themselves on loans from financial intermediaries, cannot provide.[22] Within the government sector, too, monetary policy will have a differential impact. State and local governments, faced in many cases with legal limitations on the amounts they are allowed to borrow, cannot call upon the Federal Reserve System to guarantee a market for their securities; and this makes the level of their capital expenditures somewhat the hostage of monetary policy (C. Phelps, 1963; see also Ando *et al.*, 1965; Evans and Klein, 1967; Suits, 1962).

Reliance upon monetary policy as a contracyclical tool thus serves to distort the pattern of inter-sectoral growth - in particular favoring the expansion of the oligopolistic sector at the expense of other sectors. Even if the distortion is temporary, with the long-run pattern of growth eventually reasserting itself, the effect will in any case be to accentuate the cyclical instability of demand arising within those other sectors.

Still another consequence of relying too heavily upon monetary instruments to control aggregate demand must be pointed out. Since it is only by threatening the megacorp's short-term liquidity position that the Federal Reserve System can expect to force the firms within the oligopolistic sector to cut back on their investment plans, successful implementation of the policy runs the considerable risk of creating panic in the money markets, a result which is the very abnegation of the Federal Reserve System's primary responsibility. If the monetary authorities succeed in so limiting the availability of credit that even a megacorp cannot obtain all the short-term funds it requires, the holders of near-money - megacorps especially - may be compelled to dispose of their liquid assets, such as government bonds, certificates of deposit and corporate securities in general, for cash. Alarmed by the resulting decline in value, the other holders of these types of assets may join in the rush to sell, thereby endangering the liquidity of the capital funds market and eroding confidence in the monetary system as a whole.[23] Even if the monetary authorities do not allow the situation to reach these crisis proportions - and the tight money policy will to that extent, of course, be less effective - they are nonetheless engaged in a dangerous game, that of trying to cut off the flow of funds to business firms to a degree sufficient to curtail 'excessive' capital expenditures without causing paralysis. It is somewhat like trying to restrain an unruly individual by placing one's fingers around his neck and slowly tightening the grip. One runs the risk of cutting off the circulation altogether, leaving the individual unconscious if not actually lifeless.

This is not to argue that monetary policy is unimportant or unnecessary (cf. Ball, 1965; Davidson, 1967, 1972; Minsky, 1975). It is merely to point out, on the basis of the microeconomic theory developed earlier, that a primary reliance upon monetary policy as a contracyclical tool not only may discriminate among different sectors of the economy, it may even contribute to the amplitude of cyclical fluctuations. For this reason monetary policy is likely to prove most useful when it is made subordinate to, and thus serves to reinforce, fiscal policy. But even the efficacy of fiscal policy needs to be reconsidered in light of the micro and macro theory developed earlier.

Fiscal policy. Some of the consequences arising from a change in fiscal policy have already been touched on. As pointed out, the addition of new programs or the more liberal financing of old ones, representing as it does a discrete or discontinuous increase in government expenditures, will cause an upward shift of the government sector's investment demand curve. With the rate of growth of government expenditures, $\overset{*}{I}_G$, thus exceeding the rate of growth of tax revenue, $\overset{*}{S}_G$, the warranted growth rate for the economy as a whole will necessarily rise, at least for the moment.

It would seem that the same effect would follow from a downward shift of the savings curve for the government sector. There are two points to keep in mind, however. The first is that while a change in the rate of growth of government spending will cause a shift in the government sector's investment demand curve without there necessarily being a change in the slope of that curve, a change in tax rates - the only way the government sector's savings curve can be manipulated - will primarily lead to a change in the slope of that curve. This means that the effect of any change in tax rates will not be independent of the current rate of economic expansion. The second point is that, whatever the shift that can be produced in the government sector's savings curve through a change in tax rates, the effect on the warranted growth rate will, at best, be partially countermanded. This follows from a unique characteristic of the tax as well as some of the other parameters of the various savings curves. They are parameters of two savings functions simultaneously so that the most immediate effect of any change in tax rates is to redistribute income between the affected sectors. Whatever decline in the rate of growth of discretionary income occurs in the government sector as a result of reducing a tax rate will be offset by an increase in the rate of growth of discretionary income in the benefiting sector; and *vice versa*.

The effect of a tax reduction on the aggregate growth rate will therefore depend on the extent to which a higher rate of growth of discretionary income within the benefited sector will lead to a higher rate of growth of discretionary expenditures in that same sector. Even within the household sector, where the correspondence between an increment in discretionary income and an increment in discretionary expenditures is perhaps greatest, there is certain to be some slippage between the two, especially if the increment in discretionary income appears to be merely transitory. In the oligopolistic sector, based on the evidence as to the determinants of investment demand, the slippage will be all the greater - if not total.[24] It is only with these two qualifications strongly in mind that one can regard the downward shift of the government's savings curve as the correlative of an upward shift of the same sector's investment demand curve.

The dynamic just described also works in reverse. If, following a downward shift in the government sector's investment demand curve (and/or, to a lesser extent, following an upward shift in its savings curve), the rate of growth of taxes should exceed the rate of growth of expenditures, the warranted growth rate for the economy as a whole will necessarily fall. This is because, with the government running a surplus, it will be withdrawing more claims from the income stream than it is injecting into it, the government's surplus thus having the effect of reducing the level of aggregate demand. In this case, the megacorps within the oligopolistic sector will find themselves operating below their standard ratios, the resulting excess of investment over savings serving to offset the surplus in the government sector.

From what has already been said, then, there would seem to be little question of the government's ability, acting through fiscal policy, to control the level of aggregate demand and, by this means, to determine the warranted growth rate for the oligopolistic subsector. Still, an important limitation of fiscal policy must be noted, even aside from the lesser stimulative effect of tax reductions. It has to do with the government's power to tax the megacorp directly. It should be pointed out that more than just the ability to influence the level of aggregate demand is at issue here. If the government could impose a levy of its own limiting the net after-tax revenue flows of megacorps, it would then be able to force a shift in the oligopolistic sector's savings function independently of what might be happening to the price level within the oligopolistic sector and/or the national incremental wage pattern. This would, in turn, provide the government with a more direct form of control over the oligopolistic sector. The question, then, is how much power does the government have to tax the megacorp directly?

Up to this point, no provision has been made for taxes in the oligopolistic pricing formula. This omission must now be corrected. The megacorp, in setting its price, will need to take into account both types of taxes which affect it directly. With regard to an *ad valorem* tax, the revenue received by the megacorp, given an industry price P, will be the industry price less a percentage equal to the tax rate. That is,

$$P - P(t_e) = AR \tag{7.1}$$

where AR = average revenue received by the megacorp.

If the average revenue received by the megacorp is to cover the megacorp's costs and still generate the desired amount of investment funds, the industry price must be set so that

$$P - P(t_e) = AVC + \frac{FC + CL}{SOR \cdot ERC} \tag{7.2}$$

Shifting terms, this equation becomes

$$P = \frac{1}{1 - t_e}\left(AVC + \frac{FC + CL}{SOR \cdot ERC}\right) \tag{7.3}$$

From the above equation it is possible to derive the marginal tax-price adjuster, that is, the percentage by which the industry price will have to be changed following a revision of the *ad valorem* tax rate if the megacorps in that industry are to continue earning the same after-tax revenue. The formula for this marginal tax-price adjuster, T_e, is as follows:

$$T_e = \frac{1}{1 - t_{e_1}} - \frac{1}{1 - t_{e_0}} \bigg/ \frac{1}{1 - t_{e_0}} \tag{7.4}$$

where $t_{e_0} \equiv$ the previous *ad valorem* tax rate
and $t_{e_1} \equiv$ the new *ad valorem* tax rate.[25]

When an *ad valorem* tax is being levied on the industry for the first time, the formula reduces to:

$$T_e = \frac{1}{1 - t_{e_1}} - 1 \tag{7.5}$$

since t_{e_0} will then be equal to 0.

With a corporate income tax rather than an *ad valorem* tax in effect, the oligopolistic price formula becomes slightly more complicated. If the megacorp is to cover its costs and still generate a sufficient amount of internal funds for investment, the industry price must be set so that

$$P = \frac{1}{1 - Net(t_y)}\left(AVC + \frac{FC + CL}{SOR \cdot ERC}\right) \tag{7.6}$$

As reflected by the formula, a corporate income tax has less of an impact on the price level than an *ad valorem* tax by a percentage equal to *Net* - the ratio of net income to the price that would be necessary in the absence of any tax. The marginal tax-price adjuster in this case, T_y, is as follows:

$$T_y = \frac{1}{1 - Net(T_{y_1})} - \frac{1}{1 - Net(t_{y_0})} \bigg/ \frac{1}{1 - Net(t_{y_0})} \tag{7.7}$$

In its most general form, then, the price equation for an oligopolistic industry may be written as follows:

$$P = \frac{1}{1 - t_e}\left[\frac{1}{1 - Net(t_y)}\left(AVC + \frac{FC + CL}{SOR \cdot ERC}\right)\right] \tag{7.8}$$

with t_e or t_y equal to 0 if no *ad valorem* or corporate income tax is urrently being levied. With the assistance of this revised price equation and, even more important, of the tax-price adjusters derived from it, it is possible to determine what the incidence of a tax on the megacorp is likely to be - that is, whether it will be passed along to customers in the form of a higher industry price or, alternatively, be absorbed by the megacorp itself through a reduction in the average corporate levy. In other words, it is possible to indicate the extent to which a tax on the megacorp is likely to be shifted onto others.

Incidence of the corporate income tax. If the incidence of the tax were to fall entirely on the megacorp's customers through higher prices, the tax would be little different from a personal income tax - except insofar as it were more or less regressive[26] - and the savings function for the oligopolistic sector would be left unaffected. If, however, the incidence were to fall entirely on the megacorp through a reduction in the realized corporate levy, this would be an entirely different matter. For in that case the savings function for the oligopolistic sector would necessarily shift. In the final analysis, then, the efficacy of a fiscal policy based on taxing the megacorp will depend on the ability of the affected oligopolistic industries to raise their price by a percentage, n, equal to the tax-price adjusters, T_e and T_y. This, in turn, will depend on the costs to each of the megacorp-price leaders, acting as surrogates for their industries, of raising prices by that percentage. While these costs have already been analyzed for a price increase designed simply to augment the corporate levy and for a price increase designed to offset a rise in costs stemming from acceptance of the national incremental wage pattern, they will be somewhat different for a price increase designed to neutralize the effect of an increase in excise or corporate income taxes.

The costs of any price increase, it will be recalled, are those due to the substitution effect, the entry factor and the fear of meaningful government intervention. The first of these costs will be incurred following a tax-neutralizing price increase only to the extent that the tax has been levied against particular industries, industries which produce goods and services that are not competitive with one another. Of course, to the extent that this is the case, the tax will be less effective as an instrument of aggregate economic policy - though it may be all the more effective as a means of exercising social control over particular industries. The type of tax which least meets this condition for the substitution effect to be operative is the corporate income tax. Since all meagacorp-price leaders will be similarly affected by any change in this tax,[27] and since all can be expected to try to increase their prices in response within one or two pricing periods,[28] any substitution effect will be largely nullified. Only insofar as the industries which produce competing goods and services have different tax-price adjusters, that is, only insofar as they are governed by different values for *Net*, will the ensuing percentage increases in price be different. These disparities in *n*, however, are not likely to be very great, and as a result the substitution effect is not likely to be significant.[29] In short, the cost of a price increase due to the substitution effect will be negligible for any tax on the megacorp, such as the corporate income tax, which is broadly based; while for any tax such as an *ad valorem* excise tax on a single product which is not broadly based it will have little aggregate impact.

As for the entry factor, no tax, whatever its form, is likely to make a difference. This reflects the fact that, with the exception of a sharply graduated corporate income tax, the impost will affect all firms equally, potential new ones as well as existing megacorps. It will therefore be no easier, after the tax has been levied or increased, for an outsider to overcome the barriers that have been erected against the entry of new firms. Of course, it is true that insofar as the existing megacorps are unable to shift the tax forward onto consumers, they may no longer be able to obtain all the investment funds they need through the corporate levy at below the market rate of interest. But this simply means that they will then be forced to compete for funds with any potential new entrant in the capital funds market; and in this competition, because of their established position, the existing megacorps will still be at a considerable advantage.[30] In short, the cost of a tax-neutralizing price increase due to the entry factor, will, like the cost due to the substitution effect in the case of a broadly based tax, be negligible.

This leaves only the fear of meaningful government intervention as a possible factor preventing megacorps from raising their price to neutralize the effect of a change in megacorp taxes. It is difficult to see, however, how this fear can serve as a significant restraint. Under present political and legal conditions, it is difficult enough for the government to bring sufficient pressure to bear to prevent a price increase designed clearly to augment the corporate levy (see above, pp. 77-80). How then can it be expected to bring sufficient pressure to bear to prevent a price increase designed simply to maintain the corporate levy? Of course, this is a situation which may change over time, and the virtual absence of any increase in the corporate income tax since the end of World War II, except under the unusual circumstances surrounding the Korean War build-up of American armed forces, suggests caution before making too definitive a statement. Still, it seems reasonable to conclude that, in this case, the fear of meaningful government intervention can be largely dismissed.

In summary, then, the cost of internally raised funds, *R*, will be negligible and the possibility of meaningful government intervention, ρ, less than the minimum acceptable probability of such intervention,

X_2, as long as the percentage increase in price, n, which ensues following an increase in the general taxes levied against megacorps does not exceed T_y or just simply T, the tax-price adjuster for any broadly based impost. In other words, the supply curve of investment funds is the same, under these circumstances, as the horizontal axis of the investment demand-supply graph up to the point where $n = T$ (see figure 24). Put still another way, the R and S_I curves (see figures 12-14, chapter 3) will, as a result of the increase in the tax rate, shift outward to the left and right respectively by an amount equal to T. Thus there

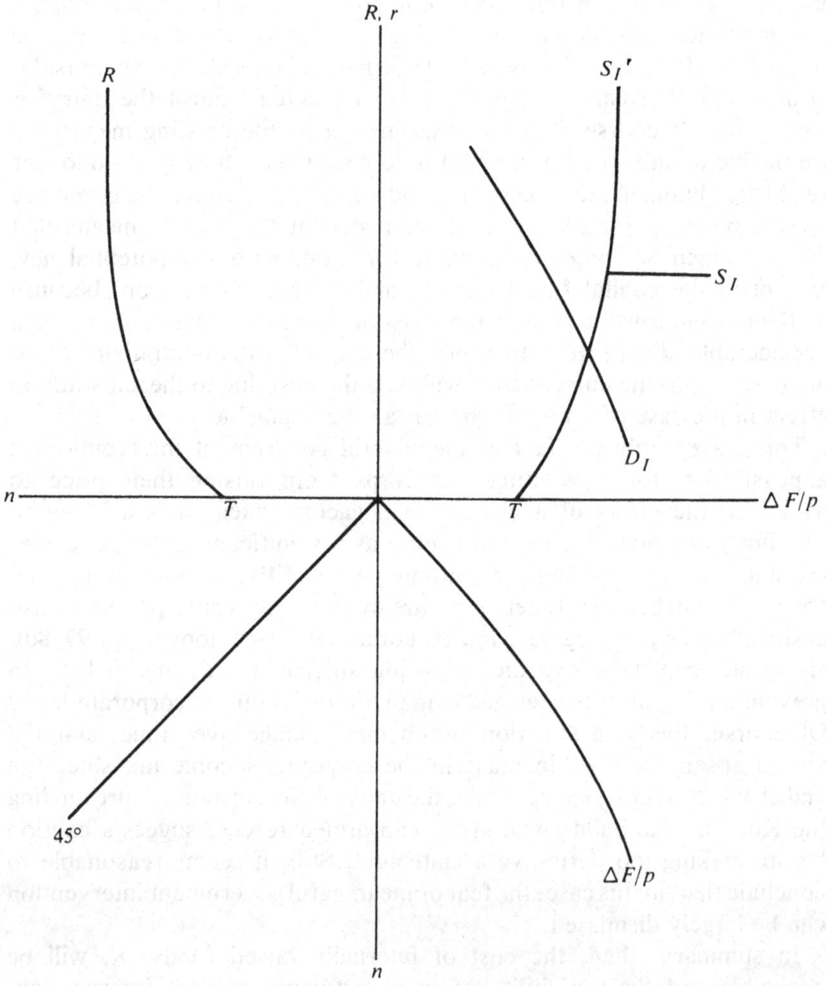

Figure 24

is every reason to expect the burden of any broadly based tax on megacorps to be shifted forward onto consumers in the form of higher prices.[31]

The obverse of this, however, does not follow. When and if the burden of the tax is lightened, those same customers are hardly likely to notice. This is because a reduction in or the elimination of any broadly based tax on megacorps will not necessarily lead to a decrease in prices with the oligopolistic sector. Just as the substitution effect, the entry factor and the fear of meaningful government intervention are all negligible factors in dissuading the megacorp from raising its prices following an increase in tax rates, so too they are negligible factors in forcing the megacorp to lower its prices following a reduction in tax rates. This makes a higher tax on megacorps doubly ineffectual as an anti-inflationary measure. If imposed to curtail aggregate demand as a means of halting the rise in price levels, it is likely to have the opposite effect. The higher the taxes imposed on megacorps, the higher the oligopolistic sector's price level is likely to be. Yet a decline in those same taxes will accomplish little toward reducing the oligopolistic sector's price level. The most that can be expected is that it will make unnecessary an increase in prices that might otherwise occur.

The government's power to force a shift in the oligopolistic sector's savings curve is therefore quite limited. The underlying explanation for this is the market power which megacorps acting collectively through the mechanism of price leadership have - a market power which enables them to control the price levels in their industries and thus offset any action by the government to reduce the average corporate levy through a change in tax rates. What this means is that, aside from the general weakness of a tax-based fiscal policy - that the shift of the savings curve in the government sector will necessarily be matched by a shift of the savings curve in some other sector, and in the opposite direction, so that the aggregate savings curve is virtually unaffected - there is an even more specific untoward consequence when such a policy is directed at megacorps. Any increase in the putative tax burden on megacorps is likely to be shifted to the household sector in the form of higher prices, this intersectoral redistributional effect exacerbating the struggle over relative income shares that underlies the wage-price inflationary spiral. For the wage-price spiral, as already implied, is simply the result of different groups in society using what economic and other power they may have to avoid the decline in real and/or relative income which threatens them when a change in the aggregate growth rate occurs.

The shortcomings of fiscal policy go even beyond these points, however. Not only is the government unable to shift the savings curve for the oligopolistic sector in the way it might wish through a change in tax rates, it is also unable to influence the price level within that sector indirectly through its admitted ability to control the level of aggregate demand. This is the second important limitation of fiscal policy - perhaps even more serious than the first. To understand it one must examine the supply curves for each of the two component parts of the business sector.

The business sector's supply curves. Just as it would be a mistake to specify but a single savings and investment demand function for the entire business sector, so too it would be erroneous to specify but a single supply curve. Indeed, in indicating the relationship between aggregate output and the price level, it is essential to distinguish the oligopolistic sector from the non-oligopolistic sector.

In the case of the latter, any upward shift in demand which requires an increase in output will necessarily give rise to a corresponding increase in the price level - assuming, of course, no change in any of the relevant parameters. This positive relationship between output and price at the aggregate level follows from the shape of the supply curve in those polypolistic and monopolistically competitive industries which comprise the non-oligopolistic sector. The shape is determined by two factors: (a) the elasticity of the marginal cost curves of the individual firms which, when aggregated, constitute the industry supply curve and (b) the rate at which firms enter or leave the industry as price varies. If the firms in the industry are subject to variable marginal costs - a condition which will be met if they are single-plant firms with U-shaped cost curves - and if any change in industry demand is not entirely supplied by marginal firms moving into or out of the industry, the industry supply curve will necessarily be positively sloped, as depicted in figure 25. In other words, any upward shift in demand will, perforce, be accompanied by an increase in price.

What must be stressed is that this positive relationship will hold even if the firms in the industry are currently operating with 'excess' capacity, that is, even if they are producing to the left of the minimum cost point on their average total cost curves. Indeed, the positive relationship will hold as long as marginal costs are positively related to output. Of course, the more pronounced the movement from operating below the cyclical norm of production to above the cyclical norm, the greater will be the relative increase in price. Put another way, the industry supply curve is likely to become increasingly steeper, that is, more inelastic, as demand shifts upward; and this is so for two reasons. (1) At levels of output below the cyclical norm, some of the firms in the industry may be temporarily shut down because the industry price is insufficient to cover their average variable costs. An upward shift in demand from such a low point, then, is likely to result in some of these firms re-entering the industry by simply resuming operations. As the upward shift in demand persists and the supply of these temporarily shut-down firms is exhausted, the rate of re-entry will necessarily slow down. (2) As the upward shift in demand continues past the level of output that constitutes the cyclical norm, the firms in the industry will find it increasingly more difficult, due to the generally high levels of demand for all goods and services, to obtain at existing price levels the variable inputs supplied by other polypolistic and monopolistically competitive industries. This means that in addition to the increase in marginal costs which ensues from the more intensive use of the fixed inputs, the firms in the industry will experience a further increase in marginal costs as a result of the consequent bidding up of variable input prices - including wage rates. The latter, as already pointed out, are likely to rise because of the upward pull of wage rates within the oligopolistic sector.

In the case of the oligopolistic sector, the situation will be quite different. An upward shift in demand may be accompanied by an increase in price - but it need not be. This is because the members of an oligopolistic industry will, under normal circumstances, have a certain amount of reserve capacity with which to supply the increased demand; and because, moreover, they will be able to bring this reserve capacity into operation at what, in the eyes of the managerial group, is viewed as constant marginal cost.

Again, the conclusion is implicit in the shape of the industry supply curve, derived in this case, too, by aggregating the supply curve of all the individual firms, or megacorps, in the industry. However, since

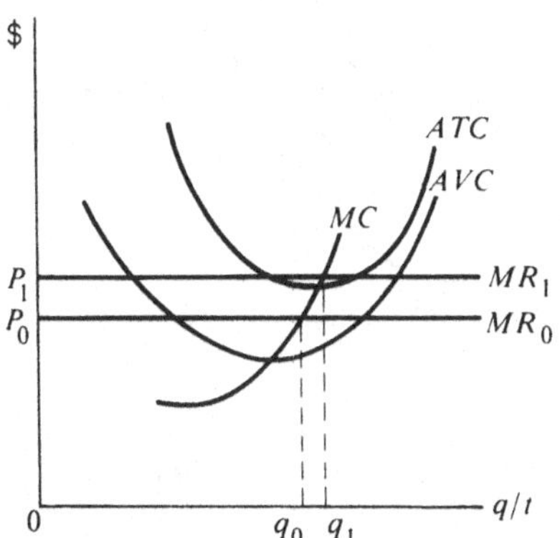

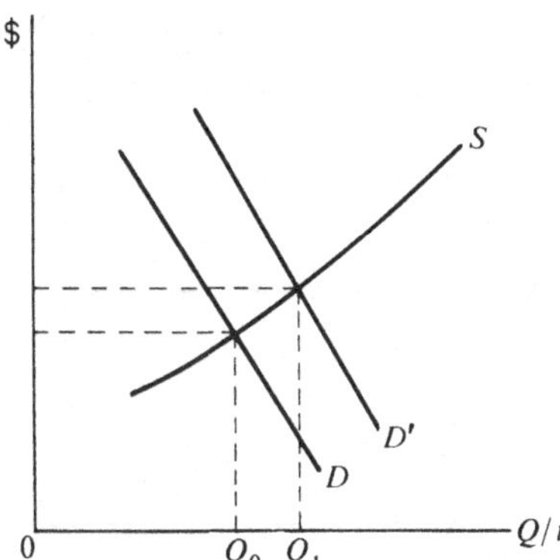

Figure 25

marginal costs cannot be equated with marginal revenue, at least in the short run, an individual megacorp's supply curve is not the same as its marginal cost curve. Rather, since the megacorp's pricing decisions are based on anticipations over the current planning period, a time horizon which largely obliterates any short-run marginal considerations, its supply curve is the same as the curve summing up its average variable and fixed costs plus the average corporate levy over the intermediate run. (See figure 6 shown here again.) This curve may be termed the average total anticipated outlays curve. Moreover, due to the difficulty of coordinating pricing decisions in an oligopolistic industry, a difficulty that leads to changes being made in the industry price only at discrete intervals, the supply curve is that one point on the average total anticipated outlays curve which represents the expected level of output during the current planning period.[32] This one point corresponds to the average total anticipated outlays at the standard operating ratio.

The megacorp, then, is prepared to supply, up to a certain point, any quantity of goods or services that may be demanded at a price just sufficient to cover its average total anticipated outlays over the current planning period. The point which marks the upper limit on the amount of goods which the megacorp is willing to supply at this fixed price is the point at which the marginal cost curve intersects the price or average revenue curve, for if the megacorp produces beyond that point it will suffer a decline in total revenue. Still, rather than try to

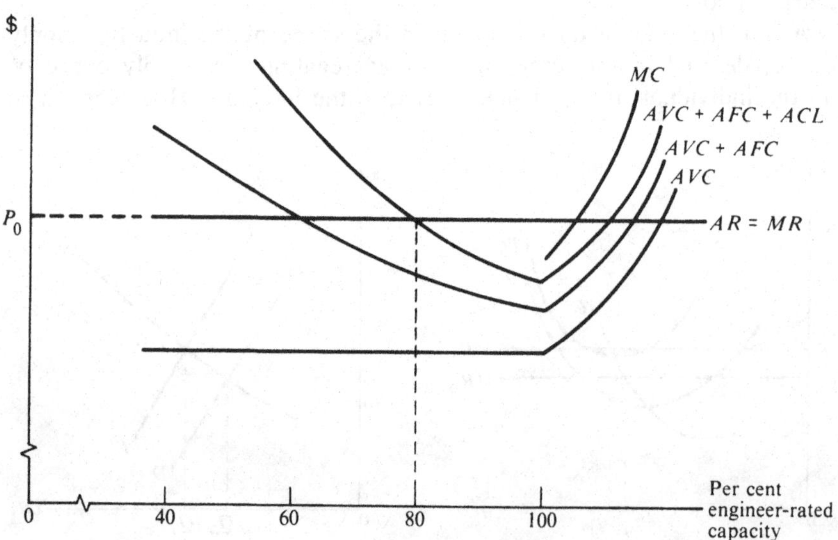

Figure 6

raise its price unilaterally when the marginal cost begins to exceed marginal revenue, the megacorp will delay filling orders and in this way avoid unprofitable operations. In effect, it will simply refuse to produce beyond the intersection point. Ordinarily, however, as already pointed out, a megacorp will have previously acquired sufficient reserve capacity to assure against its being put in such an embarrassing position.

Thus the megacorp's supply curve is coextensive with its average revenue curve - up to the point where that curve intersects the marginal cost curve. The industry's supply curve, again using per cent of engineer-rated capacity as the relevant variable, is simply the weighted average of these individual supply curves;[33] and like them it will be infinitely elastic up to a certain point, this point being the weighted average of the maximum quantities which a firm in the industry is willing to produce at the fixed industry price. What this means is that the industry's current supply price will be independent of, that is, unaffected by, short-run fluctuations in demand. The supply curve will shift up and down - though more likely up than down - only in response to the factors discussed above in chapters 3 and 5, that is, in response to a change in the demand for and supply of investment funds or to a change in average variable and fixed costs (ignoring once again the influence of taxes). These are factors not easily manipulated in the short run - at least under present institutional arrangements - for they reflect the secular growth rate as perceived by megacorps, $\overset{*}{G}_s$, and/or the national incremental wage pattern, W_p.

The supply curve for the oligopolistic sector as a whole will therefore be perfectly elastic - at least in the short run. This is in contrast to the supply curve for the non-oligopolistic sector, which is positively sloped throughout. From this difference in the respective supply curves of the oligopolistic and non-oligopolistic sectors, two important points follow. The first is that it is only within the non-oligopolistic sector that a higher growth rate will necessarily lead to a higher price level, and thus contribute to the inflationary pressure. The underlying explanation for this propensity of the non-oligopolistic sector is not, as already pointed out, the inability to obtain additional labor inputs but rather, the absence of the reserve capacity found within the oligopolistic sector - a reserve capacity which enables the megacorp, unlike the neo-classical proprietorship, to expand output up to a certain point simply by starting up some previously idle plant or plant segment. Whereas therefore any increase in the growth rate is certain to be accompanied by a rise in the price level within the non-oligopolistic sector,[34] in the case of the oligopolistic sector it need not.[35] The very fact, however, that the price level within the oligopolistic sector is for the most part unaffected by short-run changes in aggregate demand means that the government will find it extremely difficult to control the inflation likely to arise in that sector whenever the current rate of growth of investment and the current wage pattern, taken together, imply a greater claim upon the megacorp-price leader's revenue than is likely to be realized at the current anticipated rate of growth. This is the second important point, and it helps to explain why an advanced economy such as that of the United States is likely to experience, not the Golden Age upon which some economists base their analysis but rather, the bastard Golden Age described by Joan Robinson (1962a, pp. 51-9). More specifically, it provides the final element necessary for understanding the dynamics of the inflationary process manifest in the wage-price spiral.

The dynamics of the wage-price spiral

To many it will appear than an unnecessarily long and circuitous route has been followed in trying to answer the question posed at the beginning of this treatise: What has been the cause of the persistent inflation experienced since the end of World War II? The excursion has been necessary, however, in order to demonstrate two important propositions about the recent inflationary experience. They are:

(1) That the rise in price levels has not been due to any 'excess' growth of demand or, what is essentially the same thing, to pressure against the supply constraints on the rate of economic expansion;

(2) That rather it has been due to the difficulty of adjusting the several variables which together determine the aggregate savings rate so that, following a change in the secular growth path, the economy on its new course will pass safely between the Scylla of a cyclical decline and the Charybdis of a wage-price spiral.

If both those hazards are to be avoided, then the variables such as $\bar{P}_O$, W_p and T_y which determine the aggregate savings rate must be adjusted so as to achieve simultaneously the following: (a) avoid an excessive growth of savings relative to investment that will curtail the rate of economic expansion and cause a cyclical movement around the secular growth path, and (b) distribute the concurrent gains in real income in a manner that is acceptable to megacorps, trade unions, the government, or any other organized group in society with the power to press successfully for a larger nominal share of the incremental social surplus. It is when the latter condition is not satisfied, presaging a struggle over the relative distribution of real income, that a wage-price spiral is likely to be initiated.

The model developed above, predicated on the division of the business sector into oligopolistic and non-oligopolistic subsectors, helps to explain why a shortage neither of manpower nor of productive capacity is likely to curtail the secular growth rate. According to the model, the oligopolistic sector on the one hand faces a perfectly elastic supply curve for manpower, meaning that megacorps are able to obtain whatever additional workers they need at whatever are the prevailing rates of remuneration. This perfectly elastic supply curve reflects the differential in wages paid members of the laboring manpower force in the oligopolistic sector relative to what they could earn in other types of employment. The oligopolistic sector on the other hand can be expected to expand its productive capacity sufficiently in advance of demand so as to always have a certain amount of reserve capacity. This 'cushion' reflects the desire of individual megacorps to protect themselves against a possible loss of relative market position, either to rivals within the same industry able to supply customers they themselves are forced to turn away or to new firms attracted into the industry by the shortfall in supply.

The model posits a quite different situation in the non-oligopolistic sector. On the one hand the firms in that sector are seen as being able to obtain additional manpower only by drawing more heavily upon the surplus labor to be found in the countryside and, more immediately, among the urban unemployed. Faced with the need both to stem the outflow of workers into the oligopolistic sector and to attract more workers themselves when the rate of economic expansion exceeds the secular average, these firms will be forced to narrow the differential in wages between the oligopolistic and non-oligopolistic sectors. This implies a positively sloped rather than a perfectly elastic supply curve for manpower. On the other hand the firms in the sector are seen as being unlikely to expand their capacity in anticipation of growing demand. This is because, being family-based proprietorships, they are incapable of operating more than one or two plants. Instead, capacity is increased through the entry of new firms into the various industries which comprise the sector, the firms being attracted when the increased demand, pressing against a fixed amount of plant and equipment, leads to rising marginal costs and widening profit margins.

In the non-oligopolistic sector, then, momentary supply bottlenecks, due to the difficulty of obtaining manpower and/or a lack of capacity, may arise. This does not mean, however, that the overall rate of economic expansion will be significantly affected. The non-oligopolistic subsector is, after all, only a part of the business sector. Indeed, it is the less important part, constituting the periphery rather than the essential core of a modern, technologically advanced economy (cf. Averitt, 1968). With the exception of agriculture and textiles, the industries in the sector are either satellites of other, oligopolistic industries or else produce less essential types of goods. Even more significant in the present context, the non-oligopolistic subsector is characterized by less capital intensive methods of production and is marked by lower rates of growth. Whatever bottlenecks may arise therein, they are likely only to slow down the overall rate of economic expansion.

This is borne out by the empirical evidence for the United States from the post World War II period, especially the 1960s. While satisfactory manpower data have become available only recently, there is no reason to believe that megacorps have, at any time during the twenty-five years between 1946 and 1971, been forced to cut back on production because they could not obtain the workers they needed. Indeed, the job vacancy rate for all of manufacturing between April and October 1969, a period during which the economy was at a cyclical peak, averaged only 1.4 per cent, and this was at a time when the unemployment rate was 3.5 per cent (Monthly Labor Review, March 1970). There is, to be sure, scattered evidence of smaller firms being unable at times to obtain all the workers they have needed at wage rates they were willing and able to pay. But it is doubtful that this has ever led to more than a local slowdown in the delivery of goods or services. It has certainly not had much discernible effect outside the non-oligopolistic subsector.

Nor is there any reason to believe that megacorps in the United States have, at any time during the post World War II period, been forced to cut back on production for lack of capacity. Indeed, the evidence already pointed out indicates that megacorps have almost always had at least 10 per cent unutilized, or reserve, capacity - and never less than 5 per cent (see note 29 to chapter 2). Since the available data pertain almost entirely to large firms, it is not possible to say with certainty what the situation has been in the non-oligopolistic subsector. But again, there is nothing to suggest that bottlenecks in that subsector - in this case, stemming from lack of capacity - have to any significant degree restricted the overall rate of economic expansion. Thus, whether it is manpower or productive capacity which is seen as the effective constraint, there is little or no direct evidence of the pressure against supply that would be observable were the post World War II inflationary experience in the United States to be explicable in terms of 'excess' demand.[36]

The model developed above provides an alternative explanation of inflation, however. It suggests that a delicate balance is required to assure both the secular growth rate is maintained and that the national income is distributed in a manner that is acceptable to the groups in society - megacorps, trade unions and the government - with the power to command a larger nominal share. The experience of the United States during the 1960s reveals just how delicate that balance is and what happens when it is upset.

The experience of the 1960s. The American economy was only beginning to recover from its third recession in eight years - the last two at least brought on by the efforts to control inflation through conventional fiscal and monetary instruments - when the Kennedy Administration took office in 1961.[37] The new President's economic advisors devised a strategy intended not only to achieve the higher secular growth rate promised during the campaign but also to prevent any accompanying rise in price levels. The strategy called, on the one hand, for fiscal and monetary measures to stimulate the economy. Although political considerations made it inexpedient to push in Congress for an increase in the budget prepared by the outgoing Administration, the Berlin crisis in the summer of 1961 finally opened the way for an increase in Federal spending without an offsetting rise in taxes (Heller, 1966, pp. 30-5; Tobin, 1974, pp. 21-4). Led in part, but only in part, by defense outlays, Federal expenditures were to grow in real terms during the first eighteen months of the Kennedy Administration at equivalent annual rates of more than 11 per cent. The growth of total government expenditures ($\overset{*}{I}_G$ in the model set forth above) was slightly over 8 per cent.[38] Meanwhile, the less restrictive monetary policy which the Federal Reserve Board was persuaded to adopt led to a recovery and subsequent boom of residential construction.[39]

But the strategy devised by the New Frontier economists had a second aspect to it. This more novel feature of the Kennedy Administration's economic policy called for the Executive Branch to intervene in advance so as to influence, if not actually determine, the national incremental wage pattern (W_p in the above model). Thus it was that the Council of Economic Advisors in their 1962 report set forth 'guideposts' which called for wage increases to be limited to the secular growth of output per worker ($\overset{*}{Z}_s$ in the above model). According to the Council, this would not only permit wages and profits to keep pace with one another as they both rose over time, it would also hold unit labor costs constant, thereby avoiding any upward pressure on prices from the cost side (*Economic Report of the President*. 1962. pp. 185-9: Sheahan, 1967, ch. 2). Implicit in the policy, though not openly stated, was acceptance of the argument that the inflation of the 1950s had been due, at least in part, to cost-push factors.[40]

The guideposts, described in only the most general terms in the January report of the Council, soon became more specific as a result of the 'key' negotiations conducted in the steel industry later that spring. The Steelworkers' union, bowing to pressure from officials of the Kennedy Administration, settled in April for a contract which raised labor costs within the industry by less than the 3 per cent by which ouput per worker throughout the economy was estimated to have increased between 1947 and 1960. When the steel companies nonetheless shortly thereafter posted price increases of $10 a ton or 3.5 per cent, the President was faced with a choice of either intervening forcefully and directly to secure a rollback in steel prices or allowing the guideposts to become a shambles. Kennedy, of course, opted for the former course and when, under the extraordinary pressure placed on them by threats of antitrust prosecution and canceled defense contracts, the steel companies finally buckled under, the guideposts were a firmly established policy (Sheahan, 1967, ch. 4; McConnell, 1963). Not surprisingly, in view of what has been said previously, prices within the oligopolistic sector were to remain remarkably stable over the remaining three years of the then current wage round, despite the high growth rate experienced by the economy as a whole.[41]

Although that growth rate, in real terms, was to average 5.0 per cent from the second quarter of 1962 through the second quarter of 1965 (5.7 per cent from the second quarter of 1961 on), there were signs toward the end of 1962 that the recovery from the earlier recession had spent itself and that indeed the economy was about to embark on another downward movement. More alarming to officials within the Kennedy Administration that even the decline in the growth of real GNP was the failure of the unemployment rate to fall below 5.5 per cent, since it was the unemployment rate which was most widely regarded as the measure of how close to its potential the economy was operating. The rate of growth of employment (outside of agriculture), because it excludes the effect of rising demand in attracting more persons into the labor force, is undoubtedly a better measure of the economy's ability to provide jobs, but even this figure, after stabilizing during the first three quarters of 1962 at the secular average for the 1960s of about 2.5 per cent, had again dipped toward the end of the year to only slightly over 1 per cent.

The diagnosis of the problem by officials within the Kennedy Administration was similar to what has previously been described as the greater elasticity of the savings curves in the oligopolistic and government sectors relative to that of the investment curves in those two sectors. The name given to the problem, at least insofar as the government sector is concerned, by Kennedy's chief economic advisor, Walter Heller, was 'fiscal drag' and the solution which he and his colleagues on the Council of Economic Advisors succeeded in persuading the President to recommend in his 1963 economic message to Congress was a reduction in taxes, both personal and corporate.[42] It was to be more than a year, however, before this proposal was enacted into law, and then a further year was to pass before the second part of the two-stage tax reduction was to take effect. In the meantime, not only had Johnson succeeded

Kennedy as President - indeed, it was largely because of Johnson's greater skill in dealing with Congress than the tax bill was finally passed - but also the economy was once again growing at a rate approximately equal to the 5.7 per cent average for the 1961-5 period. The avoidance of anything more serious than a slight dip in the growth rate during the winter of 1962-3 was due largely to the slack taken up first by consumer durable expenditures, together with residential construction (household investment, $\overset{*}{I}_H$, in the above model), and then, as it became increasingly clear that the normal cyclical pattern of economic activity had been altered, by business fixed investment, particularly in the oligopolistic sector ($\overset{*}{I}_O$ in the model).[43]

As the fourth quarter of 1964 approached, the strategy devised by the New Frontier economists seemed to be working much better than any of them would have dared to hope in 1961. A higher secular growth rate and the virtual end of the trade cycle, political and otherwise, had both been achieved - and this without any significant rise in price levels. While the fourth quarter of 1964 would show some signs of a weakening in demand, similar to what had occurred two years earlier, the second round of the tax cut, due to take effect on 1 January, seemed certain to nudge, or 'fine tune', the economy back on its secular growth path. Nonetheless, despite the bright prospects which the future seemed to hold, 1965 was to mark the beginning of the series of events that would produce the inflation of the late 1960s.

The first of these was the establishment of a new national incremental wage pattern, W_p, under circumstances that would increase organized labor's suspicions that the Presidential guideposts were being unfairly applied. The Council of Economic Advisors had, in its 1964 annual report, calculated the secular growth rate of output per worker, $\overset{*}{Z}_s$, at 3.2 per cent based on a five-year moving average, and this figure had then been put forward as the recommended limit on increases in labor compensation (*Economic Report of the President*, 1964, pp. 114-15). When, just prior to the new contract talks in the steel industry in the spring of 1965, the five-year moving average was recalculated, it turned out to be 3.6 per cent. The Council, fearing that the unusually prolonged expansion of the economy was a distorting factor, insisted that 3.2 per cent was still the appropriate estimate of $\overset{*}{Z}_s$ (*Economic Report of the President*, 1966, p. 92; see also Sheahan, 1967, pp. 21-4, 47-8). This seemingly arbitrary shift in the basis for determining the wage standard, coming on the heels of the refusal by the automobile industry to lower its prices when, under the guideposts, it should have, left organized labor somewhat disenchanted with the wage and price stabilization program (Sheahan, 1967, pp. 46-7). The fact that wages were rising more rapidly in the sectors not covered by the major AFL - CIO unions did not increase the labor leaders' confidence in the guideposts.[44]

Even so - and despite the fact that its leadership had only recently been overturned, in part because the former president was thought to have taken too soft a bargaining position in the previous negotiations - the Steelworkers finally agreed in September, following quite forceful Presidential intervention in the deadlocked talks, to a contract which, it was estimated, would increase labor costs over each of the three years of the contract by no more than 3.2 per cent. Some of the settlements in other industries, including that by the Steelworkers' union itself in the aluminum industry, were more closely in line with the estimated 4.9 per cent increase which the Automobile Workers had obtained the year before following the refusal of the auto companies to lower their prices, but the majority of settlements that followed fell within the 3.2 per cent figure. As the Council declared in its 1966 report: 'The generally satisfactory record of 1965 wage contracts has important implications for wage trends . . . . Because of the relatively light calendar of expiring contracts, the basic pattern of wages for most key industries has already been set for 1966.' (See also Sheahan, 1967, ch. 5.) The success in moderating wage demands had been achieved, however, at the expense of undermining confidence by organized labor in the mechanism most directly responsible for the moderation. And as prices began to rise in 1965, despite the guideposts, that confidence was even further eroded.

Contrary to the popular impression, the inflation of the late 1960s did not just begin with the decision of the Johnson Administration in the summer of 1965 to intervene in Vietnam with large-scale military forces. Prices within the oligopolistic sector had begun to rise even earlier, starting around the first quarter of the year - though at the somewhat moderate rate of less than 1 per cent per annum (see fig. 26). The end of the price stability which had prevailed during the preceding four years was due in large part to the need which megacorps felt to increase their average corporate levy, a need deriving from the higher secular growth rates which had been achieved and the resulting pressure to expand plant capacity more rapidly. Indeed, beginning in the second quarter of 1963, investment in new plant and equipment had been increasing at equivalent annual rates of approximately 14 per cent, and while the rate of growth of corporate cash flow net of dividends had by and large kept pace, in the fourth quarter of 1964 it declined significantly even as the expansion of capacity continued undiminished.[45]

The decision to intervene in Vietnam did, it is true, exacerbate the problem of inflation, but not, as is sometimes assumed, by creating a general condition of excess demand and not by causing any shortage of workers. While providing more fiscal stimulus than had been counted on for 1965, the build-up of US forces in Southeast Asia was, by the end of the year, being offset by cutbacks in other areas, including, though by no means limited to, Federal spending. Indeed, as a result of both the temporary freeze placed by the Johnson Administration on non-defense expenditures and the collapse of residential construction caused by the Federal Reserve's tight money policy, the economy went into a 'mini-recession' during the first quarter of 1967, with the real growth rate actually turning out to be negative (*Economic Report of the President*, 1966, p. 78). In other words, it was during 1965 and 1966 that the Vietnam build-up was to have its greatest impact on the level of aggregate demand. And while employment outside of agriculture had grown at equivalent annual rates of 3.4 per cent during this period, well above the average for the 1960s, the unemployment rate still stood at 3.7 per cent in January 1967. The Federal Reserve Board index of capacity utilization, though holding at the unusually high level of 88.9 per cent, had meanwhile passed its peak during the preceding summer. Even more important, in terms of understanding the inflation of the late 1960s, the wholesale price index was only 5.1 per cent higher than it had been at the beginning of 1965 (reflecting an annual growth rate of 2.5 per cent) - and only 3.8 per cent higher (an annual growth rate of 1.9 per cent) if the prices of commodities are ignored. Except for the fact that prices were no longer stable, the situation was superficially similar to what it had been following the Berlin build-up in 1961-2, with the economy expanding during 1966 at an equivalent annual rate of 5 per cent.

The Vietnam build-up was nonetheless to contribute to the inflation of the late 1960s in two important ways. The first was its effect on prices in the non-oligopolistic sector. Clearly, certain inelasticities on the supply side, especially in the case of food items such as beef, played a role. But, as already pointed out, the price level in the non-oligopolistic sector, unlike that of the oligopolistic sector, is quite sensitive to demand conditions. Thus the Vietnam build-up, coming on the heels of the stimulus to household spending provided by the second installment of the tax cut in 1965, pushed the economy up well above its secular growth path. While prices in the oligopolistic sector were only minimally affected, those in the non-oligopolistic sector rose quite sharply, advancing at equivalent annual rates of 5.3 per cent between the beginning of 1965 and the end of the third quarter of 1966. This upward surge, especially of food prices, together with similar increases in the price of services, led to a significant decline in consumer purchasing power at a time when the machinists' union was negotiating what would turn out to be a 'key' contract with the airlines (*Economic Report of the President*, 1967, pp. 86-94; Sheahan, 1967, pp. 57-60).

The second effect of the Vietnam build-up was to divert an increasing portion of total resources into the government sector. Indeed, this was to be the most serious consequence of the decision taken in the summer of 1965. When the domestic programs that were part of President Johnson's other 'war' began to have a significant budgetary impact beginning in 1967, the continuing high levels of spending for the Vietnam war meant that the government was forced to press against the other sectors of the economy for available resources. With its power to engage in deficit spending, the Federal government was, of course, unlikely to come up short. But the oligopolistic sector, with the power over prices which the corporate levy reflects, was no less able to make good its claim on the national product. Indeed, with the high growth rates already realized and in prospect, the oligopolistic sector had somehow to hold on its previous share of resources if the expansion of capacity within the sector was to keep pace with the growth of demand. This left only the household sector to bear the burden of the shift in economic priorities which the war in Vietnam, on top of the war against poverty at home, implied.[46] The fact was that, with both the secular growth rate and the expansion of the public sector which the Johnson Administration's policies portended, the previous rate of growth of real income within the household sector could not be maintained - even if output per worker, instead of declining as it did in 1967, had continued growing at the same rate.

Thus, as the time approached for new contract talks in the automobile industry in the fall of 1967, even the now suspect 3.2 per cent figure no longer represented a non-inflationary national incremental wage pattern. And trade union leaders like the United Auto Workers' Walter Reuther, in the face of the substantial rise in consumer prices which, during the preceding two years, had more than halved the gains in real compensation for employees, were not about to settle for just 3.2 per cent. Although the situation demanded a lower national incremental wage pattern, W_p, if a further inflationary push was to be avoided, the guideposts established by the Council of Economic Advisors had lost all credibility. Indeed, the best advice which the Council could offer was that organized labor should not try to recoup all the losses of real income which its members had suffered during the preceding two years (*Economic Report of the President*, 1967, pp. 127-34). When, despite this warning, the United Auto Workers, following the pattern which had been set in the airline industry the year before by the machinists' union, succeeded in obtaining a contract which pushed up labor costs by an estimated 4.9 per cent, the wage-price inflationary spiral was fully under way. And while the insistence on higher wages by individual unions could, to some extent, improve the relative position of their members, it could not make the household sector as a whole better off. Whatever increase in compensation was obtained by any one group of workers trying to recover lost ground, the gains were subsequently reduced in value by the steady rise in prices. With high levels of demand again being realized, prices within the non-oligopolistic sector were to increase by 4.8 per cent in 1968. The mere 1.9 per cent rise in prices within the oligopolistic sector somewhat moderated the trend, but still the consumer price index would advance by 4.2 per cent during the year (see figure 26).[47] The representative household thus found it impossible to translate its gains in nominal income into gains in real income.

Moreover, this wage-price inflationary spiral, once set in motion, was impossible to bring to a halt either by lowering the aggregate growth rate, as the Johnson Administration tried to do toward the end of 1968,

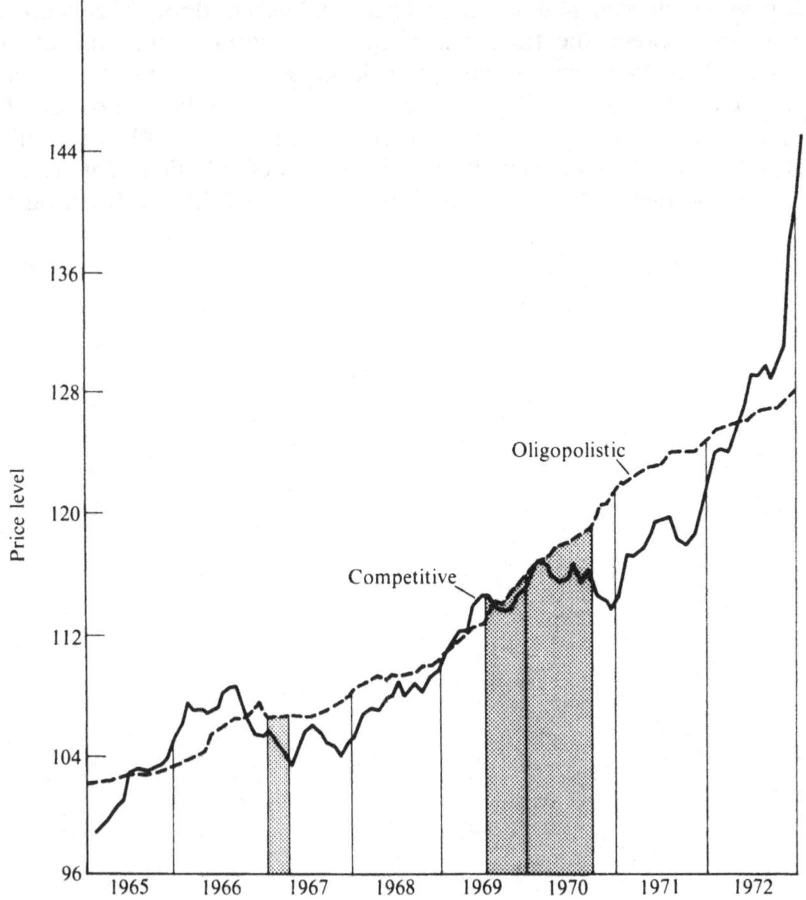

Figure 26. Wholesale prices in oligopolistic and competitive industries, 1965-73 (1957-9 = 100)

or by engineering a full-blown recession, as the incoming Nixon Administration succeeded in doing during 1969-70. The point is that the difference between the secular growth of output per worker, $\overset{*}{Z}_s$, and the national incremental wage pattern, $\overset{*}{W}_p$, determines what the change in unit labor costs will be within the oligopolistic sector, and this change in unit labor costs, together with whatever change in the average corporate levy is dictated by the secular growth rate, $\overset{*}{G}_s$, in turn determines whether there will be a change in the price level within the oligopolistic sector, $\bar{P}_O$. Thus, while the price level within the non-oligopolistic sector can be directly influenced by fiscal and monetary policy, the price level within the oligopolistic sector cannot. $\bar{P}_O$ depends not only on the secular rate of economic expansion, as set by government policy, but also on the national incremental wage pattern established through collective bargaining between the trade unions and megacorps in the bellwether industry. Efforts to control the price level in the oligopolistic sector by reducing the rate of economic expansion will not only be ineffectual, they may even, because of the effect on output per worker and the realized corporate levy, actually boost the rate of inflation. This is the lesson of the 1960s - and indeed of the entire post World War II period.[48]

8. Toward social control

The preceding chapters have sought to develop the analytical framework necessary for understanding the causes of inflation in a technologically advanced economy such as that of the United States. From the explanation just offered of how prices, along with wages and dividends, are determined in the oligopolistic sector of the American economy only one conclusion is possible - that inflation results not from any 'excess' of aggregate demand but rather from the efforts by powerful groups in society to maintain their own relative income position in the face of the redistributional effect which the inevitable change in the aggregate growth rate is certain to have. This struggle over relative income shares can be seen most clearly in the frequently observed wage-price spiral, with first trade unions and then megacorps seeking to regain whatever ground has been lost.

Were the price level the only casualty, the periodic jousting between labor and management, most directly over wages but indirectly over prices as well, would hardly warrant the attention it has received in this treatise. After all, what more harmless way is there for releasing pent-up social tensions than for the GNP deflator to take a beating? While it is true that the chief victims of the conflict are generally the less organized groups in society, even this untoward effect is a minor one compared to the actual consequences which the post World War II inflation has had for the United States. The fact is that the government, harkening to the outcry of rentier groups, has continually intervened in the economy in an effort to bring a halt to rising prices. Yet without an adequate understanding of the basic economic forces at work, this intervention has succeeded only in transforming the wage-price spiral into a political trade cycle. With aggregate demand unnecessarily curtailed, physical output has been irretrievably lost, the secular growth rate has been held far below what it should have been and - most serious of all - many Americans have been deprived of the employment opportunities which they had every right to expect. Indeed, all of the government's efforts to alleviate poverty at home have been of minor import compared to the disastrous consequences of its misguided policies to control domestic inflation.

Now that a suitable analysis of the dynamic underlying the wage-price inflationary spiral has been provided, all that remains is to draw out some of the policy implications. The primary emphasis will, of course, be on the measures which the government can take to prevent a secular rise in the price level. This will be the subject of the section immediately following. The existence of the megacorp, as part of an oligopolistic industry structure, creates other types of problems as well, however. These other problems, such as inadequate social control over investment, the distorting effect of dividends on the distribution of income, and the lack of managerial accountability, will also be touched on in this final chapter.

Alternative approaches to social control

Once it is recognized that the very structure of the American economy - specifically, its large oligopolistic sector - leads to the type of inflation which cannot be effectively controlled by the conventional tools of fiscal and monetary policy, one is forced to choose between one of two approaches - unless, of course, one is willing to remain caught on the horns of the Phillipsian dilemma. The first involves a concerted effort to change the structure of the economy, eliminating the market power of the megacorp and reducing the oligopolistic sector to insignificance. The other approach involves the search for a more effective means of regulating the megacorp than the market place alone can provide.

There is little need to dwell at length on the first approach. Despite the surviving rhetoric, the United States long ago abandoned any real attempt to restructure the economy through its antitrust laws (cf. Whitney, 1958; Dewey, 1965; Stigler, 1966b, especially p. 236). And insofar as the purpose of those laws was to make all of industry conform more nearly to the polypolistic model, it was probably wise to do so. At the time the choice was made, during World War I, Americans were most deeply impressed by the greater ability of the megacorp to mobilize resources on behalf of the then pre-eminent social goal (Eichner, 1969, ch. 11). Today, if the preceding chapters are correct in their analysis of the non-oligopolistic subsector's dynamic properties, Americans would have to be at least equally struck by the stabilizing role which megacorps play in the overall economy. It is doubtful that they would opt for a more volatile business sector, such as would exist if the savings and investment functions attributed above to the non-oligopolistic subsector were to characterize the business sector as a whole.

In any case, the antitrust laws as they are applied today have little more than a nuisance value, affording the government, it is true, some scope for the type of arbitrary intervention analyzed in chapter 3 but nonetheless without any real prospect of changing the structure, and hence the behavior, of the industries being singled out for attention. The main effect of this effort, as Galbraith (1967b) has pointed out, is to blind the lay public to the need for more effective measures to regulate the market power of the megacorp (see also Barber, 1970, ch. 12).

In contemplating what those more effective measures might be, one is likely to think first of direct control over prices. This can take any one of several forms: a general price freeze, establishment of independent regulatory commissions in individual industries, even nationalization. There are, of course, important differences between these various forms of direct control. An independent regulatory commission, for example, is more likely to be able to take into account the factors unique to any particular industry - though it is also more likely to be captured by the members of that industry and the direction of control thereby reversed. Nationalization, on the other hand, permits other objectives besides the mere control over prices to be achieved - though it also places the greatest restraint on the initiative of the individual enterprise. There is one point, however, which must be made about all these forms of direct control. Though they give public officials the power to decide what price shall ultimately prevail, they still leave those officials up in the air as to how they should exercise their power. In other words, the various forms of direct control simply beg the question of what is a socially optimum price.

If the goal is simply to curb inflation, it might seem that this is not a very important question. As long as prices can be prevented from rising, what does it matter whether they are 'socially optimum' or not? On these grounds, a general price freeze is the most effective anti-inflationary measure the government can adopt. A complete prohibition on all price changes, however, has the effect of neutralizing the price mechanism as an aid in making allocative decisions - especially the longer the freeze remains in effect. While this is hardly likely to provoke a public outcry, the parallel effect on relative income shares almost certainly will. The fact is that the longer prices remain unchanged, the greater will be the number of persons who feel that the existing structure of prices is unfair to them. And given the change in underlying economic conditions which is likely to be occurring simultaneously, they will quite often have a persuasive case. If political pressures are not going to eventually undermine whatever form of direct control has been established, prices, too, will have to change. But what new structure of prices would be fair to all? This is why the question of what is a socially optimum price cannot be avoided - even if the goal is simply to curb inflation.

The answer which economists usually give to this question - that the price should be equal to marginal (social) cost - is not very helpful insofar as the oligopolistic sector is concerned. With marginal cost equal to average variable cost, at least in the short run, this prescription fails to explain how the megacorp's overhead costs, not to mention its investment expenditures, are to be financed. If, however, the argument is modified so that long-run marginal costs are substituted for short-run marginal costs, thereby taking into account the firm's overhead expenses, the argument loses its analytical sharpness. Indeed, the prescription then reduces to the full-costing principle, and the question then becomes which of the megacorp's various disbursements are to be regarded as true social costs.[1]

There is usually no dispute about the megacorp's actual contractual expenses - wages, the cost of raw materials, fixed-interest payments and the like. What lends itself to controversy is the difference between those costs and the price currently being charged. It is this margin above costs - what is usually referred to as 'profit' - which some persons have trouble accepting as a true social cost. And their skepticism seems somewhat justified in light of the pricing discretion which the megacorp typically enjoys as a result of the market power it shares with the other oligopolists in its industry. For what is to prevent the megacorp from using that discretion to increase its own income at the expense of those dependent on it for the goods they need? The 'profit' in other words, may simply represent an unwarranted exaction on the rest of the community.

It is easy for an economist to show that in an expanding economy at least some margin above cost, whatever it might be called - 'profit', 'turn-over tax', or the enterprise's 'surplus' - is necessary, for without that margin, investment would not be possible.[2] The question still remains, however, of how much that margin need be. There are two quite different ways in which this question can be answered, and thus two quite different ways of arriving at a socially optimum price.

The first approach stems from neo-classical theory and the capital accumulation and allocation model implicit in that theory. In this view of things, growth, if it does occur, is financed from the savings which households have managed to set aside out of their income and which business firms than compete for in the capital funds market. From this it follows that households must be compensated for the income claims which they have relinquished, the payment they receive being a necessary social cost of obtaining the funds required for growth. The first approach, then, involves the determination of how much compensation households must receive to induce them to make the required amount of savings available to the business sector. It is this amount of compensation, and this amount alone, which the first, and more conventional, approach suggests must be added to the firm's contractual costs to arrive at a socially optimum price.

One may well question the relevance of this capital accumulation and allocation model in an economy such as that of the United States wherein more than two-thirds of the investment funds for the business sector as a whole, and more than 90 per cent of the funds in manufacturing alone, do not even pass through the capital funds market (see note 17 to chapter 1). Indeed, under the circumstances, it is doubtful that what economists generally see as the advantage of this model - that it leads to household savings being placed in the hands of those firms which can employ them to the best advantage - is even remotely realized in practice.[3] Yet to make the model more relevant, by adopting measures which would force a larger proportion of the total savings utilized by the business sector to pass through the capital funds market, would probably require, if the same aggregate rate of investment is to be maintained, either that the government itself provide the necessary funds through its taxing powers or that there be vastly greater inequality in the distribution of personal income. The more important point, however, is that if direct control over prices is to be established using the approach derived from this model of the capital accumulation and allocation process, it is necessary to determine, on an industry-by-industry - if not on a firm-by-firm basis - the margin above costs, or 'profit', required to induce the household sector to provide the necessary funds for investment. This is because the capital-output ratio and thus the amount of compensation paid to the household sector will itself vary from industry to industry and even from firm to firm. For this reason the above approach can be described as a microeconomic one; and it gives rise to all the problems observed in connection with public utility regulation in the United States (for a comprehensive survey of these problems see Kahn, 1970).

The alternative approach can be described as a macroeconomic one. It is based on the extension of Keynesian theory which has been developed in this treatise and on the model of the capital accumulation and allocation process which is implicit in that theory. In this view of things, growth is a continuous phenomenon, even if the rate itself varies, with the expansion being financed out of the funds which the megacorp - along with the government - is able to extract because of its power, non-economic as well as economic. From this it follows that the margin above costs on the goods produced, at least in the oligopolistic portion of the business sector, will depend on the aggregate growth rate - the higher that growth rate the higher the margin. This suggests the possibility that the margin above costs - that is, the amount of corporate and governmental levies - can be controlled through the aggregate growth rate. It is for this reason that the approach can be regarded as a macroeconomic, or post-Keynesian, one. Let us see how this approach might in practice work out.

The macroeconomic approach

As the previous chapter sought to demonstrate, the government can, through its fiscal policy, initiate any change in the secular growth rate it wishes. An increase in the rate of growth of government expenditures, holding tax rates constant, will lead to an upward shift in the investment demand function for the economy as a whole and thus to an increase in the rate of growth of aggregate output. It is this scope for discretionary action that gives the government its critically important leverage on the economy.

The new, higher aggregate growth rate will be a sustainable one, however, only as long as the government is willing to continue running the requisite deficit. Once it ceases to add to its debt burden at the same rate, the higher aggregate growth rate can be maintained only if, by coincidence, some other sector is willing to play the same role or, what is somewhat more easily arranged, only if the savings curves for all the sectors can be shifted so as to bring the rate of growth of savings in each sector into line with the rate of growth of investment. In the final analysis, then, maintaining a higher aggregate growth rate requires being able to shift the savings curves for all the individual sectors of the economy, including the oligopolistic sector, in such a way that the resulting debt burden and distribution of national income is acceptable to those groups in society with the power to change them. This, in turn, means recognizing that the national incremental wage pattern, W_p, along with the various tax rates, is an instrumental variable which can, and must, be manipulated in order to bring about the necessary macroeconomic balance.[4]

Making the national incremental wage pattern an instrumental variable can be regarded as a form of incomes policy - though not necessarily the sort which underlies the popular conception of such a policy. For many persons, an incomes policy simply means putting a restraint on the gains achieved by trade unions at the collective bargaining table. Yet, as the preceding analysis has sought to make clear, the national incremental wage pattern may be not only too high for the desired growth rate to be maintained without an upward movement of prices, it may also be too low. With the steady rise in output per worker which economic growth accompanied by technological progress implies - and it is hard to conceive of one without the other - a continuous increase in the various rates of compensation paid to household members is the only means by which the resulting marginal social surplus can, in the face of the downward rigidity in prices attributable to the oligopolistic sector, be widely distributed throughout the society. If the national incremental wage pattern is too low, with the result that the increase in the various rates of compensation is also too low, a rise in prices may be avoided but the desired secular growth rate will not be maintained. Indeed, due to insufficient demand, the secular growth rate will almost certainly decline.

It can thus be seen that determining the national incremental wage pattern involves a delicate balancing act, with a false step in one direction likely to launch the economy on a wage-price spiral and a false step in the other direction likely to produce a minor recession or worse. For this reason it is essential that a better mechanism be developed for determining the national incremental wage pattern - one which avoids the shortcomings which have already been noted in the present mechanism whereby the pattern is set through the key bargain reached in the bellwether industry.

Both the guideposts promulgated under Presidents Kennedy and Johnson and the different boards established by President Nixon under Phases II and III of his new economic policy were efforts to deal with some of those shortcomings. The guideposts eventually broke down because they were too inflexible. They simply could not deal with the new conditions created by the stepped up war effort in Southeast Asia after 1965 while still maintaining credibility with the public (cf. Sheahan, 1967; see also Heller, 1966, pp. 43-7; Schultz and Aliber, 1966). The several boards established under Phases II and III were somewhat of an improvement over the guideposts, both because of the greater flexibility which was inherent in them and because of the statutory power they had to enforce their decisions.[5] Even so, they failed to deal with the basic political problem posed by the power of the trade unions, and especially their champion in the bellwether industry, to determine the national incremental wage pattern pretty much as they wish, subject only to resistance of the companies with which they bargain. Success by the boards, as by the guideposts, required that the trade unions surrender, or at least hold in check, this power. It was not clear, however, either what the trade unions were to receive in return or what their bargaining partners, the megacorps, were on their part to surrender. The boards, then, seemed to represent what the trade unions have usually found an incomes policy to be - simply a restraint on wages alone. Since the trade unions were in effect bargaining on behalf of the entire household sector, this meant a restraint on the rate of growth of disposable income as well.

The Nixon Administration sought to counter this impression about its anti-inflationary program by imposing a similar type of restraint on the profit margins - and thus on the average corporate levy - of megacorps. How serious the government was in these efforts need not concern us. The fact is that, as the above chapters have tried to make clear, once the administration set the course of its fiscal policies, thereby determining the secular growth rate, it had already in effect decided what those profit margins had to be. The only difference made by its efforts to control profit margins directly was that, insofar as the profit margins required by the secular growth rate were greater than the profit margins allowed under Phases II and III, the fear of government intervention became a far more significant factor in the pricing decision of megacorps; and this, in turn, may have led to a somewhat greater reliance on external financing. The conclusion to which the above analysis leads is that if the trade unions are to receive anything meaningful in return for surrendering, or at least holding in check, the power they now have to determine the national incremental wage pattern, it must be a greater voice in determining the target variable which not only controls the profit margins of megacorps but also most directly affects the growth of real income for their members. That target variable is the secular growth rate.

How to give the trade unions, as well as other groups in society, a greater voice in determining the secular growth rate is easy to say - though difficult perhaps to implement. The various groups need to be brought together in a social and economic council where the implications of alternative growth rates can be discussed and some sort of consensus reached. These deliberations would be more informed, to be sure, if there were a secretariat to provide members of the council with an objective economic analysis of the possibilities, both in the short run and over a longer time period. The more important condition, however, is that the consensus reached by the social and economic council, assuming the council were a sufficiently representative body, become the basis for government policy, in the legislative branch as well as in the executive branch. What this amounts to is a form of indicative planning, such as is now carried out by several Western European countries.[6] The advantage to be gained from it is that, with broad agreement reached as to what the secular growth rate should be, the determination of the national incremental wage pattern would no longer need to involve simply a power struggle between megacorps and trade unions.

The inescapable economic fact is that, once the existing productive resources are fully utilized, progressively higher rates of growth of aggregate output, $\overset{*}{G}$, can be achieved only at the expense of progressively lower rates of growth of disposable income, $\overset{*}{Y}_D$. There is thus a fundamental trade-off between the rate of growth of aggregate output and the rate of growth of real income for the household sector; any group such as a social and economic council, in deciding on the one, is in effect deciding on the other simultaneously. The choices confronting such a group at any given point in time are similar to those shown in figure 27, with points *A*, *B*, *C*, *D* and *E* representing the alternative combinations of $\overset{*}{G}$ and $\overset{*}{Y}_D$ which are presently achievable. The task of the social and economic council would, of course, be to choose one of those combinations.

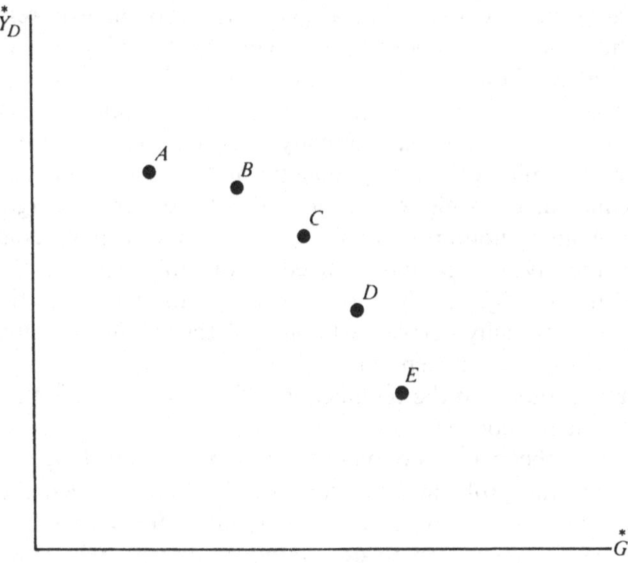

Figure 27

The rate of growth of disposable income so selected would, in turn, largely dictate what the national incremental wage pattern should be. With $\overset{*}{Y}_D$ already decided upon, only one value for W_p would, in fact, be consistent with price stability on the one hand and assure a sufficiently high level of aggregate demand to achieve the target growth rate on the other. That one, non-inflationary value for W_p is unlikely to be the same as the value for $\overset{*}{Y}_D$ already decided upon. How closely the two will correspond will depend on the allowance which must be made for what other countries have come to term 'wage drift',[7] for the differential rate of growth of wages between unionized and non-unionized workers and for the rate of growth of both transfer and rentier income. Yet, with the secular growth rate, along with the preferred rate of inflation, having already been agreed to, the exact relationship between $\overset{*}{Y}_D$ and W_p, as well as possibly the exact relationship between $\overset{*}{G}$ and $\overset{*}{Y}_D$, should be the only points actually open to dispute. This is the macroeconomic, or post-Keynesian, approach to controlling inflation. And it involves the recognition that both the rate of growth of wages and the margin above costs within the oligopolistic sector may have to vary, depending on the secular growth rate chosen by the society through its political institutions.

This macroeconomic approach is not without its problems. There is first the technical problem of determining, to the satisfaction of those whose relative income shares are at stake, the econometric relationship between the various instrumental and target variables. This is particularly difficult because of the complicated interrelationships which exist among the various sectors of the economy (Aukrust, 1970; Eichner, 1974). Some of these interrelationships have already been pointed out in contrasting the pricing dynamics of the oligopolistic and non-oligopolistic sectors. But the reality of the American economy with its separate agricultural, service, regulated, non-profit and import sectors is more complicated than even the five-sector model used throughout this treatise would suggest. What is required is a further elaboration of that five-sector model, with empirically derived estimates of the savings and investment functions for each of the separate sectors.

Far more serious than the technical problem, however, is the political one of securing the cooperation of all the groups in society whose support is necessary if the macroeconomic approach to controlling inflation is to work. Here the problem is made more difficult by what the macroeconomic approach, as so far presented, takes for granted - namely, the power of the megacorp to determine its own margin above costs, subject only to the restraint imposed by the substitution effect, the entry factor and the fear of meaningful government intervention. However well suited the macroeconomic approach may be for dealing with the problem of inflation, it seems blind to the megacorp's pricing power and the strong likelihood that that power will be abused.

Actually, however, the pricing model developed in this treatise as a microeconomic foundation for post-Keynesian theory does suggest a way in which the megacorp's pricing power can be brought under effective social control. It would require somewhat more elaborate social mechanisms than now exist, and for this reason establishing effective social control over the megacorp would not be as easy to accomplish as simply ending the wage-price spiral. Still, the megacorp can be satisfactorily tamed - and without the disadvantages which more direct forms of control, especially those based on the microeconomic approach, carry with them. This is fortunate since, unless important groups in society, the trade unions especially, can be convinced that the megacorp will not be able to abuse its pricing power, the political problem associated with the macroeconomic approach may be insoluble.

As this treatise has repeatedly pointed out, what is generally regarded as the 'profit' of the megacorp after taxes actually consists of two quite different components. The dividends paid out to the equity debt holders comprise one of these components, and the earnings retained by the megacorp comprise the other. The treatise has emphasized the dissimilarity of the two components by treating the dividends as part of the megacorp's fixed costs and the retained earnings as part of the corporate levy. Because of these two quite different components of its 'profit', effective social control over the megacorp requires two quite different tacks.

Insofar as the dividends are concerned, it is difficult to discern what it is that, from society's point of view, warrants the payment of this form of compensation. Here several important facts should be kept in mind.

The first is that only 10 per cent of the investment in the unregulated portion of the oligopolistic sector is financed externally - and less than 5 per cent is financed through new equity issues (see note 17 to chapter 1). What this suggests is that the equity debt holders are hardly indispensable as a source of investment funds. In fact, there is reason to believe that, with the effort to regulate the economy primarily through monetary policy abandoned and with a proper macroeconomic balance achieved, the role of the equity debt holders in financing new investment could be eliminated altogether.[8]

The second important fact to keep in mind is that the real return to the equity debt holders on the funds they have made available to the megacorp far exceeds the real return to the fixed-interest debt holders. For example, anyone supplying a representative megacorp with investment goods on a fixed-interest basis in 1945 would have found that, simply as a result of inflation, his rate of compensation in real terms had by 1965 fallen to approximately 57 per cent of what he had originally contracted to receive, while anyone supplying the same megacorp with investment funds on an equity basis would have found that, taking into account the rise in dividends as well as the effects of inflation, his rate of compensation in real terms had by 1965 increased by more than 2 1/2 times.[9] This nearly five-fold differential in the relative rates of compensation, even without taking into account any capital gains, is more than can be justified by any supposedly greater risk which the equity debt holders incur because they have no contractual claim on the megacorp's revenue. As proof of this contention, it would only be necessary to convert all the megacorp's common stock into non-voting, cumulative preferred shares and then see what differential, if any, still remained in the real return to the two different types of debt. Indeed, it is hard to avoid the suspicion that the greater rate of compensation presently enjoyed by the equity debt holders is due entirely to the voting power they have, a legal right which gives them an effective club over the group responsible for deciding what their rate of compensation should be.

The third important fact to keep in mind is that the equity debt holders provide little in the way of a check on the performance of the executive group. The shareholders are rarely in a position to impose their views on the executive group; and when they are, as during a take-over bid by some outside group, the criterion they are likely to follow - which of the two contending factions is apt to compensate them more generously in the future - is only tangentially related to the question of how well the company is being managed, either in the interests of the company *qua* organization or in the interests of the larger society. The substantially greater return enjoyed by the equity debt holders is thus not a necessary social payment for the work of the executive group being overseen. Indeed, as already noted, it is the fixed-interest debt holders who are likely to provide what little check there is on the executive group's performance (see above, chapter 3, pp. 58-9).

The fourth and final fact to keep in mind is that dividends are the single most important source of income inequality in the United States. In 1962, 10 per cent of all US households owned 62 per cent of the equity in those companies whose shares were publicly traded. These shares, together with other types of marketable securities, were in fact the most unequally distributed of all forms of wealth, and it is unlikely that the situation has changed significantly over the decade (Projector and Weiss, 1966; see also Lampman; 1962; Ackerman *et al.*, 1971). Inequality in the distribution of wealth, because of the property income to which it gives rise, is in turn the primary cause of inequality in the distribution of income.

One might hesitate, even in the face of these four facts, to urge elimination of dividend payments entirely - first, because it would discourage neo-classical proprietorships from evolving into megacorps, thereby eliminating an important means by which the oligopolistic sector is continually being rejuvenated, and, second, because it would generate such bitter social conflict that there would be room for little else on the political agenda. However, there seems no reason not to try to hold down the rate of growth of dividends as much as possible.

To be of practical import, any limit placed on the rate at which dividends could be increased would have to be lower than the national incremental wage pattern, W_p. How much lower would, of course, depend on the political strength of equity debt holders as members of the rentier class. The closer to zero this limit was, however, the less would be the skewing effect of dividends on the distribution of national income. It might be argued that this type of constraint would do little to eliminate the capital gains which, in some ways, are the most pernicious aspect of the present distributional arrangements (see note 39 to chapter 5). Those who take this position are, however, simply allowing themselves to be taken in by the myth that all of the megacorp's revenue after taxes accrues to the equity debt holders and that it makes no difference what proportion of the net revenue is paid out in dividends. It is precisely because so many of those who benefit from the present arrangements believe in this myth that a limit on the rate at which dividends could be increased might prove feasible politically.

An alternative ploy would be to change the law so that the federal government's social security trust fund could be used to purchase common stock in megacorps. This would end the scandalous situation in which those reserves are now invested in low-yield government bonds. Not only would the returns be greater if the social security trust fund were used instead to obtain an equity interest in the oligopolistic sector, it would also give some truth to the argument that dividends are the means by which widows, orphans and others unable to provide for themselves are spared from becoming dependent on public charity. Furthermore, as the social security trust fund increased its stock holdings, the public would gain a stronger voice in the affairs of megacorps. This second ploy is not so much an alternative to the first as a complement. Indeed the two measures may both be necessary to give assurance that the pricing power of the megacorp is not being used simply to enhance the income of one group in society at the expense of others - in this case, through the payment of dividends.

Insofar as the retained earnings component of the megacorp's 'profit' is concerned, the situation is entirely different. From what has already been said, it should be clear that the retained earnings, as part of the corporate levy, serve the important social function of enabling the megacorp to finance its investment expenditures. Indeed, its crucial role in the capital accumulation process suggests that the entire corporate levy is a true social cost. The means by which the megacorp finances most of its investment nonetheless constitutes a tax on the consuming public. As in the case of a public levy, those being taxed have every reason to insist that the funds thus obtained are being used in ways that best serve the general interest.

It is important not to exaggerate the scope of the problem. The largest part of the corporate levy, it must be realized, is used to acquire the additional productive capacity which an expanding economy requires - with much of that new plant and equipment embodying the improved technology which makes possible higher output per worker. Still, there are certain broad uses to which the corporate levy is put which raise serious social questions.

The sums spent on advertising are perhaps the least defensible of the investment outlays which the corporate levy permits. Indeed, it is hard to see what public good, if any, is served by this type of expenditure. Rather than informing the potential buyer, advertising, especially that placed in the mass media by the megacorp, merely obfuscates and confuses. The main effect, in fact, is to debase and corrupt a large part of society's informational network. The economic arguments on behalf of advertising, meanwhile, are hardly to be taken seriously. Even if it were true that advertising could shift the aggregate consumption function,[10] there are certainly better and more direct ways of avoiding a decline in the overall growth rate. In reality, the primary function of advertising - and the only reason that megacorps spend as much money on it as they do - is to protect the market position of established firms by erecting formidable barriers to entry.[11]

Advertising, however, is not the only questionable investment outlay by the megacorp. Even with regard to the sums spent on research and development, customer servicing, annual model changeovers and similar means of strengthening market position, there is good reason to believe that the social returns fall far short of the private returns.[12] Since all of these types of expenditures have some redeeming value, however small, it might not be wise to ban them outright. Besides, there is a better strategy for eliminating the undesirable effects to which these types of expenditures give rise, including their dissipation of the available social surplus. This strategy consists of forcing megacorps to undertake their advertising, R & D, customer servicing and similar activities on an industry-wide basis by placing severe restrictions on the freedom of individual firms to carry out such activities. Most of the undesirable effects of these types of investment outlays, it turns out, derive from inter-firm rivalry and would be avoided if the expenditures were to be handled by the industry as a whole.

The restrictions on the individual megacorp's freedom of action would have to take different forms depending on the type of investment outlay. In the case of advertising, for example, individual megacorps might be limited to reprinting whatever objective comparison of its product with those of other firms a newly created consumer protection agency might report. In the case of R & D, individual megacorps might be placed at a disadvantage in obtaining patent rights unless they joined in an industry-wide research effort. While the relaxation of the antitrust laws implicit in the above strategy might go against the grain of those who still feel that the Golden Age of Competition can be restored, it would in fact simply end competition in areas where it has been shown that competition has undesirable consequences.

Even if the strategy were successful in eliminating those undesirable consequences, however, a somewhat more subtle question would remain. This is whether all the uses to which the corporate levy is likely to be put at any given point in time represent the best allocation of that part of society's discretionary income. The question, really, is whether the short-circuiting of the capital funds market which results from primary reliance on internal financing does not prevent investment funds from flowing to where, from society's point of view, they will do the most good.

Conglomerate expansion, as already pointed out, is the primary means by which, under oligopolistic conditions, investment funds are shifted from less rapidly growing to more rapidly growing industries. Indeed, this means of shifting funds may be far more effective than the capital funds market which exists in a country like the United States. Even so, the necessary amount of investment funds may not always flow to where, from society's point of view, it will do the most good. A large part of the problem would, of course, be eliminated if regulated industries were to be placed on an equal footing with other industries by being permitted to finance their investment through a corporate levy also. To go beyond this reform and assure even better allocation of investment funds within the business sector would require the creation of a new type of social mechanism as an adjunct to whatever system of indicative planning might be established.

The necessary new social mechanism is a series of industry planning panels, with government officials and representatives of the consuming public joining with company executives and labor leaders to decide what type of investment program, including R & D, is going to be required if each industry is to meet the long-range goals set by the social and economic council. The investment program decided upon by the panel would be regarded as a socially optimum one, and that part of the government charged with coordinating economic policy would then see to it, both through the margin above costs allowed firms in the industry and through the credit extended by the government's own specialized lending agencies, that this amount of investment was financed. Capital expenditures other than those called for under the investment program agreed to by the industry panel could still be made by the individual firm, but no provision would be made for them in calculating the industry's necessary margin above costs.

It should be emphasized that the creation of these industry panels would make sense only as a further development of the system of indicative planning already called for. Within that context, but only within that context, they would represent the ultimate form of social control over at least the retained earnings component of the megacorp's 'profit'. However, there are more important, and more immediate, steps that would have to be taken to assure the better allocation of the current marginal social surplus.

That marginal social surplus, as already pointed out, is reflected not only in the investment funds expended by the business sector but also in the tax monies spent by the government itself - as well as in the consumer durables purchased by the household sector and in the nonmonetary capital flows abroad. The optimum allocation of the social surplus requires therefore that, at the margin, the social benefit from the use of society's discretionary income be equal in all five sectors. Yet the task of allocating the marginal social surplus among the various sectors is not one which the market mechanism, by itself, is capable of performing. The need, already indicated, for making the national incremental wage pattern an instrumental variable subject to conscious political choice is one reflection of this fact and the ability of the government, through its tax and spending powers, to determine at least the initial thrust along any expansion path is another. Indeed, the one-fifth of GNP which flows through the government sector is the most compelling evidence as to the limited ability of the market to make certain types of allocative decisions. It is these limitations of the market which argue for a system of indicative planning.

Confronting the inherent weakness of the market mechanism merely serves, however, to point out the weakness - hopefully transitory - of contemporary political institutions. How well do the decisions reached by government reflect the preferences of the general citizenry? And what reason is there to believe that, however great the unmet need may be for public services, the government is capable of making a wise choice in how it spends its money? Recent advances in public budgeting theory, especially the advent of program budgeting (Schultze, 1968; Rivlin, 1971), suggest that some progress is being made on at least the second of these two questions. Still, until there is reasonable assurance on both points, one must temper the call for a comprehensive system of indicative planning. It hardly makes sense to grant the government the power needed to eliminate the last source of misallocation within the business sector when the government lags so badly in the quality of its own decision-making. For a country like the United States, further progress in the political sphere may well be a precondition for further progress in the economic realm.

Achieving social control

The policy implications of the preceding analysis can thus be summarized as follows: with some means found either for limiting or siphoning off the growth of dividends, it is possible to establish effective social control over the megacorp to a large extent simply by establishing effective social control over investment. This means regulating the overall economy through government fiscal policy, thereby determining the secular growth rate of megacorps, and then supplementing this overall control with restrictions on some of the specific uses to which the corporate levy can be put. Indeed, with dividends limited and investment regulated, only one further step would be required to assure complete social control over the megacorp.

This would be a procedure for placing the megacorp in receivership - and thus for securing a change in the executive group - when and if its performance was found to be inadequate from a social point of view. The more precise the grounds for invoking this remedy, the less subject to abuse it would, of course, be. A number of grounds which seem sufficiently precise can be suggested, among them the megacorp's failure to maintain a certain rate of growth relative to other megacorps and the failure to meet the standards for product quality which government agencies might establish. There is another ground which can be suggested for placing the megacorp in receivership, and it is one which would provide the final stroke required for regulating the megacorp through investment. This ground would be the megacorp's failure to follow an optimal pricing rule - that is, a pricing rule based on setting a margin above costs just sufficient to finance the investment called for under a system of indicative planning.

The procedure for placing the megacorp in receivership would, if adopted along with the other measures proposed in this final chapter, go far in dealing with the key problem raised by this treatise - the largely unchecked power of the megacorp's executive group. This is a power capable of great good, as evidenced by the high rates of economic growth in the United States. But it is also a power which can work to the public detriment, as evidenced by the role of the megacorp in the recent inflationary experience, an experience which has made governments hesitate to stimulate the economy and thereby achieve higher rates of growth both of employment and of output. That power, both for good and bad, can be brought under effective social control if the critical determinants of the megacorp's behavior, along with the crucial part played by the oligopolistic sector in the overall economy, are properly understood. All that is required, at least intellectually, is a different set of theoretical models from those economists are accustomed to employing.

Notes

Chapter 1. Introduction

1. The Phillipsian dilemma refers, of course, to the Phillips curve showing the trade-off between unemployment and inflation. See Phillips (1958).

2. For example, the unemployment rate increased by 76 per cent, from 4.2 per cent to 7.4 per cent, between July (III quarter) 1957 and August (III quarter) 1958, while the GNP deflator increased by 2 per cent, from 98.0 to 100.1, over the same period. Similarly, the unemployment rate increased by 39 per cent, from 4.9 per cent to 6.8 per cent, between October (IV quarter) 1961 and May (II quarter) 1962, while the GNP deflator increased by 1 per cent, from 104.5 to 105.6 over the same period. Finally, the unemployment rate increased by 67 per cent, from 3.6 per cent to 6.0 per cent, between November (IV quarter) 1969 and December (IV quarter) 1971, while the GNP deflator increased by 9 per cent, from 130.5 to 142.7, over the same period.

3. Keynes (1936) especially the preface. See also J. Robinson (1972).

4. The advantage of this behavioral definition of oligopoly is that it avoids the unanswerable question of how many firms are a 'few'. The disadvantage is that it precludes the possibility of predicting interdependent behavior simply on the basis of industry structure. Still, since interdependent behavior is as readily observed as such structural characteristics as the concentration ratio and barriers to entry and since it is possible to predict other types of behavior on the basis of recognized interdependence, this is not a serious limitation of such a definition. Cf. Pfouts and Ferguson (1959).

5. Developments in economic theory since Keynes have proceeded along two lines. One path has involved an effort to reconcile static Keynesian macroeconomic theory with neo-classical microeconomic models, thereby preserving this part of the discipline's heritage. Those who have followed this path are apt to refer to themselves as *neo*-Keynesians. The other path has involved the dynamic extension of Keynesian analysis along Ricardian lines, meanwhile abandoning the neo-classical assumptions of perfect competition and of distribution based on marginal productivity theory. Those who have followed this path are apt to refer to themselves as *post*-Keynesians. For a comparison of the two approaches, see Kregel (1971).

6. The concept of joint profit maximization derives from Fellner (1949, chs. 4-8).

7. Machlup (1952, ch. 12). See also Fellner (1949, chs. 2, 3 and 6); Baumol (1967, ch. 3).

8. Shubik (1970, pp. 424-8). For a valiant effort along these lines, see Shubik's earlier work (1959).

9. The root word 'polypoly' is a more technical term for what is generally referred to as perfect or simply plain competition. For the origins of the usage, see Machlup (1952, pp. 85-6). The reason for using the term 'polypoly' and its derivative 'polypolistic' throughout this treatise is to avoid the ambiguities

surrounding the term 'competition'. For a discussion of those ambiguities, see Stigler (1957); McNulty (1968).

10. On the institutional economists, see Gambs (1946, ch. 1); Gruchy (1947, ch. 8, especially pp. 588-94). On Marxian theory, see Marx (1933, 1935); Sweezy (1942, part 1). For a comparison of the classical, neo-classical, Marxian and Keynesian theories of income distribution, see Kaldor (1955-6); Davidson (1960). On post-Keynesian theory, see Kregel (1971, chs. 8-12: 1973): Eichner and Kregel (1975).

11. See Baumol (1967); Marris (1964); O. Williamson (1964); Chamberlain (1962); Galbraith (1967a); Marris and Wood (1971), especially Marris, 'Introduction to Theories of Corporate Growth'. For a critical evaluation of this approach, see Machlup (1967).

12. See the citations by Bronfenbrenner and Holzman (1963, pp. 75-6).

13. The almost complete neglect of the rest-of-the-world, and hence the foreign, sector is one of the major defects of the present work. In a world of growing interdependence among nations, with the rise of the trans-national megacorp, this is a serious omission. Its rectification, however, must be left to a later time.

14. Cf., J. Robinson (1969, pp. x-xi). The above definition avoids the difficulties inherent in trying to define an industry in terms of either cross-elasticities of demand or production functions. Whether a group of firms all keep watch on the same set of price quotations is easily determined empirically, yet fails to describe any important industry grouping in the real world.

15. For a representative sample of these views, as well as their critics, see Federal Reserve Bank of Boston (1969).

16. Personal savings accounted for only 17.5 per cent of gross national savings between 1955 and 1967. Of this relatively small proportion, insurance and pension funds accounted for 55 per cent. The data on insurance and pension funds can be found in the *Federal Reserve Bulletin*, January 1960, November 1962, and May 1968; the data on gross national saving, in the *Federal Reserve Bulletin*, December 1960, June 1962, and August 1967; the data on personal savings, in the *Handbook of Basic Economic Statistics*, December 1969, p. 237.

17. Between the fourth quarter, 1948, and the third quarter, 1960, only a little more than 10 per cent of all investment in the manufacturing sector was financed through long-term external debt, with slightly more than half of that being accounted for by new fixed interest obligations and the rest by equity issues (Anderson, 1964, p. 25.). This compares with the slightly more than one-third of all investment financed through long-term debt for all US non-farm, non-financial corporations between 1948 and 1955 (*Survey of Current Business*, February 1967) and the 24 per cent so financed between 1956 and 1970 (Bosworth, 1971).

18. The inadequacies of the neo-classical theory of the firm have been brought out in critiques too numerous to list in their entirety. See, for example, Silberstein (1970); Shubik (1970, especially pp. 411-13); McGuire (1964, especially chs. 2, 4); Andrews (1964). For a historical perspective on the critiques themselves, see Nordquist (1965). For the latest attempt to refurbish the neo-classical theory of the firm to make it serviceable in the face of an inhospitable reality, see Phelps (1970). This is the neo-classical alternative to the microeconomic model developed in this treatise.

19. Leijonhufvud (1968, ch. 2); Lange (1945); Lerner (1952). Friedman (1970) has recently suggested that the essential difference between Keynesians and

non-Keynesians is precisely the question of the degree to which price adjustments can be expected to neutralize exogenous disturbances.

Chapter 2. The nature of the megacorp

1. What is meant by the term 'behavioral pattern' is the explication of the goal or goals pursued by an economic decision-making unit. A 'decision-rule' is the formula by which the goal explicit in the behavioral pattern is to be achieved. Thus, short-run profit maximization is the behavioral pattern usually assumed in the case of a business firm, and the equating of marginal cost with marginal revenue the corresponding decision rule.

2. Larner (1966, especially pp. 786-7). See also Villarejo (1962). While Villarejo argues that the control of most large corporations remains still in the hands of a few major stockholders and directors, the evidence which he presents nonetheless bears out the Berle-Means thesis (cf. Marris, 1964, p. 18, fn 34). A more sophisticated variant of the same argument is that control of most megacorps has come to be centered in the hands of a few large banks and other financial institutions which manage most of the nation's pension plans and mutual funds. This control by a small group of fiduciary agents has been termed the fourth stage of the corporate revolution by Berle (1959). The evidence on this last point is, however, inconclusive (cf. Tilove, 1959; Chevalier, 1969). Control by a small group of fiduciary agents would, in any case, bear primarily on the minimum dividend constraint discussed below, and would not necessarily alter the underlying behavioral pattern of the firm. For a critical review of the empirical evidence on the separation of management from ownership, one which demonstrates that the point is by no means a settled one, see DeVroey. unpublished.

3. Between 1952 and 1960, according to the US Securities and Exchange Commission, only fourteen proxy contests for control of one of the 500 largest industrial corporations took place, and six of these contests involved three of the same companies. Of these fourteen contests, the incumbent management group won seven and the dissident group five, two of the contests being settled by court-directed compromise (Whetten, 1961). While not all contests for control of a corporation necessarily reach the proxy stage, all those in which the stockholders are able to exercise their voting rights do. For a discussion of the other type of contest for control - the take-over bid - see below, chapter 5, pp. 164-8.

4. For studies confirming the fact of the megacorp's relative permanency, see Mermelstein (1969); Boyle and McKenna (1970).

5. Marris (1964, ch. 2, especially pp. 70-8). See also Roberts (1959, ch. 3); J. McGuire, Chin and Elbing (1962). For a further refinement of the above studies, see Baker (1969). For studies reporting contrary findings, see Lewellen and Huntsman (1970); Masson (1971). But see also Lewellen (1968, ch. 11, especially p. 241), and the 'Review' of the Lewellen book by Marris in the *Journal of Economic Literature*, June 1972.

6. R. A. Gordon (1945, p. 327). A separate matter, stockholder concern as to how profits are apportioned between dividends and retained earnings, will be taken up at a later point in this chapter and in chapter 5.

7. Katona (1951, pp. 196-7). See also R. A. Gordon (1945, pp. 305-6); Galbraith (1967a, chs. 10-15).

8. Monsen and Downs (1965); O. Williamson (1964); Papandreau (1952); Cyert and March (1956).

9. J. Robinson (1953). It should be noted that Professor Robinson does not attach the same analytical significance to the distinction between the nineteenth-century neo-classical proprietorship and the twentieth-century megacorp which this treatise does.

10. Baumol (1962) has emphasized growth in terms of sales; Marris (1964) growth in terms of assets. See the appendix to this chapter.

11. See below, chapter 5, pp. 181-2. It should be added that because of this assumed characteristic of technological change - to wit, its largely exogenous nature - the possibility of increasing growth over the long run through deliberate efforts to reduce costs will receive little attention in the discussion that follows.

12. These non-price forms of competition are discussed below, in the analysis of the demand for investment funds by the megacorp. See chapter 3, pp. 90-6.

13. For empirical evidence as to the stability of relative market shares over time, see Gort (1963); Jacoby (1964); Havrilsky and Barth (1969); Boyle and Sorensen (1971).

14. A 'rule of thumb' represents a satisfactory approximation to the optimum decision rule, that is, the decision rule which represents the precise formula by which the goal or goals implicit in the behavioral pattern can be achieved. On the significance of 'rules of thumb', see Baumol and Quandt (1964, pp. 23-9).

15. The term 'optimize' is used instead of the term 'maximize' to indicate that what is desired is the largest share of the market consistent with maximum long-run growth.

16. For a discussion of the various alternative behavioral assumptions which economists have suggested be made about the megacorp, see the appendix to this chapter.

17. The determinants of the dividend rate are discussed in greater detail below in chapter 5, pp. 164-72.

18. M. Gordon (1959); Durand (1959); Walter (1963). Although Friend and Puckett (1964, especially pp. 658, 680) have presented further evidence casting doubt on these findings, they nonetheless point out that the statistical results they are questioning 'are based on a larger number of cross-section studies utilizing linear and logarithmic (and occasionally even other) relationships . . .' and that, moreover, their own contradictory analysis 'is limited not only in coverage of industries and time periods, but also in the linearity assumed'.

19. The difference between these two alternatives behavioral assumptions, the 'managerial' or growth maximizing and the 'stockholder-welfare' or equity maximizing postulates, is brought out most sharply in Mueller (1969); Lintner (1971); Solow (1971); Marris (1971a, pp. 26-36). See also the appendix to this chapter.

20. Cf. Clark (1961, pp. 90-6); Poston (1959); Lintner (1971). See also Smithies (1939); Wan (1966). For an overview of the various efforts that have been made to deal with the inter-temporal effects of a change in price, see Scherer (1970, p. 213, fn 1). The Scherer book, it should be noted, represents perhaps the most comprehensive textbook treatment of the present field of industrial organization.

21. Cf. R. Hall and Hitch (1939); Kaplan, Dirlam and Lanzilotti (1958); Katona (1951, chs. 9-10); Leyland (1964); Hague (1949-50); Mackintosh (1963, especially pp. 134-6). These and other studies have indicated behavior which is consistent only with the maximization of net revenue over the long run - even though the survey techniques employed are open to serious methodological criticism.

22. Gort (1962, pp. 29-30). See also Fuchs (1961, pp. 283-91). The Fuchs

study is subject to the methodological criticisms discussed below, in note 34, for its use of concentration ratios.

23. That this inventory adjustment mechanism is crucial to the aggregate equilibrium determination process as well was brought out many years ago by Metzler (1947).

24. Cf. Lewis (1949, ch. 1). One can also view the services of the 'fixed' inputs as being divisible, in which case the same argument applies. In other words, the 'fixed' inputs may be 'indivisible in acquisition' but not 'indivisible in use'. Cf. Machlup (1952, p. 231); Maxwell (1965).

25. Kuh (1966). This insensitivity of the wage rate is explained more fully below in chapters 5 and 7.

26. Beckman, 1960. Even aside from the above theoretical argument, the ability of megacorps to expand continuously without seeming disadvantage would appear to be sufficient proof on this point. The fact is that large firms, such as megacorps, have, if anything, a higher rate of growth than their smaller counterparts. Mansfield (1962); Hymer and Pashigian (1962); Samuels (1965). See also Simon (1964); Hymer and Pashigian (1964). The more general point - the lack of managerial barriers to expansion - is dealt with below, chapter 4, p. 138.

27. These points are elaborated on below in chapter 3, pp. 76-7. See especially note 29.

28. It is not as yet clear which of these two categories fits the shortage of oil refining capacity experienced during the winter of 1973-4 - or even whether a third category, such as effective collusion at the international level, encouraged by high barriers to entry, needs to be added. In any case, the shortfall in refining capacity is one of those exceptions which, by its very uniqueness, helps demonstrate the validity of the general rule.

29. The Federal Reserve System develops estimates of the percentage of manufacturing capacity being utilized, based on data from the McGraw-Hill Annual Survey of Business' Plans (Enzler, 1967), and the Department of Commerce publishes these estimates quarterly in *Business Cycle Developments*. Over the 24-year period between 1948 and 1971, the average rate of capacity utilization, computed from these estimates, was 84.8 per cent. The lowest figure for any one year was 74.0 per cent (1958), and the highest figure for any one year was 94.2 per cent (1953). In only four years did the figure fall below 80 per cent, and in only three years did the figure reach as high as 91 per cent. Of course, since the data on capacity utilization obtained through the McGraw-Hill Annual Survey reflect the companies' own varying definitions of capacity and because of the conceptual difficulties pointed out above (p. 36), the 85 per cent figure is only an approximation. Nonetheless, it is the best estimate available as to the percentage of engineer-rated capacity at which megacorps typically operate.

30. Johnston himself discusses many of the criticisms (1960, pp. 169-94). See also the review of Johnston's book by Smith (1961).

31. The existence of a divisible capital stock, confirmed by the empirical evidence with regard to megacorps, is sufficient in itself to explain the constancy of average variable and marginal costs. The fixity of factor coefficients, while unnecessary to establish the same point, nonetheless reinforces it. The reason for positing the fixity of factor coefficients, however, is to lay the basis for the theory of income distribution set forth in chapter 5.

32. Means (1962a, ch. 4); US Congress, Senate Committee on the Judiciary,

Subcommittee on Antitrust and Monopoly, *Hearings, Administered Prices*, Part I, *Opening Phase, Economists' Views*, 1957. Administered pricing has sometimes been used as a synonym for oligopolistic pricing, with the result that by showing the existence of administered pricing in the polypolistic sector of the economy it has been possible to cast doubt on not only the usefulness of the term, but also on the significance of the phenomenon itself. As an unfailing characteristic of oligopoly, even if not limited to that type of market structure alone, it is, however, both useful and significant. Cf. Adelman (1961).

33. Hansen (1970, pp. 7-17, 122-4); Leijonhufvud, (1968, pp. 67-89). See also J. Robinson (1971, chs. 1-2). The analysis which follows can be said, in Hansen's terminology, to substitute the Marshallian excess price hypothesis for the customary Walrasian excess demand hypothesis.

34. For the reasons that this behavioral definition of oligopoly is to be preferred over a structural one, see above, chapter 1, note 4. An industry concentration ratio, it should be added, merely indicates the probability of interdependent behavior or, at most (see chapter 4, pp. 132-3), the probability that the price jointly determined by the industry as a whole will be maintained by each and every member of the industry. This limited predictive power which it has does mean that the concentration ratio can be used as a first approximation to study the *extent* of oligopoly. It cannot, however, be used as a measure of 'monopoly' power. There is no reason to believe that, merely because the four largest firms control 36 per cent of the market rather than 33 per cent, they have a greater degree of control over price. On the measure of 'monopoly' power, see chapter 3, p. 85.

35. This situation in which the individual firm is unable or unwilling to alter its price is reflected in the kinky oligopoly curve generally associated with Sweezy (1939). The kinky oligopoly curve, however, is merely descriptive; it is not analytical. While it correctly indicates that an oligopolist cannot unilaterally alter its price, and thus helps explain why the price in an oligopolistic industry is likely to be 'sticky', it offers no explanation of how or why the price will eventually change - as indeed it likely will. On the elasticity of the industry's short-run demand curve, see Houthakker and Taylor (1966); Stone (1954); Hirsch (1950-1). On the precursors to Sweezy, see Spengler (1965).

36. Actually, as Stigler and Kindahl (1970) point out, it is only the price listed by sellers that need be identical. The price actually paid by buyers will differ depending on the concessions which buyers are able to wrangle by virtue of their bilateral bargaining position. The point is driven home even more forcefully in Sultan's (1975) study of the electric equipment industry.

37. This historical experience is recounted, in the case of the sugar refining industry in Eichner (1969); in the case of the tobacco industry in Tennant (1950); in the case of the petroleum industry in H. Williamson and Daum (1959).

38. The difficulty in coordinating a change in price may be internal as well as external, the bureaucratic nature of the megacorp-price leader complicating the decision-making task (Burkart, 1969). See also G. Mills (1965).

39. See, for example, the hearings on administered prices conducted by the Senate Antitrust and Monopoly Subcommittee (the Kefauver committee), referred to in note 32, especially the hearings on the steel and asphalt roofing industries. See also Sultan (1975).

40. Cf. Needham (1964); Asch (1970, pp. 329-37); Scherer (1970, pp. 262-72), as well as the sources cited therein.

41. For an example of how swift that detection can be, see the Kefauver

hearings on the asphalt roofing industry, part 5, pp. 1539-79 (full reference in note 32).

42. Some economists have argued that while the quoted price may remain unchanged in oligopolistic industries, the effective price will vary as firms become more or less willing to effect transactions at below the quoted figures. This is the distinction between the seller's list price and the actual transaction price (Stigler, 1947, pp. 432-49; Alchian and Allen, 1964, pp. 375-6). There are two points to be noted about this argument. The first is that the empirical evidence bearing on the point is far from being conclusive (cf. Bailey, 1958; Kefauver hearings, part 13, *Identical Bidding*; Stigler and Kindahl, 1970; Sultan, 1975). But even if it could be conclusively demonstrated that secret price shaving is a widespread phenomenon related to aggregate demand conditions, the question would still remain as to the significance of this fact. Certainly, allocation decisions cannot be made on the basis of unknown prices. Nor can the extent of inflation be gauged in the same manner. For these purposes - and they are the only ones which have social consequences - seller-quoted prices are all that are immediately available; they are the prices upon which persons in business and in government will base their decisions. The rest of this treatise, then, can be viewed as an explanation of how in oligopolistic industries list prices are determined and how, once determined, they affect the overall performance of the economy. Discounts below those quoted prices, to the extent they occur, can be dismissed as analytically insignificant - a mere complication insofar as the arguments made below are concerned. Even so, they receive some treatment, in the discussion of the Marshallian variant of polypoly as distinct from the Walrasian variant, below, chapter 4.

43. The contrast is brought out quite dramatically in the Kefauver hearings on the steel industry, p. 295, by comparing the frequency of price changes in the steel industry with the frequency of price changes in the steel scrap industry. It was, in fact, this relative infrequency of price changes which Means had in mind when he first advanced the concept of administered prices in a memorandum to the Secretary of Agriculture in 1934. The memorandum is reprinted in Means (1962a, pp. 77ff). Unfortunately, Means also sought to correlate the frequency with which prices changed with the magnitude by which they changed, and this led to a controversy which tended to obscure his more basic finding, to wit, that some prices tend to be inflexible. Cf. Moore and Levy (1955, pp. 435-40); Ruggles (1955, pp. 441-94); Blair (1955, pp. 566-82).

44. On the use of ideal or pure types, see M. Weber (1958, 1964).

45. When it does, the megacorp is, in fact, likely to adopt a modified marginal cost approach. Orders will continue to be accepted, but the filling of those orders will be delayed or stretched out so as to avoid incurring marginal costs of production that exceed marginal revenue. This explains, for example, the occasional backlog of orders in the steel and automobile industries with no attempt made to raise prices to take advantage of the situation (cf. Zarnowitz, 1962). That marginal cost can be reduced by stretching out the date of delivery is Oi's First Theorem of dynamic production (Oi, 1967).

46. This situation - in which the cost curves of the low-cost firm determine the industry supply curve - contrasts with that in a polypolistic industry. In the latter case, it is the cost curves of the high-cost, or marginal, firms which determine the industry supply curve. See below, chapter 7, pp. 256-9.

47. In other words, the kink in the revenue curve facing the megacorp will disappear when it acts as the price leader, that is, as surrogate for the industry

as a whole. Failure to distinguish between this situation in which the megacorp is acting as surrogate for the entire industry from that in which it is acting unilaterally is a source of considerable confusion in the literature on oligopoly.

48. The slope of the megacorp-price leader's average revenue curve will be greater than that of the industry demand curve by a factor equal to the inverse of the fraction representing its current share of the market. However, the quantity of output demanded from the megacorp-price leader will be less than that demanded from the industry as a whole by the same factor. The price elasticity of demand being equal to the slope of the demand curve multiplied by the ratio of the initial quantity supplied, Q_0, to the initial price, P_0, the two factors cancel out one another. Thus, whatever the share of the market supplied by any one firm, the elasticity of its average revenue curve will be the same as that of every other firm as well as that of the industry demand curve. This means that relative market share will have no effect on the elasticity of a firm's average revenue curve as long as it can be assumed that every other firm is quoting an identical price.

49. Chamberlin (1962, ch. 5); J. Robinson (1969, chs. 2-3). Though Chamberlin was careful not to assert that the price in his 'small group' case, the one taken here to be typical of oligopolistic industries, is set so as to equate the marginal revenue implicit in a negatively sloped average revenue curve with marginal cost; and Robinson, in the preface to the latest edition of her work, admits that she 'had to make a number of limitations and simplifications which led the argument astray', it seems likely that economists will continue, as they have in the past, to fall back on that model in trying to explain oligopolistic pricing behavior.

Appendix to chapter 2. Alternative behavioral assumptions

1. For a somewhat different survey and overview, see Marris (1971a).

2. By modificatory, it is meant that the conclusion is merely qualified by substituting that assumption, not fundamentally altered. A metamorphic assumption is one which, when substituted, leads not to the same result with diminished values, but rather to an entirely different result.

3. The distinction derives from Meyerson and Banfield's taxonomy of the differing conceptions of the public interest, as applied to the megacorp (Meyerson and Banfield, 1955, p. 322-9).

4. A briefer version of the same model can be found in O. Williamson (1963a); Cyert and March (1963, ch. 9). See also Alchian and Kessel (1962).

5. See, for example, Baumol (1967, ch. 7); Sandmeyer (1964); Haveman and De Bartolo (1968). It has been suggested that firms seek to maximize profits subject to a minimum sales or market share constraint (F. Fisher, 1960). See also Osborne (1964); F. Fisher (1965).

6. It is the basis, for example, of the efforts to test the sales maximization hypothesis by examining whether management-controlled firms have a lower profit rate than stockholder-controlled firms (Pardridge, 1964; Kamerschen, 1968; Hindley, 1970; Larner, 1971, ch. 4), or whether, more generally, there is a negative correlation between sales and profits (Mabry and Siders, 1967; M. Hall, 1967). Since what is being tested is a faulty version of the sales maximization hypothesis, it is hardly surprising that these studies have led to either inconclusive or negative results. The faulty version derives, however, from Baumol's own writings, especially the earlier edition of *Business Behavior, Value and Growth.*

Cf. Shepherd (1962); Sandmeyer and Steindl (1970); Peston (1959). For a survey of the studies investigating the relationship between growth and profitability, see Eatwell. (1971).

7. Baumol (1962 and 1967, part 2). For an interesting adaptation of the sales growth maximization model along satisficing lines, see Leibenstein (1960).

8. Cf. Mueller (1969); Lintner (1971); Solow (1971). The difference in growth rates over time will be particularly significant, Lintner points out, if the risks of alternative policies increase as the policies are projected further into the future.

9. For the fullest development of mathematical models along these lines, see Marris and Wood (1971); Marris (1973, appendix II).

Chapter 3. The pricing decision

1. The pricing decision is thus part of the sequential decision-making process that occurs within the megacorp, with conditions confronting the megacorp being periodically reviewed to determine if the variables over which the firm has control, such as price, output, investment expenditures, etc., need to be adjusted (cf. Vickers, 1968, p. 185; Lachman, 1956, pp. 13-14).

2. This can be rewritten as follows:

$$P_1 = P_0 + \frac{n(P_0)}{100}$$

where $P_1 \equiv$ new industry price
$P_0 \equiv$ previously prevailing industry price
and $n \equiv$ percentage change in price, $\frac{\Delta P}{P} \times 100$.

3. This complementarity observed in practice may well reflect the rule-of-thumb established antecedently on the basis of the megacorp's optimal debt-equity ratio. See below, this chapter, note 42.

4. Of the approximately 9,000 corporations covered by Moody's Investors Service, an average of only 130 a year between 1956 and 1969 reported a reduction in their dividend rate. This represents an annual average of approximately 1.4 per cent. If data were available for the 500 largest corporations alone, the percentage would most likely be even lower. (This information comes from Moody's Investors Service.) On the reluctance of corporations to reduce the dividend, see Lintner (1956).

5. See above, chapter 2, pp. 36-7, as well as below, this chapter, note 51.

6. The average corporate levy can be equated with the turnover tax, added to the costs of production and used, as it is in Soviet-type economies, to finance subsequent capital formation (cf. Samuelson, 1971). It is also similar in concept to the variable m in Kalecki's pricing formula, $p = mu + n\bar{p}$, where p is the price charged by the firm, $\bar{p}$ the industry price, u the firm's per unit costs and n the adjustment factor taking into account any margin between the firm and industry price due to product differentiation (Kalecki, 1954, ch. 1; see also Davidson, 1960, ch. 5). It should be noted that, unlike what is about to be done below with respect to the average corporate levy, Kalecki offers no explanation of what determines the magnitude of m. The same criticism can

be made of Weintraub's variable *k*, which is analogous to Kalecki's *m* (Weintraub, 1959). Despite this failing, Kalecki's 'monopoly' model constitutes one of the important lines of development upon which not only this treatise but all post-Keynesian theory is based (cf. Kregel, 1971, ch. 7; Asimakopulos, 1974; Harris, 1974). For an analysis along the same lines as Kalecki, one that comes even closer to anticipating the arguments of this treatise, see Steindl (1952).

7. This is because only average variable costs must be subtracted from the price level to determine the marginal corporate levy while both average variable costs and average fixed costs must be subtracted to determine the average corporate levy.

8. The marginal propensity to save is the proportion of an increase in income which will be saved. For a megacorp, it becomes

$$\frac{\Delta \text{ savings}}{\Delta \text{ revenue}} = \frac{\Delta Q \cdot MCL}{\Delta Q \cdot P} = \frac{MCL}{P}.$$

This, in turn, can be rewritten as

$$\frac{P - AVC}{P}$$

or, with constant marginal costs, as $\dfrac{P - MC}{P}$.

9. At the same time, the change in price - reflected in the diagram by the vertical distance P_1P_0 - is equal to an increase in the average corporate levy; the net revenue at price P_0 - the vertical distance *BE* - is equal to the marginal corporate levy at price P_0, and the net revenue at price P_1 - the vertical distance *AE* - is equal to the marginal corporate levy at price P_1.

10. This immediate gain in any given time period, taking into account the substitution effect, may be expressed mathematically as follows:

$$G_j = n\,[(Q_j \cdot P_0) - (|e_j| \cdot Q_0 \cdot MCL_0)]$$

where $G_j \equiv$ the immediate gain in any given time period *j*, taking into account the substitution effect,
$Q_j \equiv$ quantity of output sold in any given time period *j* following the increase in price,
$|e_j| \equiv$ absolute value of the arc elasticity of demand in any given time period *j*,

and *n*, P_o, Q_o and MCL_0 are as previously defined. In the formula $(n \cdot Q_j \cdot P_0)$ is simply rectangle *BGFE* and $(n \cdot |e_j| \cdot Q_0 \cdot MCL_0)$ is rectangle P_1ABP_0. This is because $(n \cdot Q_j \cdot P_0)$ is the same as $(\Delta P \cdot Q_j)$ and $(\Delta MCL \cdot Q_j)$ while $(n \cdot |e_j| \cdot Q_0 \cdot MCL_0)$ is the same as $(\Delta Q_j \cdot MCL_0)$ where ΔP is the change in price, ΔMCL is the change in the marginal corporate levy and ΔQ_j is the change in the quantity of output sold between time period *j* and the previous time period.

11. This may be expressed mathematically as follows:

$$G = \sum_{j=1}^{s-1} \frac{n[(Q_j \cdot P_0) - (|e_j| \cdot Q_0 \cdot MCL_0)]}{(1 + r)^j}$$

where $G \equiv$ present value of the total gain from the price increase,
$s \equiv$ the time period in which the substitution effect can be expected

to become positive, that is, when $n[(e_j \cdot Q_0 \cdot MCL_0) - (Q_j \cdot P_0)] > 0$.

and $r \equiv$ megacorp price leader's marginal efficiency of investment.

The reason for using r as the discount rate is that presumably the megacorp-price leader is capable of earning a return equal to that rate on any funds it invests. Thus the advantage to the megacorp-price leader of having funds sooner rather than later is that those funds can be expected to grow at an annual rate equal to r.

12. The eventual cost, in any given time period, due to the substitution effect may be expressed mathematically as follows:

$$C_{1_j} = n[(|e_j| \cdot Q_0 \cdot MCL_0) - (Q_j \cdot P_0)]$$

where C_{1_j} $\equiv$ the cost, in any given time period j, arising from the substitution effect.

13. This may be expressed mathematically as follows

$$C_1 = \frac{1}{t-(s-1)} \sum_{j=s}^{t} n[(|e_j| \cdot Q_0 \cdot MCL_0) - (Q_j \cdot P_0) \Big/ (1+t)^{s-1}$$

where $C_1 \equiv$ cost, per time period, due to the substitution effect arising from the price increase,

and $t \equiv$ number of time periods taken into consideration when setting the industry price.

In the formula, the term

$$\frac{1}{t-(s-1)} \sum_{j=s}^{t}$$

is simply a means of obtaining the average loss of corporate levy in each of the time periods for which the substitution effect is positive. The discount formula $(1 + r)^{s-1}$ indicates the value of this eventual loss, not in the time period in which it is actually incurred but rather, in the time period immediately following the rise in price. It is the means of effectively eliminating the interval between the rise in price and the positive impact of the substitution effect, an interval which would not exist in the case of interest payments on external funds.

14. Thus,

$$R_1 = \frac{[t-(s-1)]^{-1} \sum_{j=s}^{t} (|e_j| \cdot Q_0 \cdot MCL_0) - (Q_j \cdot P_0)}{(1+r)^{s-1}} \Bigg/ \sum_{j=1}^{s-1} \frac{(Q_j \cdot P_0) - (|e_j| \cdot Q_0 \cdot MCL_0)}{(1+r)^j}$$

where R_1 $\equiv$ the implicit interest rate, due to the substitution effect, on internally derived funds.

The n terms, it should be noted, cancel one another. In the long run, especially if e_j and Q_j quickly assume the values of e_t and Q_t once the substitution effect becomes positive,

$$R_1 \rightarrow \frac{(|e_t| \cdot Q_0 \cdot MCL_0) - (Q_t \cdot P_0)}{(1+r)^{s-1}} \Big/ \sum_{j=1}^{s-1} \frac{(Q_j \cdot P_0) - (|e_j| \cdot Q_0 \cdot MCL_0)}{(1+r)^j}$$

15. The terms r and i are dealt with more extensively below.

16. It should be kept in mind that the elasticity of demand being referred to here is not the point elasticity of demand, $\left|\frac{dq}{dP} \cdot \frac{P}{Q}\right|$, but rather the arc elasticity of demand, $\left|\frac{\Delta Q}{\Delta P} \cdot \frac{P}{Q}\right|$. See Sylos-Labini (1962, pp. 37–8).

17. Actually the statement is stronger than it need be. For the conclusions that follow to hold, it is necessary only that the absolute decline in sales, not the percentage decline in sales, be greater as n increases. This, in turn, requires only that the industry demand curve, and thus the megacorp-price leader's revenue curve, be negatively sloped.

18. The value of h_j will, of course, depend on the slope of the industry demand curve.

19. Only a few studies have attempted to measure the long-run elasticity of demand as compared with the short-run elasticity. See, for example, Working, Ladd and Tedford (1959); Nerlove and Addison (1958); Waugh (1964). Without underestimating the methodological difficulties involved, it should be noted that these studies present a mixed picture as to whether industry demand is likely to become price elastic even in the long run.

20. Bain (1956). The paragraphs that follow draw heavily upon this work, a classic in the field of industrial organization.

21. For empirical studies offering evidence on the value of m for a significant sample of American industries, see Bain (1956, pp. 68–82); Mann (1966, appendix); Saving (1961); Weiss (1964, 1965).

22. For evidence on the economies of scale in advertising, see Asch and Marcus (1970). See also Doyle (1968, p. 584).

23. Cf. 'Cost and Availability of Credit' (1952); Smith (1959); M. Hall and Weiss (1967). See also Ando, Brown and Adams (1965); Evans and Klein (1967); Suits (1962).

24. The assumption here is that the new firm produces the same product or line of products as the older firms. It is, of course, possible that the new firm will enter into production with a significantly different or somewhat better variant of the basic product, thereby being able to gain a foothold in the industry without undermining the industry price structure. In this case, it becomes a question of how great a loss of sales the established members of the industry will tolerate before being moved to take some retaliatory action such as bringing out their own version of the variant to the basic product.

25. More generally, m represents a discrete decline in sales as distinct from the more gradual decline reflected in the substitution effect. It is because the impact of imports is gradual rather than discrete that that impact is not included as part of the entry factor, even though imports in a certain sense can be characterized as new competition. Because of its sales base outside the United States which enables it to achieve an optimum level of output, a foreign firm

has an advantage over a domestic firm planning to enter the same industry - assuming there is no tariff or other type of trade restriction that has to be overcome.

26. The immediate gain in any given time period j, taking into account the entry factor only, is the same as the immediate gain taking into account the substitution effect except that in this case rectangle *BGFE* in Figure 7 becomes rectangle *G′GFF′* and is equal to $(n \cdot Q_0' \cdot P_0)$ where Q_0' is the quantity of output sold in any given time period j, following the increase in price and the entry into the industry of a new firm of minimum optimal size m; and rectangle P_1ABP_0 becomes rectangle $P_1CG'P_0$ and is equal to $(n \cdot k_j \cdot m \cdot Q_0 \cdot MCL_0)$ where k is the coefficient showing the change that occurs in π as n varies such that $\pi = k \cdot n$. The variables π and m are, of course, as previously defined in the text. Thus the immediate gain in any given time period j, taking into account the entry factor only, may be expressed mathematically as follows:

$$G_j' = n[Q_j' \cdot P_0) - (k_j \cdot m \cdot Q_0 \cdot MCL_0)]$$

where $G_j' \equiv$ the immediate gain in any given time period j, taking into account the entry factor alone.

The eventual cost, in any given time period j, due to the entry factor alone is derived by making a similar modification in the equation for C_{1_j}. Mathematically, this cost, due to the entry factor, can be expressed as follows:

$$C_{2_j} = n[(k_j \cdot m \cdot Q_0 \cdot MCL_0) - (Q_j' \cdot P_0)]$$

where $C_{2_j} \equiv$ the eventual anticipated cost, in any given time period j, arising from the entry factor.

27. By making the appropriate changes in the variables of R_1, R_2 can be expressed mathematically as follows:

$$R_2 = \frac{[t-(s-1)]^{-1}\sum_{j=s}^{t}(k_j \cdot m \cdot Q_0 \cdot MCL_0) - (Q_j' \cdot P_0)}{(1+r)^{s-1}} \Bigg/ \sum_{j=1}^{s-1}\frac{(Q_j' \cdot P_0) - (k_j \cdot m \cdot Q_0 \cdot MCL_0)}{(1+r)^j}$$

where $R_2 \equiv$ the implicit interest rate, due to the entry factor, on internally derived funds.

Again, in the long run, especially if k_j and Q_j' quickly assume the values of k_t and Q_t', once the entry factor becomes positive,

$$R_2 \rightarrow \frac{(k_t \cdot m \cdot Q_0 \cdot MCL_0) - (Q_t' \cdot P_0)}{(1+r)^{s-1}} \Bigg/ \sum_{j=1}^{s-1}\frac{(Q_j' \cdot P_0) - (k_j \cdot m \cdot Q_0 \cdot MCL_0)}{(1+r)^j}$$

28. This follows from the fact that $R_2 = f(\pi)$. Thus if $\pi = k \cdot n$, $R_2 = f(n)$.

29. This is because, once capital funds have been sunk in the new enterprise, the firm will continue to produce, even if it does not cover its full costs, as long as it covers at least its average variable or 'out-of-pocket' expenses. Only

when and if the plant facilities need to be replaced or some other new commitment of capital funds becomes necessary is the entrant likely to withdraw from the industry. For a description of the difficulties that the entry of a new firm into an industry can cause, see Alemson (1969).

30. For a comparison of this approach to the entry factor with that of other writers, see the appendix to this chapter.

31. Cf. Crosland (1956, especially ch. 22); Wilcox (1966, ch. 23); Adams (1961, pp. 552-4).

32. Cf. Means (1962b, pp. 191-2); Bernstein (1955, ch. 10) Wilcox (1966, ch. 19); Shepherd and Gies (1966); Caves (1962, ch. 12, 18); Kahn (1970).

33. Since this chapter was first written, President Nixon moved to impose overall price controls on the oligopolistic sector. In some ways, this represented a more radical step than the regulation of individual industries and, in some ways, a less radical step. It was more radical in the scope of the government control thus established, covering as the regulations did virtually every business firm outside the agriculture sector. It was less radical, however, in that no effort was made to examine in detail the cost-and-price situation within any single industry. The nation's unhappy experience with utility regulation undoubtedly explains the reluctance to proceed in that direction. Be that as it may, the lately established system of wage and price controls represented a generalized approach to the problem of market power which this treatise is examining, and not something the imposition of which any one industry need fear in advance before announcing a rise in price. In other words, before they are put into effect, price controls are unlikely to deter an industry from raising its price. Of course, once the price controls have been established, the sanctions which the enabling legislation provides will indicate the type of meaningful government intervention which a megacorp need fear if it raises its price above the allowable maximum. A further discussion of overall price controls will be found below, in chapter 8.

34. In 1965, for example, the Johnson Administration forced the automobile industry to forgo an implicit price increase by threatening to seek restoration of the exise tax on automobiles unless the automobile companies passed the tax reduction along to consumers in the form of lower prices (*New York Times*, 25 July 1965). The threat, however, was not sufficient to deter the automobile companies from raising prices on the following year's models (*New York Times*, 12 October 1965). That same year, the Johnson Administration forced the aluminum industry to rescind a price increase by threatening to release government stockpiles of aluminum (*New York Times*, 11 November 1965). What is most puzzling is the evident reluctance to reduce or eliminate tariff protection for those industries in which the government wishes to restrict price increases.

35. The most important statutes are the Sherman Act of 1890 (26 Stat. 209) and the Clayton and Federal Trade Commission Acts of 1914 (38 Stat. 717, 730). However, since antitrust law is primarily case law, those statutes by themselves provide very little guidance as to what megacorps can and cannot do. For a comprehensive survey of the case law, see Neale (1960); Dewey (1959, chs. 11-16); Scherer (1970, chs. 19-21); Asch (1970, part III).

36. The total appropriation for antitrust enforcement in 1967 was $7.5 million. This enabled the Antitrust Division of the Justice Department to institute thirty-four cases, only slightly below the average for the five-year period 1965-9. The Federal Trade Commission, meanwhile, initiated another nine restraint cases (Posner, 1970).

37. This constraint on antitrust action is largely the legacy of the 'Trust-busting' era between 1906 and 1920 when the extent to which dissolution would be allowed was determined by the courts. See Eichner (1969, ch. 13); Dewey (1959, ch. 17).

38. This 'nuisance' value of antitrust was perhaps most clearly revealed during the public battle between President John F. Kennedy and the steel industry over the latter's decision to raise its prices in the spring of 1962, an action which endangered the Administration's wage-price guideposts. Cf. McConnell (1963, ch. 5, especially pp. 88-90). See also below, chapter 7, pp. 263-4.

39. The danger of government retaliation is less if prices in general are rising and if labor costs in the industry have recently increased - even if the increase in price is greater than necessary to offset the rise in costs. The importance of this point will be brought out below.

40. In mathematical terms,

$$R = \frac{\dfrac{1}{t-(s-1)} \sum_{j=s}^{t} [Q_0 \cdot MCL_0(|e_j| + k_j \cdot m)] - [P_0 \cdot Q_0(1 - n[|e_j| + k_j \cdot m])]}{(1+r)^{s-1}} \bigg/ \sum_{j=1}^{s-1} \frac{[P_0 \cdot Q_0(1 - n[|e_j| + k_j \cdot m])] - [Q_0 \cdot MCL_0(|e_j| + k_j \cdot m)]}{(1+r)^j}$$

Again, in the long run, especially if e_j and k_j quickly assume the values of e_t and k_t once the combined impact of the substitution effect and entry factor becomes positive,

$$R \rightarrow \frac{[Q_0 \cdot MCL_0(|e_t| + k_t \cdot m)] - [P_0 \cdot Q_0(1 - n[|e_t| + k_t \cdot m])]}{(1+r)^{s-1}} \bigg/ \sum_{j=1}^{s-1} \frac{[P_0 \cdot Q_0(1 - n[|e_j| + k_j \cdot m])] - [Q_0 \cdot MCL_0(|e_j| + k_j \cdot m)]}{(1+r)^j}$$

In connection with these equations, it should be noted that

$$Q_j = Q_0 - \Delta Q$$

and $Q'_j = Q_0 - \Delta Q'$.

Since $\Delta Q = n \cdot |e_j| \cdot Q_0$

and $\Delta Q' = n \cdot k_j \cdot m \cdot Q_0$,

it follows that $Q_j = Q_0 - (n \cdot |e_j| \cdot Q_0) = Q_0(1 - n \cdot |e_j|)$

and $Q'_j = Q_0 - (n \cdot k_j \cdot m \cdot Q_0) = Q_0(1 - n \cdot k_j \cdot m)$.

41. $\Delta F/p$ is simply the denominator of R divided by the number of time periods in a planning period.

$$\frac{\Delta F}{p} = \frac{1}{p}\sum_{j=1}^{s-1}\{P_0 \cdot Q_0[1 - n(|e_j| + k_j \cdot m)]\}$$
$$- [Q_0 \cdot MCL_0(|e_j| + k_j \cdot m)]$$

where $p \equiv$ number of time periods in a planning period.

42. Cf. Baumol and Malkiel (1967); Vickers (1968, ch. 4); Solomon (1963, ch. 8); Baxter and Cragg (1970).

43. This cost of external funds, i, may be expressed mathematically as follows:

$$i = (a)i_e + (1 - a)i_d^*$$

where $i \equiv$ cost of external funds,
$i_e \equiv$ rate of return which must be paid on equity debt obligations,
$i_d \equiv$ rate of return which must be paid on fixed interest obligations,
and $a \equiv$ ratio of equity to total debt.

If there are y types of equity and fixed debt obligations, there will be y rates of return which have to be weighted and averaged.

44. 'Permanent' in the sense of being expected to persist over time. The concept is a variant of that used by Friedman in his studies of the money supply (1956) and of consumption (1957). See also Eisner (1967). A change in the permanent interest rate would thus be a change in the average minimum level of interest rates over the business cycle. Marglin (1970) makes the same point, though the argument is different.

45. To allow for this factor, i would have to be adjusted by a factor, $1 + q$, where q is the additional cost, due to the risk entailed, of borrowing funds externally. The value of q is one measure of the extent to which the interests of the executive group take precedence over those of the megacorp itself. It is thus an indication of the extent to which the organic behavioral assumption adopted in this treatise (see above, chapter 2, appendix, pp. 51-4) needs to be qualified to take into account individualistic factors.

46. For a discussion of the distinction between the more generally referred to marginal efficiency of, or rate of return on, capital and the marginal efficiency of investment, as well as the argument why the latter is the more useful concept, see below, chapter 5, pp. 147-8. See also chapter 4, note 19.

47. The analogy to atomic weapons and nuclear warfare should be readily apparent, and it offers certain clues to understanding both oligopolistic behavior and international relations. In the latter context, what is termed collusion in a market situation takes on a different light.

48. Even with the price level the same for all firms, the amount of savings actually realized may, because of differing costs, diverge from the industry average. In addition, the individual firm has the option of relying on externally generated funds to a greater or lesser extent than its industry rivals.

49. On the reasonableness of this assumption, see below, chapter 5, pp. 181-2.

50. If technological change were not entirely capital embodied, the possibility would arise of being able to increase net revenue, and hence the total corporate levy realized in the long run, through investment in the development of cost-reducing methods. Similarly, if the megacorp-price leader were not committed to remain a member of but a single industry, the possibility would arise of investment in diversification. These possibilities, excluded from consideration here in the simple model, are nonetheless discussed in later chapters.

51. The amount of reserve capacity required will be equal to $(\sigma - Q_j)$ where $\sigma = (1 - SOR)/(SOR)$ and Q_j is the expected sales in time period j.

52. The analytical significance of this influence which current demand conditions have on the rate at which investment plans are actually carried out will be brought out below, in chapter 6, pp. 193–4. Here one need only note that it is one factor contributing to the flexibility of the accelerator.

53. While efforts have been made in recent years to measure the role of technology and individual skills in the process of economic growth (see, for example, Denison, 1962; Solow, 1957), the fact remains that the national income accounts measure only the growth of physical capital, and not the growth of the non-physical capital discussed above. This is not to deny the problems inherent in trying to measure these as well as other non-tangible items which do not receive a valuation by passing through a market place. Cf. Ruggles and Ruggles (1970).

54. The use of the corporate levy to purchase the stock of another firm, as part of a diversification move, would be an example of a variant II investment that would have to be included in the megacorp's overall MEI schedule. Indeed, in the case of a conglomerate megacorp, as analyzed below, chapter 4, this type of investment, as a means of gaining entry into another industry, plays a critically important role.

55. Cf. Ansoff (1965); Stemp (1970). For an especially interesting analytical framework in this connection, see Mackintosh (1963, particularly chs. 1 and 2).

56. Cf. Mao (1970). On the other hand, this does not mean that the firm will not try to make the best possible investment decision. Indeed, it is primarily in this area of capital budgeting that a megacorp is most likely to display behavior consistent with that of the postulated profit-maximizing entrepreneur. Cf. Early (1956); Early and Carleton (1962); Firestone (1960). The fact that firms pursue rational or even marginalist policies with respect to capital budgeting does not mean, however, that they set prices equal to marginal costs.

Appendix to chapter 3. Antecedent formulations of the entry factor

1. Bain (1958, 1956). A parallel line of development in Great Britain, though resulting in a less formal treatment of the entry factor, can be traced through the work of Harrod (1952, ch. 8), Andrews (1949, ch. 5), Hicks (1954) and H. Edwards (1955).

2. The weakness of Wenders' approach is that it views the substitution effect and the entry factor as establishing alternative maximum price levels rather than being complementary components of the implicit interest rate on internally generated investment funds.

3. That is,

<table>
<tr><td rowspan="3">Δ price</td><td>Δ supply curve of internally generated funds</td><td>Δ entry factor
Δ substitution effect
Δ probability of meaningful government intervention</td></tr>
<tr><td>Δ permanent interest rate</td><td></td></tr>
<tr><td>Δ demand for investment funds</td><td></td></tr>
</table>

Chapter 4. Extension of the basic model

1. See the earlier discussion of what constitutes an industry, chapter 1, p. 10.
2. Chandler (1969, especially pp. 262-75 and table 2); Gort (1966, pp. 32-3).
3. Eichner (1969, ch. 1). See also Chandler (1962).
4. For the analysis of monopoly when a megacorp is not involved, see below, this chapter, pp. 127-9.
5. Cf. Eichner (1976). While those intellectually nurtured in the University of Chicago tradition in economics are also inclined to treat oligopoly and monopoly as being fundamentally the same, they do so within the static, short-run framework that has been shown in this treatise to be inapplicable to the oligopolistic sector of the American economy. Cf. Friedman (1962, ch. 5); Stigler (1966a, chs. 11-12).
6. The above considerations help to explain the financing policies of electric power companies, quantitatively the most important type of public utility insofar as investment is concerned, in the post World War II period. As expected, electric utilities over this interval have to a far greater extent that their manufacturing counterparts been forced to rely on external financing - new securities issues accounting for approximately 52 per cent of the investment funds obtained by them between 1952 and 1966, compared with only 10 per cent for corporations in manufacturing (Plattner, 1969).
7. This, of course, is a questionable assumption since size of firm has a significant influence on access to external investment funds. See above, chapter 3, note 23.
8. Very often this is the *quid pro quo* for government control over prices.
9. Cf. Houthakker and Taylor (1966, pp. 88, 153-4); F. Fisher and Kaysen (1962, pp. 2-9, 35, 76, 234-5); Stern (1965).
10. US Securities Exchange Commission, *Statistical Bulletin*, January 1970. This figure is based on data for the first ten months of 1968 and 1969, and compares the new securities offered by corporations in the electric, gas and water, the railroad, other transportation and communications industries with those offered by all corporations.
11. This would appear to be especially true for the American Telegraph and Telephone Company, accounting as it does for approximately 38 per cent of all new equity issues and 13 per cent of all new securities issues, including fixed debt as well as equity financing. American Telephone and Telegraph Company, *Bell System Financing*, 1 July 1969.
12. Averch and Johnson (1962); Wellisz (1963). For a more complete discussion on this point, see Kahn (1970, II, pp. 49-59).
13. The theoretical point is made, in connection with investment in R & D, by Scherer (1967). As an illustration of the point, compare the reaction of two industries, both regulated but one monopolistic and the other oligopolistic, to separate incidents of technological innovation. The airline industry, faced with the development of the jet aircraft, would have preferred to wait until its existing stock of propeller-driven planes was fully depreciated before converting its fleets to all jets. The inter-firm competition, however, meant that once one airline purchased the jets the others had to follow suit, even though it led to considerable financial difficulty. On the other hand, the telephone industry, faced with the development of all electronic switching equipment, has been able to wait until the existing electro-mechanical equipment wears out. This has meant that the linking of computers to home receiving sets has been

considerably delayed. The contrast between the response of the airline industry and that of the telephone industry to the same type of technological opportunity underscores the advantage of oligopoly over monopoly. This advantage derives from the point noted earlier - namely, that though competition via price may be muted under oligopoly, competition via investment will, for that very reason, be all the more intense (see above, chapter 3, p. 88). Of course, as noted below, in chapter 8, not all the competition via investment will necessarily be beneficial to society.

14. Penrose (1959, chapter 4); Marris (1964, pp. 114-18); Leyland and Richardson (1964); Mackintosh (1963). It should be noted that expansion into a new industry involves a strain on managerial resources - and on the organizational structure itself - of a different order of magnitude from expansion within an existing industry.

15. The argument can be generalized to encompass $X + Y$ industries, where Y is the number of industries into which the megacorp is presently contemplating expansion.

16. For a discussion of the relative merits of using the payoff period and the marginal efficiency of investment in capital budgeting decisions, see M. Gordon (1953); Kaldor (1964, pp. 274-6).

17. The theory of conglomerate expansion has not been well worked out. Perhaps the best treatment is to be found in Mueller (1969); Marris (1964, chs. 2-3). Marris himself acknowledges the important prior work of Penrose (1959). See also Clemens (1951-2); M. Fisher (1961).

18. For evidence that conglomerate expansion is mainly into newer, more rapidly expanding industries, see Gort and Hogarty (1970, pp. 183-4); Alemson (1969); Kottke (1966). See also Wood (1971, appendix C).

19. If, as Joan Robinson has persistently pointed out (1953-4, 1956), there is no unambiguous way to measure capital, the rate of return on capital must necessarily be ambiguous as well. The marginal efficiency of investment, though difficult to estimate, does not suffer from the same theoretical defect, and it is in any case something which firms themselves have no choice but to try to determine. For more on the distinction between the marginal efficiency, or rate of return, on capital and the marginal efficiency of investment, see below, chapter 5, pp. 147-8.

20. This is so for two reasons: one, because the megacorp is in a better position to adjust the price in the other industries, those in which it is the price leader; and two, because the value if R is likely to be less for a price follower than for a price leader since the former can ignore with greater safety the probability of meaningful government intervention.

21. See above, chapter 2, note 33, as well as McNulty (1967); Wiles (1956, ch. 4); Machlup (1952, pp. 85-92, 111-15).

22. This means that the value of t in the formula for R (see above, chapter 3, note 39) will be equal to 1.

23. In Hicks' (1954, p. 45) language, the firm is a 'sticker' rather than a 'snatcher'.

24. This implies that the firm ignores the intervening values for $|e_j|$.

25. Cf. Orr and MacAvoy (1965). While Orr and MacAvoy deem it necessary to invoke the assumption of spatial differentiation in order to derive individual firm demand curves that are fractional shares of the industry demand curve, the assumption of price leadership, as argued above (chapter 2, pp. 47-8), leads to the same result.

26. It is precisely because this last condition is not met that public bidding by government and quasi-public bodies, including utilities, is often beset by collusion among the suppliers. See, for example, Eichner (1962); Herling (1962); Kuhlman (1967); Sultan (1975).

27. The limited relevance of the Walrasian model, except for internationally traded commodities, has been stressed by E. Brunner (1952, p. 738).

28. Chamberlin (1962). This narrowly defined case of monopolistic competition is not to be confused with oligopoly, either with product differentiation or without. See above, chapter 2, pp. 39-40). An important subgroup, within the class of monopolistically competitive firms, consists of firms supplying services.

29. On bargaining theory, see the sources cited below in the discussion of collective bargaining, chapter 5, note 12. See also Galbraith (1952).

30. The monopolistically competitive firm need not be a part of any industry - at least one that can be narrowly defined. As Triffin (1949, ch. 2) long ago noted, the concept of an industry may have little relevance in the case of monopolistic competition.

31. See the sources cited by Beckman (1960, p. 464, fn 1, 2 and 3).

32. This implies that the suppliers of services, as distinct from commodities, are unlikely to be price takers. This reinforces the point made earlier that firms supplying services are likely to be monopolistically competitive rather than polypolistic. (See above, note 28). With the growing importance of the service sector, this is not a minor point.

33. O. Williamson (1965) has argued that oligopoly is unstable in the same manner that polypoly in the Marshallian sense is - because the community of interest which characterizes the industry will tend to break down over time. The point, however, is that while the breakdown of the community of interest which characterizes an oligopolistic industry is an extraordinary event, the undermining of the price level through price shaving which characterizes polypoly in the Marshallian sense is endemic. The sense of community is far greater in oligopoly, especially when the industry consists of only a small number of megacorps.

34. The savings may come from either the household or the government sectors. If they come from the former, the question arises as to what degree of skewness in the distribution of income will be necessary in order to assure the requisite amount of savings. If the savings come from the government, then the question of social control and transformation of the socio-economic system dealt with below in chapter 8 arises. It is, of course, possible that the savings will be generated out of a permanent disequilibrium condition within the business sector, such as will occur when the growth of demand continually exceeds the expansion of supply capacity. But in this case one has not only the same problem of a skewed income distribution (to the extent that the relative gain in profits is used to augment household spending) but, in addition, all the shortcomings of a disequilibrium and, hence, indeterminate model.

35. Cf. Averitt, 1968. The oligopolistic subsector includes all oligopolistic industries (bilateral oligopolies, oligopolies with product differentiation, and all other oligopolies, including those selling to non-oligopolistic business firms) plus all regulated or nationalized enterprises. The non-oligopolistic sector includes all polypolistic industries in the Walrasian sense (producers of internationally traded commodities and suppliers to megacorps); all polypolistic industries in the Marshallian sense (newer, rapidly growing industries as well as other industries subject to stagnation and/or periodic imperfect collusion, with the construction

sector included among the latter), plus all monopolistically competitive firms (family-operated manufacturing enterprises with product differentiation, retail trade and distribution outlets benefiting from spatial differentiation, and suppliers of services).

Chapter 5. The distribution of income

1. Even with fixed technical coefficients it is still possible for changes in productivity to occur in the short run as the result of shutting down and starting up again plants with different least cost points. On this point, see above chapter 2, pp. 34–5. Even if all plants are equally efficient, a change in 'productivity' will be observed as the rate of capacity utilization is varied. This change in 'productivity', however, reflects the downward slope of the average total cost curve due to the fixed cost component rather than any real change in operating efficiency, or the direct costs of production.

2. For useful surveys of most of these theories, see Davidson (1960); Bronfenbrenner (1971); Pen (1971).

3. This is the 'adding up' problem discussed by J. Robinson (1934); Stigler (1966a, pp. 151–3); Vickrey (1964, p. 257); Bronfenbrenner (1960, p. 301, especially fn 3); Davidson (1960, pp. 29–31). If the sum of the marginal products of each of the factors does not equal the total product, then marginal productivity theory is insufficient by itself to explain all income shares.

4. Cf. Harcourt (1969, 1972) together with the sources cited therein; Ferguson and Nell (1972); Kregel (1971); Kaldor (1966); J. Robinson (1953–4, 1957). If one is not prepared to accept the arguments of these admittedly hostile critics of marginal productivity theory, then one should examine the far more devastating comments of friendly interpreters. See, for example, Ferguson (1969, especially ch. 15); Bronfenbrenner (1971, especially chs. 7, 8, 16). It should be added that there is a long history of criticism of marginal productivity in the United States going back to Veblen and continuing through other institutional economists (Veblen, 1919; Gruchy, 1947, pp. 588ff).

5. What must be left deliberately ambiguous is whether each of the separate increases is to be measured in absolute or in percentage terms. As a practical matter, in order to maintain adequate but minimum differentials in compensation for different types of jobs, it will be necessary to alternate between absolute and percentage changes in the rates of compensation since complete reliance on the former leads eventually to differentials that are too small and a complete reliance on the latter to differentials that are too large. When to shift from one to the other basis is likely to be the greatest source of disharmony within an organization, whether relative rates of compensation are determined entirely by the employing firm, entirely by a trade union or by the two acting jointly.

6. The fixed-interest debt holders will themselves be receiving a uniform rate of return on their investment, this uniform rate of return being the result of the differential capital gains or losses which serve to equalize bond yields over time.

7. Recognition of this fact goes back at least to Pareto, as pointed out by Georgescu-Roegen (1935). See also Fukuoka (1955, pp. 25–9).

8. Even in this most favorable case, marginal productivity theory may be misleading. This is the point of the double-switching controversy between the Cambridge, England, post-Keynesians and the Cambridge, Mass., neo-classical

growth theorists (J. Robinson, 1956, pp. 411-30; Kregel, 1973, ch. 7; Harcourt, 1972).

9. The production work force - whether organized into a trade union or not - is to be regarded as that portion of the total laboring manpower force whose wages are included as part of the firm's direct costs of production. The remaining portion of the laboring manpower force is to be regarded as the overhead work force or, more simply, overhead personnel.

10. Such an occurrence, it should be noted, is a historical rarity and one which is generally associated, to the extent that it does occur, with the sector in which the megacorp first appeared, railroad transportation.

11. Two exceptions to the general case may be noted. One, the trade union, in an effort to gain a bargaining advantage, may insist on conducting negotiations with one of the lesser firms in the industry before taking on the price leader or 'industry giant'. Second, and as a means of avoiding the 'whipsawing' or playing of one firm off against the others which the first exception gives rise to, the entire industry may bargain collectively with the trade union. Even in this latter case, it is likely to be a representative of the price leader who conducts the actual negotiations on behalf of the entire industry.

12. The literature on bargaining is partially summarized by Pen (1959); Coddington (1968). See also Cartter (1959, ch. 9); Dunlop (1958); Walton and McKersie (1965, chs. 1-3); Bronfenbrenner (1971, ch. 10).

13. The more capital-intensive methods of production are, after all, the ultimate source of higher wages. While this is little solace to the worker who, in the short run, either loses his job or fails to find one because of a relative decline in the demand for labor inputs, pressure on the government to pursue policies leading to a higher rate of growth of employment is likely to be of more help to the displaced worker than for the trade union to trim its own wage demands.

14. The clearest exceptions have been in the time of war or in the case of workers who provide essential public services - with results that have not recommended an expansion of the practice to other situations. Even the procedures set up under the Railroad Employees Act, the closest that the United States has come to establishing compulsory arbitration of labor disputes in peacetime outside the public sector, have been careful, at least until recently, to avoid imposing terms on one of the parties.

15. While this provides a quantitative definition of the trade union's goals, comparable to those assumed to be pursued by the megacorp, strictly speaking the trade union tries to hold on to categories of jobs and not to a specific proportion of the total available employment when the proportion of the laboring manpower force in different job categories - particularly blue and white collar - changes.

16. In some cases it is possible for a worker to remain formally outside the trade union, yet be forced through a mandatory dues check-off system to contribute to the union's treasury. The fact that such a compulsory dues check-off system is sometimes the bargaining goal of the trade union is confirming evidence, though not very strong evidence, of the empirical relevance of the behavioral pattern postulated above.

17. These figures are compiled from data found in US Bureau of the Census (1966). The list of oligopolistic industries is taken from Shepherd (1970).

18. For the delineation of the wage rounds prior to the 1960s, see Eckstein and Wilson (1962). See also Youtsler (1956, pp. 70-81). As for the subsequent wage rounds, see below, chapter 7, pp. 263-70.

19. That is,

$$\frac{\Delta AVC}{AVC} = L_1 \cdot W_p$$

where $L_1 \equiv$ ratio of production labor compensation to total direct costs, and AVC and W_r are as defined above.

20. That is,

$$c_d = f(W_p)$$

where $c_d \equiv$ percentage increase in direct costs other than labor historically associated with an increase in the rate of compensation for the production work force.

More specifically,

$$c_d = d \cdot W_p$$

where $d > 0$ and is statistically determinable from past data. It should be noted that by allowing for other determinates besides W_p in this equation it is possible to enlarge the model to encompass such phenomena as (1) the setting of commodity prices in world markets (see above, chapter 4, p. 135) as part of the interdependency among various national economies, and (2), more specifically, the relationship between commodity-importing developed nations and commodity-exporting less developed nations.

21. That is,

$$\frac{\Delta AVC}{AVC} = L_1 \cdot W_p + (1 - L_1) \cdot d \cdot W_p.$$

The above equation may be rewritten as follows:

$$\frac{\Delta AVC}{AVC} = W_p[L_1 + (1 - L_1) \cdot d]$$

22. That is,

$$\frac{\Delta FC}{FC} = L_2 \cdot U_2 \cdot W_p$$

where, $U_2 \equiv$ ratio of the compensation paid that portion of the overhead work force whose wages are keyed to the trade union agreement to total overhead labor compensation, and

$L_2 \equiv$ ratio of overhead labor compensation to total fixed costs, and FC is as defined previously.

23. The difficulty of organizing a successful proxy fight has already been pointed out. See above, chapter 2, note 3.

24. It might be added that the elimination of X-inefficiency is what constitutes the curriculum, at least as an ideal, in the American business school, an institution almost unique to the United States.

25. Purchase by a company of its own stock in the open market serves to keep up the price of those shares and thus makes a take-over bid more expensive - even if the incumbent management is precluded from voting those shares in any subsequent proxy battle. On the extent of stock repurchases, see Bierman and West (1966); Elton and Gruber (1968).

26. See above, chapter 2, pp. 25-8, and note 19, and chapter 2, appendix, pp. 53-4.

27. This point brings out the principal difference between the model of the firm developed by Marris and the model upon which this treatise is based. Marris assumes that the price level is exogenously determined, and that what needs to be explained is the rate of growth of dividends or, in his framework, the valuation ratio. (See Baumol, 1962; Marris, 1964; J. Williamson, 1966; Marris and Wood, 1971; Marris, 1973, appendix II.) In the model developed in this treatise, it is assumed that the rate of growth of dividends is determined exogenously (by the socio-economic factors described in the next section), and that it is the price level which needs to be explained. The two managerial models are therefore each an elaboration, or refinement, of the other.

28. This minimum condition, that the firm need only maintain a rate of growth in dividends equal to that of other megacorps, helps explain why the possibility of a take-over bid does not vitiate the influence which the separation of management from ownership has on the executive group's motivation (cf. Alchian and Kessel, 1962, p. 160; Manne, 1965).

29. M. Gordon (1959); Durand (1959); Walter (1963). See also the criticism by Friend and Puckett (1964) of these empirical findings that an increase in dividends, relative to net revenue, will lead to a disproportionate increase in the price of common shares and therefore a decline in the price-dividend ratio.

30. The timing of the increase in dividends will be influenced by numerous factors, including when any major trade union agreements expire. An increase in the dividend rate, for example, is least likely just prior to the negotiation of a new contract, particularly in a bellwether industry. In addition, the likelihood of an increase in dividends will reflect cyclical business conditions, the high rates of capacity utilization associated with periods of strong aggregate demand producing large revenues which, together with any previously negotiated labor contracts that keep labor costs constant, make payment of the higher dividend rate possible. Finally, if the increase in dividends requires an increase in price as explained below, its timing will be governed by political considerations, that is, by when the possible retaliatory action of government will be minimized.

31. See below, note 33.

32. If only some industries raise their price to cover the higher dividend payments, they will be subject to greater competition from other products via the substitution effect; if they decide instead to allow the average corporate levy to fall, the firms within those industries will be without the funds they need to assure maximum growth, and at the very least the entry of new firms into those industries will be facilitated. Thus it is only if all, or nearly all, industries raise their price that the individual megacorp will not be placed at a competitive disadvantage. But in that case, because reported net earnings can be expected to increase in the bellwether industry, the size of the national incremental wage pattern, as explained later in this chapter, is likely to increase also.

33. The empirical evidence already in hand with regard to dividend behavior - which shows that megacorps on the average increase their dividends by a certain small percentage each year, at the same time avoiding any cutback in the amount of payment if at all possible - is not inconsistent with the argument just presented, namely, that dividends within the oligopolistic sector will be increased steadily over time at a rate dictated by the growth of wages. For the empirical evidence on dividend behavior, see Lintner (1956); Brittain (1966), as well as the equations

for dividends found in Keynesian macroeconomic models such as the Wharton (Evans and Klein, 1967) and the Brookings (Duesenberry *et al.*, 1965) models. The same empirical evidence is, however, not inconsistent with the alternative stockholder welfare, or equity maximizing, behavioral hypothesis if the effects of uncertain future income are taken into account (cf. Lintner, 1971). To distinguish between the two dynamic models, it would be necessary to determine whether, within the oligopolistic sector, the rate of growth of dividends corresponded more closely to the rate of growth of wages or more closely to the rate of growth of output (and investment).

34. That is,

$$\frac{\Delta FC}{FC} = L_2 \cdot U_2 \cdot W_p + Div \cdot W_p$$

where $Div \equiv$ ratio of dividend payments to fixed costs.

Alternatively, this may be written as follows:

$$\frac{\Delta FC}{FC} = W_p[L_2 \cdot U_2 + Div]$$

35. That is,

$$\frac{\Delta C}{C} = v \cdot \frac{AVC}{AVC} + (1 - v) \cdot \frac{AFC}{AFC}$$

$$= W_p\left[v(L_1 + (1 - L_1) \cdot d) + (1 - v)\frac{(L_2 \cdot U_2 + Div)}{SOR \cdot ERC}\right]$$

where $C \equiv AVC + AFC$

and $v \equiv \dfrac{AVC}{C}$.

36. In other words, that n exceeds $\Delta C/C$ as calculated in the equation in note 35.

37. The argument presented so far explains the strong correlation which has been found to exist between the rate of growth of wages on the one hand and trade union organizations and oligopolistic market structure on the other hand. The empirical literature is summarized and synthesized in Levinson (1967).

38. While Marx's theories on value are presented in their most comprehensive form in *Capital* (1933), they are set forth much more clearly and succinctly in *Value, Price and Profit* (1935). They are also discussed with intelligence and sympathy in Sweezy (1942, part 1). The best critique of the Marxian theories of value is still Bohm von-Bawerk (1949). See also Samuelson (1967) and the several essays on Marx by Joan Robinson (1951), especially the two entitled 'The Labour Theory of Value' in volumes I and II.

39. The myth is fostered by the distorting effect which capital gains have on the distribution of income in the short run. By itself, an increase in the price of a company's shares would not be a matter of concern. After all, what one rentier gains by selling his stock at a higher price is another rentier's loss. But in fact the higher price paid for a company's shares, if part of a general rise in the price of common shares, may also be due to the effects of monetary policy. The Federal Reserve Board, by seeing to it that credit is more readily

available, may well be financing the higher stock prices. The resulting capital gains will, in turn, enable equity debt holders to increase their purchasing power relative to other groups in society. Between 1960 and 1964, persons with $200,000 a year or more income realized almost two-thirds of their income from capital gains. (Bhatia, 1970, p. 363, fn 1). Even if a subsequent tightening of monetary policy should produce a break in stock market prices so that the value of outstanding shares more closely approximates the present discounted value of the likely future dividend stream, the equity debt holders will have had their consumption fling.

40. For an interesting attempt to do so, see Stanfield (1973).

41. See, however, Keynes (1930, vol. 1, pp. 139-40). It should be noted that Joan Robinson is the source of this description of Keynes' views. The entire section on Keynesian and post-Keynesian macroeconomic distribution theory has been informed by the criticisms of earlier drafts made by Mrs Robinson in a series of private communications.

42. Kaldor (1955-6, pp. 94-100); Boulding (1950, ch. 14); Weintraub (1959, 1966). For a summary treatment of these several models, see Davidson (1960, chs. 6-8).

43. J. Robinson (1956, Book II, especially chs. 7-9); Kregel (1971, chs. 10-12 and 1973, part 2); Kaldor (1955-6). For an overview see Eichner and Kregel (1975).

44. The argument is made by Kalecki (1938, p. 76) reprinted in Kalecki (1971) but the quotation itself is not to be found in any English work of Kalecki. What happens when capitalists consume rather than save or, alternatively, when workers save rather than consume has been explored most fully by Pasinetti (1962, 1974). On Pasinetti's contribution, see Kregel (1971, ch. 10).

45. See below, chapter 8, p. 282. The distorting effect which the capital gains derived from stock ownership have on the distribution of incomes has already been pointed out. See above, note 39.

46. For the delineation of the business sector into the oligopolistic and non-oligopolistic subsectors, see above, chapter 4, note 35.

47. In this last case, there will be a monetary effect of the sort discussed below, chapter 7, pp. 245-7.

48. Not just the relative distribution of income between the laboring manpower force and the equity debt holders, but also the aggregate growth rate is likely to be affected by any one of the three possible divergences.

49. It would appear, on the basis of both surveys and other data, that megacorps devote only a small portion of their research and development effort to the task of reducing their own costs of production. Most of the R & D funds - approximately 80 to 90 per cent, depending on the industry - go for either new product development or product improvement. Gustafson (1962, pp. 178-9); Scherer (1965, pp. 260-1); Comanor (1967, p. 647); Mansfield (1968, p. 59).

50. While there is considerable empirical evidence in support of this point, most of it cannot be taken seriously because the evidence comes from studies based on fitting a neo-classical production function to aggregate data. (On the objection to the use of an aggregate neo-classical function, see above, p. 146, and note 4.) For a study which avoids this problem but nonetheless finds strong evidence that technological progress is capital embodied, see Shen (1968). The main shortcoming of the Shen study is that it is based entirely on data from the state of Massachusetts alone.

51. The judgments reflected in this overview have been shaped to a large

extent by the author's participation in the Columbia University Seminar on Technology and Social Change. The more important proceedings of this seminar have been published by the Columbia University Press. See Ginzberg (1964); Warner, Morse and Eichner (1965); Warner and Morse (1966). See also Jewkes, Sawers and Stillerman (1958); Mansfield (1968); Nelson, Peck and Kalachek (1967); Scherer (1970, ch. 15); Blaug (1963).

52. Both the Presidential guideposts established during the Kennedy-Johnson administrations and the several wage determination boards set up under President Nixon represented efforts to develop an alternative to the contract settlement in the bellwether industry as the basis for the national incremental wage pattern. So far, however, these efforts have served merely to supplement the key bargain reached privately in either the steel or automobile industry rather than to supplant it. For a further discussion of the guideposts and the Nixon policies, see below, chapters 7 and 8, pp. 263-6, 277.

53. Eckstein and Wilson (1962); Eckstein (1968). For a critique of the Eckstein-Wilson empirical studies upon which this chapter is largely based, see T. McGuire and Rapping (1967); Hamermesh (1970). See also Eckstein (1967).

54. Bronfenbrenner and Holzman (1963, pp. 75-6), as well as the sources cited therein.

Chapter 6. Micro and macro

1. Indeed, Keynes' attack was directed primarily at Pigou, not Marshall, which represents more than just a courtesy to Keynes' mentor. Marshall had not insisted that unemployment was generally 'voluntary' in the sense that a willingness on the part of workers to accept lower wages would enable them to find employment.

2. J. Robinson (1956, 1962a); Kaldor and Mirrlees (1962). The best introduction to this body of work is Kregel (1971, 1973); Eichner and Kregel (1975). For Professor Robinson's own efforts to provide a more useful microeconomic foundation for macrodynamic analysis, see, not *The Economics of Imperfect Competition*, the work most clearly identified with her name in the minds of most economists, but rather J. Robinson (1962c) as well as (1971, ch. 7); Robinson and Eatwell (1974).

3. Cf. Kaldor (1951); Matthews (1959, chapter 3); Waud (1967). The critical factor here is the tendency of investment to vary less sharply than the amount of corporate levy - or savings in the oligopolistic sector - being realized. (On the greater variability of the realized corporate levy, see above, chapter 3, pp. 64-5. With investment thus less responsive than savings to changes in aggregate demand, the expansion process is bounded, meaning that there is a single rate of growth toward which the economic system will tend to converge. The point is elaborated on below in this chapter. It should be noted that the positing of a lagged accelerator model of this sort, with the implications for aggregate stability which such a model has, marks a significant departure from the analysis of Kalecki - which this treatise has, up to this point, closely paralleled - and even to some extent a departure from the analysis of J. Robinson. This point, too, is elaborated on below.

4. While the studies to be cited in this section pertain to investment in the manufacturing sector as a whole, the proportion of capital expenditures accounted for by megacorps is so great that the studies can more truthfully be said to

apply primarily to the oligopolistic subsector. See below, note 31.

5. The reason, as Smyth (1964) has argued, is undoubtedly that the accelerator models used were improperly formulated.

6. Earlier, Chenery (1952) and Koyck (1954) had also developed lagged accelerator models, though of a different sort.

7. Eliminating the past profits variable which he found to be unnecessary and ignoring the error and constant terms, Eisner's (1963) estimating equation is as follows:

$$i_t = \sum_{j=1}^{7} b_{1_j} \Delta s_{t+1-j} + b_2 d_{53}$$

where, $i_t \equiv$ gross capital expenditures deflated by gross fixed assets, a measure of the relative change in capital stock,

$$\Delta s_t \equiv \frac{S_t - S_{t-1}}{S_{52} + S_{53} + S_{54}}$$ = the change in sales deflated by average sales over the base period 1952-4, a measure of the relative change in demand.

and d_{53} = 1953 depreciation charges divided by 1953 gross fixed assets, a measure of (the inverse of) the durability of capital and replacement requirements.

D_{I_1}, as indicated above in chapter 3, pp. 89-90 is a function of the expected increase in industry sales during the current planning period, this expected increase being but a forward projection of the industry's past sales trend. If Eisner's i_t term is redefined as net capital expenditures and the depreciation or replacement variable is accordingly eliminated, the Eisner estimating equation would be but a separate form of D_{I_1}.

8. Cf. Anderson (1964); Leeuw (1962); Jorgenson (1963); Fromm and Klein (1965); Liu (1963); Meyer and Glauber (1964); Resek (1966). For a concise summary of the findings of some of these studies with respect to the interest elasticity of investment, see Evans (1969, pp. 136-7).

9. See Meyer and Kuh (1959, ch. 2) for a review of the literature up to the date of its publication. See also Eisner and Strotz (1964) for a later though less thorough summary.

10. Even so, the effect of the long-term interest rate on investment seems to be confined to cyclical peak periods when internally generated funds are no longer adequate to finance investment needs. Meyer and Glauber (1964, pp. 235-6); Anderson (1964, ch. 2). Evans (1967) found that the effect of the long-term interest rate was further limited to certain industries.

11. See below, chapter 7, pp. 245-8, for a more extended discussion of the role played by monetary factors in investment decisions.

12. It should be added that this emphasis on the past trend of sales, rather than the past trend of profits, serves to distinguish further the investment demand function for the oligopolistic sector from that of the non-oligopolistic sector. See below, p. 212.

13. $\overset{*}{G}_s$ can be identified with the secular growth of GNP, as presently measured in the national income and product accounts. It is preferable, however, to identify

$\overset{*}{G}_s$ with the secular growth of physical output and marketable services, thereby excluding the government's wage bill from the production account. This makes the relation between $\overset{*}{G}_s$ and $\overset{*}{I}_0$ more direct. This is how $\overset{*}{G}_s$ will be used throughout this chapter. It makes the government's wage bill analogous to a transfer payment to the household sector.

14. In terms of the oligopolistic price formula.

$$P = AVC + \frac{FC + CL}{SOR \cdot ERC}, \; Net = \frac{[Div]\; FC + [1 - Dep]\; CL}{P \cdot SOR \cdot ERC}$$

where *Div* is the percentage of the fixed costs accounted for by dividend payments and *Dep* is the percentage of the corporate levy accounted for by depreciation allowances. Once it is recognized, however, that the oligopolistic price formula must be modified to take into account the taxes already in effect (see below, pp. 250–1), it is no longer possible to define *Net* in terms of *P*. If this denominator is not to expand indefinitely as a result of including the taxes themselves in the oligopolistic price formula, it is necessary to substitute instead

$$AVC + \frac{FC + CL}{SOR \cdot ERC}$$

or, in the terminology adopted below, average expected non-tax outlays. Since this involves either awkward mathematics or awkward language and since, in the case of a corporate income tax, the practical difference is not that great, it is perhaps best to continue describing *Net* as the ratio of net income to total income, thereby ignoring the effect of taxes on the oligopolistic price formula.

15. Eichner (1975). If the rate of growth of savings in the oligopolistic sector exceeds the rate of growth of investment, assuming that savings and investment were equal initially, megacorps will be under no pressure to raise prices. But, as was brought out earlier, they will be under no pressure to lower prices either. This condition, with the rate of growth of savings exceeding the rate of growth of investment, is not consistent with macrodynamic stability either, as will soon be made clear. If the excess of savings does not lead to an increase in the national incremental wage pattern, W_p, or to some action by the government which has the effect of reducing savings in the oligopolistic sector, it will be eliminated through a slowing down of the aggregate growth rate itself.

16. The exceptional case, requiring that the savings generated in some sector be tapped, is discussed below, pp. 245–8.

17. Cf. Pierson (1972, pp. 387–8). The process by which savings and investment are brought back into balance is explained by Metzler (1947).

18. The secular growth rate is simply the past growth rate with the cyclical fluctuations eliminated in the same manner as in deriving the standard operating ratio (see above chapter 3, p. 62). It thus depends on the trend of the growth rate as perceived by megacorps themselves.

19. As noted earlier (chapter 2, note 29), the Department of Commerce now regularly reports the rate of capacity utilization in manufacturing. That figure can be compared with the standard ratio cited above in chapter 2. The source of information for the change in liquid assets by megacorps is the flow of funds accounts published by the Board of Governors of the Federal Reserve System. For a description of these accounts, see J. Cohen (1972) and the sources cited therein.

20. Anderson (1964, ch. 2). The statement needs to be qualified to the extent that the expansion of the economy continues for an extended period of time, for then other factors are not likely to remain constant. In fact, wages and dividends are likely to rise due to pressure from the laboring manpower and capital debt-holding constituencies; and as a collateral matter the megacorp may be forced to revise its investments plans upward. This point will be elaborated on shortly.

21. The exception, of course, is the work of the post-Keynesian economists, for whose long-run macrodynamic models this treatise is intended to provide both the microeconomic foundations and the short-run disequilibrium analysis. But as was noted above in chapter 5, pp. 179–80, even in the writings of other post-Keynesian economists the savings function is not always specified in precisely the same terms as it is here. On this point, see Eichner and Kregel (1975).

22. While the increase in the realized corporate levy from raising the industry price will be less than proportional over the long run, this being due to both the substitution effect and the entry factor (see above, chapter 3, pp. 67–77, as well as p. 84), in the shorter time period covered by the savings function as just defined this combined influence is likely to be negligible and therefore can be ignored.

23. See, especially, Kuh (1960); Schultze (1964); Evans (1969, pp. 287–9). Scitovsky (1964) has directly related this evidence to the Keynesian cyclical theory of income distribution discussed in the preceding chapter. See also Denison (1964). A savings function of the sort just specified is also consistent with the empirical evidence from some of the studies of investment behavior showing the influence exerted by the availability of external funds. See, in this connection, Anderson (1964); Meyer and Glauber (1964); Kuh (1963); Evans (1967); Jorgenson (1971).

24. This is because the price of capital goods probably does not vary sufficiently from the general price level to make any real difference in investment decisions.

25. The slope of the line I_0 thus measures the 'flexibility' of the accelerator, at least with respect to increases in sales or output. What is 'flexible' is the weight given the sales experience in any one time period in estimating the secular trend of industry sales.

26. The warranted growth rate is a concept which was introduced into macrodynamic analysis by Harrod (1948). On this point see Kregel (1971, pp. 106–10).

27. To the extent that a firm finds itself with prospects of rapid growth – and has succeeded in overcoming the managerial limitations on expansion – the proportion of profits retained by it may begin to approximate that of megacorps in general, and its own individual savings curve will, of course, bow upward. This, however, should be viewed as the marginal, rather than the typical, case within the non-oligopolistic sector, the firm itself representing a megacorp *in embryo*.

28. This is precisely the type of investment demand function assumed by Kalecki in his macrodynamic analysis. See Kalecki (1954, pp. 96–108). An important difference between Kalecki's work and this treatise therefore lies in the fact that while Kalecki posits an investment demand function of this sort for the entire business sector, this treatise assumes that it pertains at most only to the non-oligopolistic subsector. See also Steindl (1952). Although Steindl calls attention to many of the same characteristic features of oligopolistic

industries pointed out in this treatise in a similar effort to build on Kalecki's earlier work, he nonetheless winds up with the same type of investment demand function. It differs from Kalecki's only in that it uses the rate of capacity utilization instead of past profits as the independent variable; but given the strong correlation between the two, this difference is more apparent than real.

29. It should be emphasized that what is critical here is the slope of the investment demand curve relative to the slope of the savings curve - that is, the coefficient of $\overset{*}{G}$ in the function $\overset{*}{I} = f(\overset{*}{G}\text{-}G_s)$, with r and whatever other variables may be relevant held constant, relative to the coefficient of $\overset{*}{G}$ in the function $\overset{*}{S} = f(\overset{*}{G}\text{-}G_s)$, with W_p and whatever other variables such as $\bar{P}_o$ or t_y may be relevant also held constant. If the slope of the investment demand function is greater than the slope of the savings function, that sector and/or the economy as a whole will be dynamically unstable in the manner just described.

30. This may be the reason why the empirical evidence fails to disclose any greater cyclical instability of investment in the non-oligopolistic sector than in the oligopolistic sector (cf. Hastay, 1954, pp. 13-16).

31. 60 to 75 per cent of all the investment undertaken in the manufacturing sector is accounted for by the 1,000 largest manufacturing firms, the great majority of which would probably qualify as megacorps (Anderson, 1964, pp. 66-7). Looked at from a somewhat different perspective, the oligopolistic industries previously defined (see Shepherd, 1970) account for approximately 52 per cent of all investment in manufacturing. This sector, in turn, accounts for approximately 60 per cent of business fixed investment in the United States (*Statistical Abstract of the United States*, 1967, p. 497). If to manufacturing are added the communications, mining and transportation (other than railroads) sectors, areas of the American society in which megacorps also predominate, the percentage rises to approximately 93 per cent.

32. Evans (1969, ch. 6) has even gone so far as to treat expenditures on household durables as an investment decision.

33. This is the import of Evans' finding that households apparently sacrifice savings, or liquid assets, in order to maintain the desired growth in the stock of consumer durables when cyclical conditions require that a choice be made between them. (Evans, 1969, ch. 6, section 5, especially p. 171, where the long-run income elasticity of demand for consumer durables was estimated to be 1.2.)

34. Hamberg (1963). This is the basis of the 'fiscal drag' argument popularized by Heller in the early 1960s and used to justify the Federal tax cut of 1964 (see Heller, 1966, pp. 65-6, as well as below, p. 264).

35. How far up along the savings function will depend on (a) the size of the deficit created by the shift of the investment demand function in the other sector, and (b) the extent to which the deficit is offset by the disproportionate increase in the rate of growth of savings outside the oligopolistic sector. The difference between (a) and (b) will reflect the excess of savings over investment within the oligopolistic sector itself.

36. It should be noted that, for the United States from 1968 to 1970, the government's purchase of goods and services - the category in the national income accounts which is closest to what has been defined here as discretionary expenditures, that is, investment, by the government, or I_G - represented on average 23 per cent of GNP. This compares with the 11 per cent of GNP represented by business fixed investment (I_N and I_O together, with I_N probably

accounting for 60 per cent of that figure); the 13 per cent of GNP represented by residential construction and consumer durables (I_H), and the 6 per cent of GNP represented by exports (I_F).

37. To anticipate all the intersectoral effects, one would need to estimate econometrically the savings and investment demand functions for all five sectors, each based on the aggregate growth rate, $\overset{*}{G}$, as one of the independent variables. For more on this point, see below, chapter 7, note 48.

Chapter 7. Conventional policy instruments

1. The term 'potential' growth rate is taken from J. Robinson (1956, p. 405).

2. In addition to Kuhn (1959) and Reynolds (1960, pp. 199-200), see Schultze (1959, pp. 59-71, 113-21); Schlesinger (1958); Segal (1961, especially pp. 179-80); Bowen (1960).

3. See Ginzberg (1976) for an elaboration of this point. It represents a synthesis of Lewis' (1954) emphasis on the role played within underdeveloped countries by disguised unemployment in the countryside and Karl Marx's (1933, vol. 1, ch. 25, sections 3-5) emphasis on the role played in more developed economies by what he termed the industrial reserve army. This synthesis means that in Sweezy's (1942, p. 91) diagram of labor flows the entry of new workers into the industrial process must be seen as reflecting not only the natural increase of population within the industrial sector itself but also the migration from the rural areas of the world (Eichner, 1973b). It should be noted that, in the theory of manpower, what Marx termed the industrial reserve army is referred to as the peripheral work force, and it consists of those workers subject to lay-off when aggregate demand declines (cf. Morse, 1969).

4. The point is dealt with at greater length in Eichner (1973b).

5. Implicit in the argument is the supposition that wage rates behave differently in the oligopolistic and non-oligopolistic sectors, and indeed depend on quite different factors. There is also the supposition that differentials in wage rates between the two sectors vary over the cycle. For evidence supporting these propositions, see Wachter (1970).

6. Services, including governmental ones, are, of course, the important execption since, as suggested above (chapter 5, p. 175), a more refined version of the labor theory of value probably applies in their case. The construction industry may be another exception.

7. The positing of excess labor reserves in the form of a partially unemployed peripheral labor force is an essential difference between a neo-classical analysis which assumes 'full' employment and a post-Keynesian analysis such as this one which does not. On this point, see Davidson (1967).

8. What seem to be gains to the household from higher wages are often, in fact, only a sign that income within the sector has been redistributed. This is true when, for instance, the increase in real wages within the oligopolistic sector exceeds the increase in output per worker throughout the economy, but these relative gains are then balanced by a lesser increase in real wages outside the oligopolistic sector. As implied, it is the increase in output per worker, throughout the economy and not just within the oligopolistic sector, which determines the extent to which the representative household - at least one with working members - can have its economic position improved; and this points out another source of conflict over the distribution of income which can have inflationary consequences. It should be added that what is meant

here by resources being less than optimally allocated includes the situation in which the secular growth rate is above the socially optimum level as defined below in chapter 8, and thus the average corporate levy has been set too high.

9. It should be pointed out that in order to carry out this analysis in terms of only three sets of curves, those for the oligopolistic subsector, those for the government sector, and those for the economy as a whole - without taking explicit account of the curves for the non-oligopolistic, household and foreign sectors - some of the important intersectoral effects must be glossed over (see above, chapter 6, note 37).

10. The argument as to the several ways in which the savings curve for the oligopolistic sector, and thus the savings curve for the economy as a whole, can be shifted serves to meet the criticism which has been made by Marris and others of the so-called Kaldor effect - namely, that the mechanism by which the aggregate savings rate is adjusted to determine the aggregate growth rate in post-Keynesian macrodynamic models has not been adequately specified. Marris (1964, p. 309); Modigliani (1964, especially p. 41). See also Moore (1967) where an attempt is made to meet the Marris criticism in a way not too dissimilar from the argument being offered here.

11. Promulgation of the Presidential guideposts in the early 1960s and the resurrection of the guideposts most recently as part of the Nixon Administration's new economic program both represent an alternative way of establishing the national incremental wage pattern, one that seeks to avoid this particular source of difficulty.

12. Incomes policy may be regarded as a third contracyclical tool, even though its purpose is to control price levels, and not to regulate real flows.

13. This ignores, as being empirically insignificant any 'real balances' effect. Cf. Johnson (1962, pp. 27-8); Friedman (1968); Tobin (1969). See also Davidson (1972); K. Brunner (1971); Silber (1969). The Davidson book, it should be noted, provides the best treatment of money in the post-Keynesian literature - despite, or rather because of, its professed aim of correcting the relative neglect of monetary factors in that literature. Indeed, it employs the same macrodynamic framework as this treatise. In this connection, see also Minsky (1975).

14. That is, the resulting change in the cost of money (the short-term interest rate) must lead to a change in the cost of fixed-interest obligations (the long-term interest rate). This argument, it should be noted, implies a somewhat more variegated set of debt instruments - cash, bills, bonds and equities - than the original Keynesian division of monetary assets into either money or bonds (cf. J. Robinson, 1952, pp. 6-7; Johnson, 1962, pp. 11-12). Recognizing the existence of separate short- and long-term interest rates, the one equating the demand for and supply of cash and the other equating the demand for and supply of fixed-interest obligations, has a number of theoretical advantages. First, it supplies the missing fourth price relative in the original five-equation Keynesian model, thereby avoiding the need to make an implicit, and unwarranted, assumption about the degree of substitutability between two of the aggregate flows (see Leijonhufvud, 1968, ch. 3). Second, it disposes of the supposed conflict between the liquidity preference theory of the interest rate and the loanable funds theory - without invoking Walras' law. There are, in fact, two interest rates to be explained, and these two interest rates, with the monetary system constantly subject to exogenous disturbances, can be expected to change independently of one another. Cf. Johnson (1962, pp. 23-8); Hansen (1970, ch. 12); Lloyd (1969).

15. It also depends on the degree of intermediation. Cf. Tobin and Brainard (1963); Meltzer (1969, pp. 30–2).

16. The monetary authorities are, for example, most likely to take measures to lower interest rates, and thus attempt to stimulate investment, during a period of depressed overall stock prices. This, in turn, will increase the cost of raising equity capital. Which effect of depressed business conditions will be the stronger will depend, among other things, on the value of *a* in the equation in chapter 3, note 42, above. This is not to argue against a compensatory monetary policy, for clearly in its absence, the composite cost of external funds would be even higher. It is merely to reinforce the point made below, that monetary policy has to be viewed as the handmaiden of other measures.

17. In this implicit model of the monetary sector there are, then, three separate and distinct interest rates, with a change in one producing only a partial, or muted, response in another. This series of positive but diminishing linkages between the short-term interest rate and the long-term interest rate on the one hand and between the long-term interest rate and the permanent interest rate on the other hand is what enables the monetary system, under normal circumstances, to play a stabilizing role in the economy (cf. Lange, 1970, ch. 4; see also E. Edwards, 1966). While the extensive body of empirical evidence on the term structure of interest rates can be interpreted as contradicting this model of the monetary sector, the evidence is actually quite consistent with the model if one keeps in mind that what the studies show is a long-run tendency for the monetary sector to move from a disequilibrium towards an equilibrium position. The studies have, in fact, been stimulated by the need to explain the substantial differential movement of interest rates in the short run. For a similar interpretation of the evidence, see Silber (1970). See also Kane (1970).

18. See above, chapter 6, notes 8 and 9, and the works therein, especially the concluding comments of Eisner and Strotz in their survey article (1964).

19. Cf. Roosa (1951); Tucker (1968); Catt (1965); J. Cohen (1968). The point here is that the inability of firms to obtain the money they need may slow down the rate at which transactions are carried out, and this slowing down of the rate at which transactions are carried out is the same, in a time-related model, as a decrease in the rate of transactions.

20. See above, note 19 for an elaboration of this point. See also Hicks (1969, especially pp. 312–13). For evidence that even the largest firms may face credit rationing, see Federal Reserve System (1958, pp. 420–36). Of course, those firms' access, as multinational corporations, to Eurodollar and similar sources of foreign funds, mitigates this control which the Federal Reserve System is able to exercise.

21. The evidence on this point is mainly from the 1955–7 period of credit restraint. It indicates that commercial bank loans to small business increased by a smaller percentage than loans to large businesses, even though small businesses are far more dependent on bank credit to meet their financing needs (Federal Reserve System, 1958, pp. 420–39; US Congress, Joint Economic Committee, 1959, pp. 378–81). The Federal Reserve System, in its study, attributed the smaller percentage increase in commercial bank loans to small businesses to the fact that they were less able to meet traditional credit standards, necessarily made more stringent than in earlier years by the general monetary restraint. But see also Meltzer (1960); Bach and Huizenga (1961); Silber and Polakoff (1970); Christian and Mazek (1969).

22. The experience of the housing industry since 1966 confirms the validity

of previous empirical studies emphasizing the importance of credit conditions within that sector. See, for example, the studies cited in Grebler and Maisel (1964) as well as the econometric models in Rhomberg and Boissonneualt (1965); Evans and Klein (1967); Evans (1969, ch. 9, section 1); Suits (1962); Maisel (1965).

23. Conditions in the money markets during September 1966, when the Federal Reserve System sought to curtail, through monetary policy alone, what was considered to be the effects of excess demand may well have approximated this situation; and only the timely reversal of the Federal Reserve Board's policies prevented an incipient money panic from getting out of hand.

24. This is the implication of the empirical studies showing that the rate of investment is influenced little, if any, by the availability of internal funds. See above, chapter 6, p. 196. It should be noted this last point represents a generalization and extension of the conventional argument as to the lower multiplier effect of a reduction in taxes relative to an increase in government expenditures.

25. The mathematical proof is as follows:

$$T_e = \frac{\Delta P}{P} (\text{given}\, \Delta t_e) = \frac{P_1 - P_0}{P_0}$$

$$= \frac{1}{1-t_{e_1}}\left(AVC + \frac{FC+CL}{SOR \cdot ERC}\right) - \frac{1}{1-t_{e0}}\left(AVC + \frac{FC+CL}{SOR \cdot ERC}\right) \Big/ \frac{1}{1-t_{e0}}\left(AVC + \frac{FC+CL}{SOR \cdot ERC}\right)$$

The term $\left(AVC + \frac{FC+CL}{SOR \cdot ERC}\right)$ cancels out, leaving

$$\frac{1}{1-t_{e_1}} - \frac{1}{1-t_{e0}} \Big/ \frac{1}{1-t_{e0}}$$

26. While it is usually assumed that an excise or sales tax is more regressive than a personal income tax, this is a piece of conventional wisdom in need of re-examination. Clearly, it depends on the particular items covered by the excise tax, as well as the progressiveness of the personal income tax. It is therefore necessary to compare a specific excise tax with a specific income tax, a comparison which can be made quite readily with the help of budget studies from different income groups. In the case of the corporate income tax as a whole, its progressiveness will depend on the extent to which different income groups are dependent on oligopolistic industries for the items they customarily purchase, assuming that it is only oligopolistic industries which are able to shift the tax.

27. It is, of course, possible to have such a sharply graduated corporate income tax that the megacorp-price leaders of the different sizes encountered in different industries will be affected differentially. The present corporate income tax, however, which imposes its maximum rate of 48 per cent on any corporation with net income of $25,000, is not of this type.

28. This postulated lag of one or two pricing periods can be largely ignored since the full substitution effect will, as already pointed out in chapter 3, take

considerably longer to be felt. As for whether the expectation that other industries will also raise their prices will be sufficient to induce any one industry to raise its price, the experience in the post World War II period with changes in the corporate income tax has been too limited and too much influenced by larger events to say with any certainty. The assumption that the expectation is sufficiently strong is therefore, at this point, no more than a hypothesis. That is, there is no reason to believe that an oligopolistic industry will be deterred from raising its price following an increase in the corporate income tax rate by the fear that other industries will not do the same.

29. Even if the values for *Net* are 15 per cent and 5 per cent respectively, the resulting differences in the tax-price adjusters, for an increase in the corporate income tax rate from 45 per cent to 60 per cent, would be 2.42 per cent less 0.78 per cent, using the formulas developed above. In other words, the percentage increase in price in the first industry would be greater than that in the second industry by only 1.64 per cent. The values chosen in the example, it should be noted, are extreme ones.

30. See above, note 21.

31. The empirical evidence on this question is both contradictory and unreliable. See, for example, Mieszkowski (1969). Whether one finds that the corporate income tax is shifted in its entirety (Krzyzaniak and Musgrave, 1963; Kilpatrick, 1965) or that it is absorbed completely by corporations (R. J. Gordon, 1967; C. Hall, 1964) depends largely on the model employed to test the hypothesis, that is, on the variables that are statistically held constant. For a discussion of the methodological issues involved, see Slitor (1966); Goode (1966); Krzyzaniak and Musgrave (1966). See also Cragg, Harberger and Mieszkowski (1967); Krzyzaniak and Musgrave (1970); Moffat (1970).

32. While the industry price can be changed more frequently than the interval of a planning period (the planning period will normally encompass several pricing periods), the price will not be altered in one direction if it is expected that it will subsequently have to be altered in the other direction. In other words, as already argued, an oligopolistic industry will try to minimize the number of price changes.

33. Weighted in the sense that the per cent of engineer-rated capacity at which $AR = MC$ for each firm must be multiplied by its relative market share expressed as a decimal fraction. If the per cent of engineer-rated capacity being utilized is replaced by quantity produced per unit of time as the variable to be measured along the horizontal axis, the individual firms' supply curves are aggregated rather than averaged to derive the industry's short-run supply curve.

34. Except, of course, in the unlikely event that the firms in the industry were previously producing at a point of falling marginal costs and/or that the increase in demand is met entirely by either new firms entering the industry or old firms resuming operations.

35. The difference can be seen quite clearly by comparing the change in the price level for the oligopolistic sector over time with the change in the price level for the non-oligopolistic sector. This is done on p. 269, for the 1960s.

36. Some economists would cite as indirect evidence of manpower stringencies the tendency of wages to rise during periods of relatively rapid economic expansion. This 'evidence' however, is only as good as the assumption upon which the interpretation is predicated, namely, that rising wages are caused by stringencies or 'tightness' in labor markets. As chapter 5 has tried to argue,

such an assumption is by no means warranted and that in fact rising wages can be better explained in terms of a quite different dynamic.

37. The imminent recovery as the Kennedy Administration took office can be explained both by the outgoing Administration's belated moves to increase Federal spending and ease monetary conditions just prior to the election and by the stabilizing effect of the oligopolistic and government sectors described above.

38. Defense expenditures, it should be noted, grew at equivalent annual rates of only 10.4 per cent. The term 'equivalent annual rate' refers to the percentage change in any one quarter, adjusted to an annual basis by applying a compound interest factor. This adjusted figure can then be averaged over any number of periods to obtain the mean value of the equivalent annual rates over that interval. All percentage figures given below have been computed in this manner from data obtained through the National Bureau of Economic Research data bank. They have also been deflated by an appropriate price index so that the equivalent annual rates reflect real rates of growth.

39. Residential construction, after declining at equivalent annual rates of more than 12 per cent between mid-1959 and the end of 1960, grew by 3 per cent during the first six months of 1961 and then by nearly 14 per cent during the succeeding twelve-month period.

40. A belief in the importance of cost-push factors in the inflation of the 1950s was by no means shared by all the economic advisors to President Kennedy. The strongest proponents of this view were undoubtedly Otto Eckstein and Charles Schultze, both of whom had done much to develop the argument during the Eisenhower years. See Eckstein and Fromm (1959); Schultze (1959).

41. See the wholesale price index for these years as well as the *Economic Report of the President*, 1965, pp. 57-9, and 1966, pp. 66-7.

42. Heller (1966, p. 66); *Economic Report of the President*, 1963, pp. xii-xxii and ch. 3. See also Stein (1969, ch. 15-17). It should be pointed out that while the notion of 'fiscal drag' was advanced at a time of concern over the faltering growth rate, the problem was seen as a secular rather than just a cyclical one (Heller, 1966, p. 35). This is also the point made earlier in this chapter. The slowdown in the rate of economic expansion toward the end of 1962, incidentally, can be explained to some degree by the end of the military build-up that followed the Berlin crisis. The 9.3 per cent decline in defense expenditures during the second half of 1962 contributed to the slight decrease in total Federal spending and the less-than-normal increase in overall government spending at the time.

43. Consumer durable expenditures were growing at equivalent annual rates of better than 10 per cent from the end of the second quarter of 1962 through the end of the second quarter of 1963 while residential construction, after declining at an equivalent annual rate of 6.6 per cent in the fourth quarter of 1962, increased at an equivalent annual rate of nearly 8 per cent during the first half of 1963. Expenditures on new plant and equipment in manufacturing, following a decline in the winter of 1962-3, rose at equivalent annual rates of better than 18 per cent from the beginning of the second quarter of 1962 through the end of the first quarter of 1964.

44. In retail trade, for example, gross hourly earnings were increasing at average annual rates of 3.9 per cent, compared with the 3.2 per cent figure for manufacturing (*Economic Report of the President*, 1966, p. 78).

45. After having previously increased at equivalent annual rates of 15.0 per cent, corporate cash flow net of dividends decreased at an equivalent annual

rate of 4.2 per cent during the fourth quarter of 1964. And while recovering during the first quarter of 1965, it would throughout the next two years consistently fall below the rate of growth of expenditures on new plant and equipment in manufacturing.

46. The government sector's share of GNP increased from 18.5 per cent to 21.0 per cent between the second quarter of 1965 and the second quarter of 1968, while the household sector's share - including residential construction - fell from 68.3 per cent to 66.9 per cent. Investment in new plant and equipment, which had accounted for 10.6 per cent of GNP in the second quarter of 1965, still accounted for about the same proportion in the second quarter of 1968 - though this was slightly higher than the 9.1 per cent of GNP which it represented in the second quarter of 1962. These changes, though slight, are nonetheless significant.

47. *Economic Report of the President*, 1970, p. 54. For the basis upon which the price level in the oligopolistic sector has been distinguished from that of the non-oligopolistic sector, see Eichner (1973a).

48. Cf. Bowen (1960); Eckstein (1964); Schultze (1959); Ferguson (1962); Goodwin (1952). It would, of course, be even more convincing if the above point could be demonstrated by means of an econometric model based on statistically derived savings and investment functions for each of the five sectors. This however, remains a future project - one which, hopefully, would provide the final empirical confirmation of the theories outlined above, both micro and macro. It should be added that, while the same lesson can be drawn from the experience of the United States since 1971, the successive devaluations of the dollar since that date have been an important complicating factor, causing a substantial rise in the price of commodities which has greatly overshadowed the rise in the price level of the oligopolistic sector.

Chapter 8. Toward social control

1. Cf. Bonbright (1961, ch. 20); Kahn (1970, I, chs. 3-5), and the sources cited in the footnotes of these two works.

2. This is perhaps the most fundamental point which emerges from any post-Keynesian macrodynamic analysis. See J. Robinson (1956, 1962); Kaldor (1956); Eichner and Kregel (1975).

3. There are, of course, other reasons for questioning the efficacy of the capital funds market as an allocator of savings, all of which reasons reflect various types of imperfections in the market. The two most important of these imperfections are the differential access which some firms have to the market (see above, chapter 3, note 23, and chapter 7, note 21) and the difficulty of equalizing the social rate of return among private and public investment projects. On the latter point, see Prest and Turvey (1966); Eckstein (1961); Baumol (1968).

4. An instrumental variable is one which is subject to direct control by public authorities. A target variable is one that reflects a goal of society. (Tinbergen, 1952).

5. *New York Times*, 8 October 1971, and 12 January 1973.

6. While the experience with indicative planning in Western Europe has not been without its difficulties, it has been far more successful than is realized in the United States. For a critical evaluation of that experience, see Shonfield (1965); MacLennon, Forsyth and Denton (1968). Though Lutz (1969) takes a less sanguine view of that experience, her point is primarily a theoretical one

- that merely announcing projections beforehand cannot make them come true, and that indeed the market mechanism provides a more effective means of correcting faulty projections than does a system of indicative planning. What is important, however, is not whether the projected rates of growth in individual industries are realized but rather, whether the economy as a whole achieves higher rates of growth, together with other desired objectives, than would otherwise be possible. For a discussion of indicative planning in the American context, in what is an elaboration of the present argument, see Eichner (1973c).

7. D. Robinson (1968, ch. 2); Parish and Hennessy (1964, pp. 21-3, 66); Brown (1962).

8. This is based on the fact that, during the first half of the 1960s, when less emphasis was being placed on monetary policy and the economy was on a relatively stable growth path, most manufacturing corporations were able to dispense entirely with external financing (Bosworth, 1971).

9. This comparison is based both on the change in the consumer price index between 1945 and 1965, and on the change in the index for dividends per share of Moody's 125 industrials over the same interval.

10. Cf. Taylor and Weiserbs (1972). In presenting evidence that the aggregate consumption function can be shifted through advertising, evidence they admit can hardly be taken as conclusive because of the limitations inherent in the test designed by them, Taylor and Weiserbs (1972, p. 642) note the absence of any previous empirical studies on the question. See also Doyle (1968, pp. 577-8, 583). Taylor and Weiserbs view their study as a direct test of the Galbraith argument (1967, especially pp. 272-3) that large corporations can, through advertising, control the level of aggregate demand. It should be noted that skepticism on this point is the one substantive difference between the arguments made by Galbraith and those found in this treatise. On this point, see the exchange between Galbraith, Robert Solow and Robin Marris in the fall 1967 and spring 1968 issues of *The Public interest*.

11. Cf. Kaldor (1950-1). Backman's apologia (1967) for advertising fails to deal adequately with Kaldor's arguments. Telser's response (1966b) is somewhat more to the point but nonetheless suffers from the unrealistic nature of the assumptions underlying his argument - in particular, the high informational content he assigns advertising messages.

12. Cf. Usher (1964); Scherer (1967); Comanor (1967, pp. 652-7); Mueller and Tilton (1969); F. Fisher, Griliches and Kaysen (1962); Menge (1962).

References

Abramowitz, Moses. 1938. 'Monopolistic Selling in a Changing Economy', *Quarterly Journal of Economics* **52,** 191-214.

Ackerman, Frank, Birnbaum, Howard, Wetzler, James and Zimbalist, Andrew. 1971. 'Income Distribution in the United States', *Review of Radical Political Economics* **3,** 20-43.

Adams, Walter. 1961. *The Structure of American Industry.* 3rd ed., New York: Macmillan.

Adelman, Morris A. 1961. 'Steel, Administered Prices and Inflation', *Quarterly Journal of Economics* **75,** 16-40.

Alchian, Armen A., and Allen, William R. 1964. *University Economics.* Belmont, California: Wadsworth.

Alchian, Armen A., and Kessel, Reuben A. 1962. 'Competition, Monopoly and the Pursuit of Pecuniary Gain', in National Bureau of Economic Research, *Aspects of Labor Economics.* Princeton, NJ: Princeton University Press.

Alemson, M. A. 1969. 'Demand, Entry, and the Game of Conflict in Oligopoly Over Time: Recent Australian Experience', *Oxford Economic Papers* **21,** 220-47.

American Economic Association. 1958. *Readings in Industrial Organization and Public Policy.* Chicago: Irwin.

American Economic Association and Royal Economic Society. 1966-7. *Surveys of Economic Theory.* 3 vols. New York: St Martin's Press.

Anderson, W. Locke. 1964. *Corporate Finance and Fixed Investment: An Econometric Study.* Boston: Graduate School of Business Administration, Harvard University.

Ando, Albert, Brown, E. Cary, and Adams, Earl W. Jr. 1965. 'Government Revenues and Expenditures', in Duesenberry *et al.*, 1965.

Andrews, P. W. S. 1949. *Manufacturing Business.* London: Macmillan.

Andrew, P. W. S. 1964. *On Competition in Economic Theory.* London: Macmillan.

Ansoff, H. Igor. 1965. *Corporate Strategy, An Analytical Approach to Business Policy for Growth and Expansion.* New York: McGraw-Hill.

Asch, Peter. 1970. *Economic Theory and the Antitrust Dilemma.* New York: Wiley.

Asch, Peter, and Marcus, Matityahu. 1970. 'Returns to Scale in Advertising', *Antitrust Bulletin* **15,** 33-42.

Asimakopulos, A. 1974. 'A Kaleckian Theory of Income Distribution', *Canadian Journal of Economics* **8,** 313-33.

Aukrust, Odd. 1970. *PRIM I, A Model of the Price and Income Distribution Mechanism of an Open Economy.* Oslo: Norwegian Central Bureau of Statistics, reprint no. 35. Reprinted with some new material added, from *Review of Income and Wealth* **16,** 51-78.

Averch, Harvey, and Johnson, Leland. 1962. 'Behavior of the Firm Under Regulatory Restraint', *American Economic Review* **52,** 1052-69.

Averitt, Robert T. 1968. *The Dual Economy: The Dynamics of American Industry Structure.* New York: Norton.

Bach, George L., and Huizenga, C. J. 1961. 'The Differential Effects of Tight

Money', *American Economic Review* **51,** 52-80.
Backman, Jules. 1967. *Advertising and Competition.* New York: New York University Press.
Bailey, Martin J. 1958. 'Administered Prices in the American Economy', in US Congress, Joint Economic Committee, *The Relationship of Prices to Economic Stability and Growth: A Compendium of Papers Submitted by Panelists Appearing Before the Joint Economic Committee, March 13, 1958,* 85th Congress, 2nd Session. Washington: Government Printing Office.
Bain, Joe S. 1956. *Barriers to New Competition.* Cambridge, Mass.: Harvard University Press.
Bain, Joe S. 1958. 'A Note on Pricing in Monopoly and Oligopoly', *American Economic Review* **29,** 448-64, reprinted in American Economic Association, 1958.
Baker, Samuel H. 1969. 'Executive Incomes, Profits, and Revenues: A Comment on Functional Specification', *Southern Economic Journal* **35,** 379-83.
Ball, Robert J. 1965. *Inflation and the Theory of Money.* Chicago: Aldine Press.
Barber, Richard J. 1970. *The American Corporation: Its Power, Its Money, Its Politics.* New York: Dutton.
Baumol, William J. 1958. 'On the Theory of Oligopoly', *Economica* **25,** 187-98.
Baumol, William J. 1959. *Business Behavior, Value and Growth.* London: Macmillan.
Baumol, William J. 1962. 'On the Theory of the Expansion of the Firm', *American Economic Review* **52,** 1078-87.
Baumol, William J. 1967. *Business Behavior, Value and Growth.* Revised edition, New York: Harcourt, Brace and World.
Baumol, William J. 1968. 'On the Social Rate of Discount', *American Economic Review* **58,** 788-802.
Baumol, William J., Hein, Peggy, Malkiel, Burton G., and Quandt, Richard E. 1970. 'Earnings Retention, New Capital and the Growth of the Firm', *Review of Economics and Statistics* **52,** 345-55.
Baumol, William J., and Malkiel, Burton G. 1967. 'The Firm's Optimal Debt-Equity Combination and the Cost of Capital', *Quarterly Journal of Economics* **81,** 547-78.
Baumol, William J., and Quandt, Richard E. 1964. 'Rules of Thumb and Optimally Imperfect Decisions', *American Economic Review* **54,** 23-46.
Baxter, Nevins D., and Cragg, John G. 1970. 'Corporate Choice Among Long-Term Financing Instruments', *Review of Economics and Statistics* **52,** 225-35.
Beckman, Martin J. 1960. 'Some Aspects of Returns to Scale in Business Administration', *Quarterly Journal of Economics* **74,** 464-71.
Berle, Adolf A. 1959. *Power Without Property: A New Development in American Political Economy.* New York: Harcourt, Brace and World.
Berle, Adolf A., and Means, Gardiner C. 1933. *The Modern Corporation and Private Property.* New York: Macmillan.
Bernstein, Marver H. 1955. *Regulating Business by Independent Commission.* Princeton, NJ: Princeton University Press.
Bhagwati, Jagdish N. 1970. 'Oligopoly Theory, Entry-prevention, and Growth', *Oxford Economic Papers* **22,** 297-310.
Bhatia, Kul B. 1970. 'Accrued Capital Gains, Personal Income and Saving in the United States, 1948-64', *Review of Income and Wealth* **16,** 363-78.
Bierman, Harold Jr., and West, Richard. 1966. 'The Acquisition of Common

Stock by the Corporate Issuer', *Journal of Finance* **21,** 687-96.

Blair, John. 1955. 'Economic Concentration and Depression Price Stability', *American Economic Review* **45,** 566-82.

Blaug, M. 1963. 'A Survey of the Theory of Process-Innovations', *Economica* **30,** 13-32.

Bohm-Bawerk, Eugene von. 1949. *Karl Marx and the Close of His System.* New York: Augustus Kelley.

Bonbright, James C. 1961. *Principles of Public Utility Rates.* New York: Columbia University Press.

Bonner, J., and Lees, D. S. 1963. 'Consumption and Investment', *Journal of Political Economy* **71,** 64-75.

Bosworth, Barry. 1971. 'Patterns of Corporate External Financing', *Brookings Papers on Economic Activity* **1,** 253-84.

Boulding, Kenneth. 1950. *A Reconstruction of Economics.* New York: Wiley.

Bowen, William G. 1960. *The Wage Price Issue; A Theoretical Analysis.* Princeton, NJ: Princeton University Press.

Boyle, Stanley E., and McKenna, Joseph P. 1970. 'Size Mobility of the 100 and 200 Largest U.S. Manufacturing Corporations, 1919-1964', *Antitrust Bulletin* **15,** 505-20.

Boyle, Stanley E., and Sorenson, Robert L. 1971. 'Concentration and Mobility: Alternative Measures of Industry Structure', *Journal of Industrial Economics* **19,** 118-32.

Brittain, John A. 1966. *Corporate Dividend Policy.* Washington: Brookings Institution.

Brody, Andrew. 1966. 'A Simplified Growth Model', *Quarterly Journal of Economics* **80,** 137-46.

Bronfenbrenner, Martin. 1960. 'A Reformulation of Naive Profit Theory', *Southern Economic Journal* **26,** 301-9.

Bronfenbrenner, Martin. 1971. *Income Distribution Theory.* Chicago: Aldine.

Bronfenbrenner, Martin, and Holzman, Franklyn D. 1963. 'A Survey of Inflation Theory', *American Economic Review* **53,** 593-661, reprinted in American Economic Association and Royal Economic Society, 1966-67, vol. I, 46-107.

Brown, E. H. Phelps. 1962. 'Wage Drift', *Economica* **29,** 339-56.

Brunner, Elizabeth. 1952. 'Competition and the Theory of the Firm (Part II)', *Economia Internaxionale* **4,** 727-47.

Brunner, Karl. 1971. '"Yale" and Money', *Journal of Finance* **26,** 165-74.

Buchanan, Norman S. 1940. *The Economics of Corporate Enterprise.* New York: Holt.

Burkart, A. J. 1969. 'Some Managerial Influences on a Firm's Pricing Policy', *Journal of Industrial Economics* **17,** 180-7.

Cartter, Allan M. 1959. *Theory of Wages and Employment.* Chicago: Irwin.

Cassady, Ralph Jr. 1963. *Price Warfare in Business Competition: A Study of Abnormal Competitive Behavior.* Occasional Paper no. 11, Lansing, Mich.: Bureau of Business and Economic Research, Graduate School of Business Administration, Michigan State University.

Catt, A. J. L. 1965. '"Credit Rationing" and the Keynesian Model', *Economic Journal* **75,** 358-72.

Caves, Richard E. 1962. *Air Transport and Its Regulators.* Cambridge, Mass.: Harvard University Press.

Chamberlain, Neil. 1962. *The Firm: Micro-Economic Planning and Action.* New York: McGraw-Hill.

Chamberlin, Edward H. 1962. *The Theory of Monopolistic Competition; A Reorientation of the Theory of Value.* 8th ed., Cambridge, Mass.: Harvard University Press (1st ed., 1933).

Chandler, Alfred D. Jr. 1962. *Strategy and Structure: Chapters in the History of Industrial Enterprise.* Cambridge, Mass.: MIT Press.

Chandler, Alfred D. Jr. 1969. 'The Structure of American Industry in the Twentieth Century: A Historical Overview', *Business History Review* **43,** 255-98.

Chenery, Hollis B. 1952. 'Overcapacity and the Acceleration Principle', *Econometrica* **20,** 1-28.

Chevalier, Jean-Marie. 1969. 'The Problems of Control in Large American Corporations', *Antitrust Bulletin* **14,** 163-80.

Christian, James W., and Mazek, Warren F. 1969. 'Corporate Debt Structure and the Differential Effects of Monetary Policy', *Southern Economic Journal* **35,** 359-68.

Clark, James M. 1961. *Competition as a Dynamic Process.* Washington: Brookings Institution.

Clemens, Eli W. 1951-2. 'Price Discrimination and the Many Product Firm', *Review of Economic Studies* **9,** 1-11.

Coddington, Alan. 1968. *Theories of the Bargaining Process.* Chicago: Aldine.

Cohan, Avery B. 1962. 'On the Inequality of the Rate of Profit and the Rate of Interest: Comment', *Southern Economic Journal* **28,** 387-99.

Cohen, Jacob. 1968. 'Integrating the Real and Financial via the Linkage of Financial Flow', *Journal of Finance* **23,** 1-28.

Cohen, Jacob. 1972. 'Copeland's Moneyflows After Twenty-Five Years: A Survey', *Journal of Economic Literature* **10,** 1-26.

Comanor, William S. 1967. 'Market Structure, Product Differentiation and Industrial Research', *Quarterly Journal of Economics* **81,** 639-57.

Cooper, William W. 1949. 'The Theory of the Firm: Some Suggestions for Revision', *American Economic Review* **39,** 1204-22.

'Cost and Availability of Credit and Capital to Small Business', 1952. Staff Report to the Board of Governors of the Federal Reserve System, Submitted to the Subcommittee on Small Business, October 30, 1952, Subcommittee Print no. 8, 82nd Congress, 2nd Session.

Creamer, Daniel B. 1964. 'Estimates of Capacity and Capacity Utilization in Manufacturing: A Description and Appraisal', in Commission on Money and Credit, *Inflation, Growth and Employment.* Englewood Cliffs, NJ: Prentice-Hall, 289-343.

Cragg, John G., Harberger, Arnold C., and Mieszkowski, Peter. 1967. 'Empirical Evidence on the Incidence of the Corporation Income Tax', *Journal of Political Economy* **75,** 811-21.

Crosland, Charles A. 1956. *The Future of Socialism.* London: Jonathan Cape.

Cyert, Richard M., and DeGroot, Morris H. 1971. 'Interfirm Learning and the Kinked Demand Curve,' *Journal of Economic Theory* **3,** 272-87.

Cyert, Richard M., and March, James G. 1956. 'Organizational Factors in the Theory of Oligopoly', *Quarterly Journal of Economics* **70,** 44-64.

Cyert, Richard M., and March, James G. 1963. *A Behavioral Theory of the Firm.* Englewood Cliffs, NJ: Prentice-Hall.

Davidson, Paul. 1960. *Theories of Income Distribution.* New Brunswick, NJ: Rutgers University Press.

Davidson, Paul. 1967. 'A Keynesian View of Patinkin's Theory of Employment', *Economic Journal* **77,** pp. 559-78.

Davidson, Paul. 1972. *Money and the Real World.* London: Macmillan.

Day, Richard H. 1967. 'Profits, Learning and the Convergence of Satisficing to Marginalism', *Quarterly Journal of Economics* **81,** 302-11.

Day, Richard H., and Tinney, E. Herbert. 1968. 'How to Cooperate in Business Without Really Trying: A Learning Model of Decentralized Decision Making', *Journal of Political Economy* **76,** 583-600.

Denison, Edward F. 1962. *The Sources of Economic Growth in the United States and the Alternatives Before Us.* New York: Committee for Economic Development.

Denison, Edward F. 1964. 'Comment: A Survey of Some Theories of Income Distribution', National Bureau of Economic Research, 1964.

DeVroey, Michel R. Unpublished. 'The Measurement of the Separation of Ownership and Control in Larger Corporations: A Critical Review'.

Dewey, Donald. 1959. *Monopoly in Economics and Law.* Chicago: Rand McNally.

Dewey, Donald. 1965. 'Competitive Policy and National Goals: The Doubtful Relevance of Antitrust,' in *Perspectives on Antitrust Policy,* Almarin Phillips, ed., Princeton, NJ: Princeton University Press, 62-87.

Dewey, Donald. 1969. *The Theory of Imperfect Competition: A Radical Reconstruction.* New York: Columbia University Press.

Downie, Jack. 1958. *The Competitive Process.* London: Gerald Duckworth.

Doyle, Peter B. 1968. 'Economic Aspects of Advertising: A Survey', *Economic Journal* **76,** 823-60.

Duesenberry, James S. 1958. *Business Cycles and Economic Growth.* New York: McGraw-Hill.

Duesenberry, James S. *et al.*, eds. 1965. *The Brookings Quarterly Econometric Model of the United States.* Chicago: Rand McNally.

Dunlop, John T. 1950. *Wage Determination Under Trade Unions.* New York: Augustus Kelley.

Dunlop, John T. 1957. 'The Task of Contemporary Wage Theory', in *The Theory of Wage Determination,* John T. Dunlop, ed., Proceedings of a Conference held by the International Economic Association. London: Macmillan.

Dunlop, John T. 1958. *Industrial Relations Systems.* New York: Holt and Rinehart.

Durand, David. 1959. 'The Cost of Capital, Corporation Finance, and the Theory of Investment: Comment', *American Economic Review* **49,** 639-55.

Dye, Howard S. 1967. 'A Bargaining Theory of Residual Income Distribution', *Industrial and Labor Relations Review* **21,** 40-54.

Earley, James S. 1956. 'Marginal Policies of "Excellently Managed" Companies', *American Economic Review* **46,** 44-70.

Earley, James S., and Carleton, Willard T. 1962. 'Budgeting and the Theory of the Firm: New Findings', *Journal of Industrial Economics* **10,** 165-73.

Eatwell, John. 1971. 'Growth, Profitability and Size: The Empirical Evidence', in Marris and Wood, eds., 1971, Appendix A, pp. 389-421.

Eckstein, Otto. 1961. 'A Survey of the Theory of Public Expenditure Criteria', in National Bureau of Economic Research, *Public Finances: Needs, Sources and Utilization.* Princeton, NJ: Princeton University Press.

Eckstein, Otto. 1964. 'A Theory of the Wage-Price Process in Modern Industry', *Review of Economic Studies* **31,** 267-86.

Eckstein, Otto. 1967. 'The Determination of Money Wages in American Industry: Reply', *Quarterly Journal of Economics* **81,** 690-4.

Eckstein, Otto. 1968. 'Money Wage Determination Revisited', *Review of Economic Studies* **35,** 133-44.

Eckstein, Otto, and Fromm, Gary. 1959. 'Steel and the Postwar Inflation', in US Congress, Joint Economic Committee, *Employment, Growth and Price*

Levels, Study Paper no. 1, Washington: Government Printing Office.
Eckstein, Otto, and Fromm, Gary. 1968. 'The Price Equation', *American Economic Review* **58,** 1159-83.
Eckstein, Otto, and Wilson, Thomas S. 1962. 'Determination of Money Wages in American Industry', *Quarterly Journal of Economics* **76,** 379-414.
Edwards, Edward O. 1961. 'An Indifference Approach to the Theory of the Firm', *Southern Economic Journal* **28,** 123-9.
Edwards, Edward O. 1966. 'The Interest Rate in Disequilibrium', *Southern Economic Journal* **33,** 49-57.
Edwards, H. R. 1955. 'Price Formation in Manufacturing Industry and Excess Capacity', *Oxford Economic Papers* **7,** 94-118.
Eichner, Alfred S. 1962. 'Trial by Myth', *Second Coming* **1,** 46-50.
Eichner, Alfred S. 1969. *The Emergence of Oligopoly: Sugar Refining as a Case Study*. Baltimore: Johns Hopkins Press.
Eichner, Alfred S. 1973a. 'A Theory of the Determination of the Mark-up under Oligopoly', *Economic Journal* **83,** 1184-2000.
Eichner, Alfred S. 1973b. 'Human Resource Planning', in *New York Is Very Much Alive - A Manpower View,* Eli Ginzberg, ed. New York: McGraw-Hill, pp. 247-69.
Eichner, Alfred S. 1973c. 'Manpower Planning and Economic Planning: The Two Prerequisites', in *The Localization of Federal Manpower Planning,* Robert L. Aronson, ed. Ithaca, NY: New York School of Industrial and Labor Relations, pp. 65-80.
Eichner, Alfred S. 1974. 'Price Policies of Oligopolistic Companies: The Larger Dynamic', Regional Trade Union Seminar on Prices Policy, *Final Report*. Paris: Organization for Economic Cooperation and Development, 78-92.
Eichner, Alfred S. 1975. 'The Geometry of Macrodynamic Balance', unpublished paper.
Eichner, Alfred S. 1976. 'A Generalized Pricing Model', in *Growth, Profit and Property, Essays in the Revival of Political Economy*, Edward J. Nell, ed. Cambridge: Cambridge University Press.
Eichner, Alfred S., and Kregel, J. A. 1975. 'An Essay on Post-Keynesian Theory: A New Paradigm in Economics', *Journal of Economic Literature* **13,** 1293-1314.
Eisner, Robert. 1960. 'A Distributed Lag Investment Function', *Econometrica* **28,** 1-29.
Eisner, Robert. 1963. 'Investment: Fact and Fancy', *American Economic Review* **53,** 237-46.
Eisner, Robert. 1967. 'A Permanent Income Theory for Investment - Some Empirical Explorations,' *American Economic Review* **57,** 363-91.
Eisner, Robert, and Strotz, Robert. 1964. 'Determinants of Business Investment', in Commission on Money and Credit, *Impacts of Monetary Policy*. Englewood Cliffs, NJ: Prentice-Hall.
Eldridge, Clarence E. 1958. 'Advertising Effectiveness - How Can It Be Measured?', *Journal of Marketing* **22,** 241-51.
Elton, Edwin J., and Gruber, Martin J. 1968. 'The Effect of Share Repurchases on the Value of the Firm', *Journal of Finance* **23,** 135-50.
Encarnacion, Jose Jr. 1964. 'Constraints and the Firm's Utility Function', *Review of Economic Studies* **31,** 115-20.
Enzler, Jared. 1967. 'Revised Indexes of Manufacturing Capacity and Capacity Utilization', *Federal Reserve Bulletin* **53,** 1096-7.
Evans, Michael K. 1967. 'A Study of Industry Investment Decisions', *Review*

of Economics and Statistics **49,** 151-64.

Evans, Michael K. 1969. *Macroeconomic Activity: Theory, Forecasting and Control, An Econometric Approach.* New York: Harper and Row.

Evans, Michael K., and Klein, Lawrence R. 1967. *The Wharton Econometric Forecasting Model.* Philadelphia: Economic Research Unit, Department of Economics, Wharton School of Finance and Commerce, University of Pennsylvania.

Fair, Ray C. 1971. 'Sales Expectations and Short Run Product Decisions', *Southern Economic Journal* **37,** 267-75.

Federal Reserve Bank of Boston. 1969. *Controlling Monetary Aggregates: Proceedings of the Monetary Conference Held at Nantucket Island, June 8-10.* Boston: Federal Reserve Bank of Boston.

Federal Reserve System. 1958. *Financing Small Business,* Report to the Committees on Banking and Currency and the Select Committees on Small Business, US Congress. Washington: Government Printing Office.

Fellner, William J. 1949. *Competition Among the Few: Oligopoly and Similar Market Structures.* New York: Knopf.

Ferber, Robert. 1962. 'Research on Household Behavior', *American Economic Review* **52,** 19-63, reprinted in American Economic Association and Royal Economic Society, 1966-7, vol. III, pp. 114-54.

Ferguson, Charles E. 1962. 'Inflation, Fluctuations, and Growth in a Dynamic Input-Output Model', *Southern Economic Journal* **28,** 251-64.

Ferguson, Charles E. 1965. 'The Theory of Multi-Dimensional Utility Analysis in Relation to Multiple-Goal Business Behavior: A Synthesis', *Southern Economic Journal* **32,** 169-75.

Ferguson, Charles E. 1969. *The Neoclassical Theory of Production and Distribution.* Cambridge: Cambridge University Press.

Ferguson, Charles E., and Nell, Edward J. 1972. 'Two Review Articles on Two Books on the Theory of Income Distribution', *Journal of Economic Literature* **10,** 437-53.

Finkel, Sidney R., and Tarascio, Vincent J. 1969. 'A Theoretical Integration of Production and Wage Theory', *Western Economic Journal* **7,** 371-8.

Firestone, Frederic N. 1960. *Marginal Aspects of Management Practices.* East Lansing, Mich.: Michigan State University Press.

Fisher, Franklin M. 1960. 'Review: Business Behavior, Value and Growth by William J. Baumol', *Journal of Political Economy* **68,** 314-15.

Fisher, Franklin M. 1965. 'On the Goals of the Firm: Comment', *Quarterly Journal of Economics* **79,** 500-3.

Fisher, Franklin M., Griliches, Zvi, and Kaysen, Carl. 1962. 'The Costs of Automobile Model Changes Since 1949', *Journal of Political Economy* **70,** 433-51.

Fisher, Franklin M., and Kaysen, Carl. 1962. *A Study in Econometrics: The Demand for Electricity in the United States.* Amsterdam: North-Holland.

Fisher, Malcolm. 1961. 'Towards a Theory of Diversification', *Oxford Economic Papers* **13,** 293-311.

Forrester, Jay. 1971. *World Dynamics.* Cambridge, Mass.: Wright-Allen Press.

Friedman, Milton. 1956. 'The Quantity Theory of Money – A Restatement', in *Studies in the Quantity Theory of Money,* Milton Friedman, ed. Chicago: University of Chicago Press.

Friedman, Milton. 1957. *A Theory of the Consumption Function.* Princeton, NJ: Princeton University Press.

Friedman, Milton. 1962. *Price Theory, A Provisional Text.* Chicago: Aldine.

Friedman, Milton. 1968. 'Money: Quantity Theory', *International Encyclopedia of the Social Sciences*, 2nd ed. New York: Crowell Collier and Macmillan. Vol. 10.

Friedman, Milton. 1970. 'A Theoretical Framework for Monetary Analysis', *Journal of Political Economy* **78,** 193-238.

Friend, Irwin, and Puckett, Marshall. 1964. 'Dividends and Stock Prices', *American Economic Review* **54,** 656-82.

Fromm, Gary, and Klein, Lawrence R. 1965. 'The Complete Model: A First Approximation', in Duesenberry *et al.*, eds., 1965.

Fukuoka, Masao. 1955. 'Full Employment and Constant Coefficients of Production', *Quarterly Journal of Economics* **69,** 23-45.

Fuchs, Victor R. 1961. 'Integration, Competition and Profits in Manufacturing Industries', *Quarterly Journal of Economics* **75,** 278-91.

Galbraith, John Kenneth. 1952. *American Capitalism: The Concept of Countervailing Power.* Boston: Houghton Mifflin.

Galbraith, John Kenneth. 1957. 'Market Structure and Stabilization Policy', *Review of Economics and Statistics* **39,** 124-33.

Galbraith, John Kenneth. 1967a. *The New Industrial State.* Boston: Houghton Mifflin.

Galbraith, John Kenneth. 1967b. 'The New Industrial State', *Antitrust Law and Economics* **1,** 11-20.

Gambs, John S. 1946. *Beyond Supply and Demand: A Reappraisal of Institutional Economics.* New York: Columbia University Press.

Gaskins, Darius W., Jr. 1971. 'Dynamic Limit Pricing: Optimal Pricing under Threat of Entry, *Journal of Economic Theory* **3,** 306-22.

Georgescu-Roegen, Nicholas. 1935. 'Fixed Coefficients of Production and the Marginal Productivity Theory', *Review of Economic Studies* **3,** 40-9, reprinted in Georgescu-Roegen, 1966.

Georgescu-Roegen, Nicholas. 1966. *Analytical Economics, Issues and Problems.* Cambridge, Mass.: Harvard University Press.

Georgescu-Roegen, Nicholas. 1971. *The Entropy Law and the Economic Process.* Cambridge, Mass.: Harvard University Press.

Gift, Richard E. 1968. *Estimating Economic Capacity, A Summary of Conceptual Problems.* Lexington, Ky: University of Kentucky Press.

Ginzberg, Eli. ed. 1964. *Technology and Social Change.* New York: Columbia University Press.

Ginzberg, Eli. 1976. *The Human Economy, A Theory of Manpower Development and Utilization.* New York: McGraw-Hill.

Gold, Bela. 1966. 'New Perspectives on Cost Theory and Empirical Findings', *Journal of Industrial Economics* **14,** 164-89.

Goode, Richard. 1966. 'Rates of Return, Income Shares and Corporate Tax Incidence', in Krzyzaniak, 1966, pp. 209-46.

Goodwin, Richard M. 1952. 'A Note on the Theory of the Inflationary Process', *Economia Internazionale* **5,** 1-22.

Gordon, Myron J. 1953. 'The Payoff Period and the Rate of Profit', *Journal of Business* **28,** 253-60, reprinted in Solomon, 1959.

Gordon, Myron J. 1959. 'Dividends, Earnings and Stock Prices', *Review of Economics and Statistics* **41,** 99-105.

Gordon, Robert A. 1945. *Business Leadership in the Large Corporation.* Washington: Brookings Institution.

Gordon, Robert J. 1967. 'The Incidence of the Corporation Income Tax in

U.S. Manufacturing, 1925-62', *American Economic Review* **57,** 731-58.

Gort, Michael. 1962. *Diversification and Integration in American Industry.* Princeton, NJ: Princeton University Press.

Gort, Michael. 1963. 'Analysis of Stability and Change in Market Shares', *Journal of Political Economy* **71,** 51-63.

Gort, Michael. 1966. 'Diversification, Mergers and Profits', in *The Corporate Merger,* William W. Albert and Joel E. Segall, eds. Chicago: University of Chicago Press.

Gort, Michael, and Hogarty, Thomas F. 1970. 'New Evidence on Mergers', *Journal of Law and Economics* **13,** 167-84.

Grebler, Leo, and Maisel, Sherman J. 1964. 'Determinants of Residential Construction: A Review of Present Knowledge', in Commission on Money and Credit, *Impacts of Monetary Policy.* Englewood Cliffs, NJ: Prentice-Hall.

Gruchy, Allan G. 1947. *Modern Economic Thought; The American Contribution.* New York: Prentice-Hall.

Gustafson, W. Eric. 1962. 'Research and Development, New Products, and Productivity Change', *American Economic Review* **52,** 177-85.

Hague, Douglas C. 1949-50. 'Economic Theory and Business Behavior', *Review of Economic Studies* **16,** 144-57.

Hahn, Frank H., and Matthews, Robert C. O. 1964. 'The Theory of Economic Growth: A Survey', *Economic Journal* **74,** 779-902, reprinted in American Economic Association and Royal Economic Society, 1966-7, vol. II, 1-124.

Hall, Challis A. Jr. 1964. 'Direct Shifting of the Corporation Tax in Manufacturing', *American Economic Review* **54,** 258-71.

Hall, Marshall. 1967. 'Sales Revenue Maximization: An Empirical Examination', *Journal of Industrial Economics* **15,** 143-56.

Hall, Marshall, and Weiss, Leonard. 1967. 'Firm Size and Profitability', *Review of Economics and Statistics* **49,** 319-31.

Hall, Robert L., and Hitch, Charles J. 1939. 'Price Theory and Business Behaviour', *Oxford Economic Papers* **2,** 12-45, reprinted in Wilson and Andrews, 1951.

Hamberg, Daniel. 1963. 'Fiscal Policy and Stagnation since 1957', *Southern Economic Journal* **29,** 211-17.

Hamermesh, Daniel S. 1970. 'Wage Bargains, Threshold Effects and the Phillips Curve', *Quarterly Journal of Economics* **84,** 501-17.

Hansen, Bent, 1970. *A Survey of General Equilibrium Systems.* New York: McGraw-Hill.

Harcourt, Geoffrey C. 1969. 'Some Cambridge Controversies in the Theory of Capital', *Journal of Economic Literature* **7,** 369-405.

Harcourt, Geoffrey C. 1972. *Some Cambridge Controversies in the Theory of Capital.* Cambridge: Cambridge University Press.

Harris, Donald J. 1974. 'The Price Policy of Firms, the Level of Employment and Distribution of Income in the Short Run', *Australian Economic Papers* **13,** 144-51.

Harrod, Roy F. 1948: *Towards a Dynamic Economics: Some Recent Developments of Economic Theory and Their Application to Policy.* London: Macmillan.

Harrod, Roy F. 1952. *Economic Essays.* London: Macmillan.

Hastay, Milard. 1954. 'The Cyclical Behavior of Investment', in Universities - National Bureau for Economic Research, *Regularization of Business Investment,* Proceedings of a Conference. Princeton, NJ: Princeton University Press, pp. 3-30.

Haveman, Robert, and De Bartolo, Gilbert. 1968. 'The Revenue Maximization Oligopoly Model: Comment', *American Economic Review* **58,** 1355-8.

Havrilsky, Thomas, and Barth, Richard. 1969. 'Tests of Market Share Stability in the Cigarette Industry, 1955-1960', *Journal of Industrial Economics* **17,** 145-50.

Haynes, W. Warren. 1964. 'Pricing Practices in Small Firms', *Southern Economic Journal* **30,** 315-24.

Heflebower, Richard B. 1954. 'Toward a Theory of Industrial Markets and Prices', *American Economic Review* **44,** 121-39.

Heller, Walter W. 1966. *New Dimensions of Political Economy*. Cambridge, Mass.: Harvard University Press.

Henderson, Alexander M. 1954. 'The Theory of Duopoly', *Quarterly Journal of Economics* **68,** 565-84.

Herling, John. 1962. *The Great Price Conspiracy; The Story of the Antitrust Violations in the Electrical Industry*. New York: R. B. Luce.

Hicks, John R. 1954. 'The Process of Imperfect Competition', *Oxford Economic Papers* **6,** 41-54.

Hicks, John R. 1969. 'Automatists, Hawtreyans, and Keynesians', *Journal of Money, Credit and Banking* **1,** 307-19.

Higgins, Benjamin H. 1939. 'Elements of Indeterminancy in the Theory of Non-Perfect Competition', *American Economic Review* **29,** 468-79.

Hindley, Brian. 1970. 'Separation of Ownership and Control in Modern Corporations', *Journal of Law and Economics* **13,** 185-221.

Hines, Howard H. 1957. 'Effectiveness of "Entry" by Already Established Firms', *Quarterly Journal of Economics* **71,** 132-50.

Hirsch, Werner Z. 1950-1. 'A Survey of Price Elasticities', *Review of Economic Studies* **19,** 50-8.

Horowitz, Ira. 1969. 'The Price Quoter Under Risk', *Western Economic Journal* **7,** 129-36.

Houthakker, Hendricks S., and Taylor, Lester D. 1966. *Consumer Demand in the United States, 1929-1970: Analysis and Projections*. Cambridge, Mass.: Harvard University Press.

Hymer, Stephen, and Pashigian, Peter. 1962. 'Firm Size and the Rate of Growth', *Journal of Political Economy* **70,** 556-63.

Hymer, Stephen, and Pashigian, Peter. 1964. 'Firm Size and the Rate of Growth: Reply', *Journal of Political Economy* **72,** 83-4.

Jacoby, Neil H. 1964. 'The Relative Stability of Market Shares: A Theory and Evidence from Several Industries', *Journal of Industrial Economics* **12,** 83-107.

Jastrom, Roy W. 1955. 'A Treatment of Distributed Lags in the Theory of Advertising Expenditure', *Journal of Marketing* **20,** 36-46.

Jenner, R. A. 1966. 'An Information Version of Pure Competition', *Economic Journal* **76,** 786-805.

Jewkes, John, Sawers, David and Stillerman, Richard. 1958. *The Sources of Invention*. New York: St Martin's Press.

Johns, B. L. 1962. 'Barriers to Entry in a Dynamic Setting', *Journal of Industrial Economics* **11,** 48-61.

Johnson, Harry G. 1962. 'Monetary Theory and Policy', *American Economic Review* **52,** 335-84, reprinted in American Economic Association and Royal Economic Society, 1966-7, vol. I, pp. 1-45.

Johnston, John. 1960. *Statistical Cost Analysis*. New York: McGraw-Hill.

Johnston, John. 1961. 'An Econometric Study of the Production Decision', *Quarterly Journal of Economics* **75,** 234-61.
Jorgenson, Dale W. 1963. 'Capital Theory and Investment Behavior', *American Economic Review* **53,** 247-59.
Jorgenson, Dale W. 1971. 'Econometric Studies of Investment Behavior: A Survey', *Journal of Economic Literature* **9,** 1111-47.
Kahn, Alfred E. 1970. *The Economics of Regulation.* New York: Wiley. 2 vols.
Kaldor, Nicholas. 1950-1. 'The Economic Aspects of Advertising', *Review of Economic Studies* **18,** 1-27, reprinted in Kaldor, 1960a.
Kaldor, Nicholas. 1951. 'Mr. Hicks on the Trade Cycle', *Economic Journal* **61,** 833-47.
Kaldor, Nicholas. 1955-6. 'Alternative Theories of Distribution', *Review of Economic Studies* **23,** 83-101, reprinted in Kaldor, 1960a.
Kaldor, Nicholas. 1957. 'A Model of Economic Growth', *Economic Journal* **67,** 591-624.
Kaldor, Nicholas. 1960a. *Essays on Value and Distribution.* Glencoe, Ill.: Free Press.
Kaldor, Nicholas. 1960b. 'A Rejoinder to Mr. Atsumi and Professor Tobin', *Review of Economic Studies* **27,** 121-3.
Kaldor, Nicholas. 1964. 'A Memorandum on the Value-Added Tax', *Essays in Economic Policy.* London: Duckworth.
Kaldor, Nicholas. 1966. 'Marginal Productivity and the Macro-Economic Theories of Distribution', *Review of Economic Studies* **33,** 309-19.
Kaldor, Nicholas, and Mirrlees, James A. 1962. 'A New Model of Economic Growth', *Review of Economic Studies* **29,** 174-92.
Kalecki, Michal. 1938. *Essays in the Theory of Economic Fluctuations.* London: Allen and Unwin.
Kalecki, Michal. 1943. 'Political Aspects of Full Employment', *Political Quarterly* **14,** 322-31, reprinted in Kalecki, 1971.
Kalecki, Michal. 1954. *Theory of Economic Dynamics, An Essay on Cyclical and Long-Run Changes in Capitalist Economy.* New York: Rinehart.
Kalecki, Michal. 1971. *Selected Essays on the Dynamics of the Capitalist Economy, 1933-1970.* Cambridge: Cambridge University Press.
Kamerschen, David R. 1968. 'The Influence of Ownership and Control on Profit Rates', *American Economic Review* **58,** 432-47.
Kamien, Martin J., and Schwartz, Nancy L. 1971. 'Limit Pricing and Uncertain Entry', *Econometrica* **39,** 441-54.
Kane, Edward J. 1970. 'The Term Structure of Interest Rates: An Attempt to Reconcile Teaching with Practice', *Journal of Finance* **25,** 361-74.
Kaplan, Abraham H., Dirlam, Joel B., and Lanzillotti, Robert F. 1958. *Pricing in Big Business: A Case Approach.* Washington: Brookings Institution.
Katona, George. 1951. *Psychological Analysis of Economic Behavior.* New York: McGraw-Hill.
Kaysen, Carl, and Turner, Donald F. 1959. *Antitrust Policy: An Economic and Legal Analysis.* Cambridge, Mass.: Harvard University Press.
Kefauver Hearings - See US Congress, Senate, Committee on the Judiciary, Subcommittee on Antitrust and Monopoly, *Hearings: Administered Prices.*
Keynes, John Maynard. 1930. *A Treatise on Money.* London: Macmillan. 2 vols.
Keynes, John Maynard. 1936. *The General Theory of Employment, Interest and Money.* London: Macmillan.

Kilpatrick, Robert W. 1965. 'The Short-Run Forward Shifting of the Corporate Income Tax', *Yale Economic Essays* **5,** 355–422.

Klein, Lawrence R., and Ball, R. J. 1959. 'Some Econometrics of the Distribution of Absolute Prices and Wages', *Economic Journal* **69,** 465–82.

Klein, Lawrence R., and Goldberger, Arthur S. 1955. *An Econometric Model of the United States, 1929-52.* Amsterdam: North-Holland.

Koot, Ronald S., and Walker, David A. 1970. 'Short-Run Cost Functions of a Multi-Product Firm', *Journal of Industrial Economics* **18,** 118–28.

Kottke, Frank J. 1966. 'Market Entry and the Character of Competition', *Western Economic Journal* **4,** 24-43.

Koyck, Leendert M. 1954. *Distributed Lags and Investment Analysis.* Amsterdam: North-Holland.

Kregel, J. A. 1971. *Rate of Profit, Distribution and Growth: Two Views.* Chicago: Aldine.

Kregel, J. A. 1973. *The Reconstruction of Political Economy: An Introduction to Post-Keynesian Economics.* New York: Halstad.

Krzyzaniak, Marian, ed. 1966. *Effects of Corporation Income Tax.* Detroit: Wayne State University Press.

Krzyzaniak, Marian, and Musgrave, Richard A. 1963. *The Shifting of the Corporate Income Tax, An Empirical Study of Its Short-run Effect Upon the Rate of Return.* Baltimore: Johns Hopkins Press.

Krzyzaniak, Marian, and Musgrave, Richard A. 1966. 'Discussion,' in Krzyzaniak, ed., 1966.

Krzyzaniak, Marian, and Musgrave, Richard A. 1970. 'Corporation Tax Shifting: A Response', *Journal of Political Economy* **78,** 768–73.

Kuh, Edwin. 1960. *Profits, Profit Markups and Productivity - An Examination of Corporate Behavior Since 1947.* US Congress, Joint Economic Committee, Study paper no. 15. Washington: Government Printing Office.

Kuh, Edwin. 1963. *Capital Stock Growth: A Micro-Econometric Approach.* Amsterdam: North-Holland.

Kuh, Edwin. 1965. 'Income Distribution and Employment', in Duesenberry *et al.*, eds., 1965.

Kuh, Edwin. 1966. 'Unemployment, Production Functions, and Effective Demand', *Journal of Political Economy* **74,** 328–49.

Kuh, Edwin, and Meyer, John R. 1963. 'Investment Liquidity and Monetary Policy', in Commission on Money and Credit, *Impacts of Monetary Policy.* Englewood Cliffs, NJ: Prentice-Hall.

Kuhlman, John M. 1967. 'Theoretical Issues in the Estimation of Damages in a Private Antitrust Action', *Southern Economic Journal* **33,** 548–58.

Kuhn, Alfred. 1959. 'Market and Wage-Push Inflation', *Industrial and Labor Relations Review* **12,** 243–51.

Lachmann, Ludwig M. 1956. *Capital and Its Structure.* London: Bell.

Lampman, Robert J. 1962. *The Share of the Top Wealth-holders in National Wealth, 1922-56.* Princeton, NJ: Princeton University Press.

Lange, Oskar. 1945. *Price Flexibility and Employment,* Cowles Commission for Research in Economics, Monograph no. 8. Bloomington, Ind.: Principia Press.

Lange, Oskar. 1970. *Introduction to Economic Cybernetics.* New York: Pergamon Press.

Lanzillotti, Robert F. 1958. 'Pricing Objectives in Large Corporations', *American Economic Review* **48,** 921–40.

Lapp, Ralph E. 1973. *The Logarithmic Century*. Englewood Cliffs, NJ: Prentice-Hall.

Larner, Robert J. 1966. 'Ownership and Control in the 200 Largest Nonfinancial Corporations, 1929-1963', *American Economic Review* **56,** 777-87, reprinted in Larner, 1971.

Larner, Robert J. 1971. *Management Control and the Large Corporation*. New York: Dunellen.

Leeman, Wayne A. 1956. 'The Limitations of Local Price-Cutting as a Barrier to Entry', *Journal of Political Economy* **64,** 329-35.

Leeuw, Frank de. 1962. 'The Demand for Capital Goods of Manufacturers: A Study of Quarterly Time Series', *Econometrica* **30,** 407-23.

Leibenstein, Harvey. 1960. *Economic Theory and Organizational Analysis*. New York: Harper.

Leijonhufvud, Axel. 1968. *On Keynesian Economics and the Economics of Keynes: A Study in Monetary Theory*. New York: Oxford University Press.

Lerner, Abba P. 1952. 'The Essential Properties of Interest and Money', *Quarterly Journal of Economics* **66,** 172-93.

Levinson, Harold M. 1967. 'Unionism, Concentration, and Wage Changes: Toward a Unified Theory', *Industrial and Labor Relations* **20,** 198-206.

Lewellen, Wilbur G. 1968. *Executive Compensation in Large Corporations*. New York: National Bureau for Economic Research.

Lewellen, Wilbur G., and Huntsman, Blaine. 1970. 'Managerial Pay and Corporate Performance', *American Economic Review* **60,** 710-20.

Lewis, W. Arthur. 1949. *Overhead Costs, Some Essays in Economic Analysis*. London: Allen and Unwin.

Lewis, W. Arthur. 1954. 'Economic Development with Unlimited Supplies of Labor', *Manchester School of Economic and Social Studies* **22,** 131-91.

Leyland, Norman H. 1964. 'Growth and Competition', *Oxford Economic Papers* **16,** 3-9.

Leyland, Norman H., and Richardson, G. B. 1964. 'Growth of Firms', *Oxford Economic Papers* **16,** 1-3.

Lintner, John. 1956. 'Distribution of Incomes of Corporations Among Dividends, Retained Earnings and Taxes', *American Economic Review* **46,** 97-113.

Lintner, John. 1971. 'Optimum or Maximum Corporate Growth under Uncertainty', in Marris and Wood, eds., 1971.

Liu, Ta-Chung. 1963. 'An Exploratory Quarterly Econometric Model of Effective Demand in the Postwar U.S. Economy', *Econometrica* **31,** 301-48.

Livernash, E. Robert. 1957. 'The Internal Wage Structure', in *New Concepts in Wage Determination*, George W. Taylor and Frank C. Pierson, eds. New York: McGraw-Hill.

Lloyd, Cliff. 1969. 'Lord Preference and Lord Funds', *Economic Journal* **74,** 578-81.

Luce, Robert Duncan, and Raiffa, Howard. 1957. *Games and Decisions*. New York: Wiley.

Lutz, Freidrich A. 1945. 'The Criterion of Maximum Profits in the Theory of Investment', *Quarterly Journal of Economics* **60,** 56-77.

Lutz, Vera C. 1969. *Central Planning for the Market Economy: An Analysis of the French Theory and Experience*. London: Longmans.

Lydall, H. F. 1955. 'Conditions of New Entry and the Theory of Price', *Oxford Economic Papers* **7,** 300-11.

Mabry, Bevars S., and Siders, David L. 1967. 'An Empirical Test of the Sales

Maximization Hypothesis', *Southern Economic Journal* **33,** 367-77.
McConnell, Grant. 1963. *Steel and the Presidency, 1962.* New York: Norton.
McGuire, Joseph. 1964. *Theories of Business Behavior.* Englewood Cliffs, NJ: Prentice-Hall.
McGuire, Joseph, Chiu, John S. Y. and Elbing, Alvar O. 1962. 'Executive Income, Sales and Profits', *American Economic Review* **52,** 753-61.
McGuire, Timothy W., and Rapping, Leonard A. 1967. 'The Determination of Money Wages in American Industry: Comment', *Quarterly Journal of Economics* **81,** 684-9.
Machlup, Fritz. 1952. *The Economics of Sellers' Competition: Model Analysis of Sellers' Conduct.* Baltimore: Johns Hopkins Press.
Machlup, Fritz. 1967. 'Theories of the Firm; Marginalist, Behavioral, Managerial', *American Economic Review* **57,** 1-34.
MacLennan, Malcolm, Forsyth, Murray, and Denton, Geoffrey. 1968. *Economic Planning and Policies in Britain, France and Germany.* New York: Praeger.
McKinnon, Ronald I. 1966. 'Stigler's Theory of Oligopoly: A Comment', *Journal of Political Economy* **74,** 281-5.
Mackintosh, Athole S. 1963. *The Development of Firms.* Cambridge: Cambridge University Press.
McNulty, Paul J. 1967. 'A Note on the History of Imperfect Competition', *Journal of Political Economy* **75,** 395-9.
McNulty, Paul J. 1968. 'Economic Theory and the Meaning of Competition', *Quarterly Journal of Economics* **82,** 639-56.
Maher, John E. 1961. 'The Wage Pattern in the United States, 1946-57', *Industrial and Labor Relations Review* **15,** 3-20.
Maisel, Sherman J. 1965. 'Nonbusiness Construction', in Duesenberry *et al.*, eds., 1965.
Mann, H. Michael. 1966. 'Seller Concentration, Barriers to Entry, and Rates of Return in Thirty Industries, 1950-1960', *Review of Economics and Statistics* **48,** 296-307.
Manne, Henry G. 1965. 'Mergers and the Market for Corporate Control', *Journal of Political Economy* **73,** 110-20.
Mansfield, Edwin. 1962. 'Entry, Gibrat's Law, Innovation and the Growth of Firms', *American Economic Review* **52,** 1023-51.
Mansfield, Edwin. 1968. *The Economics of Technological Change.* New York: Norton.
Mao, James C. T. 1970. 'Survey of Capital Budgeting: Theory and Practice', *Journal of Finance* **25,** 349-60.
Marglin, Stephen A. 1970. 'Investment and Interest: A Reformulation and Extension of Keynesian Theory', *Economic Journal* **80,** 910-31.
Margolis, Julius. 1958. 'The Analysis of the Firm: Rationalism, Conventionalism, and Behavioralism', *Journal of Business* **31,** 187-99.
Markham, Jesse W. 1951. 'The Nature and Significance of Price Leadership', *American Economic Review* **41,** 891-905.
Marris, Robin. 1963. 'A Model of Managerial Enterprise', *Quarterly Journal of Economics* **77,** 185-209.
Marris, Robin. 1964. *The Economic Theory of 'Managerial' Capitalism.* New York: Free Press.
Marris, Robin. 1968. 'Galbraith, Solow, and the Truth About Corporations', *Public Interest* **11,** 37-46.
Marris, Robin. 1971a. 'An Introduction to Theories of Corporate Growth,' in

Marris and Wood, eds., 1971, pp. 1-36.
Marris, Robin. 1971b. 'Preface for Social Scientists', in Marris and Wood, eds., 1971, pp. xv-xxvi.
Marris, Robin. 1972. 'Review: The Ownership Income of Management by Wilbur G. Lewellen', *Journal of Economic Literature* **10,** 491-3.
Marris, Robin. 1973. 'Why Economics Needs a Theory of the Firm', *Economic Journal* **83** (supplement), 321-52.
Marris, Robin, and Wood, Adrian, eds. 1971. *The Corporate Economy, Growth Competition and Innovative Potential.* Cambridge, Mass.: Harvard University Press.
Marshall, Alfred. 1920. *Principles of Economics,* 8th ed. London: Macmillan.
Marshall, Alfred. 1923. *Money, Credit and Commerce.* London: Macmillan.
Marx, Karl. 1933. *Capital.* London: Charles Kerr and Company, vol. I (1st German ed., 1867; 1st English ed., 1886).
Marx, Karl. 1935. *Value, Price and Profit,* Address Delivered June, 1865. New York: International Publishers.
Masson, Robert T. 1971. 'Executive Motivations, Earnings, and Consequent Equity Performance,' *Journal of Political Economy* **79,** 1278-92.
Matthews, R. C. O. 1959. *The Business Cycle.* Chicago: University of Chicago Press.
Maxwell, William David. 1965. 'Short Run Returns to Scale and the Production of Services', *Southern Economic Journal* **32,** 1-14.
Means, Gardiner C. 1962a. *The Corporate Revolution in America: Economic Reality vs. Economic Theory.* New York: Crowell-Collier.
Means, Gardiner C. 1962b. *Pricing Power and the Public Interest, A Study Based on Steel.* New York: Harper and Bros.
Meltzer, Allan H. 1960. 'Mercantile Credit, Monetary Policy and Size of Firm,' *Review of Economics and Statistics* **42,** 429-37.
Meltzer, Allan H. 1969. 'Money, Intermediation, and Growth', *Journal of Economic Literature* **7,** 27-56.
Menge, John A. 1962. 'Style Change Costs as a Market Weapon', *Quarterly Journal of Economics* **76,** 632-47.
Mermelstein, David. 1969. 'Large Industrial Corporations and Assets Shares', *American Economic Review* **59,** 531-41.
Metzler, Lloyd. 1947. 'Factors Governing the Length of Inventory Cycles', *Review of Economics and Statistics* **29,** 1-15.
Meyer, John R., and Glauber, Robert R. 1964. *Investment Decisions, Economic Forecasting and Public Policy.* Boston: Graduate School of Business Administration, Harvard University.
Meyer, John R., and Kuh, Edwin. 1959. *The Investment Decision: An Empirical Study.* Cambridge, Mass.: Harvard University Press.
Meyerson, Martin, and Banfield, Edward C. 1955. *Politics, Planning and the Public Interest, The Case of Public Housing in Chicago.* New York: Free Press.
Mieszkowski, Peter. 1969. 'Tax Incidence Theory: The Effects of Taxes on the Distribution on Income', *Journal of Economic Literature* **7,** 1103-24.
Mill, John Stuart. 1965. *Principles of Political Economy; With Some of Their Applications to Social Philosophy,* 7th ed. Edited with an introduction by W. J. Ashley. New York: Augustus Kelley (1st ed., 1848).
Mills, C. Wright. 1959. *The Power Elite.* New York: Oxford University Press.
Mills, Gordon, 1965. 'Uncertainty Cost Interdependence and Opportunity-Cost

Pricing', *Journal of Industrial Economics* **13,** 235-42.

Minsky, Hyman P. 1975. *John Maynard Keynes*. New York: Columbia University Press.

Modigliani, Franco. 1964. 'Comment: Some Theories of Income Distribution', in National Bureau for Economic Research, 1964, pp. 39-50.

Modigliani, Franco, and Miller, Merton H. 1958. 'The Cost of Capital, Corporation Finance and the Theory of Investment', *American Economic Review* **48,** 261-97.

Moffat, William R. 1970. 'Taxes in the Price Equation: Textiles and Rubber', *Review of Economics and Statistics* **52,** 253-61.

Monsen, R. Joseph Jr., and Downs, Anthony. 1965. 'A Theory of Large Managerial Firms', *Journal of Political Economy* **73,** 221-36.

Moore, A. M. 1967. 'A Reformulation of the Kaldor Effect', *Economic Journal* **77,** 84-99.

Moore, John R., and Levy, Lester S. 1955. 'Price Flexibility and Industrial Concentration', *Southern Economic Journal* **21,** 435-40.

Morse, Dean. 1969. *The Peripheral Worker*. New York: Columbia University Press.

Moyer, Reed. 1968. 'The Relation of Profit Rates to Operating Rates,' *Journal of Industrial Economics* **16,** 178-85.

Mueller, Dennis C. 'A Theory of Conglomerate Mergers', *Quarterly Journal of Economics* **83,** 643-59.

Mueller, Dennis C., and Tilton, John E. 1969. 'Research and Development Costs as a Barrier to Entry', *Canadian Journal of Economics* **2,** 570-9.

National Bureau for Economic Research. 1964. *The Behavior of Income Shares, Selected Theoretical and Empirical Issues*. Studies in Income and Wealth, vol. 27. Princeton, NJ: Princeton University Press.

Neale, Alan D. 1960. *The Antitrust Laws of the United States of America: A Study of Competition Enforced by Law*. Cambridge: Cambridge University Press.

Needham, Douglas. 1964. 'The Rationale of Basing Point Prices', *Southern Economic Journal* **30,** 309-14.

Nelson, Richard R., Peck, Merton J., and Kalachek, Edward D. 1967. *Technology, Economic Growth and Public Policy*. Washington: Brookings Institution.

Nerlove, Marc, and Addison, W. 1958. 'Statistical Estimation of Long-Run Elasticities of Supply and Demand', *Journal of Farm Economics* **40,** 892-902.

Nordhaus, William D. 1973. 'World Dynamics: Measurement Without Data', *Economic Journal* **83,** 1156-83.

Nordquist, Gerald L. 1965. 'The Breakup of the Maximization Principle', *Quarterly Review of Economics and Business* **5,** 33-46.

O'Brien, D. P. 1964. 'Patent Protection and Competition in Polyaminds and Polyester Fibre Manufacture', *Journal of Industrial Economics* **12,** 224-35.

Oi, Walter. 1967. 'The Neoclassical Foundations of Progress Functions', *Economic Journal* **77,** 579-94.

Orr, Daniel, and MacAvoy, Paul W. 1965. 'Price Strategies to Promote Cartel Stability', *Economica* **32,** 186-97.

Osborne, Dale K. 1964. 'On the Goals of the Firm', *Quarterly Journal of Economics* **78,** 592-603.

Osborne, Dale K. 1965. 'On the Goals of the Firm: Reply', *Quarterly Journal of Economics* **79,** 50-4.

Paish, F. W., and Hennessy, Joseleyn. 1964. *Policy for Incomes?* London: Institute for Economic Affairs.

Palda, Kristian S. 1964. *The Measurement of Cumulative Advertising Effects.* Englewood Cliffs, NJ: Prentice-Hall.

Palda, Kristian S. 1966. 'The Hypothesis of a Hierarchy of Effects', *Journal of Marketing Research* **3,** 13-25.

Papandreau, Andreas G. 1952. 'Some Basic Problems in the Theory of the Firm', in *A Survey of Contemporary Economics,* Bernard F. Haley, ed. Homewood, Ill.: Irwin, vol. II.

Pardridge, William D. 1964. 'Sales or Profit Maximization in Management Capitalism', *Western Economic Journal* **2,** 137-41.

Pashigian, B. Peter. 1968. 'Limit Price and the Market Share of the Leading Firm', *Journal of Industrial Economics* **16,** 165-77.

Pasinetti, Luigi. 1962. 'Rate of Profit and Income Distribution in Relation to the Rate of Economic Growth', *Review of Economic Studies* **29,** 167-79, reprinted in Pasinetti, 1974.

Pasinetti, Luigi. 1974. *Growth and Income Distribution - Essays in Economic Theory.* Cambridge: Cambridge University Press.

Pen, Jan. 1959. *The Wage Rate Under Collective Bargaining.* Cambridge, Mass.: Harvard University Press.

Pen, Jan. 1971. *Income Distribution, Facts, Theories, Politics.* New York: Praeger.

Penrose, Edith T. 1959. *The Theory of the Growth of the Firm.* New York: Wiley.

Peston, Maurice H. 1959. 'On the Sales Maximisation Hypothesis', *Economica* **26,** 128-36.

Pfouts, Ralph W., and Ferguson, Charles E. 1959. 'Market Classification Systems in Theory and Policy', *Southern Economic Journal* **26,** 111-18.

Phelps, Charlotte DeMonte. 1963. 'The Impact of Monetary Policy on State and Local Government Expenditures in the United States', Commission on Money and Credit, *Impacts of Monetary Policy.* Englewood Cliffs, NJ: Prentice-Hall.

Phelps, Edmund S., ed. 1970. *Microeconomic Foundations of Employment and Inflation Theory.* New York: Norton.

Phillips, Almarin. 1961. 'Policy Implications of the Theory of Interfirm Organization', *American Economic Review* **51,** 245-54.

Phillips, Almarin. 1962. *Market Structure, Organization and Performance, An Essay on Price Fixing and Combinations in Restraint of Trade.* Cambridge, Mass.: Harvard University Press.

Phillips, Almarin. 1964. 'A Theory of Interfirm Organization', *Quarterly Journal of Economics* **74,** 602-13.

Phillips, A. W. 1958. 'The Relation Between Unemployment and the Rate of Change of Money Wages in the United Kingdom', *Economica* **25,** 283-99.

Pierson, Gail. 1972. 'Money in Economic Growth', *Quarterly Journal of Economics* **86,** 383-95.

Plattner, Robert H. 1969. 'Dividend Policy and External Funds', *Public Utilities Fortnightly* **83,** 15-22.

Pollack, Robert A. 1970. 'Habit Formation and Dynamic Demand Functions', *Journal of Political Economy* **79,** 745-65.

Porter, Glenn P. 1970. 'The Changing Distributional System in American Manufacturing, 1770-1900', unpublished doctoral dissertation, Johns Hopkins University.

Porter, Glenn P. 1973. *The Rise of Big Business, 1860-1910.* New York: Thomas Y. Crowell.

Porter, Glenn P., and Livesay, Harold C. 1971. *Merchants and Manufacturers:*

Studies in the Changing Structure of Nineteenth-Century Marketing. Baltimore: Johns Hopkins Press.

Posner, Richard A. 1970. 'A Statistical Study of Antitrust Enforcement', *Journal of Law and Economics* **13,** 365-420.

Prest, A. R., and Turvey, R. 1965. 'Cost-Benefit Analysis: A Survey', *Economic Journal* **75,** 683-735, reprinted in American Economic Association and Royal Economic Society, 1966-7, vol. I, pp. 155-203.

Projector, Dorothy S., and Weiss, Gertrude S. 1966. *Survey of Financial Characteristics of Consumers.* Washington: Board of Governors of the Federal Reserve System.

Pyatt, F. Graham. 1971. 'Profit Maximization and the Threat of Entry', *Economic Journal* **81,** 242-55.

Rapoport, Anatol, and Chammah, Albert M. 1965. *Prisoners' Dilemma.* Ann Arbor, Mich.: University of Michigan Press.

Reder, Melvin W. 1947. 'A Reconsideration of the Marginal Productivity Theory', *Journal of Political Economy* **55,** 450-8.

Resek, Robert W. 1966. 'Investment by Manufacturing Firms: A Quarterly Time Series Analysis of Industry Data', *Review of Economics and Statistics* **48,** 322-47.

Reynolds, Lloyd G. 1960. 'Wage Push and All That', *American Economic Review* **50,** 195-204.

Reynolds, Lloyd G. 1964. *Labor Economics and Labor Relations,* 4th ed. Englewood Cliffs, NJ: Prentice-Hall.

Rhomberg, Rudolf R., and Boissonneualt, Lorette. 1965. 'The Foreign Sector', in James S. Duesenberry *et al.*, eds., 1965.

Ripley, Frank C. 1966. 'An Analysis of the Eckstein-Wilson Wage Determination Model', *Quarterly Journal of Economics* **80,** 121-36.

Rivlin, Alice. 1971. *Systematic Thinking for Social Action.* Washington: Brookings Institution.

Roberts, Benjamin C. 1958. *National Wages Policy in War and Peace.* London: Allen and Unwin.

Roberts, David R. 1959. *Executive Compensation.* Glencoe, Ill.: Free Press.

Robinson, Derek. 1968. *Wage Drift, Fringe Benefits and Manpower Distribution, A Study of Employer Practices in a Full-employment Labour Market.* London: Organization for Economic Cooperation and Development.

Robinson, Joan, 1934. 'Euler's Theorem and the Problem of Distribution', *Economic Journal* **44,** reprinted in J. Robinson, 1951, 1960, 1965, vol. I, pp. 1-19.

Robinson, Joan. 1950. 'The Labour Theory of Value', Review of Eugen von Bohm Bawerk's *Karl Marx and the Close of His System* and Ladislaus von Bortkiewicz's *On the Correction of Marx's Fundamental Theoretical Construction in the Third Volume of Capital,* in *Economic Journal,* June, 1950, reprinted in J. Robinson, 1951, 1960, 1965, vol. I, pp. 146-51.

Robinson, Joan. 1951, 1960, 1965. *Collected Economic Papers.* Oxford: Blackwell. 3 vols.

Robinson, Joan. 1952. 'The Rate of Interest', in *The Rate of Interest and Other Essays.* London: Macmillan.

Robinson, Joan. 1953. 'Imperfect Competition Revisited', *Economic Journal* **63,** 579-93, reprinted in J. Robinson, 1951, 1960, 1965, vol. II, pp. 222-38.

Robinson, Joan. 1953-4. 'The Production Function and the Theory of Capital', *Review of Economic Studies* **21,** 81-106, reprinted in J. Robinson, 1951, 1960, 1965, vol. II, pp. 114-31.

Robinson, Joan. 1954. 'The Labour Theory of Value,' *Science and Society*, **18,** 141-51, reprinted in J. Robinson, 1951, 1960, 1965, vol. II, pp. 49-58.
Robinson, Joan. 1956. *The Accumulation of Capital*. London: Macmillan.
Robinson, Joan. 1957. 'La Theorie de la Repartition', ('The Theory of Distribution'), *Economie Applique* **10,** 523-38, reprinted in English in J. Robinson, 1951, 1960, 1965, vol. II, pp. 145-58.
Robinson, Joan. 1962a. *Essays in the Theory of Economic Growth*. London: Macmillan.
Robinson, Joan. 1962b. *Economic Philosophy*. Chicago: Aldine.
Robinson, Joan. 1962c. 'The Basic Theory of Normal Prices', *Quarterly Journal of Economics* **76,** 1-19.
Robinson, Joan. 1962d. 'Marxism: Religion and Science', *Monthly Review* **14,** 423-35, reprinted in J. Robinson, 1951, 1960, 1965, vol. III, pp. 148-57.
Robinson, Joan. 1969. *The Economics of Imperfect Competition*. London: Macmillan, 2nd ed. (1st ed., 1933).
Robinson, Joan. 1971. *Economic Heresies: Some Old-Fashioned Questions in Economic Theory*. New York: Basic Books.
Robinson, Joan. 1972. 'The Second Crisis of Economic Theory', *American Economic Review* **62,** 1-15.
Robinson, Joan, and Eatwell, John. 1974. *An Introduction to Economics*. London: McGraw-Hill.
Robinson, Romney. 1961. 'The Economics of Disequilibrium Price', *Quarterly Journal of Economics* **75,** 199-233.
Roll, Eric. 1942. *A History of Economic Thought*. Englewood Cliffs, NJ: Prentice-Hall.
Roosa, Robert V. 1951. 'Interest Rates and the Central Bank', in *Money, Trade, Economic Growth; In Honor of John Henry Williams*. London: Macmillan.
Rosen, Sherwin. 1969. 'Trade Union Power, Threat Effects and the Extent of Organization', *Review of Economic Studies* **36,** 185-96.
Rostow, Eugene V. 1959. 'To Whom and For What Ends are Corporate Managements Responsible?', in *The Corporation in Modern Society*, Edward S. Mason, ed. Cambridge, Mass.: Harvard University Press.
Ruggles, Nancy, and Ruggles, Richard. 1970. *The Design of Economic Accounts*. New York: National Bureau for Economic Research.
Ruggles, Richard. 1955. 'The Nature of Price Flexibility and the Determinants of Relative Price Changes in the Economy', in Universities-National Bureau for Economic Research, *Business Concentration and Public Policy*. Princeton, NJ: Princeton University Press.
Salter, W. E. G. 1960. *Productivity and Technological Change*. Cambridge: Cambridge University Press.
Samuels, J. M. 1965. 'Size and the Growth of the Firms', *Review of Economic Studies* **32,** 105-12.
Samuelson, Paul A. 1967. 'Marxian Economics as Economics', *American Economic Review* **57,** 616-23.
Samuelson, Paul A. 1971. 'Understanding the Marxian Notion of Exploitation: A Summary of the So-called Transformation Problem Between Marxian Values and Competitive Prices', *Journal of Economic Literature* **9,** 399-431.
Sandmeyer, Robert L. 1964. 'Baumol's Sales Maximization Model: Comment', *American Economic Review* **54,** 1073-80.
Sandmeyer, Robert L., and Steindl, Frank G. 1970. 'Conjectural Variation, Oligopoly and Revenue Maximization', *Southern Economic Journal* **37,** 40-4.
Saving, Thomas R. 1961. 'Estimation of Optimum Size Plant by the Survivor

Technique', *Quarterly Journal of Economics* **75**, 569-607.

Scherer, Frederick M. 1965. 'Size of Firm, Oligopoly, and Research: A Comment', *Canadian Journal of Economics and Political Science* **31**, 256-67.

Scherer, Frederick M. 1967. 'Research and Development Resource Allocation under Rivalry', *Quarterly Journal of Economics* **81**, 359-94.

Scherer, Frederick M. 1970. *Industrial Market Structure and Economic Performance.* Chicago: Rand McNally.

Schlesinger, James R. 1958. 'Market Structure, Union Power and Inflation', *Southern Economic Journal* **24**, 296-312.

Schneider, Norman. 1966. 'Product Differentiation, Oligopoly, and the Stability of Market Shares', *Western Economic Journal* **5**, 58-63.

Schultz, George P., and Aliber, Robert Z. 1966. *Guidelines, Informal Controls and the Market Place.* Chicago: University of Chicago Press.

Schultze, Charles L. 1959. *Recent Inflation in the United States.* US Congress, Joint Economic Committee, Study paper no. 1. Washington: Government Printing Office.

Schultze, Charles E. 1964. 'Short-Run Movements of Income Shares', in National Bureau for Economic Research, 1964, pp. 143-88.

Schultze, Charles E. 1968. *The Politics and Economics of Public Spending.* Washington: Brookings Institution.

Schultze, Charles L., and Tryon, J. L. 1965. 'Prices and Wages', in James S. Duesenberry *et al.*, 1965.

Schumpeter, Joseph. 1939. *Business Cycles, A Theoretical, Historical and Statistical Analysis of the Capitalist Process.* New York: McGraw-Hill. 2 vols.

Schumpeter, Joseph. 1955. *History of Economic Analysis.* New York: Oxford University Press.

Scitovsky, Tibor. 1943. 'A Note on Profit Maximization and Its Implications', *Review of Economic Studies* **11**, 57-60.

Scitovsky, Tibor. 1964. 'A Survey of Some Theories of Income Distribution', in National Bureau for Economic Research, 1964, pp. 15-31.

Segal, Martin. 1961. 'Unionism and Wage Movements', *Southern Economic Journal* **28**, 174-81.

Sheahan, John. 1967. *The Wage-Price Guideposts.* Washington: Brookings Institution.

Shen, T. Y. 1968. 'Competition, Technology and Market Shares', *Review of Economics and Statistics* **50**, 96-102.

Shepherd, William G. 1962. 'On Sales-Maximizing and Oligopoly Behavior', *Economica* **29**, 420-4.

Shepherd, William G. 1970. *Market Power and Economic Welfare: An Introduction.* New York: Random House.

Shepherd, William G., and Gies, Thomas G., eds. 1966. *Utility Regulation: New Directions in Theory and Policy.* New York: Random House.

Shonfield, Andrew. 1965. *Modern Capitalism, The Changing Balance of Public and Private Power.* New York: Oxford University Press.

Shubik, Martin. 1959. *Strategy and Market Structure.* New York: Wiley.

Shubik, Martin. 1970. 'A Curmudgeon's Guide to Microeconomics', *Journal of Economic Literature* **7**, 405-34.

Sibson, Robert E. 1960. *Wages and Salaries; A Handbook for Line Managers.* New York: American Management Association.

Silber, William L. 1969. 'Monetary Channels and the Relative Importance of Money Supply and Bank Portfolios', *Journal of Finance* **24**, 81-7.

Silber, William L. 1970. 'The Term Structure of Interest Rates: Discussion', *Journal of Finance* **25**, 380-1.

Silber, William L., and Polakoff, Murray E. 1970. 'The Differential Effects of Tight Money: An Econometric Study', *Journal of Finance* **25**, 83-98.

Silberstein, Aubrey. 1970. 'Price Behaviour of Firms', *Economic Journal* **80**, 511-82.

Simon, Herbert A. 1955. 'A Behavioral Model of Rational Choice', *Quarterly Journal of Economics* **39**, 99-118.

Simon, Herbert. 1964. 'Firm Size and the Rate of Growth: Comment', *Journal of Political Economy* **72**, 81-2.

Skinner, R. C. 1970. 'The Determination of Selling Prices', *Journal of Industrial Economics* **18**, 201-17.

Slitor, Richard E. 1966. 'Corporate Tax Incidence: Economic Adjustments to Differentials under a Two-Tier Tax Structure', in Krzyzaniak, ed., 1966, pp. 136-208.

Smith, Caleb A. 1961. 'Review of *Statistical Cost Analysis* by J. Johnston', *American Economic Review* **51**, 417-19.

Smith, Harold T. 1959. *Equity and Loan Capital for New and Expanding Small Business*. Kalamazoo, Mich.: W. E. Upjohn Institute for Employment Research.

Smithies, Arthur. 1939. 'The Maximization of Profits Over Time with Changing Cost and Demand Functions', *Econometrica* **7**, 312-18.

Smyth, D. 1964. 'Empirical Evidence on the Acceleration Principle', *Review of Economic Studies* **31**, 185-202.

Soffer, Benson. 1959. 'On Union Rivalries and the Minimum Differentiation of Wage Patterns', *Review of Economics and Statistics* **41**, 53-61.

Solomon, Ezra, ed. 1959. *The Management of Corporate Capital*. Glencoe, Ill.: Free Press.

Solomon, Ezra. 1963. *The Theory of Financial Management*. New York: Columbia University Press.

Solow, Robert M. 1957. 'Technical Progress and the Aggregate Production Function', *Review of Economics and Statistics* **39**, 312-20.

Solow, Robert M. 1968. 'The Truth Further Refined: A Comment on Marris', *The Public Interest* **11**, 47-52.

Solow, Robert M. 1971. 'Some Implications of Alternative Criteria for the Firm', in Marris and Wood, eds., 1971, pp. 318-42.

Sorrentino, Constance. 1972. 'Unemployment in Nine Industrialized Countries', *Monthly Labor Review* **95**, 39-43.

Spengler, Joseph J. 1965. 'Kinked Demand Curves, By Whom First Used?' *Southern Economic Journal* **32**, 81-4.

Sraffa, Piero. 1960. *Production of Commodities by Means of Commodities; Prelude to a Critique of Economic Theory*. Cambridge: Cambridge University Press.

Stanfield, J. Ronald. 1973. *The Economic Surplus and Neo-Marxism*. Lexington, Ky: D. C. Heath.

Steele, Henry. 1964. 'Patent Restrictions and Price Competition in the Ethical Drugs Industry', *Journal of Industrial Economics* **12**, 198-223.

Stein, Herbert. 1969. *The Fiscal Revolution in America*. Chicago: University of Chicago Press.

Steindl, J. 1952. *Maturity and Stagnation in American Capitalism*. Oxford: Basil Blackwell.

Stemp, Isay. 1970. *Corporate Growth Strategies*. New York: American Management Association.

Stern, Carl. 1965. 'Price Elasticity of Local Telephone Service Demand', *Public Utilities Fortnightly* **75,** 24-34.

Stigler, George J. 1939. 'Production and Distribution in the Short Run', *Journal of Political Economy* **47,** 305-27, reprinted in Stigler, 1968.

Stigler, George J. 1941. *Production and Distribution Theories, The Formative Period.* New York: Macmillan.

Stigler, George J. 1947. 'The Kinky Oligopoly Demand Curve and Rigid Prices', *Journal of Political Economy* **55,** 432-49, reprinted in Stigler, 1968.

Stigler, George J. 1950. 'Monopoly and Oligopoly by Merger', *American Economic Review* **40,** 23-34, reprinted in Stigler, 1968.

Stigler, George J. 1957. 'Perfect Competition, Historically Contemplated', *Journal of Political Economy* **65,** 1-17.

Stigler, George J. 1964. 'A Theory of Oligopoly', *Journal of Political Economy* **72,** 44-61, reprinted in Stigler, 1968.

Stigler, George J. 1966a. *The Theory of Price.* New York: Macmillan (1st ed., 1942).

Stigler, George G. 1966b. 'The Economic Effects of the Antitrust Laws', *Journal of Law and Economics* **9,** 225-58.

Stigler, George G. 1968. *The Organization of Industry.* Homewood, Ill.: Irwin.

Stigler, George J., and Kindahl, James K. 1970. *The Behavior of Industrial Prices.* New York: National Bureau of Economic Research.

Stocking, George W., and Watkins, Myron W. 1951. *Monopoly and Free Enterprise with a Report and Recommendation of the Twentieth Century Fund.* New York: Twentieth Century Fund.

Stone, Richard. 1954. *The Measurement of Consumers' Expenditures and Behaviour in the United Kingdom, 1920-38.* Cambridge: Cambridge University Press.

Stonier, Alfred W., and Hague, Douglas C. 1953. *A Textbook of Economic Theory.* London: Longmans Green.

Suits, Daniel B. 1962. 'Forecasting and Analysis with an Econometric Model', *American Economic Review* **52,** 104-32.

Sultan, Ralph G. 1975. *Pricing in Oligopoly.* Cambridge, Mass.: Harvard University Press.

Sutton, Francis X., *et al.* 1956. *The American Business Creed.* Cambridge, Mass.: Harvard University Press.

Sweezy, Paul. W. 1939. 'Demand Under Conditions of Oligopoly', *Journal of Political Economy* **47,** 568-73.

Sweezy, Paul W. 1942. *The Theory of Capitalist Development; Principles of Marxian Political Economy.* New York: Monthly Review Press.

Sylos-Labini, Paolo. 1962. *Oligopoly and Technical Progress.* Cambridge, Mass.: Harvard University Press.

Taylor, Lester D., and Weiserbs, Daniel. 1972. 'Advertising and the Aggregate Consumption Function', *American Economic Review* **62,** 642-55.

Telser, Lester G. 1966a. 'Cutthroat Competition and the Long Purse', *Journal of Law and Economics* **9,** 259-77.

Telser, Lester G. 1966b. 'Supply and Demand for Advertising Messages', *American Economic Review* **56,** 457-66.

Tennant, Richard B. 1950. *The American Cigarette Industry: A Study in Economic Analysis and Public Policy.* New Haven: Yale University Press.

Tilove, Robert. 1959. *Pension Funds and Economic Freedom: A Report to the Fund for the Republic.* New York: Fund for the Republic.

Tinbergen, Jan. 1952. *On the Theory of Economic Policy*. Amsterdam: North-Holland.
Tinbergen, Jan. 1968. *Statistical Testing of Business Cycle Theories*. New York: Agathon (1st ed., 1939).
Tobin, James. 1960. 'Towards a General Kaldorian Theory of Distribution', *Review of Economic Studies* **27,** 119-20.
Tobin, James. 1969. 'A General Equilibrium Approach to Monetary Theory', *Journal of Money, Credit and Banking* **1,** 15-30.
Tobin, James. 1974. *The New Economics One Decade Later.* Princeton, NJ: Princeton University Press.
Tobin, James, and Brainard, William. 1963 'Financial Intermediaries and the Effectiveness of Monetary Controls', *American Economic Review* **53,** 383-400.
Triffin, Robert. 1949. *Monopolistic Competition and General Equilibrium Theory.* Cambridge, Mass.: Harvard University Press.
Tucker, Donald P. 1968. 'Credit Rationing, Interest Rate Lags, and Monetary Policy Speed', *Quarterly Journal of Economics* **82,** 54-84.
Tugwell, Rexford, ed. 1924. *The Trend of Economics.* New York: Knopf.
Turner, H. A., and Zoeteweij, H. 1966. *Prices, Wages and Income Policies in Industrialized Market Economies.* Geneva: International Labor Office.
US Bureau of the Census. 1966. *Concentration Ratios in Manufacturing Industry in 1963.* Report Prepared for the Subcommittee on Antitrust and Monopoly, Committee on the Judiciary, US Senate. Washington: Government Printing Office.
US Congress. Joint Economic Committee. 1959. *Staff Report on Employment, Growth and Price Levels.* Washington: Government Printing Office.
US Congress. Senate. Committee on the Judiciary, Subcommittee on Antitrust and Monopoly. 1957-63. *Hearings: Administered Prices.* Parts 1-24. 85th Congress, 1st Session-88th Congress, 1st Session. Washington: Government Printing Office.
US President. 1960-71. *Economic Report of the President.* Washington: Government Printing Office.
Usher, Dan. 1964. 'The Welfare Economics of Invention', *Economica* **31,** 279-87.
Veblen, Thorstein. 1919. *The Place of Science in Modern Civilization.* New York: R. W. Huebsch.
Vickers, Douglas, 1968. *The Theory of the Firm, Production, Capital and Finance.* New York: McGraw-Hill.
Vickrey, William S. 1964. *Microstatics.* New York: Harcourt, Brace and World.
Villarejo, Don. 1962. 'Stock Ownership and the Control of Corporations', *New University Thought* **2,** 47-65.
Wachter, Michael L. 1970. 'Relative Wage Equations for U.S. Manufacturing Industries, 1947-67', *Review of Economics and Statistics* **52,** 405-10.
Walter, James E. 1963. 'Dividend Policy: Its Influence on the Value of the Enterprise', *Journal of Finance* **18,** 280-91.
Walters, Alan A. 1963. 'Production and Cost, An Econometric Survey', *Econometrica* **31,** 1-66.
Walton, Richard E., and McKersie, Robert B. 1965. *A Behavioral Theory of Labor Negotiations, An Analysis of a Social Interaction System.* New York: McGraw-Hill.
Wan, Henry Y. 1966. 'Intertemporal Optimization with Systematically Shifting Cost and Revenue Functions', *International Economic Review* **7,** 204-25.

Warner, Aaron W., and Morse, Dean, eds. 1966. *Technological Innovation and Society*. New York: Columbia University Press.

Warner, Aaron W., Morse, Dean, and Eichner, Alfred S., eds., 1965. *The Impact of Science on Technology*. New York: Columbia University Press.

Waud, Roger N. 1967. 'An Expectations Model of Cyclical Growth: Hicks on the Trade Cycle Revisited', *Oxford Economic Papers* **9**, 213-27.

Waugh, Frederick. 1964. *Demand and Price Analysis; Some Examples from Agriculture*. Washington: US Department of Agriculture.

Weber, Arnold R. 1963. 'The Structure of Collective Bargaining and Bargaining Power: Foreign Experiences', *Journal of Law and Economics* **6**, 79-151.

Weber, Max. 1958. *From Max Weber: Essays in Sociology*. New York: Oxford University Press.

Weber, Max. 1964. *The Theory of Social and Economic Organization*. New York: Free Press.

Weintraub, Sidney. 1959. *A General Theory of the Price Level, Output, Income Distribution, and Economic Growth*. Philadelphia: Chilton.

Weintraub, Sidney. 1966. *A Keynesian Theory of Employment, Growth and Income Distribution*. Philadelphia: Chilton.

Weintraub, Sidney. 1968. 'Rate Making and an Incentive Rate of Return', *Public Utilities Fortnightly* **81**, 23-33.

Weintraub, Sidney. 1973. *Keynes and the Monetarists*. New Brunswick, NJ: Rutgers University Press.

Weiss, Leonard W. 1964. 'The Survivor Technique and the Extent of Suboptimal Capacity', *Journal of Political Economy* **72**, 246-61.

Weiss, Leonard W. 1965. 'Correction: The Survival Technique and the Extent of Suboptimal Capacity', *Journal of Political Economy* **73**, 300-1.

Wellisz, Stanislaw H. 1963. 'Regulation of Natural Gas Pipeline Companies: An Economic Analysis', *Journal of Political Economy* **71**, 30-43.

Wenders, John T. 1967. 'Entry and Monopoly Pricing', *Journal of Political Economy* **75**, 55-60.

Whetten, Leyland C. 1961. *The Influence of Recent Proxy Contests on Social and Economic Trends*. Bureau of Business and Economic Research, Georgia State College of Business Administration.

Whitin, Thomas M. 1968. 'Dynamic Programing Extensions to the Theory of the Firm', *Journal of Industrial Economics* **16**, 81-98.

Whitney, Simon N. 1958. *Antitrust Policy: American Experience in Twenty Industries*. New York: Twentieth Century Fund.

Whittington, G. 1972. 'The Profitability of Retained Earnings', *Review of Economics and Statistics* **54**, 152-60.

Wilcox, Clair. 1966. *Public Policies Toward Business*. Homewood, Ill.: Irwin. 3rd ed. (1st ed., 1955).

Wiles, Peter J. 1956. *Prices, Cost and Output*. Oxford: Basil Blackwell.

Williamson, Harold F., and Daum, Arnold F. 1959. *The American Petroleum Industry*. Evanston, Ill.: Northwestern University Press.

Williamson, John. 1966. 'Profit, Growth and Sales Maximization', *Economica* **33**, 1-16.

Williamson, Oliver E. 1963a. 'Managerial Discretion and Business Behavior', *American Economic Review* **53**, 1032-57.

Williamson, Oliver E. 1963b. 'Selling Expense as a Barrier to Entry', *Quarterly Journal of Economics* **77**, 112-28.

Williamson, Oliver E. 1964. *The Economics of Discretionary Behavior: Managerial*

Objectives in a Theory of the Firm. Englewood Cliffs, NJ: Prentice-Hall.

Williamson, Oliver E. 1965. 'A Dynamic Theory of Interfirm Behavior', *Quarterly Journal of Economics* **79,** 579-607.

Wilson, T., and Andrews, P. W. S. 1951. *Oxford Studies in the Price Mechanism.* Oxford: Clarendon Press.

Wood, Adrian. 1971. 'Diversification, Merger and Research Expenditures: A Review of Empirical Studies', in Marris and Wood, eds., 1971, Appendix C, pp. 428-53.

Worcester, Dean A. Jr. 1957. 'Why "Dominant Firms" Decline', *Journal of Political Economy* **65,** 338-46.

Working, Elmer J., Ladd, G. W., and Tedford, J. R. 1959. 'A Generalization of the Working Method for Estimating Long-Term Elasticities', *Journal of Farm Economics* **41,** 221-33.

Youtsler, James S. 1956. *Labor's Wage Policies in the Twentieth Century.* New York: Twayne Publishers.

Zarnowitz, Victor. 1962. 'Unfilled Orders, Price Changes and Business Fluctuations', *Review of Economics and Statistics* **44,** 367-94.

Zeman, Harry. 1966. 'Trends in White-Collar Salaries, 1961-66', *Monthly Labor Review* **89,** 1250-5.

Zudak, L. S. 1970. 'Productivity, Labor Demand and Production Facility', *Journal of Industrial Economics* **18,** 255-74.

Zudak, L. S. 1971. 'Labor Demand and Multi-Product Cost in Semi-Continuous and Multi-Process Facilities', *Journal of Industrial Economics* **19,** 267-90.

Index

Abramowitz, M., 51
accelerator models of investment, 7, 194-6, 218, 304, 315, 317
accountability, by megacorp's executive group, 272
ad valorem taxes, 198-9, 238, 250-1
administered prices, 38, 42, 293
advertising, ability of to shift consumption function, 284, 326; as barrier to entry, 72, 73, 107; as investment, 90-6, 191, 283-4; as part of corporate levy, 13, 58, 60, 61; social benefits from, 284, 326
aggregate demand, effect of on price level, 8, 180, 210, 259-60; theories of income distribution, 145, 177-81, 201
aggregate output, rate of growth of, 191, 197, 201-4, 207-9, 217, 226, 278-9; rate of growth of, change in, 236, 255, 275-6; rate of growth of, change in, effect of on price level, 259-60, 271; rate of growth of, government control over, 199, 222-4, 234-44, 248-50, 271, 275-6
airline industry, 305
aluminum industry, 301
American economy, in the 1960s, 263-70
anthropogenic system, 226
antitrust laws, 40, 41-2, 272, 284
antitrust prosecution, 77, 79-80, 106, 272
arbitration, compulsory, 155, 159
assumptions, metamorphic vs. modificatory, 50, 51, 54, 295; of oligopolistic pricing model, 3, 18, 126
AT & T, predominant role of in capital funds market, 305
Australia, 159
automobile industry, 159-62, 265-6, 301
auto-steel orbit, 160, 172
automatic stabilizers, 205
autonomous shifts in sectoral curves, 210, 220-3, 234-44, 248-9

backlog, of orders, 259, 294
Bain, J., 4, 71, 104
bargaining (*see* collective bargaining)
barriers to entry, 71-4, 103-7, 112, 116, 253, 288; investment in increasing, 92-3
basic research, 93
basing point system, 43
Baumol, W., 4, 52
behavioral theories of the firm (*see* theories of the firm, behavioral)
benefits, private vs. social, 95-6, 283-4
bellwether industry (*see* industry, bellwether)
Berle, A., 19, 50
Bhagwati, J., 103
boom and bust cycle, 214
bottlenecks (*see* supply constraints)
Buchanan, N., 53
budgeting, capital, 97, 304; public, 286
bureaucratic nature, of the megacorp (*see* megacorp, bureaucratic nature of
business sector, 9, 260, 318
buyer, type of found in market, 133-6, 141-2

Cambridge School in economics, 146, 177-81, 190-1, 308
capacity, expansion of, 90, 137-8, 181-2, 192-3, 204, 211, 245, 283; reserve, 35, 36-7, 90, 106-7, 195, 257, 259, 261, 304; shortages of, 260-2; (*see also*, engineer-rated capacity; utilization, rate of)
capital accumulation process, 14, 95, 115; alternative models of, 111-16, 274-5
capital bias, under regulation, 116
capital debt holders, 147, 152 (*see*

also equity debt holders; fixed interest debt holders)
capital expenditures, decisions with respect to, 117 (*see also* investment, by megacorp)
capital funds market, 111-12, 120, 125, 237, 152, 187-90, 193, 200, 245, 253, 274-5, 284-5, 325
capital gains, from stock ownership, 282, 308, 312
capital goods, cost of, 20
capital goods industry, role of in technological progress, 181-2
capitalism, changes in, 20, 179
capitalists, 178-9
cartels, 40
cash flow (*see* corporate levy
Cassel, G., 38
ceiling, on price increases (*see* upper limit, on price increases)
Chamberlin, E., 135, 295
Chicago tradition in economics, 305
classical tradition in economics, 175
collective bargaining, 6, 151-62, 176-7, 182-8
collusion, 303, 307 (*see also* joint profit maximization)
commodities, internationally traded, 135, 310
compensation, of capital debt holders, 146-9, 274, 276, 281; of equity debt holders, 144-5, 148-9, 168-72, 179, 186, 242, 281; of fixed interest debt holders, 148, 281; of laboring manpower force, 144-5, 146-7, 175, 179, 186, 242, 276; of laboring manpower force, effect of on dividends, 168-72 (*see also* dividend payments; wages)
competition, inter-industry, 120; non-price, 43, 88, 181, 291; perfect (*see* pricing models, polypolistic); via investment, 88, 306
competition limits, on bargaining, 153-6
competitive sector (*see* non-oligopolistic sector)
computers, 305
concentration ratios, 288, 293
conglomerate expansion, 106, 112, 118-22, 142, 191, 285, 303
conglomerate megacorp, 5, 23, 108, 117-26; as price follower, 123; as price leader, 122
consumer durables, 215, 247, 265, 319
consumer goods, 39, 67, 135
consumer prices (*see* cost of living)
consumption, 203
contractionary phase of business cycle, 202, 205, 243
contracyclical policy, 244-60, 320
control, of megacorp (*see* decision-making power, locus of within megacorp; megacorp, social control over)
corporation (*see* megacorp)
corporate income tax, 13-14, 198-9, 217-18, 238, 240, 251-3, 322; incidence of, 250-6
corporate levy, 13, 23-5, 52-3, 56, 61-5, 66, 88, 101-3, 115, 117, 120, 140, 179, 185, 206, 280-1, 283; average, 62-5, 102-3, 171, 197, 240, 277; allocation of by conglomerate megacorp, 118-22; derivation of from different industries, 122-4; elimination of, 137-41, 143; growth of (*see* maximands, growth of corporate levy); marginal, 63, 64-5, 91-3; prohibition of under regulation, 110-11, 285; restriction of under polypoly, 126, 132-3, 137-40, 210, 247; realized, sensitivity of to actual operating ratio, 64-5, 130, 179-80, 196, 201-2, 206; restrictions on use of, 283-5, 286
cost advantages, absolute, as barrier to entry, 72-3, 74
cost-compensating price changes (*see* price level, cost-compensating changes in)
cost curves, U-shaped, 30-1, 36, 129-31, 256; under monopoly, 109; under oligopoly, 3, 31-7
cost of living, 267; as factor in collective bargaining, 183-4, 186, 242
cost reduction, investment to achieve, 191, 291, 303, 313
costs, changes in, 6, 103, 144-88, differential in among plants, 34-5,

129, 308; direct labor, 163, fixed, 31, 33-6, 41, 58-61, 63, 110-11, 114, 144, 163-4, 292; impact of wage pattern on, 162-75, 270; material inputs, 32-33, 152, 163, 274; of raising funds internally, 66-80, 253, 273-4; overhead personnel, 163-4, 273; social, 274, 283; variable, 31, 33-7, 57-8, 129-30, 141, 143-4, 162-3 (*see also*, marginal cost)
Council of Economic Advisors, President's, 263-6
Cournot duopoly model, 3
credit, availability of, 246-8, 285, 321
cyclical behavior of income shares, 178, 180-1, 184-5, 201-2, 243
cyclical fluctuations, 184, 201-2; proclivity of economy toward, 16-17, 62, 96, 195, 248, 260
Cyert, R., and March, J., 5, 49

dealer-franchise systems (*see* distribution systems)
debt, willingness to incur, 234, 236-8, 245, 276
debt-equity ratio, 86
debt service, cost of additional, 114
debt structure, 86-7, 149
decision-making power, locus of within megacorp, 20-1, 58, 117, 179
decision rules, 290
defense expenditures, 324
deficits, 234, 236-7, 268, 276, 318
demand, industry, 43-4, 89, 106, 136-7, 210; need to anticipate, 89, 106 (*see also*, elasticity of industry demand)
demand curve, for investment funds, 56, 89-103, 113, 124-5, 244
demand curve, individual oligopolist's, 43-4; kinked, 293-4
depreciation allowances, 61, 110-11, 126
determinateness, of oligopolistic pricing model, 3-4, 46-9, 97-103
Dewey, D., 106-7
discretionary expenditures, 215; relative proportions of among different sectors, 318 (*see also*, investment)
discretionary income, 215 (*see also* savings)
disguised unemployment, 229, 319
disposable income, rate of growth of, 216, 277-9
distribution systems, as barrier to entry, 72, 92
differentiating the industry's product, 90-2
diversification (*see* conglomerate expansion)
dividend payments, as part of fixed costs, 34, 58-60, 110, 179, 280; change in, 7, 54, 59, 111, 149, 164-72, 282, 296; effect of on relative income distribution, 179, 272, 282; limitations on, 282-3, 296, growth of, 164-72, 186, 281, 286, 311; reductions in, 296; relationship to change in net revenue, 25-7, 53-4
Downs, A., 49
Duesenberry, J., 51
dynamic analysis, distinguished from static analysis, 193, 198

earnings (*see* net earnings; profit)
economic development, 15, 229
economic growth, 14-15, 96
economic history, 1960s, 263-70
economic welfare, 17
economies of scale, as barrier to entry, 72-4
Eisner, R., 7, 194
elasticity of demand curve for investment funds, 113, 115-16
elasticity of industry demand, as factor determining substitution effect, 69-71, 82, 85, 90-1, 112, 123-4, 128; in Chamberlin-Robinson model, 48-9, 127; long-run, 299; under oligopoly, 5, 48, 69, 71; under regulated monopoly, 114
elasticity of revenue curves, 44-5, 48, 127, 132
elasticity of substitution, 106, 108, 289
elasticity of supply curve for internally generated funds, 85, 113-14

empirical evidence, on cost curves, 35, 37; on investment demand, 194-6; on shifting of corporate income tax, 323, on supply shortages, 262

employees (*see* laboring manpower force)

employment, rate of growth of, 226, 230, 264, 267

employment effects, 154, 227-31

endogenous processes, 193, 199, 205, 237

engineer-rated capacity, 29, 62, 259

entrepreneurial function, within the megacorp, 58-9

entry, as means of expansion under polypoly, 137-8, 141, 212, 261; ease of, 134-9, 140, 256-7 (*see also*, barriers to entry)

entry factor, 4, 28, 37, 71-7, 80-4, 92-3, 98, 103-7, 112, 127, 137, 280, 317; in case of cost-compensating price increase, 172-3; in case of tax-neutralizing price increase, 252-3, 255; probabilistic nature of, 74-7, 104, 106

entry-limiting models (*see* pricing models, stay-out)

equalization, of growth rate among megacorps, 120-1, 123-4; of implicit cost of internally generated funds, 123-4; of MEI among industries, 118, 120-1, 124

equity debt, 86, 245, 289

equity debt holders, 6, 20-1, 53, 58-9, 61, 148-9, 164-72, 175, 179, 280-2, 313; claim of on megacorp's net revenue, 25-7, 61, 281-2; right of to depose incumbent management, 149, 281

excess capacity (*see* capacity, reserve)

excess demand explanation for inflation, 260-2, 266, 271

excess investment, relative to savings, 16-17, 200, 205, 208, 213-14, 220, 222, 234, 245, 249-50

excess savings, relative to investment, 16-17, 205, 208, 213-14, 220, 222, 242, 250, 260

excise taxes, 13 (*see also ad valorem* taxes)

executive group, 6, 20-3, 51, 58, 118, 168-71, 179, 311; empathy of with equity debt holders, 152, 168-9, 171, 186; fiduciary role of, 169; threat to control by, 34, 87, 111, 149, 164-8, 170, 281-2; replacement of, 287

executives, development of, 33, 138; selection of by conglomerate firm, 117 (*see also* management)

exogenous factors, 16

expansionary phase of business cycle, 202, 205

expectations, 197, 209, 237, 244-6

exports (*see* investment, foreign sector)

external funds, access to, 59, 101, 111-12, 200, 247-8, 253, 303, 305; demand for, 115, 179, 278; regulated firm's dependence on, 115, 247 (*see also*, interest rate, permanent)

external financing, significance of, 206, 274, 281, 289 (*see also*, internal financing)

factor coefficients, fixed nature of, 3, 5, 28-30, 57, 61, 127, 144, 146, 149-50, 155; variability of, 129, 141

factor prices, influence of on technological change, 150, 181-2

factor pricing (*see* income distribution)

'fair return' principle, 110

'fair share,' labor's, 182-3, 185, 186, 228, 242

Federal expenditures, 263-70

Federal Reserve Board, 12, 245, 263, 267, 313, 322

Fellner, W., 40

Ferguson, C., 50

financial intermediaries, 59, 87, 112, 247, 290

firms, number of, 2, 132, 140; size of, 19, 132, 140, 167

fiscal drag, 264, 318

fiscal policy, 1, 130, 199, 224, 244-5, 248-56, 272, 275, 277, 286

fixed interest debt holders, 20, 58-9, 148, 282

fixed interest obligations, 86, 148, 195, 245, 274, 289, 320

flow of funds accounts, 316
fluctuations in aggregate demand, firm's adjustment to, 62-3, 72; sensitivity of prices to, 180 (*see also* aggregate demand, rate of growth of, changes in)
foreign sector, 209, 216-17, 289; stability characteristics of, 217-18
full-costing principle, 110-16, 273 (*see also* pricing models, cost-plus)
full employment, 225, 230

Galbraith, J., 5, 272
game theory, 3
General Theory, The, 189, 195, 197, 200, 206, 225
Golden Age, 260
government, ability of to allocate resources, 286
government intervention, 4, 28, 77-81, 93-4, 98, 113-14, 127, 278, 280; in collective bargaining, 161, 185-6, 266; probability of, 80, 93-4, 104, 123-4, 174, 253-4; probability of in case of cost-compensating price increase, 172-4; probability of in case of tax-neutralizing price increase, 252-3, 255; to halt inflation, 271
government sector, 9-10, 209, 247; rate of growth of, 218; rate of growth of during Johnson Administration, 267-8; role of in initiating changes in aggregate growth rate, 222-3, 234-7, 248-50; share of total discretionary spending, 318; stabilizing characteristics of, 217-18; wage bill, 316
growth of the firm, through expansion of capacity, 181 (*see also,* maximands, growth of the firm)
growth-price stability trade-off (*see* Phillipsian dilemma)
growth rate, deviation of actual from secular, 197, 201-3; 'natural,' 226; potential, 8, 15-16, 222, 224-33; secular, 197, 209, 259, 277, 278-9; secular, change in, 184-92, 202, 206-7, 221-3, 229, 270, 275-6; secular, change in, difficulty in achieving, 8, 220, 224, 234-44, 260; secular, change in, difficulty in distinguishing from cyclical movements, 184-5, 243-4; secular, effect of change in on technological progress, 232-3; warranted, 208-9, 219, 240, 249-50, 317 (*see also* aggregate output, rate of growth of)
guideposts, Presidential, 263-6, 277, 314, 320

haggling, under polypoly, 44-5
Hale, R., 150
Harrod, R., 178, 317
Heflebower, R., 51
Heller, W., 264
Hicks, J., 38, 306
Higgins, B., 50
history of the 1960s (*see* economic history, 1960s)
Horowitz, I., 50
household sector, 9-10, 152, 209, 215-16, 247, 268, 277-8; redistribution of income within, 320; stability characteristics of, 216, 218
human resource development, theory of, 226

ideal types, 45, 294
imports, 67, 173, 299 (*see also* savings, foreign sector)
incidence of corporate income tax (*see* corporate income tax, incidence of)
income, distribution of, 144-88, 276, 307; distribution of within megacorp, 5, 51, 103; distribution of, struggle over, 103, 255, 260, 271, 276; distribution of, theories of, 5, 145-59, 175-82
income, redistribution of, 197, 243, 275
incomes policy, 276, 321
increasing returns, 240
independence in pricing, 131-43
independence, of savings, and investment functions, 204
indicative planning, 9, 278-88, 325-6
indivisibilities, technical, 29, 72
industrial reserve army, 319
industry, bellwether, 159-62, 174, 176, 187, 242-3; definition of, 10,

289; planning panels, 285
inflation, 1-2, 190, 233, 263, 266-70, 272, 279, 281, 288; cost-push, 2, 263; effects of, 59; sources of, 233-44, 260-70, (*see also*, wage-price spiral)
institutional advertising, 93
institutional economics, 5, 145, 150-1, 155, 175, 289
instrumental variables, 276, 280, 325
interdependence, conjectural, 104, 133; of firms in oligopoly, 38-40, 43, 45, 71, 79, 89, 92, 93, 103, 131, 135, 288 (*see also*, joint profit maximization)
interest, paid fixed debt holders, 58, 110
interest elasticity, of investment, 245-6; of investment by regulated firms, 115
interest rate, implicit, on internally generated funds, 4, 69-71, 76-7, 80-5, 88, 94, 113, 122-6, 174, 253-4
interest rate, permanent, 4, 66, 70, 76, 86-8, 100-1, 110, 124-6, 164, 168, 195, 245-6
interest rate theory, liquidity preference vs. loanable funds, 320
interest rates, 245-6; as determinant of investment, 195; long-term vs. short-term, 245-6, 320; term structure of, 321
intermediation, 321
internal financing, importance of, 13, 112 (*see also* external financing
internal growth, 138, 143
internally generated funds, 13, 66, 245 (*see also* corporate levy)
intersectoral effects, 209, 247-8, 255, 280, 320
intertemporal revenue flows, 56, 107, 291
inventories, role of in adjusting production, 31, 132, 292
investment, as link between micro and macro models, 190; by megacorp, 7, 88-96; continuous nature of, 193; effect of on relative income distribution, 178; foreign sector, 217, 319; government sector, 217, 318-19; in erecting a more favorable public image, 89, 93-6, 191, 245; in differentiating industry's product, 89, 90-2, 94-6, 191, 245; in erecting higher barriers to entry, 89, 92-3, 94-6, 191, 245; need to regulate, 9, 283-5; on new plant and equipment, 89-90, 283; predominant influence of, 206; role of in pricing, 2-3, 5, 52-3, 56, 65, 107, 130, 193, 275; share of by non-oligopolistic sector, 214; social control over, 9, 272, 286; socially optimum, 285; varying definitions of, 94-6, 214
investment demand, rate of growth within aggregate economy, 236-7, 276; rate of growth within foreign sector, 217, 276; rate of growth within government sector, 218, 236-7, 249, 275-6; rate of growth within household sector, 215-16, 276; rate of growth within non-oligopolistic sector, 212-14, 276; rate of growth within oligopolistic sector, 191-7, 199, 204, 206-7, 236-8, 265, 276
investment demand curve, aggregate, 218; foreign sector's, 217, 221; government's 221-2, 245, 249-50; non-oligopolistic sector's, 212-14, 221; oligopolistic sector's, 191-7, 203, 208-9, 218, negatively sloped, 191-2
investment funds, access to, 113; additional amounts generated internally, 68-70, 84-5, 123-5; allocation of, 111-16, 120; demand for, 65, 88-96; supply cost of, 65-88, 114-15, 196; sources, 59, 87-8, 91-3, 197-8, 283
investment strategy, 90, 97

Johns, B., 106
Johnson administration, 264-9, 277, 301, 314
Johnston, J., 37
joint profit maximization, 40, 102, 131, 133, 141, 288

Kaldor, N., 7, 191, 232
Kaldor effect, 320
Kalecki, M., 1, 178, 296-7, 314, 317-18

Kamien, M., and Schwarz, N., 106-7
Kennedy administration, 263-5, 277, 314
key bargain, 159, 183-8, 264-8 (*see also* national incremental wage pattern)
Keynes, J., 1, 9, 178, 189-91, 193, 200, 225, 288
Keynesian effect, short-run, 177-81, 184, 201-3, 317
Keynesian theory, 2-3, 16, 145, 177-81, 189-91, 200-1, 203, 206, 275, 288, 289, 317, 320

labor force, peripheral, 319, 320
labor reserves, 228-9, 261, 320
labor theory of value, 175, 319
laboring manpower force, 5, 20, 145, 146-7, 151-6; growth rate of, 226; specific to each megacorp, 32; unorganized portion, 151-2, 175, 186
lag effects, 197, 203; in response to change in secular growth rate, 191; of investment relative to sales, 191, 193, 207
laissez-faire, 127
lay-offs, 32
learning process, 40, 43, 133
Leibenstein, H., 165
lending, by megacorp, 119
less developed nations, 229, 310
Lindahl, E. 38
Lintner, J., 54
liquid assets, accumulation of as threat to management, 120, 166, 168; change in, 202, 316
long run, 15, 65, 133, 139, 154 (*see also*, time horizon)
Lutz, F., 53
Lydall, H., 106

macro theory, micro foundations of, 189-91
macrodynamic balance, 8, 200, 240-4, 276, 281
macrodynamic behavior, 204-23, 248-50, 260-70
macroeconomic approach to control, 275-88
management, competence of, 165-6; divergence of interests, 21-2, 51; effecting change in, 59, 287; generalized utility function of, 50; separation of from ownership, 3, 19-28, 45, 49, 109, 127-9, 290, 311; techniques, 33
managerial class, 20, 138
managerial compensation, 58
managerial costs, as overhead expense, 58, 72
managerial resources, as limit on firm's expansion, 30, 33, 118, 129, 137-8, 306
managerial theories of the firm (*see* theories of the firm, managerial)
manpower, demand for, 226; supply of, 226, 261
manpower constraints, on growth rate, 224-31, 260-1
manpower resources, 9, 15, 73, 226
manufacturing, extent of oligopoly in, 11; reliance of on external funds, 289
margin, above costs, 7, 33, 56, 63, 71, 88, 185, 197, 244, 274-5, 277-8, 280, 285, 287; changes at the, 102, 177
marginal cost, 30, 32-7, 46, 57-8, 127, 129-31, 136-7, 141, 210, 256-8; constancy of, 33-7, 46-7, 57-8, 63, 109, 127, 129, 257, 292; equation of with marginal revenue, 28, 35, 46-7, 48, 66, 128, 130-1, 257-8, 290, 295; equation of with price, 273
marginal efficiency of investment, 146-8, 191-3, 196, 208; megacorp's, 4, 70, 76, 88-9, 91-6, 118-26, 146-8, 191-2, 195, 204, 244
marginal product, differentiated from marginal efficiency of investment, 146-8, 306
marginal productivity theory, 5, 145-50, 189, 288
marginal propensity to consume, 216
marginal propensity to save, 179; megacorp's, 65
market mechanisms, limitations of, 286
market power, megacorp's 2, 12, 56, 67, 85, 142, 199, 245, 255, 272, 274-5, 280, 293; constraints on, 4, 66-80, 109, 127, 172; role of in

inflation, 6, 262, 268, 272, 277, 280-1,
market share, retention of, 25, 39-41, 51-2, 89-90, 117-18, 192, 194, 245, 261; stability in, 25, 63, 291
Marris, R., 4, 52, 167, 311, 320
Marshall, A., 139, 175, 189-90, 314
Marx, K., 20, 145, 175, 319
Marxian theory, 5, 6, 175-7, 289
maximands, firm's present net worth, 25-7, 53; growth of the corporate levy, 23-5, 27, 52-4, 88-9, 117; growth of the firm, 3, 23-5, 27, 51-4, 88, 117, 119, 171; long-run net revenue, 25, 51, 53-4; market share, 51-2, 89, 97, 117; sales, 51, 52, 295; short-run net revenue, 21, 27-8, 48-51, 141, 290
maximands, trade unions', 155
Means, G., 19, 50
megacorp, and trade unions, 151-62, 271, 278; as monopolist, 108-16, 122; as representative firm in oligopoly, 3, 10, 19, 45, 291; as a price setter, 38; availability of inputs to, 262; behavioral pattern of, 3, 7, 20-5, 28, 45, 48, 109, 117, 290; bureaucratic nature of, 146-7; constituencies of, 5, 20-1, 58, 144, 152, 169-70, 175-6, 179, 198; control of, 165, 290; cost curves of, 3, 19, 31-7, 45; cumulative decline of, 120; differential returns from direct investment of funds, 66, 119-20; emphasis on growth, 120-1; entrepreneurial abilities of, 120; entrepreneurial function within, 58-9; essential characteristics of, 3, 19-45; goals of, 23-4, 28, 156, 171, 194; growth curve of, 89-90, 120; inability to alter price unilaterally, 43-4; multiplicity of plants, 3, 19, 28-37, 45, 109, 127, 129-31, 138; multiplicity of plants, economies from, 72; normal operating range of, 37, 46-7; planning within, 89, 138; public image of, 80, 93-4; relative permanence of, 290; residual income of, 6, 58-9, 67, 179, 198, 260; revenue curve of, 3, 19, 44-5; savings, 7, 13, 65, 198; short-run pricing situation of, 45-6; size of as deterrent to take-over bid, 167; social control over, 171-80, 280-1, 285-6; supply curve of, 258-9; taxes on, 198, 203, 250-6; time horizon of, 21, 49, 52-3, 127, 258 (*see also*, conglomerate megacorp; corporate levy; oligopoly; oligopolistic sector)
microeconomic approach to control, 274-5, 280
micro foundation of Keynesian theory, 189-91, 280, 317
middleman network, 134-6, 141-3
monetary flows, 12, 195
monetary policy, 1, 12-13, 131, 224, 244-8, 263, 267, 272, 281, 312; effect of on regulated industries, 115
monetary system, 12, 201, 206
money supply, 201, 244, 245
monopolistic competition, 209-14 (*see also* pricing models, monopolistic competition)
monopoly, bilateral, 136; regulated, 108-16, 285; unregulated, 5, 107-9, 127-31
monopoly power (*see* market power)
monopsony (*see* oligopsony)
Monsen, R., 49
multi-plant operation (*see* megacorp, multiplicity of plants)
myth, regarding role of stockholders, 26-7, 58, 167-70, 176, 282, 312

national incremental wage pattern, 6-9, 159-88, 197-9, 242-4, 250, 259, 263, 265-6, 268, 276-9, 282, 286; effect of on savings in oligopolistic sector, 197-8, 203, 238-44; relationship of to inflation, 241-4, 268, 270
nationalization, 77-8, 273
natural growth rate (*see*, growth rate, natural)
natural resources, as limiting factor in economic growth, 233
neo-classical production function, 8, 313
neo-classical proprietorship, 140; as price taker, 131-2; as representative

firm in polypolistic industries, 10-11, 45, 127, 291; as representative firm under monopolistic competition, 135-6; behavioral rule of, 20, 127, 132; effect of fluctuating demand on, 210-11; managerial limits on, 30, 33, 137, 211-12, 261; revenue curve of, 44-5; residual income of, 137, 143, 210-11; single-plant operation of, 129-31; 137-8, 211, 256; time horizon of, 127-9, 130, 132 (*see also*, polypoly; polypolistic sector)
neo-Keynesians, 288
net earnings, growth of, 166, 168; growth of, effect of on wage rates, 183-5, 242-3 (*see also*, maximands, short-run net revenue)
1960s experience (*see* economic history, 1960s)
Nixon administration, 270, 277-8, 301, 313, 320
non-oligopolistic sector, 10, 136, 209-14, 247, 260-2, 307, 315, 319; demand for manpower in, 226; growth rate of, 211, 214, 218, 261-2; manpower drain on, 227-8, 261; stability characteristics of, 213-14, 218, 272
non-price competition (*see* competition, non-price)
normative theory of income distribution, 145, 156-9, 175
norms, group, 169; societal, 5, 158-9, 173

oligopolistic sector, 2, 10, 249, 260, 268, 272, 307; delineation of, 136, 143; demand for manpower in, 226-7; differential ability of to obtain manpower, 227; difficulty in shifting savings curve of, 224, 234, 250-6; effect of on use of conventional policy instruments, 224, 272; growth rate of, 207, 218; share of investment, 318, 319; significance of, 11-12, 272, 293; social surplus arising in, 6-7; stabilizing characteristics of, 193, 205, 209, 234-44, 272
oligopoly, essential nature of, 2, 38-9, 288; emergence of, 11, 107, 142, 293; joint profit maximization within, 3; dominant firm model of, 40-1; price leadership model of, 40, 306; recognized interdependence within, 3, 38-9; regulated, 109-16, 285; with product differentiation, 39-40, 307
oligopsony, 134-5, 136, 141
operating capacity (*see* capacity; engineer-rated capacity)
operating ratio, actual, 64, 180, 184-5
opportunity cost of capital, 110
organizational factors, 49, 229
organized labor (*see* trade unions)
outlays, average total anticipated, 258 (*see also*, megacorp, revenue curve of)
output per worker, 144, 181-3, 198, 202, 231-3, 238, 240-1, 263, 265, 270, 276, 283, 320

parameters, of investment function, 197; of savings function, 203, 222, 238, 240, 249, 255, 260
Pashigian, B., 107
Patinkin, D., 38
pattern bargaining (*see* national incremental wage pattern)
pay-off period, 118-19
personal income tax, 252, 322
Phillipsian dilemma, 225, 272, 288
Pigou, A., 314
planning (*see* indicative planning; megacorp, planning within)
planning period, 15, 65, 86, 128, 180-1, 184-5, 201, 206, 258
plant and equipment, investment in new (*see* investment, in new plant and equipment; capacity, expansion of)
plant size, minimal optimal, 72, 74-6, 123, 124
plants, multiplicity of (*see* megacorps, multiplicity of plants)
policy implications, of macrodynamic model, 271-80
policy instruments, conventional, 1, 8-9, 224, 244-60, 263, 272
political institutions, weakness of, 286
political trade cycle, 1, 265, 271

polypoly, 209-14, 288-9 (*see also*, pricing models, polypolistic)
population growth, as measuring natural growth rate, 226
post-Keynesian theory, 2-3, 7-8, 178-82, 184, 188, 190-1, 193, 275, 288, 289, 308, 317, 320
potential growth rate (*see* growth rate, potential)
power relationships, 5, 150-6
power theory of income distribution, 145, 150-6
price, actual transaction (effective), 294; 'just,' 156, 158; 'normal,' 134-5, 139, 141; seller's list (quoted), 294; socially optimum, 273-5
price changes, frequency of, 294; minimization of, 42, 98-9, 258, 323
price competition, avoidance of, 24, 40-3, 55, 88, 141
price controls, 273, 277-8, 301 (*see also* price regulation)
price coordination, 40-2, 77, 97, 109, 258, 293
price determination, under oligopoly, 2-3, 45-9
price differentials, 39-40
price-dividend ratio, 86, 164, 168, 311
price freeze, 273
price leader, as surrogate for the industry, 43, 47, 55, 97, 152, 294; cost curves of, 47, 55; disciplinary action of, 41; revenue curves of, 47-8, 55
price leadership, 4, 40-2, 63, 131, 255, 306
price level, aggregate, 8-9, 267, 271; absolute, 55-65, 71; changes in, 4, 55-6, 65-107, 122-4, 244-5, 202, 204, 244; cost-compensating changes in, 172-5, 186, 242-4; effect of aggregate demand on, 256, 259-60, 271; effect of investment on, 2-3, 5, 52-3, 56, 65, 107, 130, 193; government's ability to control, 259-60, 270; in non-oligopolistic sector, 231, 267, 269; in oligopolistic sector, 8, 55-107, 145, 197, 203, 204, 206, 238, 244, 250, 259-60, 266-7, 269-70, 271; in oligopolistic sector, effect on savings, 197-8; relative, 67; under regulation, 109-11, 114-6
price list, open, 42-3
price maintenance, 42-3, 45, 132, 135, 136, 140, 143
price mechanism, as a means of altering intertemporal revenue flows, 56, 70; as a stabilizing factor, 16
price reductions, under oligopoly, 67, 98-9, 103, 240, 255
price regulation, 77, 78, 109-16, 272-5
price shaving, 43, 47, 105-6, 131-3, 139, 294
price stability, 279
price taker, firm as, 126, 131-3, 135-6, 140-1, 143
price wars, 41, 104
prices, downward rigidity of in oligopolistic sector, 276; identical, 42-3, 293
pricing, by conglomerate firm, 124-6
pricing discretion (*see* market power)
pricing dynamic, oligopolistic, 144, 280
pricing formula, oligopolistic, 57, 101, 110, 140; oligopolistic, role of taxes in, 250-2
pricing independence (*see* independence of pricing)
pricing models, behavioral assumptions of, 49-54; Chamberlin-Robinson monopoly, 5, 48-9, 129, 131; cost-plus, 3-4, 56, 130; cost-plus, objections to, 63; Cournot, 3; Marshallian polypoly, 126-7, 132-4, 140-3, 293; monopolistic competition, 135-6, 138, 307; oligopolistic, 55-102, 108-9, 129, 131, 139, 191, 194-6, 197; polypolistic, 38, 49, 126-43, 272, 288; satisficing, 5, 49-50, 53; stay-out, 104, 106; Walrasian polypoly, 126-7, 131-3, 141-3, 293
pricing period, 15, 42
pricing rule, optimum, 287
prisoners' dilemma, 133
probability, of entry, 74-7, 82, 85, 92, 104-7, 123-4, 138-40, 143; of independent pricing, 140 (*see also*

government intervention, probability of)
product differentiation, 135-6; as barrier to entry, 72-4
product line, 39
production techniques, 67, 69
productivity, 65, 144, 308 (*see also*, output per worker; technological progress)
profit, as a per cent of sales, 166, 168; avoidance of term, 60; relationship of to corporate levy, 61-2, 179, 274, 277, 280-1; as a determinant of investment, 195-6, 212
profit maximization (*see* maximands, short-run net revenue)
promotional expenses, 73
proxy battles, 165, 290, 310
public goods, 218
public image, of megacorp (*see* megacorp, public image)
public utilities (*see* monopoly, regulated; price level, under regulation)

R & D, as barrier to entry, 72; as investment, 90-6, 191, 284-5; as part of corporate levy, 13, 58, 60-1
railroads, 309
rate of return, on investment (*see* marginal efficiency of investment)
raw materials control, as barrier to entry, 73 (*see also*, costs, material inputs)
'real balances' effect, 321
receivership, 287
recession, 263, 267, 277
redistributive effect, of change in savings curve parameters, 249, 255; of divergence between savings and investment, 223, 241
regulatory bodies, 109-16, 273
regulation, by commission, 78, 109-11, 116, 273, 275, 285
rentier income, 279 (*see also*, compensation, equity debt holders)
replacement, of less efficient plant and equipment, 90
reserve capacity (*see* capacity, reserve)
residential construction, 215, 247, 263, 265, 267, 319, 322
residual income (*see* corporate levy)
rest-of-the-world sector (*see* foreign sector)
retained earnings, 26-7, 60, 111, 137, 280, 283
retaliation, for price shaving, 41, 74, 132
retention rate, 66, 111
revenue curve, 3, 44-5, 127
risk, of lending funds to others, 119-20
risk-bearing, within megacorp, 58-9
Robinson, J., 1, 7, 15, 191, 207, 260, 295, 306, 313, 314
rules of thumb, 25, 86, 91, 119, 291, 296

safety valve, price level as, 9, 186
sales, loss of due to entry factor, 74-7, 81; loss of due to substitution effect, 67-71, 81; industry, rate of growth of, 191, 192-4, 196, 204-5
sales tax, regressive nature of, 322
Samuelson, P., 38
satisficing behavior (*see* pricing models, satisficing)
savings, 7, 13, 112-13, 197-204, 214-15; business, 197, 203, 214; foreign sector, 216; government, 14, 217, 307; household, 7, 13, 179, 197, 200, 203, 215-16, 274-5, 289, 307; non-oligopolistic sector, 137, 143; oligopolistic sector, 65, 179, 197-204, 236; planned (*ex ante*), 201, 206; rate of growth within aggregate economy, 276; rate of growth within foreign sector, 217, 276; rate of growth within governmental sector, 217-18, 236, 249, 276; rate of growth within household sector, 215-16, 276; rate of growth within non-oligopolistic sector, 210-14, 216, 276; rate of growth within oligopolistic sector, 191-204, 207-9, 236, 276; realized (*ex post*), 201-2, 204-5, 206
savings curve, aggregate, 218, 236, 240; difficulty in shifting oligopolistic sector's, 234, 238-44,

255, 276; government sector's 218, 221, 245, 249-50, 264; household sector's, 216, 220; non-oligopolistic sector's, 211-14, 220; oligopolistic sector's 208-9, 234-44, 250, 255, 264, 320
savings curves, shifting of, 276, 320
savings function, oligopolistic sector's 191, 197-204, 317
savings-investment adjustment process, 7, 17, 190, 200-2, 204-9, 212-14, 217-18
savings rate, aggregate, difficulty in adjusting, 234-44, 260, 320; under oligopoly, 88, 197
savings ratio, 8, 88
Say's Law, 189
Schumpeterian grand invention, 221-2
scrapping (*see* replacement, of less efficient plant and equipment)
secular behavior of relative income, 178
secular growth rate (*see* growth rate, secular)
services, 175, 307, 320
Sherman Act (*see* antitrust laws)
shift variable, 197, 203, 237, 238
shifting, of corporate income tax (*see* corporate income tax, incidence of)
shortages of labor, 226, 230, 259, 260-2, 266-7
Simon, H., 5, 49
skill vector, 226-7, 230
skills, 226
slack, in American economy, 154
slope of savings and investment curves, change in, 249; relative, 210, 212-13, 216-18, 264, 304, 314, 318
social and economic council, 278, 285
social control, over megacorp, 9, 169, 250-6, 271-88
social security trust fund, 283
social surplus, 6-7, 176-7, 198, 240, 243, 260, 276, 285-6
Solow, R., 38
speculators, role of, 134-5, 141, 143
stability, of polypolistic model, 142-3
standard operating ratio, 62, 64, 180, 184, 201, 206-7, 258
standards, for combining inputs, 29-31
stay-out pricing (*see* pricing models, stay-out)
steel industry, 159-62, 263-4
Steindl, J., 297, 317
stock, company's purchase of own, 166, 310
stock options, 21, 169
stockholders (*see* equity debt holders)
stockpiles, release of government's, 77-8
strikes, industrial, 155, 157, 174
structure of the American economy, role of in inflationary process, 272
substitution effect, 4, 5, 67-71, 80-4, 90-1, 98, 104, 106, 112, 114, 127-8, 280, 317; in case of cost-compensating price increase, 172-3; in case of tax-neutralizing price increase, 252-3, 255, 322-3
supply constraints, short-run, 140-1; as source of inflation, 260-2; on economic expansion, 225-33, 260-2
supply cost of internally generated funds, 56
supply curve, aggregate, 256; industry, 1, 8, 47, 131, 140-1, 143, 256-60; non-oligopolistic sector, 256, 259; oligopolistic sector, 256-60
supply curve for all investment funds, 85-8, 97-103, 113, 124-5, 244, 254
supply curve for external funds, 87
supply curve for internally generated funds, 5, 80-5, 87-8, 97-104, 113-14, 124
supply curve for manpower, non-oligopolistic sector's 261; oligopolistic sector's, 261
surplus value, 5, 6, 145, 176-7, 181-4
Sweden, 159
Sylos-Labini, P., 4, 104, 106

Taft-Hartley injunction, 161
take-over bids, 60, 120, 164-8, 169, 282, 311
target variables, 278-9, 280, 325
tariff reduction, 77-8
taste preferences, 67, 69
tax-based fiscal policy, 249-56
tax cut, under Kennedy-Johnson administration, 264-5, 267
tax-price adjusters, 251-6, 323

tax rates, 197, 198-9, 203, 249, 276
taxation, 77-8, 217, 250-6
technical coefficients (*see* factor coefficients)
technical progress function, 232
technological progress, 144, 150, 175, 181-2, 211-12, 228, 231-3, 240-1, 276, 283, 291; capital embodied nature of, 182, 240; rate of, 224-33
technology, influence of on firm's costs, 29, 283; labor-saving, 150, 54, 283
telephone industry, 305
theories of the firm, behavioral, 49-50; equity maximizing, 25-7, 53, 149, 167, 291, 312; growth maximizing, 23-4, 52-4, 167, 291; individualistic, 50, 51; managerial, 6, 50-4, 311; neo-classical, 15-18, 49, 289; organic, 50-1, 303
time, as a determinant of the entry factor, 74-5; as a factor in the substitution effect, 67, 70-1
time horizon, for pricing decisions, 4, 49, 55, 127-9, 130, 132-3, 258
trade union, in bellwether industry, 176, 182-8, 199, 242-4, 277
trade unions, 6, 151-64, 173, 176, 182-8, 199, 228, 265-6, 268, 276-8, 280; effect of on production techniques, 30, 154, 182; goals of, 155-7, 183-4
training, of work force, 153-4
transactions demand for money, 246, 321
transfer income, 279
turn-over tax, 274, 296

unemployment, 225-6, 264, 267, 288
United Automobile Workers, 266, 268
United Steelworkers' union, 263, 266
upper limit on price increases, 76-7, 80, 83-4, 104, 173, 253-4
US economy, 1960s, 263-70
utilization, rate of, 29-31, 43-4, 129, 143, 202, 206-7, 243, 292, 316; rate of, as determinant of investment, 194-5; rate of, effect of on relative income distribution, 141-4, 178
utility regulation (*see* regulation by commission)

valuation ratio, 311 (*see also*, retention rate)
variable returns, law of, 30-1
Veblen, T., 20
vertical integration, as barrier to entry, 72, 92
Vickers, D., 54
Vietnam war, 266-8, 277

wage contours, 160-1, 172
wage drift, 279
wage pattern (*see* national incremental wage pattern)
wage rates, changes in, 6-7, 151-6, 159-64, 181-8; changes in, effect of on price levels, 231, 241-4; differential in paid by megacorp, 32, 227, 261; differentials in within firm, 308; effect on of changing demand for labor, 230-1, 261; 'equitable,' 158-62, 173; in non-oligopolistic sector, 227-31, 257, 320; in oligopolistic sector, 151-6, 159-64, 227-8, 271, 320; nominal, change in, 187-8; real, 7, 183, 187-8, 278, 320
wage rounds, 161, 264
wage structure, internal, 147
wage-price spiral, 9, 199-200, 220, 223-4, 234, 241, 255, 260-2, 268-70, 271, 277, 280
Walras, L., 38, 320
Walrasian model, 38 (*see also*, pricing models, Walrasian polypoly)
Weintraub, S., 297-8
Wenders, J., 104
whipsawing, 309
Williamson, J., 54
Williamson, O., 51, 106-7
Worcester, D., 41
work force (*see* laboring manpower force)

X-inefficiency, 165-6, 310